Managing in the
Global Economy

THE EUROPEAN UNION

Managing in the Global Economy

THE EUROPEAN UNION

HARRY COSTIN

International Organization New Acropolis
Universidad San Jorge

THE DRYDEN PRESS
Harcourt Brace College Publishers

Fort Worth   Philadelphia   San Diego   New York   Orlando   Austin   San Antonio
Toronto   Montreal   London   Sydney   Tokyo

Acquisitions Editor: *Ruth Rominger*
Developmental Editor: *Dona Hightower*
Project Editor: *Jim Patterson*
Art Director: *Brian Salisbury*
Production Manager: *Eddie Dawson*
Art & Literary Rights Editor: *Adele Krause*
Product Manager: *Lise W. Johnson*
Marketing Coordinator: *Sam Stubblefield*
Electronic Publishing Coordinator: *Cathy Spitzenberger*

Copy Editor: *Dee Salisbury*
Indexer: *Sylvia Coates*
Text Type: Weiss 10/12

Cover Image: *Ben Britt*

Address for orders:
The Dryden Press
6277 Sea Harbor Drive
Orlando, FL 32887-6777
1-800-782-4479, or 1-800-433-0001 (in Florida)

Address for editorial correspondence:
The Dryden Press
301 Commerce Street, Suite 3700
Fort Worth, TX 76102

ISBN: 0-03-015347-6

Library of Congress Catalog Card Number: 95-67303

Printed in the United States of America

5 6 7 8 9 0 1 2 3 4   067   9 8 7 6 5 4 3 2 1

The Dryden Press
Harcourt Brace College Publishers

THE DRYDEN PRESS SERIES IN MANAGEMENT

Preface

This book provides a broad overview of issues related to Western European economic and political integration. The process of integration became a focus of global concern in the late 1980s, as governments and companies attempted to assess the potential opportunities and threats of the Europe 1992 program. Europe 1992 has attempted to remove existing physical, technical, and fiscal barriers throughout the Community. This process was formally begun in 1987 with the implementation of the Single European Act (SEA), that served to modify the Treaty of Rome (1957) which was the founding Charter of the European Economic Community.

The process of European unification has been complex, going through several stages since its inception in post WWII Europe. It can be best understood in a brief chronological outline:

1949–1957	Institutions such as the Council of Europe and NATO provide a framework for cooperation between Western European countries.
1950	Robert Schuman, the French Prime Minister, proposes the pooling of Europe's coal and steel industries under a supranational High Authority.
1957	Signing of the Treaty of Rome, the founding charter of the European Economic Community by Belgium, the Netherlands, Luxembourg, France, West Germany, and Italy. The Treaty enters into force on January 1, 1958.
1957–1968	Most tariffs on intra-Community trade are eliminated. Customs Union completed on July 1, 1968.
1973–1985	"Eurosclerosis": European industries experience lack of competitiveness.
1973	Britain, Ireland, and Denmark become members of the Community.
1979	European Monetary System (EMS) becomes operative.
1981	Greece becomes a member of the Community.
1985	The Commission White Paper on Completion of the Single Market provides an agenda to eliminate remaining physical, technical and fiscal barriers by December 31, 1992.
1985–1992	Planning and implementation of the Europe 1992 program.
1986	Spain and Portugal become members of the Community.
1987	The Single European Act (SEA), a modification of the Treaty of Rome, enters into force. The SEA also enshrines the broad objectives of the Europe 1992 program.
1990	Reunification of Germany.
1992	Treaty on European Union signed in Maastricht. The Maastricht Treaty, building on the SEA of 1987, further modifies the Treaty of Rome.

1993	Maastricht Treaty enters into force.
1994	European Monetary Institute, the future "Eurofed," is established. European Union accession negotiations completed with Austria, Finland, Norway, and Sweden.

This synthesis of events relevant to European unification does not detail the true complexity of the process and the disruptive impact of unforeseen events such as the reunification of Germany in 1990, the Danish veto to the Maastricht Treaty in 1992, or of the global economic recession in the early 1990s.

The book attempts not only to provide an overview of European unification from a multi-disciplinary perspective, but also to illustrate the complexities and uncertainties inherent in such a process. The latter concern motivated the editor to select seven surveys from *The Economist* on the Europe 1992 program. These surveys, published between 1988 and 1994, provide a real-time overview of the topics. They describe the process of unification with the immediacy of depicting events as they occurred.

The topics included should be of interest to diverse audiences such as students and scholars of international business, international affairs, contemporary history, area specialists, as well as to the public at large. The understanding of contemporary developments in Europe concerns all of us.

Only a multi-disciplinary perspective could even begin to attempt to illustrate the complex process of European integration. At the very least, the following disciplines deserve mention for the insights and conceptual frameworks they have provided to the analysis of European integration in this book: Economics, International Business (Strategy, Marketing and Finance), Political Science (Institutional Development), and History have all contributed methods of analyzing and comprehending European developments.

STRUCTURE OF THE BOOK

Part I provides a historical overview of European integration, describing the current framework provided by the Maastricht Treaty, and the objectives of the Social Charter.

Part II focuses on the process of European integration under the Europe 1992 program and the Maastricht Treaty negotiations.

Part III provides a framework for country analysis, with Germany, Austria, and the Nordic Countries as examples. These countries were selected as useful cases for country analysis, because the reunification of Germany significantly altered the balance of power in the Community, and the other countries have been the first to join the Community since the launching of Europe 1992 and the signing of the Maastricht Treaty.

Part IV illustrates discipline-based (Business, Political Economics) analysis of issues related to European integration. The first reading discusses the concept and applications of industrial policy at a European level while the readings on marketing describe the impact of Europe 1992 upon markets and companies operating in those areas.

The **Appendix** provides useful suggestions for on-line research on European issues.

SUPPLEMENTS

The Dryden Press will provide complimentary supplements or supplement packages to those adopters qualified under our adoption policy. Please contact your sales representative to learn how you may qualify. If as an adopter or potential user you receive supplements you do not need, please return them to your sales representative or send them to:

Attn: Returns Department
Troy Warehouse
465 South Lincoln Drive
Troy, MO 63379

ACKNOWLEDGMENTS

I am indebted to Katherine Kominis and Nicolas Flattes, who provided significant help editing the manuscript. I also would like to thank the students at Boston University and the University of Massachusetts Dartmouth who participated in my seminars on European integration; they provided the main inspiration for this project. Finally, I owe a debt of gratitude to Shirley Williams and Raymond Vernon at the Harvard Kennedy School of Government for their profound insights on European political and economic integration.

INTRODUCTION: THE UNCERTAIN FUTURE OF WESTERN EUROPE

As Europe approaches the year 2000, her future can best be described as uncertain. Uncertainty has come to characterize not only Europe, but the entire world. The "New World Order" has brought an end to relative global stability in a world formerly ruled by two superpowers. The demise of the Soviet Empire, the reunification of Germany, and renewed ethnic conflicts in the Balkans and northern Eurasia are examples of a global landscape in process of redefinition.

Today, the only remaining element of certainty is that more change will occur. As rapid change continues, the political, economic, demographic and social environment of Europe becomes ever more different from the once-familiar setting of the post WWII Cold War era. Change has affected the goals of the Europe 1992 program, as well as the framework of the political and economic integration delineated by the Maastricht Treaty. It has created considerable differences between the daily lives of European citizens and those goals.

One important change has been the increase in unemployment in the Community, from 12 million in the late 1980s to 17 million in the mid 1990s. Also, Europe's greatest economic achievement, the Welfare System maintained by most Western European countries, is being strained by an aging population and the political impossibility to finance it with an increased tax burden to citizens and corporations. Some progress is to be expected as the recession of the early 1990s begins to recede. However, high unemployment and budget deficits are structurally ingrained and therefore unlikely to fade away,

Such economic problems with related socio-political stresses do not mean that the Europe 1992 program failed. Much has already been achieved by the almost 300 Directives of the program to complete the internal market. However, as progress is achieved in one area, new, ever greater challenges seem to loom in the horizon. The collapse of the Soviet Empire, the unification of Germany, the war in the former Yugoslavia, are all events that were not, and indeed could not have been foreseen as Europe 1992 was launched in the mid 1980s.

GLOBAL CHANGES: THE NEW WORLD ORDER

As recently as 1980 it would have been difficult to imagine or predict the collapse of the post WWII bipolar balance of power. At the time only a few visionaries, such as French theorist Edgar Morin, dared to conceive of such notions as the potential collapse of the Soviet Union from within, and thus of the bipolar system upon which all post WWII stability was built. The reunification of Germany in 1990 was also an event inconceivable just a year before. The new Germany, with 80 million citizens, has significantly altered the existing demographic, economic, and political balance in the European Community.

To understand the world of the 1990s, in all its complex political, social, and economic features we must first learn to live with ambiguity and unanswered questions. Gone are the days when answers to most of the salient issues of the day could have beeen provided if one only had access to the secret archives of the CIA or the KGB. In the post WWII bipolar system, global political and economic dynamics could largely be explained by the overt or covert interests of the Soviet Union and the United States. Today, however, with the fragmentation of political and economic power, a bipolar framework is no longer an accurate depiction of reality. The New World Order faces global challenges such as saturated markets, famines, and the threat of massive migration from poor to less poor areas.

Another important factor which can be placed in the column labeled "uncertainty" is the geopolitical will of the United States, the only remaining superpower. The U.S. is currently struggling with internal problems and with the need to redefine her foreign policy. The ever increasing fiscal debt burden, and the lack of political will to summon economic resources to provide for all her citizens health care needs, are only two examples of unresolved issues even the greatest nation in the world has to face. Also, with the demise of the Soviet Union, U.S. foreign policy is increasingly driven by economic pragmatism, rather than military dominance.

The shape of the new global landscape is difficult to define since it varies greatly in relation to the vantage point chosen for observation. The economic, political, military, and technological landscapes are all different, and, in some cases contradict each other. Japan has no nuclear capabilities, but is an economic power second only to the United States, with continual strengthening of her economic leverage. Russia and the Ukraine are economically weak, but hold nuclear capability. Technology crosses borders as if the world were a flatland, while the difference between rich and poor resembles the distance between the peaks of mountains and deep valleys.

This ever more complex panorama has weakened the predictive power of existing theoretical frameworks. The world of the mid 1990s is not only complex, but also dangerous: we still live in an era when armed confrontation seems the rule rather than the exception. It would be naive to pretend that we are headed for a promised land of unlimited bounty. Rather, it appears as if uncertainty and short planning horizons will become the foundation of any new theoretical framework we may develop to describe the world of the XXIst century.

EUROPEAN TRENDS

For Europeans, uncertainty in the New World Order takes many forms, some of which seem all too familiar problems: skyrocketing unemployment, decreasing standards of living, the threat of massive immigration from poor countries, and war in the Balkans all challenge Europe's resources and cooperative capacities. These events have tested existing policies and intra-European cooperation. Countries with liberal immigration policies for political and economic refugees, such as Germany or France, are beginning to shut their doors to former cultural, linguistic and/or colonial relatives. Also, the war in the former Yugoslavia has shown that political cooperation and foreign policy coordination among the members of the Community, enshrined in the Maastricht Treaty of 1992, remain elusive goals.

Despite these unresolved conflicts it is undeniable that many positive steps have been made under the auspices of the Community, and lately under the program that came to be known as Europe 1992.

EUROPE 1992

Europe 1992, a program launched in the mid 1980s to bring about the completion of the Internal Market, promised significant economic progress as a result of cooperation among the twelve member states of the Community. Some 300 European laws (Directives) were to be passed under the Europe 1992 program to complete the internal market and guarantee four freedoms: free movement of people, capital, goods, and services. These freedoms would be achieved through the elimination of existing physical, fiscal, and technical barriers among the members of the Community.

The key advantage of the Europe 1992 program, enshrined in the Single European Act of 1987 was focus. A clear timetable and legislative agenda, largely achieved as planned, provided a framework for an unprecedented degree of cooperation among the member states of the Community. However, a series of dramatic events destabilized the very foundations of cooperation within the Community. Beginning with the collapse of the Soviet Empire, continuing with the reunification of Germany, war in the Balkans, and global economic recession in the early 1990s, Europe experienced unforeseen setbacks.

Three options, none without risks, were possible. First, to settle for modest, purely economic goals of cooperation. Second, to consolidate existing gains and the framework provided by the Single European Act. Third, to strive for a new, unprecedented degree of cooperation that would integrate new dimensions such as a coordinated foreign policy, a common defense policy, and eventually a single European currency (hard ECU) and monetary policy independently led by a European Central Bank. The third option, a real departure from the past, was chosen. The European Union was based on the foundations of the former European Community. The Maastricht Treaty, a further modification to the Treaty of Rome, signed in 1992 and enacted in 1993, provided the necessary legislative framework for the Union.

It is too early to evaluate the results of the 1992 program, and the new programs to be developed under the Maastricht Treaty. Nevertheless, some inherent dilemmas have already appeared. In 1992, a timetable was being set to integrate monetary policies under a single European Central Bank by the end of the century, with a single currency for members of the future Monetary Union (EMU). But the existing European Monetary System (EMS) established in 1979, which provides for a managed float of currencies within pre-established ranges, virtually collapsed.

The 1992 Danish veto of the original Maastricht Treaty rang out as another tocsin of warning, as did Switzerland's refusal to join the Union. Further, though real employment and income benefits were promised to European citizens through the Europe 1992 program, this promise was unfulfilled. Instead, unemployment has risen from 12 million in the late 1980s to an unprecedented 17 million in 1993.

EUROPE: TOWARD THE XXI CENTURY

At what point might the harsh realities of the New World Order contradict the lofty goals of the European Union, to the extent where the whole system might collapse or retreat to long-outdated forms of economic cooperation? Nobody can provide clear answers to such a difficult question, but it is undeniable that tensions, such as the ones mentioned, do exist and have not been resolved, nor are they likely to do so in the near future.

At present, several critical issues occupy European decisionmakers, legislators, and the Community's institutions. Some of these issues deal with *principles*, others with the *implementation* of the framework and mechanisms for European political and economic coperation.

ENLARGEMENT

As expected, the Community has begun a new round of enlargement. Austria's admission in 1995 will provide a template for accession to the Union for all other potential members. Scandinavian countries will follow immediately, and Eastern European countries will probably have to wait for a further round of enlargement in the next decade. Turkey, a member of NATO, remains a borderline example of a country that wants to join the Community, but will most likely not be considered "European," and therefore not allowed to join.

Concerning enlargement, countries fall into the following categories:

- Small countries, such as the Scandinavian ones which have economies similar to the ones of developed western European countries, and are small enough not to disturb greatly the distribution of economic and political power in the Community. Most of these countries are members of the European Free Trade Area (EFTA).

- Countries which share the demographic and economic characteristics of the first group, but have refused to join the Community. In the past, this group included Norway, and currently, Switzerland, a country that withdrew her application for membership.

- Eastern European countries that would like to join the Community. Their current economies are not up to the standards required by the Community. Future membership will be a function of their economic development and stability.

- The final group includes countries at Europe's borders which would like to join the Community, but are not likely to be accepted. This group includes Turkey and some former European colonies in Northern Africa.

INSTITUTIONAL DEVELOPMENT

Closely related to enlargement is institutional development. The Commission will be particularly affected by enlargement. It currently comprises 17 Commissioners (two from each of the five large Community members and one from each of the other seven member states). After expected enlargement, the Commission will probably become a collegiate body with 21 Commissioners.

The European Parliament is gradually acquiring new legislative powers, although the Commission remains the key institution, at the heart of the formulation and implementation of the European economic and political agenda. The Commission is now in a state of transition with the departure of Jacques Delors, President of the Commission since 1985. His successor, Jacques Santer, the long-standing Prime Minister of Luxembourg and a compromise candidate chosen after long debate, is unlikely to have the stature or effective power of Mr. Delors. An eventual weakening of the Commission is a trend welcomed by member states such as the United Kingdom, a country that has vigorously opposed any movement toward European federalism (it vetoed the inclusion of the word *federal* in the Maastricht Treaty).

SUBSIDIARITY

The principle of *subsidiarity* is the key guideline for transfer of sovereignty from the member states to the institutions of the Community. *Subsidiarity* means that only those issues (mainly legislation) that cannot be addressed effectively at the national level will become the competence of supranational European institutions. It has been argued that no transfer of sovereignty from individual member states to the Community ever takes place, and the member states will agree on measures in their own self-interest. However, institutions such as the Commission or the European Court of Justice can effectively fine member states and block support for national industries or country legislation that contradicts Community laws.

The new distribution of power among the Community institutions and voting rights at the European Council will be addressed before the end of the decade, beginning with a revision of the Maastricht Treaty in 1996. What is decided will depend, among other factors, on the success of the framework for decision making provided by the Maastricht Treaty.

THE SOCIAL CHARTER

The Social Charter covers a wide range of issues such as the right to proportional benefits for part-time workers or the right of workers to be represented at their companies' board of directors. In brief, the Social Charter proposes to extend the benefits of the welfare state to all Community citizens. The Social Charter has been agreed on, in principle, but has been difficult to implement. The United Kingdom has blocked many of the more progressive measures, arguing economic necessity and self-interest, and has opted out of the Social Charter provisions of the Maastricht Treaty. Implementation issues were addressed in a mid-1994 White Paper by the Commission.

THE FUTURE OF THE EUROPEAN MONETARY UNION (EMU)

The Maastricht Treaty provides the framework for the EMU, which includes as objectives a single European currency and an independent European Central Bank. As a proposed date of achieving these goals, 1999 remains over-ambitious. It is possible that full monetary integration by only a few Community members may occur next, with other member states integrating in the future. This scenario has been referred to as a "two-speed Europe."

EUROPEAN COMPETITIVENESS

How to increase the competitiveness of European industries remains one of the critical items on the European agenda. Closely tied to unemployment, which rose by 40 percent over the last five years, it has been addressed in a 1993 White Paper of the Commission. The document calls for heavy investment in infrastructure for state-of-the-art industries such as information processing. Also, the existing infrastructure for transportation, one of the key competitive advantages of Western Europe, is to be strengthened. Of particular interest is the emphasis on the promotion of small- and medium-size enterprises as one of the most viable options for the much needed creation of sources of employment.

The issues discussed above are examples of those the Community will have to deal with in the coming decade. The current recession will gradually recede, reducing polical pressures within the member states to act mostly on short-term self-interest. However, the global context in the mid 1990s and beyond is clearly different from that of ten years ago, when Europe 1992 was launched. The New World Order presents a fragmented landscape with shifting priorities and diverses crises that need to be dealt with immediately. The future may not necessarily be bleak, but much remains uncertain. Forecasting has become a difficult and even potentially dangerous activity.

CONTENTS

Managing in the
Global Economy

THE EUROPEAN UNION

PART I

From Rome to Maastricht

European Unification: The Origins and Growth of the European Community

KLAUS-DIETER BORCHARDT

INTRODUCTION: TOWARDS EUROPEAN UNIFICATION

Even before the founding of the European Community the idea of a closely knit association of European States had found political expression in a variety of ways. There had been attempts to impose unity by force, notably by Napoleon and Hitler—Napoleon seeking to unite the Continent under French hegemony, Hitler to subjugate Europe under the dictatorship of the Third Reich. But there had also been peaceful schemes, especially after the harrowing experience of the First World War, for a voluntary grouping of States on terms of equality.

In 1923, for instance, the Austrian leader of the Pan-European Movement, Count Coudenhove Kalergi, had called for the creation of a United States of Europe, citing examples such as the success of the Swiss struggle for unity in 1648, the forging of the German Empire in 1871 and, first and foremost, the recognition of the independence of the United States of America in 1776. Then on September 29, 1929, in a now famous speech before the League of Nations Assembly in Geneva, the French Foreign Minister, Aristide Briand, with the backing of his German counterpart, Gustav Stresemann, proposed the creation of a European Union within the framework of the League of Nations. The immediate aim was merely to promote closer cooperation between the States of Europe, leaving their national sovereignty intact.

But all these efforts for peaceful unification failed to make any real headway against the still dominant tide of nationalism and imperialism. Only after Europe had yet again been devastated by war was the disastrous futility of constant national rivalry truly appreciated. Europe's complete collapse and the political and economic exhaustion of the European States with their outdated national structures set the stage for a completely fresh start and called for a far more radical approach to the reordering of Europe.

The subsequent moves towards integration sprang from three main factors. First was Europe's realization of her own weakness. As a result of her internal dissensions and wars she

Monique Giallombardo, Coedition and Copyright Unit, Office for Official Publications of the European Communities, Luxembourg.

had lost her age-old position at the center of the world stage. Her place was taken by the two new superpowers, the United States of America and the Soviet Union, each of which now wielded far greater military, political, and economic might than a divided, patchwork Europe of individual States could muster. Second was the conviction, summed up in the motto 'Never again!', that renewed military conflict must be avoided. Emerging from the terrible experience of two world wars—both of which had begun as European 'civil wars' and in which Europe had been the main battlefield and principal sufferer—this took shape as the guiding principle of all political action. Third was the earnest desire for a better, freer, juster world in which social and international relations would be conducted in a more orderly way.

Taken together the post-war moves towards European unification offer a picture so confusing as to baffle anyone but the most knowledgeable expert on European affairs. A multitude of different organizations, all formally quite unconnected with each other, have come into existence side by side: the Organization for Economic Cooperation and Development (OECD), the Western European Union (WEU), the North Atlantic Treaty Organization (NATO), the Council of Europe, and the European Communities (comprising the European Coal and Steel Community, the European Atomic Energy Community and the European Economic Community). Their membership ranges from seven in the WEU to 23 in the Council of Europe. Looking at their underlying concrete aims, however, a clear pattern begins to emerge, revealing three major groups.

The *first group* consists of the 'transatlantic' organizations which grew out of the close links forged between Western Europe and the USA after the war. Not surprisingly, it was an American initiative that led to the founding in 1948 of the first post-war European organization, the OEEC (Organization for European Economic Cooperation), after the then US Secretary of State, George Marshall, had called on the countries of Europe to pool their efforts for economic reconstruction, promising them American aid (which eventually took shape in the Marshall Plan). In 1960 the members of the OEEC, together with the USA and Canada, agreed to extend the organization's activities to include development aid for the Third World and, with those two countries becoming members that same year, the OEEC was renamed the OECD (Organization for Economic Cooperation and Development).

The founding of the OEEC was followed in 1949 by NATO—a military pact between the USA, Canada and the majority of the free States in Europe. Then in 1954 the Western European Union was founded. Intended to strengthen security cooperation between the countries of Europe, it extended the existing Brussels Treaty between Britain, France, Belgium, Luxembourg and the Netherlands to include the Federal Republic of Germany and Italy. Recently Portugal also applied for membership.

The WEU offers its members a platform for closer cooperation on security and defense, helping them to forge a European identity in this field and so lend greater weight to the European voice in the Atlantic alliance. The characteristic feature of the *second group* of European organizations is that their structure is designed to allow as many countries as possible to participate. Consequently it had to be accepted that their activities would not extend beyond the scope of normal international cooperation. Their prime concern is to accommodate countries which are unable or unwilling to become members of an organization endowed with supranational powers, either because their traditional neutrality—as in the case of Sweden, Austria, or Switzerland—or because of their reluctance to cede any part of their sovereignty.

This group comes under the umbrella of the Council of Europe, which was founded on May 5, 1949, as political organization. The Statute of the Council of Europe contains no reference to any such goals as federation or union, nor does it provide for any transfer or pooling of areas of national sovereignty. Decision-making power resides solely with a Committee of Ministers and unanimity is required for all decisions on matters of substance. This means that any country can use its veto to block a decision, as in the United Nations Security Council. There is also a Parliamentary Assembly, but it is a purely consultative body with no legislative powers. It can do no more than make recommendations to the Committee of Ministers; and as the Committee is not answerable to the Assembly, a recommendation can be rejected by a single dissenting vote. Even after a proposal has been adopted by the Committee of Ministers it has to be ratified by the national parliaments before it can have legal effect. By its very structure, then, the Council of Europe is merely an instrument of inter-governmental cooperation.

Nevertheless, its contribution to the cause of European unity, in particular in fostering European solidarity, cannot be rated highly enough. Its aim is to create closer links among the countries of Europe and to promote their economic and social progress. In this it has succeeded. Its membership has grown from the 10 original founders to 23 (Britain, France, Belgium, Netherlands, Luxembourg, Italy, Ireland, Denmark, Norway, and Sweden being subsequently joined by Iceland, Greece, Turkey, the Federal Republic of Germany, Austria, Cyprus, Switzerland, Malta, Portugal, Spain, Liechtenstein, Finland and San Marino). Under its auspices numerous economic, cultural, social and legal conventions have been adopted by the member States. The most significant and most widely known of these is the European Convention for the Protection of Human Rights and Fundamental Freedoms, adopted on 4 November 1950. This not only laid down a practical minimum standard of human rights to be applied in the member States but also established a system for legal remedy, empowering the institutions set up under the Convention—the European Commission for Human Rights and the European Court of Human Rights—to condemn infringements of human rights by the signatories.

The *third group* of European organizations comprises the European Coal and Steel Community, the European Atomic Energy Community and the European Economic Community. From the legal point of view, the three Communities exist separately side by side. From the point of view of political reality, however, they can be treated as a single entity. Their creation can be regarded as marking the birth of 'the European Community'.

The major innovative feature of the European Community compared with other international bodies is that its members have ceded to it a part of their national sovereignty, with the goal of forming a cohesive, indissoluble organizational and political unit. They have endowed it with sovereign powers of its own, independent of the Member States, which it can exercise to adopt acts which have the force of national law. This novel approach of pooling national sovereignty and policies is commonly referred to as "integration." The European Community, then, offers the most advanced example of European integration.

THE ORIGINS OF THE EUROPEAN COMMUNITY

The foundation stone in the building of the European Community was laid on May 9, 1950, when Robert Schuman, the French Foreign Minister, put forward a plan worked out by himself and Jean Monnet for France and Germany to pool all their coal and steel production under a joint High Authority within an organization open to any other country in Europe that wished to join.

Behind this proposal lay a twofold realization: on the one hand it was pointless to impose unilateral restrictions on Germany; but at the same time a fully independent Germany was still perceived as a potential threat to peace. The only way out of this dilemma was to bind Germany politically and economically into a firmly based grouping of European States. The plan thus took up the idea put forward by Winston Churchill in his famous Zurich speech of September 19, 1946, in which he had called for the creation of a United States of Europe, singling out Franco-German cooperation as the essential prerequisite. Churchill, however, had envisaged Britain's role as a promoter rather than as an active participant.

On April 18, 1951, six countries (Belgium, Germany, France, Italy, Luxembourg and the Netherlands) signed a Treaty establishing the European Coal and Steel Community (ECSC) and with the Treaty's entry into force on July 23 1952, the Schuman Plan became practical reality. The new Community's founding fathers hoped that it would be the seed from which the further political integration of Europe would grow, culminating in the emergence of a European Constitution.

In October 1950, before the ECSC Treaty had been signed, the French launched the idea of a European Defense Community (EDC). The outbreak of the Korean war and mounting East-West tension showed the need for a greater defense effort by the Western European countries, and this meant that West Germany had to be included. But the wounds of the Second World War had hardly begun to heal and the idea of a German national army, especially in French eyes, was quite unacceptable. Known as the Pléven Plan, the answer once again was to bind Germany into a supranational Community (this time covering defense as well) which would ensure adequate control of a re-armed Germany. In August 1954, however, the plan was dashed when the French National Assembly, unwilling to countenance such a far-reaching curb on French sovereignty as to relinquish the right to maintain a national army, refused to ratify the Treaty.

The failure of the European Defense Community also dealt a severe blow to efforts aimed at the political unification of Europe. For a while optimism gave way to resignation. But then, in June 1955, the Foreign Ministers of the ECSC countries launched a new initiative for the 'creation of a United Europe' The governments of the Six had come to realize that it was in their interest to progress further along the path on which they had embarked with the founding of the ECSC.

For the Federal Republic of Germany involvement in the integration process signified its political rehabilitation within the community of nations. As a major exporter, Germany was—and still is—economically dependent on the European market. The creation of the European Economic Community made this market more secure, substantially reducing the dangers of its reliance on foreign trade. The figures for German trade with the other Member States give eloquent testimony to the resulting economic benefits. The proportion of German exports going to other Community countries rose from 27% at the outset to 48% today.

For France the founding of an economic community that included Germany was the political expression of its readiness for reconciliation and of its desire for lasting peace in Europe. Moreover, membership of the Community offered a welcome opportunity to stimulate much-needed industrial expansion. Access to a large European trading area also opened up vital new markets for its agricultural industry.

Belgium, like Germany, relies heavily on foreign trade and hence on secure export markets, and so the idea of a common market was very attractive from the economic point of view. The country's interest in the establishment of close economic ties in Europe was reinforced by the fact that in the 1950s its industry was still centered almost totally on coal and steel. A European internal market was potentially very significant, partly because of the immediate prospect of boosting its sales of coal and steel products, but above all with a view to establishing and developing new industries.

Italy had already begun a drive to industrialize and saw the planned European internal market primarily as a unique opportunity for growth. It also counted on financial assistance from Community regional aid schemes to develop the more backward parts of the country and so reduce the high level of unemployment there.

The Netherlands also had great expectations. Involvement in the integration process would give a boost to its industrialization effort and—given its position as the major European freight carrier, with large ports and a tailor-made infrastructure—opened up bright new prospects for the future. Last but not least, the Dutch, too, were faced with the need to secure and expand their markets for agricultural produce. The government's European policy found widespread public support, not so much because of the economic advantages which beckoned as because of the prospect of security and peace in Europe and free and unstriced travel to neighboring countries.

Owing to its geographical situation, Luxembourg had, throughout history, been at the mercy of the rivalries between its great neighbors. European integration appeared to offer a way to protect its political, economic and social interests.

Given these coinciding interests, the logical place to resume the task of European unification was at the point where the ECSC had left off, in other words with the less emotionally charged question of economic integration. The EDC plan had obviously been over-ambitious. Now the aim was more modest, but more realistic The Foreign Ministers of the six founder members of the ECSC, meeting at the Messina Conference, asked a committee under the chairmanship of the Belgian Foreign Minister, Paul-Henri Spaak, to look into the prospects for further integration. In 1956 the Spaak Committee presented its report. This formed the basis for negotiations on the Treaties establishing the European Atomic Community (Euratom) and the European Economic Community (EEC) which were signed by the Six in March 1957 and entered into force on January 1, 1958.

The Treaties had not yet taken effect, however, when the British Government provoked a fierce quarrel within Europe over the best approach to European economic integration. The British idea was to set up a European free trade area which would involve no sacrifice of national sovereignty. Tariffs between the members would be dismantled, but each country would retain its freedom of action in respect of trade with non-members. Although Britain was able to win over Denmark, Norway, Iceland, Austria, Portugal, and Switzerland, the initiative eventually failed in the face of the continued determination of the Six to press ahead with their scheme for the European Economic Community (now underpinned by a treaty). Subsequent British efforts to create a large European free trade area embracing the European Economic Community and the other OEEC countries finally broke down in late 1958 because of irreconcilable differences between France and Britain. Their response was to found the European Free Trade Association (EFTA) in 1959, comprising Britain, Norway, Sweden, Denmark, Austria, Portugal, Iceland and Switzerland, together with Finland as an associate member.

Impressed by the initial successes of the EEC, the British Government very soon began to reconsider its refusal to play an active part in the process of European integration. It realized that Britain could not be sure of making its political influence felt simply by virtue of its pre-eminent position in the Commonwealth. EFTA was an equally unsuitable medium through which to work since its objectives were purely economic—unlike those of the Community, which were also political. It was rightly felt that Britain risked political isolation by remaining outside the Community. Because of the changing pattern of world trade it found itself, like all the major trading nations, under considerable pressure to protect its existing export markets and to open up new ones. The rapidly growing Community market offered an ideal opportunity, presenting British firms with a chance to mobilize their reserves of strength in the fiercely competitive European arena and so help to revitalize the economy as a whole. In August 1961 Britain made its first formal application for full membership of the Community. Three other countries—Denmark and Norway from EFTA, together with Ireland—followed suit.

The attraction of Community membership for the Scandinavian countries derived from their long-held view that they stood to gain more from free trade than they might lose. Given this basic attitude, the strongest factor behind Denmark's application was the prospect of free access to the common market. Danish food production was sufficient to feed 15 million people—three times the country's population; it was therefore a matter of vital interest to be able to export this substantial surplus freely to a common internal market at guaranteed prices. The argument for membership was reinforced by Britain's application, since Britain was Denmark's largest export market. Another major factor was the longer-term prospect of new openings for Danish industrial goods. The country's years as a member of EFTA had shown that its industry would be able to exploit the opportunities. All these factors outweighed the doubts and fears about the consequences of integration and the loosening of national control over important aspects of economic policy.

Ireland had a tradition of close and wide-ranging cultural, religious and military ties with the Continent and the Irish attitude was therefore very open to participation in the process of European integration. It, too, saw entry into the Community as a chance to boost its vital farm exports. Ever since independence in 1922, Irish agricultural trade had remained largely geared towards the British market, but this was not large enough to allow Irish agriculture to exploit its full productive potential. The importance of agriculture for the Irish economy is demonstrated by the fact that it employs one in every five workers and accounts for a third of all exports, while the associated food industry provides almost a quarter of all industrial jobs. The industrialization process begun in the mid-1930s had led to strong industrial growth, and this also called for new markets. At the same time, improved competitiveness gave Irish industry good cause to expect a healthy increase in trade and wealth as a result of joining the common market. Yet another significant factor from the Irish point of view was the Community's Social and Regional Funds, which both promised further economic benefits.

However, in 1963 the accession of the applicant countries was blocked when General de Gaulle abruptly broke off the negotiations because of his deep mistrust of the intentions behind Britain's application for membership.

In 1967 Britain applied for the second time—again followed by Ireland, Denmark and Norway—and once again the attempt foundered against French reservations. Only after de Gaulle stepped down in April 1969 did the final breakthrough come at the Hague

Summit later that year. Following lengthy negotiations the Treaties of Accession were eventually signed on January 22, 1972, and on January 1, 1973—after successful referenda in Ireland and Denmark and ratification by the national parliaments—Britain, Ireland and Denmark became members of the Communities. A referendum was also held in Norway, but there the idea of membership failed to gain acceptance and the result was a 53.49% vote against accession.

During the course of the accession negotiations the question had, of course, arisen as to what should happen with the remaining EFTA countries (Sweden, Switzerland, Austria, Portugal, Finland, Iceland, and—following its decision against membership—Norway), some of whom could not join the Community because of their neutral status while others could not be accepted as members because of their non-democratic regimes. The solution eventually adopted was for them to conclude free trade agreements with the Community, and these were signed in July 1972.

With their return to democracy, Greece (1975) followed by Portugal and Spain (1977) applied for membership of the Community. Greece saw this as a means of stabilizing its newly restored democracy and enhancing its standing and influence on the international stage. In economic terms the hope was that, through modernization of agriculture and industry, membership would help to put the economy back on its feet. Widely held reservations about the resulting limitation of national sovereignty and fears of increased foreign intervention in Greek domestic affairs were not allowed to overshadow these economic interests, and on January 1, 1981, Greece became the 10th member of the Community.

The accession of Spain and Portugal also raised numerous difficulties, but these were eventually settled in negotiations and, after the signing of the accession treaties in June 1985 and their ratification by the Parliaments of the Member States and the applicant countries, Spain and Portugal duly became the 11th and 12th members of the Community on January 1, 1986.

For Spain, this is the fulfilment of an old ambition, even though since Franco's death its isolation from Europe has already largely come to an end. From the economic point of view the main impact of accession, thanks to the funds this will make available, will give an appreciable boost to an already highly competitive agricultural industry with considerable reserves of productive capacity. Spain's share in Community regional programs will, it is hoped, help it to bridge the differences in living standards between the various regions. In the industrial sector it will, with the assistance of its new partners, be in a better position to initiate the painful but necessary process of structural adjustment and so close the long-standing gap between itself and the other countries of Europe.

For Portugal, after the loss of its colonies and recovery from domestic political upheaval, membership of the Community means a return to its basic European roots. The Community offers both an opportunity to escape from political isolation and the best prospect for economic recovery. The confidence inspired by membership has revived investment activity by large firms—essential especially for the country's industrial development, and an area where progress has been very hesitant since the revolution. Equally the Portuguese look to the Community for stimulus and support—not least financial—for economic restructuring, especially in agriculture.

The latest enlargement by no means marks the end of the Community's expansion. Indeed, the prospect of completion of the single European market by the end of 1992 has added to its attractions. Turkey and Austria have already formally applied for membership, while Malta and Cyprus have clearly indicated that they intend to do so too. But it will be some time before any of them actually joins, as the Community is still at the consolidation stage following Spanish and Portuguese accession and the most pressing item on the agenda right now is setting up the single European market among the Twelve.

In February 1982, by contrast, the Community had to accept a move away from expansion, when the people of Greenland voted by a narrow majority against continued membership. Greenland had become part of the Community in 1973 by virtue of its belonging to Denmark. Although the Treaties make no provision for withdrawal, in February 1984 the Ten agreed to allow Greenland to leave the Community with effect from January 1, 1985, granting it the status of an associated overseas territory instead.

The European Union: A Guide

CHRONOLOGY

1950 *May 9* Robert Schuman proposes pooling Europe's coal and steel industries.

1951 *April 18* European Coal and Steel Community (ECSC) Treaty signed.

1957 *March 25* European Economic Community (EEC) and European Atomic Energy Community (Euratom) Treaties signed.

1965 *April 8* Treaty merging the institutions of the three European Communities.

1968 *July 1* Customs union completed 18 months early.

1973 *January 1* Denmark, Ireland, and the United Kingdom join the Community.

1975 *February 28* First Lome Convention with African, Caribbean and Pacific countries is signed.

1979 *March 13* European Monetary System (EMS) becomes operative.

June 7-10 First direct elections to the European Parliament.

1981 *January 1* Greece joins the Community.

1985 *June 29* European Council endorses "White Paper" plan to complete the single market by 1992.

1986 *January 1* Spain and Portugal join the Community.

1987 *July 1* Single European Act enters into force.

1989 *June 26-27* Madrid European Council endorses plan for Economic and Monetary Union.

1990 *October 3* The five Laender of the former German Democratic Republic enter the Community as part of united Germany.

November 20 Transatlantic Declaration adopted by the Community and the United States.

1991 *October 21* European Community and European Free Trade Association (EFTA) agree to form the European Economic Area (EEA), a single market of 19 countries.

December 11 Maastricht European Council agrees to Treaty on European Union.

December 16 Poland, Hungary and Czechoslovakia sign first Europe Agreement on trade, political and economic cooperation.

1992 *February 7* Treaty on Union signed in Maastricht.

June 2 First Danish referendum rejects Maastricht Treaty.

1993 *January 1* European Single Market enters into force.

May 18 Second Danish referendum approves Maastricht Treaty, following declarations by Edinburgh European Council.

November 1 Treaty on European Union enters into force.

1994 *January 1* European Economic Area enters into force.

January 1 European Monetary Institute established.

March 16 EU accession negotiations completed with Austria, Finland, Norway, and Sweden.

Editor's note: The European Union was created in November 1993, with the implementation of the Maastricht Treaty. The term European Union (EU) is used in this brochure whenever appropriate. Other terms, such as European Community (EC) and European Coal and Steel Community (ECSC), are used when the historical context is appropriate, or to describe the statutory functions of organizations which still have legal identities within the EU.

Published by European Commission Delegation to the United States ©1994. Reproduction authorized preferably with acknowledgement of source.

PART I   *From Rome to Maastricht*

WHAT IS THE EUROPEAN UNION?

The European Union is an institutional framework for forging unity and cooperation among the peoples and nations of Europe. It is a new stage in a process begun in the 1950s with the creation of the three original European Communities, which came to be known collectively as the European Community.

The Community was created in the wake of World War II, as a devastated Western Europe sought ways to rebuild its economy and prevent future wars. It constitutes a unique relationship between nations. It used to be referred to as the "Common Market" because it is a single trading entity. But it was always much more than that. The European Community was a political creation from the outset, committed by its founding treaties to seek an ever closer union among the peoples of Europe.

The Union is often compared to the United States, and there are some similarities. Member countries have agreed to pool some of their sovereign powers for the sake of unity, just as American states did to create a federal republic. In the fields where such delegation of national sovereignty has occurred—for example, in trade and agriculture—the Union acts as a full-fledged country, and negotiates directly with the united States and other countries. Member states retain their full sovereign powers in such fields as security and defense matters, although they have agreed to take joint actions in foreign and security policy under the new Union. Although the U.S. federal model continues to inspire the search for political unity, Europe is constructing its own model for unification, ensuring respect for its richest asset—the historical, cultural and linguistic diversity of the European nations.

THE UNION'S ORIGINS

On May 9, 1950, the French Foreign Minister, Robert Schuman, put forward a bold plan for lifting Europe out of the rubble of World War II. Schuman proposed to pool European coal and steel industries as a first step towards a centuries-old ideal that in the past had been attempted or achieved only by force—a united Europe. Declaring that "the gathering of the nations of Europe requires the elimination of the age-old opposition of France and Germany," it proposed that Franco-German coal and steel production—at that time every country's war arsenal—be placed under a common authority within an organization open to other European countries. The long-term objective of the Schuman Declaration was to provide a structure to pursue the political unification of Europe through concrete economic

The original treaties, still in existence, established three entities: the European Coal and Steel Community (ECSC), the European Atomic Energy Community (Euratom) and the European Economic Community (EEC). The EEC has been formally renamed the European Community by the Treaty on European Union.

The Maastricht Treaty on European Union, which entered into force on November 1, 1993, creates the European Union, "founded on the European Communities, supplemented by the policies and forms of cooperation established by this Treaty".

The Maastricht Treaty creates European citizenship, and provides the European Parliament with additional powers under the co-decision procedure.

"Pillar 1" of the Maastricht Treaty provides a detailed plan for Economic and Monetary Union, amends the founding Treaties of Rome and Paris, renames the EEC the European Community (EC), and supplements the statutory powers of the Community in certain policy areas such as environment, research and technology, and education and training.

"Pillar 2" gives statutory authority to the Common Foreign and Security Policy, and sets out the procedures for policymaking and joint action in foreign and security affairs (see the section entitled "Europe—World Partner").

"Pillar 3" deals with justice and home affairs, including issues of asylum policy, the crossing of external borders, immigration, combating drug addiction and fraud on an international scale, judicial cooperation in civil and criminal matters and customs and police cooperation in areas such as terrorism.

Policy in Pillars 2 and 3 is handled by intergovernmental cooperation rather than by the original Community procedures laid down in the founding treaties, which govern Pillar 1.

integration—starting with coal and steel. According to the Declaration this would constitute the first step towards a European federation.

Belgium, the Federal Republic of Germany, Italy, Luxembourg and the Netherlands accepted the French proposal, signing the European Coal and Steel Community (ECSC) Treaty in Paris on April 18, 1951. The Six set up a novel institution, the ECSC High Authority, to which member governments transferred portions of their sovereign powers. The ECSC was so successful that coal and steel trade between the Six increased by 129 percent in the first five years.

The United States was among the first countries to accredit a diplomatic representation to the ECSC High Authority (and to the EEC and Euratom). Secretary of State Dean Acheson declared that, in matters of coal and steel, the United States would deal directly with the ECSC, rather than with the individual member states.

EUROPEAN ECONOMIC COMMUNITY AND EUROPEAN ATOMIC ENERGY COMMUNITY

Encouraged by the success of the ECSC, the Six attempted to pursue integration in the military and political fields. A Treaty establishing a European Defense Community (EDC) was signed by the Six on May 27, 1952, and even more ambitious plans for the creation of a European Political Community (EPC) were launched. However, these plans were abandoned when the French Parliament rejected the EDC in August 1954. European leaders decided to continue the unification of Europe through further economic integration, which was relaunched at a historic meeting in Messina, Italy, in June 1955. The six Foreign Ministers began to negotiate treaties to establish both:

- A European Economic Community (EEC) to merge separate national markets into a large single market that would ensure the free movement of goods, people, capital and services with a wide measure of common economic policies
- A European Atomic Energy Community (Euratom) to further the use of nuclear energy for peaceful purposes.

On March 25, 1957, in Rome, the Six signed the treaties creating these two Communities. Both were ratified before the end of the year by the parliaments of the six member countries.

ENLARGEMENT

Union membership, which is open to European democracies, has doubled from six to twelve since the first treaty was signed.

On January 1, 1973, Denmark, Ireland and the United Kingdom joined. Norway had signed an accession treaty, but its parliament refused ratification after voters rejected accession in a referendum. Greece joined the European Community in 1981, and Spain and Portugal in 1986. On October 3, 1990, the five Laender of the former German Democratic Republic entered the Community as part of a united Germany.

Turkey applied for membership in 1988, Austria in 1989, Malta and Cyprus in 1990, Sweden in 1991 and Finland, Norway and Switzerland in 1992. The new democracies of Central and Eastern Europe have also stated their interest in eventual EU membership. Hungary and Poland formally applied for membership in April 1994.

POLITICAL UNION

Although the founding treaties focus on the economic sphere, political union has been an aspiration from the outset. The Single European Act (SEA) of 1987 amended the founding treaties to facilitate concrete progress towards European unity through more majority voting, strengthened common action in the economic and social fields, and increased cooperation in the sphere of foreign policy. The SEA also gave a more prominent legislative role to the European Parliament.

The European Council in Dublin on April 28, 1990, declared that "further, decisive steps should be taken towards European unity as envisaged in the Single European Act." On December 14, 1990, in Rome, EC leaders launched an Intergovernmental Conference on Political Union. Its task was to draft a treaty incorporating new provisions to give the Community a political dimension commensurate with its economic power and international responsibilities. The Conference, which was conducted in parallel with a separate one on Economic and Monetary Union, concluded on December 11, 1991, in Maastricht, the Netherlands, where EC leaders agreed on a "three pillar" Treaty on European Union, establishing a framework for a common foreign and security policy, common action in the field of justice and home affairs, and the legal basis for full EMU.

The Treaty on European Union was signed in Maastricht on February 7, 1992, and entered into force on November 1, 1993, following ratification by the twelve Member States. The Danish electorate voted against ratification in a first referendum on June 2, 1992, but in favor in a second referendum on May 18, 1993, after a series of declarations adopted at the European Council summit meeting in Edinburgh in December 1992. The ratification process in the United Kingdom Parliament was marked by a protracted debate, but eventually completed following an affirmative parliamentary vote on August 2, 1993. Germany was the last State to deposit instruments of ratification in Rome, on October 13, 1993, after the German Constitutional Court ruled in favor of the Treaty's constitutionality following a challenge by Treaty opponents.

In December 1991, President Bush, commenting on the results of the Maastricht summit, reaffirmed United States support for a United Europe and commended EC assistance to the new democracies of Central and Eastern Europe:

> A more united Europe offers the United States a more effective partner, prepared for larger responsibilities ... A strengthened EC has a vital role to play in assuring a stable and prosperous Europe and a humane world order. Already today, the European Community and its member states are taking a major role, working with us, to help the citizens of Central and Eastern Europe transform their societies.

Continuing the longstanding U.S. policy of support for European unity, on October 18, 1993 President Clinton commended the ratification of the Treaty on European Union:

> On behalf of the American people, I offer congratulations to the Community on this occasion and reiterate our commitment to a strong and vibrant partnership. The Maastricht Treaty marks a milestone in the progress of the European Community toward political and economic union, a goal which the United States strongly supports and encourages.

EUROPEAN UNION INSTITUTIONS AND LAWMAKING

The European Union is governed by a quadripartite institutional system, including a Commission, a Council of Ministers, a European Parliament and a Court of Justice. A fifth institution, the Court of Auditors, monitors EU budget spending.

This system, novel in its conception, unique in its assignment of powers, differs from all previous national and international models. It is different from the U.S. constitutional arrangement, since the EU is not founded on a constitution, but on international treaties among sovereign nations. The power to enact laws that are directly binding on all EU citizens throughout the EU territory also distinguishes the Union from international organizations.

The Union has been described as a supranational entity. The member states have relinquished part of their national sovereignty to the EU institutions. The member states work together, in their collective interest, through the joint administration of their sovereign powers. The Union also operates according to the principle of "subsidiarity," which characterizes most federal systems. Under this principle, the Union is granted jurisdiction only for those policies that cannot be effectively handled at lower levels of government, i.e., national, regional, or local.

Overall, the EU system is flexible and inherently evolutionary, since it is designed to allow for the gradual development of European unification and has not yet achieved its final form.

European Investment Bank

Among the Union's financial instruments, the European Investment Bank (EIB) provides low interest loans for public and private investment projects that help its poorer regions, modernize industry or introduce new technology, support the energy policy, improve communications and protect the environment. The EIB is playing a major role in meeting long-term financing needs, particularly in relation to adaptation to the single market.

The EIB's capital, which is subscribed by the twelve member states, amounted to 57.6 billion ecu as of January 1, 1993. Its lending totalled 17 billion ecu in 1990. The EIB also finances projects in Mediterranean countries, in African, Caribbean and Pacific nations under the Lomé Convention and, since 1989, in the countries of Central and Eastern Europe.

Commission

The Commission is the executive and the policy engine. It proposes legislation, is responsible for administration, and ensures that the provisions of the treaties and the decisions of the institutions are properly implemented. It has investigative powers, and can take legal action against persons, companies or member states that violate EC rules. The Commission manages the budget and represents the Union in international trade negotiations.

Until 1992, the 17 Commissioners—two each from France, Germany, Italy, Spain and the United Kingdom, and one from each of the other member states—were appointed for a 4-year term by agreement among the member states. Exceptionally in 1993 the Commission was appointed to a two year term to bring it into alignment with the terms of the European Parliament. From January 1995, the Commission will be appointed to 5-year terms, conterminously with the European Parliament which has new powers under the Maastricht Treaty to approve the appointment of the Commission as a body. Under the Maastricht Treaty, the President of the Commission is appointed by agreement among the member governments in consultation with the European Parliament for a term of five years and up to two Vice-Presidents are appointed from among the Commissioners. With the implementation of the Maastricht Treaty, the Commission adopted the name "European Commission" for general usage, but it remains the Commission of the European Communities for legal purposes when acting under the statutory authority of the treaties.

The Commissioners act in the Union's interest, independently of the national governments which nominated them. Each is assigned one or more policy areas and each is assisted by a small "cabinet" or team of aides. The Commission's administrative staff, based mainly in Brussels, numbers about 13,000, divided among more than 20 "directorates-general" and other administrative services.

Council of Ministers

The Council adopts laws acting on proposals submitted by the Commission. With the implementation of the Maastricht Treaty, it is now the "Council of the European Union." It is composed of ministers representing the national governments of the member states.

FIGURE 2-1

The European Parliament

The European Parliament Grows from 518 to 567 Members in 1994.

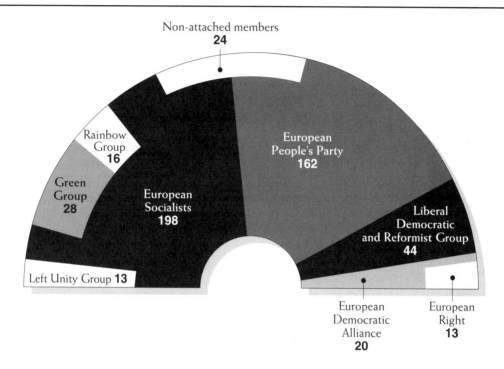

Different ministers participate in the Council according to the subject under discussion. Agricultural Ministers, for instance, discuss farm prices, and Economic and Finance Ministers discuss monetary affairs. The Ministers for Foreign Affairs coordinate the more specialized work of their colleagues. They are also responsible for foreign policy within the framework of the Common Foreign and Security Policy under the second pillar of the Treaty on Union.

Each Government acts as President of the Council for six months in rotation. The Council can take certain decisions by majority vote; others require unanimity. When decisions are taken by majority, France. Germany, Italy and the United Kingdom have ten votes each; Spain has eight votes; Belgium, Greece, the Netherlands and Portugal have five votes each; Denmark and Ireland have three votes each; and Luxembourg has two votes. Out of a total of 76 votes, 54 (a "qualified majority") are needed to approve a Commission proposal and enact it into law. Since the entry into force of the Single European Act, majority voting has been extended particularly in relation to the completion of the single market, research and technology, regional policy and the workplace, and under the Maastricht Treaty it is extended to additional measures of worker protection, education and training. Unanimity is still required for the Council to take decisions in certain sensitive areas, notably taxation.

The Council can alter the Commission's legislative proposals only by unanimous agreement. The Council is assisted in its work by the Committee of Permanent Representatives,

COMMON FOREIGN AND SECURITY POLICY (CFSP)

The CFSP succeeds European Political Cooperation (EPC), which began in 1970 and was formalized by the Single European Act in 1987. It is a framework for member states to coordinate their foreign policies, and is assisted by a small secretariat in Brussels. EPC and CFSP procedures are distinct from those of the EC. Within CFSP, Foreign Minister of the twelve member states and a representative of the Commission meet regularly to formulate joint positions on international issues and to discuss the political and economic aspects of security. The Maastricht Treaty on European Union provides for certain CFSP decisions to be taken by qualified majority vote and for the first time for the Union to develop a role in security and, eventually, defense. The Western European Union (WEU) will be the vehicle for military cooperation and for the coordination of European Union positions within NATO.

Coreper, which is composed of member states' government officials holding ambassadorial rank. The Council also has a general secretariat, with a staff of about 2000 people.

EUROPEAN COUNCIL

The European Council brings together Heads of State and Government and the President of the Commission. It meets at least twice a year, at the end of each EU member state's six-month presidency of the Council. In 1987, the Single European Act formalized the existence of this institution, which was not contemplated in the original EC treaties.

EUROPEAN PARLIAMENT

The European Parliament was composed of 518 members, directly elected by universal suffrage for five-year terms. The number of members increased to 567 in the 1994 elections reflecting the enlargement of the Federal Republic of Germany following German unification. The President of the Parliament is elected for a term of two-and-a-half years. The members of the European Parliament (MEPs) form political rather than national groups.

Thanks to the **cooperation procedure** introduced by the Single European Act—whereby the Parliament acts in cooperation with the Council and the Commission—the European Parliament enjoys an increased legislative role and has the power to amend proposals for legislation in a number of areas. Through the **assent procedure**, the Single European Act has also given the Parliament a veto power over the accession of new member states and the conclusion of association agreements with third countries. The Parliament also questions the Commission and the Council. It can amend, or reject, the Community budget. It can also dismiss the Commission through a vote of censure (a power it has never exercised). Under a new **co-decision procedure**, the Maastricht Treaty provides the European Parliament the right to veto legislation in certain policy areas, e.g. the environment (action programs), research and development (framework programs), culture, education, vocational training and youth.

The Parliament normally holds its plenary sessions in Strasbourg. Its 19 committees, which prepare the work for plenary meetings, and its political groups meet for the most part in Brussels.

FIGURE 2-2

The Co-Decision Procedure

The European Parliament always has the possibility of rejecting a proposal and so enjoys the right of veto in the decision-making process. The Maastricht Treaty thus increases Parliament's rights, but not to the extent that Parliament had wanted. Time limits are set on all the stages of the procedure. A proposal can be adopted very quickly if the Commission, Parliament, and the Council are all in agreement, where this is not the case the procedure lasts a maximum of 13 months, calculated from the date of the common position in the Council.

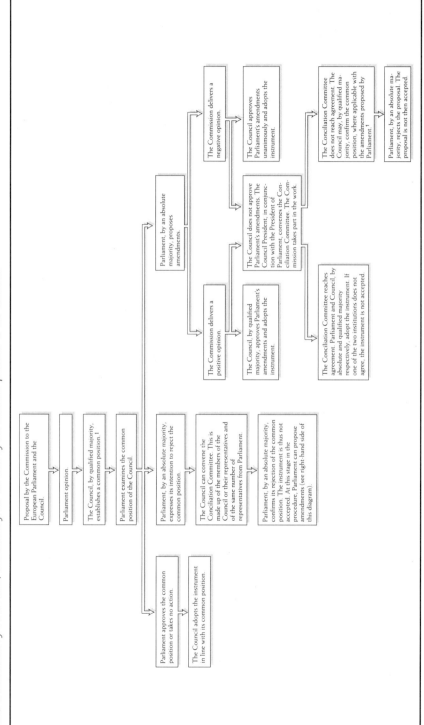

[1] The Council acts unanimously if its recommendation differs from that made by the Commission.

NB: (a) Each stage of the procedure is subject to time-limits which run from the moment a common position is adopted.

   (b) In addition to the co-decision procedure (Article 189b) there is also the cooperation procedure (Article 189c), which is similar but does not involve conciliation.

Text boxes in figure:

- Proposal by the Commission to the European Parliament and the Council.
- Parliament opinion.
- The Council, by qualified majority, establishes a common position.[1]
- Parliament examines the common position of the Council.
- Parliament approves the common position or takes no action.
- The Council adopts the instrument in line with its common position.
- Parliament, by an absolute majority, expresses its intention to reject the common position.
- The Council can convene the Conciliation Committee. This is made up of the members of the Council or their representatives and of the same number of representatives from Parliament.
- Parliament, by an absolute majority, confirms its rejection of the common position. The instrument is thus not accepted. At this stage in the procedure, Parliament can propose amendments (see right-hand side of this diagram).
- Parliament, by an absolute majority, proposes amendments.
- The Commission delivers a positive opinion.
- The Commission delivers a negative opinion.
- The Council, by qualified majority, approves Parliament's amendments and adopts the instrument.
- The Council does not approve Parliament's amendments. The Council President, in conjunction with the President of Parliament, convenes the Conciliation Committee. The Commission takes part in the work.
- The Council approves Parliament's amendments unanimously and adopts the instrument.
- The Conciliation Committee reaches agreement. Parliament and Council, by absolute and qualified majority respectively, adopt the instrument. If one of the two institutions does not agree, the instrument is not accepted.
- The Conciliation Committee does not reach agreement. The Council may, by qualified majority, confirm the common position, where applicable with the amendments proposed by Parliament.[1]
- Parliament, by an absolute majority, rejects the proposal. The proposal is not then accepted.

COURT OF JUSTICE

The Court of Justice, sitting in Luxembourg, is the Community's "Supreme Court." The Court, whose rulings are binding, ensures that the treaties are interpreted and applied correctly by the other institutions and the member states. The Court is comprised of 13 judges, one from each member state plus a President of the Court, and six advocates-general. Both groups are appointed for renewable terms of six years by mutual consent of the member states. Judgements of the Court in the field of EC law overrule those of national courts.

Through its judgments and interpretations, the Court of Justice has created a body of law which applies to EU institutions, member states, national courts, companies and private citizens.

Since 1988 the Court of Justice has been assisted by a Court of First Instance, consisting of 12 members. The new court has power to hear actions brought by EU officials, competition and coal and steel cases, and actions for damages. Its decisions are subject to appeal to the Court of Justice on points of law only.

ECONOMIC AND SOCIAL COMMITTEE

The Economic and Social Committee is a 189-member consultative body, based in Brussels. It represents the various categories of economic and social activity, such as labor, employers, agriculture, consumer and professional associations. It is consulted by the Commission and the Council for advice on EU policies and proposals for legislation.

COMMITTEE OF THE REGIONS

A Committee of the Regions was created in the Maastricht Treaty on European Union. It comprises representatives of regional and local bodies from each member state, and has statutory responsibility to advise the Commission and the Council on cultural policy, economic and social cohesion, public health, trans-European networks, and other appropriate areas of policy.

COURT OF AUDITORS

The Court of Auditors, based in Luxembourg, supervises expenditures. Its twelve members are appointed by the Council, after consulting the Parliament, for renewable six-year terms. The Court of Auditors began operating in 1977. It has extensive powers to examine the legality and regularity of receipts and expenditures and the sound financial management of the budget.

LEGISLATION

Legislation takes different forms, depending on the objectives to be achieved:

Regulations are binding in their entirety, are self-executing and directly applicable and obligatory throughout the EU territory. They can be compared to federal laws.

Directives are binding in terms of the results to be achieved, and are addressed to the member states, which are free to choose the best forms and methods of implementation.

Decisions are binding in their entirety upon those to whom they are addressed—member states natural and/or legal persons.

SINGLE MARKET—ECONOMIC AND MONETARY UNION

The Treaty of Rome stated as primary goals "a harmonious development of economic activities, a continuous and balanced expansion, an increase in stability, an accelerated raising of the standard of living and closer relations between the (Member) States" (Art. 1. EEC Treaty).

These goals were to be achieved through the progressive approximation of economic policies and the establishment of a common market.

The first step towards a common market was the creation of a customs union. This entailed removing duties on trade between member states and fixing a common external tariff—a process that was completed by July 1968, 18 months earlier than required by the EEC Treaty. The result was a massive increase in trade among the Six—from $6.8 billion in 1958, when the EEC was born, to $60 billion in 1972, just before the first enlargement. Despite these achievements, some old barriers remained and new ones were erected during the 1970s—a period of poor economic performance and "stagflation" for most industrialized countries. In addition, the Community was preoccupied with the difficult process of adapting to the first enlargement after the United Kingdom, Denmark and Ireland joined. Squabbles over the Common Agricultural Policy (CAP) and the British contribution to the EC budget obscured EC achievements in other areas and seemed to absorb all the Community's energies.

By the mid 1980s, the Community recognized that its primary aim—the creation of a true common market—had not been accomplished, and that the inability of European business to rely on an integrated market of continental dimensions was the main source of the Community's poor economic performance. The answer was the Commission's 1985 White Paper, which mapped out the road for completion of the internal market by the end of 1992.

EC 92

EC 92 was an unparalleled exercise in deregulation and liberalization. Intra-EC national borders are now no greater a barrier to trade and free movement than state borders within the United States—and in some areas even less. The EC 92 program was designed to create a unified economic area "without internal frontiers" within which people, goods, capital and services can circulate freely. The 1985 White Paper launching EC 92 listed almost 300 legislative measures needed to eliminate all physical, technical and fiscal barriers still hindering the EC economy, including:

- An end to intra-EC customs checks and border controls
- The harmonization or mutual recognition of technical standards
- The mutual recognition of professional diplomas
- An EC-wide market for services, such as banking, insurance, securities and other financial transactions
- The approximation of the national rates and assessment criteria for the EC's indirect taxes.

The positive impact of these measures was originally expected to produce a medium-term rise in European Gross Domestic Product (GDP) of between 4.5 and 7.0 percent, an increase of between 1.8 and 5 million new jobs, and a lowering of consumer prices by an average of 6 percent. By 1990, the Community's economy was clearly strengthened, thanks to job-creating growth fed by investment. Between 1984 and 1990, production rose by 20 percent and 8.5 million new jobs were created. Businesses adapted to the single market by merging, acquiring interests and developing joint ventures with businesses in other member states. Many more European firms now think and act "European."

Economic growth began to slow in the 1990s, however, turning into a serious recession by mid-1993, with unemployment above 10 percent and expected to continue to rise. The European Council adopted a coordinated economic stimulus package at its December 1992 meeting in Edinburgh, and at its Copenhagen meeting in June 1993 called for a Commission Study in response to mounting concern about structural problems in the European Community economy. A White Paper, *Growth, Competitiveness, Employment,* was presented to the Brussels European Council in December 1993.

Almost all the legislation foreshadowed in the 1985 White Paper has been enacted. As of December 1993, the Community had adopted 95 percent of the planned measures at Community level, and 84 percent had been transposed into national legislation in the twelve Member States. There are 18 measures still pending before the Council, 13 of which the Commission regards as essential for the effective implementation of the Single Market, including fiscal measures and measures dealing with company law. The abolition of frontier controls on people also remains incomplete. Implementation of the Schengen Agreement on the free movement of people, which has been signed by only nine of the EU 12, is delayed pending the completion of physical modifications to airport arrival terminals and the completion of a computerized system for monitoring arrivals at the Union's external frontiers.

THE SINGLE EUROPEAN ACT

The member states signed the Single European Act (SEA) in February 1986. After ratification by the twelve national Parliaments, the SEA entered into force on July 1, 1987. The SEA contains the amendments to the treaties necessary to ensure the timely achievement of the EC 92 program. But the Single Act is not limited to the completion of the internal market. It provides for significant developments in economic and monetary policy, social policy, research and technology, and the environment. The SEA also formalized the procedures for cooperation in the sphere of foreign policy which, although operational since 1970, had never been institutionalized. Finally, the SEA renewed the commitment to transform relations among the member states into a European Union.

THE EXTERNAL DIMENSION OF EC 92

After an initial period of careful analysis of the 1992 program, during which fears of an emerging "Fortress Europe" were expressed, the United States voiced support for the completion of the EC internal market. Secretary of State Baker said in his 1989 Berlin speech:

We think that Americans will profit from access to a single European market, just as Europeans have long profited from their access to a single American market.

In order to make EC 92 fully transparent and accessible to American businesses, the EC institutions multiplied their contacts with the relevant U.S. public and private authorities (see Reading 6). Foreign firms, especially from the United States, Japan, and the European Free Trade Association (EFTA), positioned themselves to take full advantage of the European single market. For example, they increased their direct investment in the European Community and entered into joint ventures with EC partners.

The single market benefits European and foreign companies alike. For most commercial purposes there is now one frontier instead of twelve; standards, testing and certification procedures are either uniform or equivalent; and economies of scale are possible thanks to the existence of a market of 347 million consumers. It is an open, not a closed market. As the world's biggest exporter, accounting for one-fifth of world trade, the Union could not afford to lean towards protectionism.

As in previous decades, when each step towards European integration was accompanied by a move toward greater liberalization of the multilateral system, completion of the single market was accompanied by EU efforts toward the successful completion of the Uruguay Round of multilateral negotiations. In fact, the single market and the Uruguay Round are complementary since both aim at opening world markets.

FIGURE 2-3

Composition of the ECU
The ECU, now an accounting unit, is expected to become the single currency of the ECU by the end of the century.

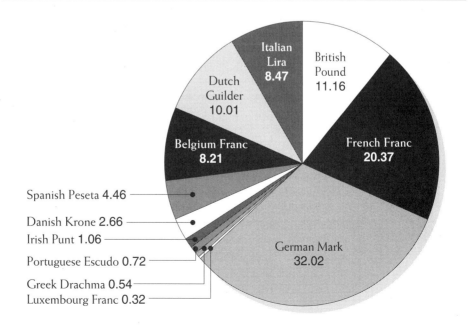

WHAT IS AN ECU?

The ecu (European Currency Unit) is a "basket" of specified amounts of each EU currency. Amounts are determined in accordance with the economic size of the member countries, and were revised every five years, until the implementation of the Maastricht Treaty. The value of the ecu is determined by using the current market rate of each member currency. The average exchange rate against the dollar in 1993 was 1 ecu = $1.17. All the member states' currencies participate in the ecu basket. In addition to its functions within the EMS, the ecu is the Union's accounting unit. It has also become popular as a private financial instrument. There are ecu-denominated traveler's checks, bank deposits and loans, and the ecu is used by some businesses as a currency for invoicing and payment. Significant amount of ecu denominated bonds have been placed on international markets. The first public offering of these bonds in the United States was launched in 1984. Currently, the ecu ranks among the top ten currencies in international bond issues. The ecu will probably become the new single European currency within the EMU.

BEYOND 1992: ECONOMIC AND MONETARY UNION

The single market has opened up new prospects for European integration, including that of Economic and Monetary Union (EMU). Without it, the internal market would remain fragmented by 12 different currencies, involving exchange rate risks and unnecessary transaction costs for citizens and businesses.

EMU is a three-step process. On July 1, 1990, the European Community entered Stage One, which aimed to improve economic and monetary policy convergence among member states. It also saw the removal of exchange controls in most member states. The Maastricht Treaty provides the legal basis for Stage Two, which began on January 1, 1994, and involves creation of a European Monetary Institute. This will pave the way for a European System of Central Banks at the beginning of Stage Three, which envisages the introduction of a single currency, probably the ecu, in qualifying countries by no later than January 1, 1999. The EMI and its successor, the European Central Bank, will be located in Frankfurt, Germany, a decision made by the European Council on October 29, 1993.

The European Monetary System (EMS), which has been operational since 1979, helped to reduce currency fluctuations in the 1980s with the goal of encouraging trade and investment across national borders, and was widely seen as another step towards EMU. The EMS is based on a system of fixed but adjustable exchange rates, resting on a variety of intervention and credit mechanisms. Its core is the ecu (see box), which is used to fix bilateral central rates for the currencies participating in the Exchange Rate Mechanism (ERM).

As of July 1, 1990—the start of Stage One—all member states had signed the EMS agreement. Under the ERM, participating currencies were allowed to fluctuate no more than 2.5 percent (or in some cases 6 percent) around the central rate. In August 1993, however, the bands within which currencies are allowed to fluctuate were widened to 15 percent around the central rate, following severe market pressure on some of the currencies in the system. In September 1992, Italy and the United Kingdom left the EMS Exchange Rate Mechanism following a round of severe pressure on their currencies. Greece and Portugal are members of the EMS but have not so far joined the ERM.

EUROPEAN UNION POLICIES

The EEC Treaty mandated common policies in certain areas, such as foreign trade, agriculture, competition and transport. In other areas, such as technology and the environment, the member states are developing common strategies in response to economic developments. The Community administers its policies and programs through its own budget. EC policies cover a broad spectrum of economic and social activities, from agriculture to transport.

AGRICULTURE

The Common Agricultural Policy (CAP) was established in 1962, in line with the objectives set out in the EEC Treaty. Its basic aims are to guarantee the security of food supplies at stable and reasonable prices, to improve productivity through technical progress and more rational agricultural production, and to ensure a fair standard of living for farmers (Art. 39, EEC Treaty). Since the CAP's inception, its fundamental objectives have been largely achieved. Food supplies are secure, markets are stable for most products and food costs have diminished as a percentage of the average household budget.

However, the CAP has faced some major challenges. Productivity increases and stagnating demand led to huge surpluses in some sectors, such as the highly publicized "wine lakes" and "butter mountains." The growth in farm surpluses became a heavy burden on the Community budget, since the CAP revolves around a system of price support. Reform was inevitable.

In the mid-1980s, the Community adopted a restrictive pricing policy, scaling down financial support for products in surplus. Among the many measures taken to make European agriculture more market-oriented, agricultural stabilizers—automatic price cuts—were adopted within the February 1988 "Delors package." Although these helped reduce agricultural spending and some stocks of basic commodities, they did not achieve lasting balance in the sector.

Faced with new surpluses and escalating budgetary costs, the Commission in February 1991 called on the Council to fundamentally reform the CAP, and submitted a full proposal to EC agricultural ministers in July. A comprehensive CAP reform plan agreed in July 1992 introduced price cuts to severely penalize overproduction, severed the link between price support and production, and gave direct income aids to small producers in affected product sectors in return for the role they play in preserving the environment and rural society.

COMPETITION

EU competition policy has a dual objective: to prevent member states from distorting competition by giving favored treatment to certain businesses, and to prevent firms from forming cartels or abusing a dominant market position.

Rules prohibit agreements to restrict competition—for example, fixing prices using a dominant position on the market for unfair advantage. They also place under the Commission's supervision national subsidies (state aids) to individual firms or industrial sectors that could distort the market. The Commission may punish anti-trust violators with heavy fines.

An efficient competition policy has a key role to play in the post-1992 Union, since the expected benefits of the single market, "optimal allocation of resources, increased productivity, lower prices and greater employment opportunities," will not be realized unless free and fair competition is ensured.

EDUCATION AND CULTURE

Education and training play a central role in securing a highly trained workforce, which is essential to Europe's international competitiveness.

Education programs include:

- **ERASMUS**: European Action Scheme for the Mobility of University Students
- **COMETT**: Community Program in Education and Training for Technology
- **LINGUA**: Action Program to Promote Foreign Language Competence in the European Union
- **YES**: Youth for Europe.

The Union's educational programs complement the EU system for the mutual recognition of diplomas, which guarantees professionals the right to practice in any member state, under the same conditions as the host country allows its own citizens.

To help European citizens acquire a revived sense of belonging to a shared European culture—rich in its diversity and based on the values of democracy, justice and liberty, the

FIGURE 2-4

The Budget
The EC budget currently comprises a little over 1 percent of total GNP and only about 3 percent of total government spending.

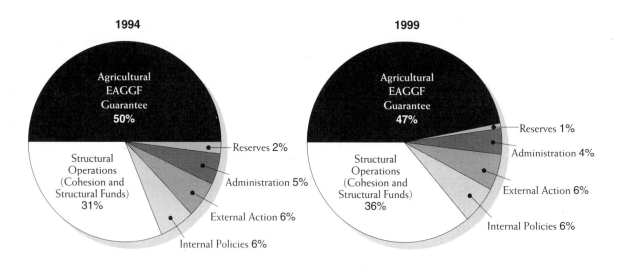

COMMUNITY REVENUE AND BUDGET

Unlike international organizations, which rely on their members' financial contributions, the Community has its own automatic sources of revenue. The Community's "own resources" are comprised of a part of the Value Added Tax (VAT) collected by the member states, customs duties on industrial products and levies on agricultural imports, as well as a contribution by each member state based on its Gross National Product (GNP).

The Community budget is adopted every year by the joint budgetary authority (the Council and the Parliament). Compared with national spending, the EC budget is very small, representing approximately 1 percent of the Community's GNP.

Union promotes the creation of a European cultural area. This entails, for example, the free circulation of cultural goods and services, business sponsorship of cultural projects and a policy on publishing. The Union also promotes the emergence of a European audio-visual industry through the adoption of common technical standards for satellite broadcasting, the "free movement" of broadcasts and the encouragement of the production and distribution of European audio-visual works.

ENERGY

In the field of energy, since the twin oil shocks of the 1970s, Europe has aimed at ensuring security of energy supply and at diversifying its energy product mix. It has greatly reduced its dependence on energy imports.

In 1988, the Commission completed an inventory of the remaining obstacles to free trade in the energy market, as a step towards the establishment of a single internal market for energy.

The EC also played a major role in the creation of a European Energy Charter which more than 36 countries, including the United States, the former Soviet Union, Canada and Japan, signed in The Hague (Netherlands) on December 17, 1991.

The Charter, which sets out the principles of pan-European energy cooperation, envisages using Western "know-how" to create a Europe-wide energy network as a means of developing Eastern European energy resources and of aiding the region's reconstruction. The Charter's principles will be implemented through specific protocols.

ENVIRONMENT

The Community's environmental policy was launched at a 1972 meeting of EC Heads of State and Government. However, it was not until the Single European Act that environmental policy was given its own place in the treaties. The Act provides that "action shall be based on the principles that preventive action shall be taken, that environmental damage should as a priority be rectified at source, and that the polluter should pay" and that "environmental protection requirements shall be a component of the Community's other policies."

EC R&TD Programs

- **ESPRIT**: European Strategic Program for Research and Development in Information Technologies
- **RACE**: Research in Advanced Communications in Europe
- **BRITE**: Basic Research in Industrial Technologies for Europe
- **EURAM**: European Research in Advanced Materials
- **SCIENCE**: Plan to Stimulate the International Cooperation and Interchange needed by European Research Scientists
- **SPES**: European Stimulation Plan for Economic Science
- **STEP**: Science and Technology for Environmental Protection
- **DELTA**: Development of European Learning through Technological Advance

Beginning in 1972, the Community developed a substantial body of environmental law, to protect against water and air pollution and the harmful effects of noise, and to control risks related to chemicals, biotechnology and nuclear energy. The European Community also participated in international conventions to protect natural resources, wild flora and fauna.

The EU is establishing stricter environmental standards targeting the polluter ("polluter pays" principle), ensuring the strict implementation of legislation, developing investment to improve the environment, and supporting environmental information campaigns.

A European Environment Agency is being established in Copenhagen to provide reliable scientific data and evaluations. According to the initial agreement in 1990, the Agency will be open to participation by other European countries. Environmental policy also constitutes a priority within the assistance programs that the Union is providing to Eastern and Central Europe.

REGIONAL AND SOCIAL AFFAIRS

In the Preamble of the EEC Treaty the member states declared their aim of "reducing the differences between the various regions and the backwardness of the less-favored regions." But there is still a wide gulf between the Union's poorest and most prosperous areas. The Union tackles regional and social disparities through the so-called Structural Funds, which comprise the European Social Fund (ESF), the European Regional Development Fund (ERDF) the Guidance section of the European Agricultural Guidance and Guarantee Fund (EAGGF), and the Cohesion Fund.

Since January 1, 1989, assistance has been targeted to national schemes to stimulate investment and create jobs in less developed regions in accordance with the principle of "Economic and Social Cohesion" mandated by the Single European Act. The key element in this reform is the virtual doubling of the Fund's resources between 1987 and 1993 to 14.1 billion ecu. The money is allocated among regions that are underdeveloped, affected by industrial decline or unemployment or in need of structural agricultural adjustment. A further increase in these resources to 31.8 billion ecu by 1999 was agreed at the Edinburgh summit of December 1992.

RESEARCH AND TECHNOLOGICAL DEVELOPMENT

The Union's activities in the field of Research and Technological Development (R&TD) used to be confined to coal, steel and nuclear energy. Since 1974, they have expanded into many other fields. The Single European Act provided specific legal powers in this field, which has become crucial to international competitiveness.

Through a pluriannual framework program, currently authorized at a total of 12 billion ecu from 1994–98, the Union conducts its R&TD activities mainly in three forms:

- **In-house research** at the Joint Research Centers
- **Shared-cost or contract research** whereby the EU contributes up to 50 percent of the cost of the research undertaken by firms, universities and research centers
- **Concerted action projects**, where the EU only ensures the coordination of the work carried out at national level.

The EU is thus promoting scientific cooperation among industry, universities and research centers across Europe to help boost its industrial competitiveness.

The Union also participates in EUREKA, which is a Europe-wide high-tech venture aimed at developing products—high-definition television, semiconductors, etc.—in response to market demand. Finally, the Union cooperates with its European neighbors, as well as with the United States and Japan, on a variety of other R&TD projects.

TRANSPORT

The EEC Treaty provides for a common transport policy. However, until the late 1980s, individual types of transport—road haulage, railways, inland waterways and aviation—continued to rely on the old national structures. In the wake of the 1992 program, the common transport policy prescribed by the EEC Treaty is finally being achieved.

Considerable progress has already been achieved for road, air and maritime transport. These sectors are being deregulated through the introduction of the freedom to provide road, air and maritime transport services, better access to the market and the application of rules of competition. Under a program to reinforce the infrastructure of the single market known as Trans-European Networks, integrated networks in road, rail, air traffic control, high speed data transmission, and energy supply lines are under development.

EUROPE—WORLD PARTNER

From the outset, the Community had wide powers for shaping its economic relations with the outside world through its common commercial policy. Political relations with the rest of the world were carried out, from 1970, through European Political Cooperation. For example, it is through EPC that the member states united to condemn human rights abuses throughout the world, to propose a solution to the Arab-Israeli conflict, to impose, and lift, economic sanctions against South Africa and to encourage the emergence of democracy in Central and Eastern Europe.

Since November 1, 1993, political relations are conducted under the Common Foreign and Security Policy in Title V (known as the "Second Pillar") of the Treaty on European

FIGURE 2-5

EU Trade, 1992

The U.S. enjoyed trade surpluses with the EU of more than $11 billion in 1990, and $17 billion in 1991.

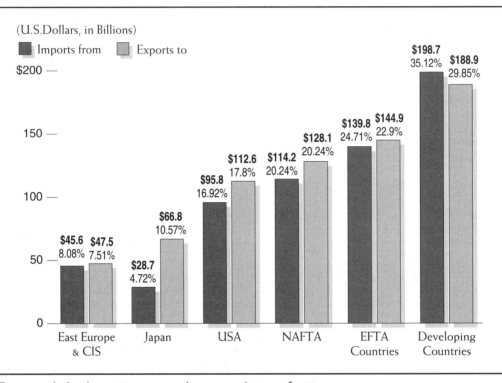

(U.S.Dollars, in Billions)

■ Imports from   ▨ Exports to

Source: Eurostat; calculated on 1992 average exchange rate of 1 ecu = $1.17.

Union, which provides for joint actions to be decided intergovernmentally and undertaken in the name of the European Union.

EUROPEAN COMMUNITY-EFTA RELATIONS

The European Free Trade Association (EFTA) was formed in 1960. Its current members are Austria, Finland, Iceland, Liechtenstein, Norway, Sweden, and Switzerland. Although its combined population is only about 32 million, EFTA is the Community's main trading partner, taking nearly 25 percent of EU exports and furnishing about 23 percent of EU imports. In comparison, the United States takes roughly 17 percent of EU exports and provides 18 percent of EU imports.

In 1973, the European Community and the EFTA countries agreed to gradually establish a free trade area for industrial products by abolishing customs duties and restrictions on trade in manufactured goods. The Community and EFTA also cooperated in the field of science and technology, transport, the environment, and education.

In October 1991, the European Community and EFTA agreed to merge their free trade zones into one European Economic Area (EEA) for people capital, goods and services.

Switzerland decided in a referendum not to ratify the EEA Treaty, but following ratification by the remaining eighteen countries of EFTA and the EU, the EEA Treaty came into force on January 1, 1994. This will oblige the EU and EFTA to share the EU's single market legislation for the removal of all physical, technical and fiscal barriers to trade. EFTA will adopt in particular:

- EU competition rules in matters of anti-trust, mergers, public procurement and state aids
- EU rules in company law, consumer protection, environment, research and development, education and social policy
- EU rules on mutual recognition of professional qualifications, underpinning the principle of freedom of movement of people.

In return for unrestricted access to the EU's single market of 347 million consumers, and to offset any repercussions for poorer EU member states, EFTA countries will also contribute to the EU's structural funds (see the section entitled "European Union Policies"). The EEA is the world's largest trading block. In 1992, it accounted for 27 percent of world exports and 30 percent of imports. EU and EFTA countries will act separately, however, in cases concerning anti-dumping trade actions and participation in international negotiations such as the GATT.

The EEA will be a gateway not only to the EU market, but also to eventual membership for EFTA members. Already accession negotiations have been completed with Austria, Sweden, Finland and Norway.

CENTRAL EASTERN EUROPE

Until the events of 1989, progress in relations between the European Community and state-trading countries of the Council of Mutual Economic Assistance (Comecon) had been slow. By June 1990, economic and cooperation agreements were signed with the Soviet Union, Hungary, Poland, Czechoslovakia, Bulgaria and the German Democratic Republic. An equivalent agreement was concluded with Romania in October 1990.

To speed up the process of reform, and to pave the way for eventual membership, the European Community signed a new set of agreements with Poland, Hungary and Czechoslovakia in December 1991. Following the breakup of Czechoslovakia in 1992 separate agreements were signed with the Czech Republic and Slovakia. Similar agreements were signed with Bulgaria and Romania. Known as "Europe Agreements," they are the most far-reaching of their kind and include provisions establishing: political dialogue through high-level meetings with the aim (where possible) of coordinating foreign policy positions, and a free trade area, in which people, capital, goods and services move freely. To allow time for adjustment, the agreements include some trade concessions in favor of the Central and Eastern European countries, and grant transitional periods for fulfillment of other principles (such as the reciprocal right of establishment for professionals and citizens), economic and financial cooperation, and cultural cooperation.

In 1992 the EU imported $47.5 billion from Central and Eastern Europe, compared with U.S. imports of $1.2 billion.

The EU also has trade and cooperation agreements with the Baltic states and Albania.

The EU has also played a significant role in the multilateral programs to promote economic and political reform in the countries of Central and Eastern Europe. Since the Western economic summit in Paris in July 1989, the Commission has been coordinating Western

FIGURE 2-6

Aid to the Third World

The EU and its member states are the largest donors of development aid.

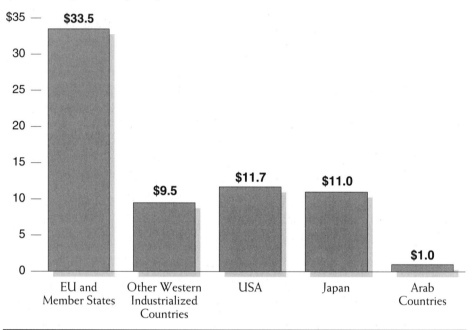

Public Aid from Prinicipal Donor Countries
(U.S. Dollars, in Billions, 1992)

Source: OECD.

aid efforts for the Group of 24 (the Community and EFTA nations plus the United States, Canada, Japan, New Zealand, Australia and Turkey). G-24 programs and projects aim to contribute to the growth of a healthy private sector in the new European democracies.

The Union and its member states are the majority shareholder in the $12 billion capital of the European Bank for Reconstruction and Development (EBRD), the aim of which is to promote economic development in the states of Central and Eastern Europe. The United States is also a major shareholder among the EBRD's 42 participating countries.

At the Copenhagen Summit in June 1993, the European Council pledged eventual EU membership for countries of Central and Eastern Europe which so desire and which are associated with the EU through the Europe Agreements.

THE COMMONWEALTH OF INDEPENDENT STATES

The EU is at the forefront of efforts to support the former Soviet Union in carrying out political and economic reforms.

In 1989, the EC and the Soviet Union signed a wide-ranging trade and cooperation agreement, granting both partners Most Favored Nation (MFN) status for their exports and

THE EU AND GATT

Because of its dependence on international trade, the EU has always been a strong advocate of free trade. The foundation of the EEC provided a major impetus for the far-reaching tariff cuts of the Dillon Round in 1960–61, and especially of the Kennedy Round of 1964–67. In the 1970s, the EC made an active contribution to the success of the Tokyo Round (1973–79), which lowered tariffs even further and regulated non-tariff trade barriers through specific codes. The EU played a leading role in the Uruguay Round of multilateral trade negotiations, which reached a successful conclusion in Geneva on December 15, 1993. The new Agreement covers such areas as agriculture, tropical products, textiles, services, intellectual property rights, investment, and dispute settlement. Today, the EU customs duties on industrialized goods are among the lowest within the GATT.

targeting key sectors for economic cooperation (standardization, energy, the environment, financial services and farming). In 1990, the EC and its member states set up programs to provide the country and constituent republics with emergency food and humanitarian aid, medical assistance, technical assistance, and credit guarantees for the purchase of food and medical products. The EU and its member states provide 73 percent of all foreign assistance to the CIS, including medical and food aid, loans and loan guarantees, strategic assistance (withdrawal of Russian troops) and technical and other assistance (commitments September 1990–end 1992).

Following the disintegration of the Soviet Union and the establishment of the new Commonwealth of Independent States (CIS) a review of the various instruments of aid and cooperation was undertaken, and separate agreements are being negotiated with some of the newly independent states of the former Soviet Union. A joint political declaration was signed in Brussels on December 9, 1993, by the Presidents of Russia, the European Council, and the European Commission, prior to the conclusion of a Partnership and Cooperation agreement. The EU is the major trading partner for Russia and most of the newly independent states, accounting for 40–50 percent of their global trade (in 1992 the EU imported from Russia 27 times more than the US and exported 4 times more than the US to Russia).

THE MEDITERRANEAN

There are cooperation agreements with twelve countries in the framework of a global Mediterranean policy designed to assist the region's economic development. The accords provide one-way, duty-free access for industrial exports to the EU, agricultural trade concessions, financial grants and European Investment Bank loans.

In the northern Mediterranean, the Community signed a cooperation agreement with Yugoslavia in 1980, and association agreements with Turkey (1964), Malta (1971) and Cyprus (1973). In the southern Mediterranean, trade, industrial, technical and financial cooperation agreements were concluded with Algeria, Morocco, Tunisia, Egypt, Israel, Jordan, Lebanon and Syria.

Since 1975, contact with the Arab countries has also been conducted through the Euro-Arab Dialogue, which covers such areas as technology transfer, investment incentives, trade cooperation, agricultural development, labor problems and cultural exchanges. In 1984, a non-preferential agreement was concluded with North Yemen, covering trade, economic cooperation and development. The Community and the Gulf Cooperation Council (Bahrain, Kuwait, Oman, Qatar, Saudi Arabia and the United Arab Emirates) signed a cooperation agreement in 1988, and establishment of a free-trade area is under discussion.

In September 1993, the Community announced a program of aid and technical assistance amounting to ecu 500 million over five years to assist the implementation of the peace agreement signed by Israel and the PLO.

THE THIRD WORLD

The Union remains strongly committed to the development of the Third World.

Lomé, Model Agreement: The Union is linked to 69 African, Caribbean and Pacific (ACP) countries by a unique pact that many consider a model approach to North-South cooperation. The Lomé Convention, launched in 1975 and renewed in 1979, 1984 and, for a ten-year period, in 1989, creates a stable legal framework for development cooperation involving negotiations between equal partners. It addresses the ACP states as a group so that aid to individual countries is not affected by political considerations. It provides for permanent dialogue through common institutions, including an Assembly, a Council of Ministers and a Committee of Ambassadors. The Lomé Convention frees the ACP countries from all customs duties on 99.5 percent of their exports to the EU, with no reciprocal concessions for EU exports. EU financial aid amounts to $15.0 billion for the period 1990-1995. The Convention has also set up a system for the stabilization of export earnings (STABEX) and a system to help the ACP countries to maintain their mineral export potential (SYSMIN).

Asia: A cooperation agreement covering trade, economic and development matters was signed in 1980 with the countries of ASEAN, the Association of South-East Asian Nations (Brunei, Indonesia, Malaysia, the Philippines, Singapore and Thailand). Contacts between the EU and ASEAN include regular political dialogue.

Between 1974 and 1976, the Community concluded non-preferential trade agreements with Bangladesh, India, Pakistan and Sri Lanka. The agreements with India (1981) and Pakistan (1986) were extended to cover economic and development cooperation. The Community opened diplomatic relations with the People's Republic of China in 1975. A 1985 trade and economic agreement set the stage for cooperation in sectors such as industry, mining, agriculture, science and technology, energy, transport, communications and environmental protection.

Latin and Central America: As a trading partner of Latin America, the Union is second only to the United States, taking roughly 20 percent of the region's exports. All Latin American countries benefit from a Generalized System of Preferences and other measures that help their exports. The EU and its member states are a leading source of development aid to this region.

The EU has trade and economic cooperation agreements with several Latin and Central American countries. It has also instituted a political dialogue with the countries of Central America, the Contadora Group and, more recently, the Rio Group, with the aim of promoting democracy, peace and economic development in Central and Latin America.

Generalized System of Preferences: The Generalized System of Preferences, the first such scheme to be established in line with the recommendation of the second United Nations Conference on Trade and Development(UNCTAD), has operated since 1971.

Under this framework, Third World countries are allowed duty-free exports of a large range of finished and semi-finished goods to the Union.

JAPAN

The EU has encouraged Japan to become more integrated into the world economy and to shoulder the responsibilities of a great economic power. To this end, the EU argues that Japan should reduce its export dependency, move towards an economy based on domestic demand and market liberalization and therefore reduce its structural trade surplus on a long-term basis. The EU aims at reducing its bilateral trade deficit, which in 1992 exceeded $40 billion. It has also taken measures to promote its exports to Japan and has obtained promises, in a number of sensitive sectors, that Japanese exports will be restrained.

EU-Japanese cooperation has been increased in the areas of industry, science and technology, telecommunications and information technology. Japanese investment in the European Union has been rising steadily, especially in depressed regions.

Political dialogue has also been deepened through the signing of a Joint Declaration with Japan in July 1991. The Declaration lays down the principles and objectives of relations between the two powers, both bilaterally and in the global context, and sets out the framework for regular consultations. The Declaration also formalizes the exchange of information on foreign policy.

CANADA

In 1976, the Community and Canada concluded a commercial and economic cooperation agreement—the Community's first such accord with a major industrialized country. It established mechanisms for cooperation in areas such as trade, industry and science. The two parties also have agreements on nuclear cooperation, medical research cooperation, and fishing. A Declaration on EC-Canada Relations, laying down the principles and framework for consultation and cooperation between the two parties was adopted on November 20, 1990.

INTERNATIONAL ORGANIZATIONS

The EU participates in the work of the Organization for Economic Cooperation and Development (OECD), in which the industrialized countries meet. It has observer status at the United Nations and in some of its specialized organizations. In November 1991, it became a member of the UN's Food and Agricultural Organization (FAO).

The EU takes part in the annual Western Economic Summits with the United States, Canada, Japan and four of its own member states (France, Germany, Italy and the United Kingdom). It is represented by the President of the Commission and the President of the Council. It also meets with the United States, Canada and Japan to discuss trade problems in the annual "Quadrilaterals," which were initiated in 1981.

THE EUROPEAN UNION AND THE UNITED STATES

The European Union and the United States are linked by a common heritage and a shared commitment to democracy. Since World War II, the United States has consistently supported the emergence of a strong, politically united Europe, founded on democratic values.

In fact, the United States provided the stimulus for the first form of organized cooperation among European nations, when Secretary of State George Marshall launched the European Recovery Program, in 1947. The "Marshall Plan" provided vast amounts of U.S. financial aid for the reconstruction of Europe, on condition that the beneficiary countries agreed to administer the American aid jointly.

In the 1950s, the Eisenhower Administration gave strong support to the newly formed European Communities and, on July 4, 1962, President Kennedy said in a historic address in Philadelphia:

> We do not regard a strong and united Europe as a rival, but a partner—developing coordinated policies in all economic and diplomatic areas.

EU-U.S. DIALOGUE

The formal EU-U.S. dialogue occurs in meetings held alternately in the United States and Europe:

- Bi-annual consultations between the President of the United States and, on the other side, the President of the European Council and the President of the Commission
- Bi-annual consultations between the U.S. Secretary of State and, on the other side, the twelve EU Foreign Ministers and the Commission, to discuss foreign policy issues
- Bi-annual ministerial-level meetings between the U.S. Government and the Commission.

Other briefings and ad hoc consultations take place especially with regard to foreign policy matters. In addition, the European Parliament maintains a Standing Delegation for relations with the United States, which meets twice yearly with members of the U.S. Congress.

AREAS OF COOPERATION

Specific accords have been concluded in the following areas:

- Peaceful use of nuclear energy, 1958
- Environmental matters, 1974
- Worker health and safety, 1979
- Mineral technology; fisheries (rights and market access), 1984
- Research and development in energy; controlled thermonuclear fusion research in radiation protection, 1986
- Biotechnology (Biotechnology Task-Force), 1990
- Competition and anti-trust (enforcement);
- Financial securities, 1991.

Informal cooperation takes place through regular discussions also, but not exclusively, in the following areas:

- Maritime transport
- High technology (since 1983)
- Scientific research
- Telecommunications
- Standardization, testing and certification
- Regulation of food and drugs
- Customs.

The European Union and the United States have agreed to strengthen their cooperation in the existing areas and to extend it to new sectors, such as financial services, education and vocational training, non-nuclear energy, and marketing opportunities for small and medium-sized enterprises.

EU-U.S. TRADE RELATIONS

The European Union and the United States account for more than 30 percent of world trade, and for more than 70 percent of the industrialized world's Gross Domestic Product (GDP). The Union is the largest trading partner of the United States, taking about 22.9 percent of total U.S. exports ($102.8 billion in 1992) and providing 17.7 percent of U.S. imports ($94.1 billion in 1992). The United States takes 16.9 percent of EU exports ($95.7 billion) and provides 17.8 percent of EU imports ($112.6 billion). The Union takes 17 percent of U.S. farm exports.

The EU has traditionally run a trade deficit with the United States in the agricultural field. EU exports to the United States mainly consist of machinery, motor vehicles, precision equipment, iron and steel and other manufactured products. U.S. exports to the EU also consist of machinery and transportation equipment, as well as agricultural products, organic chemicals and mineral fuels.

As competitors in the trade sphere, the EU and the United States are occasionally at odds on some issues. For example, steel used to be a major bone of contention, with the United States complaining of unfair competition from Europe. However, following a series of negotiations ending in September 1986, the Community agreed to regulate virtually all of its steel exports to the United States. Telecommunications and agricultural and aircraft manufacturing subsidies are among recent issues. The EU, for its part, has expressed concern about certain U.S. export controls, imposed for national security reasons, that affect European companies. In recent years it has objected to various U.S. trade laws and unfair trade practices that, in the Union's view, hamper free trade. The EU also objects to U.S. unilateral action in trade disputes and to sub-federal protectionism.

The European Union and the United States share common problems in the agricultural sector: overproduction, stagnating world demand and high levels of government support. The two parties compete on world markets for certain exports, mainly wheat and dairy products. The United States complains that the Common Agricultural Policy gives EU farmers an unfair advantage in world trade through export subsidies. The EU responds that its subsidies comply fully with GATT rules, and that the United States also subsidizes its farmers.

Despite their occasional trade conflicts, the United States and the European Union share a fundamental commitment to the international trading system that has contributed to their postwar prosperity. In fact, they have traditionally been able to resolve sectoral disagreements—"chicken wars," pasta and citrus disputes, etc.—to their mutual benefit, without jeopardizing the overall Atlantic partnership.

EU-U.S. INVESTMENT

The United States sends some 40 percent of its foreign investment to the EU. With the launching of the single market program, U.S. total investment in the member states grew from $83.9 billion in 1985 to $200.5 in 1992. EC investment in the United States grew to $219 billion in 1992—well ahead of Japanese investment, which totaled $96.7 billion.

FIGURE 2-7
Trade Statistics

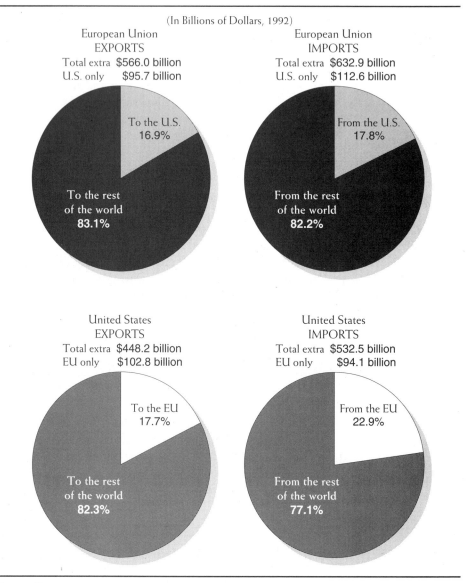

(In Billions of Dollars, 1992)

European Union
EXPORTS
Total extra $566.0 billion
U.S. only $95.7 billion

To the U.S.
16.9%

To the rest
of the world
83.1%

European Union
IMPORTS
Total extra $632.9 billion
U.S. only $112.6 billion

From the U.S.
17.8%

From the rest
of the world
82.2%

United States
EXPORTS
Total extra $448.2 billion
EU only $102.8 billion

To the EU
17.7%

To the rest
of the world
82.3%

United States
IMPORTS
Total extra $532.5 billion
EU only $94.1 billion

From the EU
22.9%

From the rest
of the world
77.1%

Source: Eurostat.

THE UNITED STATES AND THE EUROPEAN SINGLE MARKET

The United States recognized the economic and business opportunities offered by "EC 1992"—a single market bound by common rules and standards, comprising 347 million consumers with a purchasing power of over $4 trillion. In the words of the former U.S. Secretary of Commerce Robert Mosbacher, "This is a very different structure from the fragmented one U.S. businesspeople have dealt with in the past."

ACCORDING TO A 1990 GALLUP POLL:

- 47 percent of American adults have "heard or read about" the EC, compared to only 29 percent in 1987;
- 73 percent express support for the integration of Western Europe;
- 84 percent would like to receive more information on EC developments through the media; and
- 75 percent believe that the U.S. should develop a "special relationship" with the European Community.

The advantages that the United States draws from the Single Market are not limited to investment opportunities and increased exports of goods. As a strong service-oriented economy, the United States also profits from the liberalization of banking, insurance and investment services. In particular, the liberalization of financial services allows American banks in Europe a much broader scope of opportunities than permitted in the United States owing to U.S. restrictions on interstate banking and on banks' activities.

Responding to U.S. concerns, the EU has also ensured maximum transparency in standard-setting procedures for goods in order to allow non-EU companies to comment on proposed requirements at an early stage. Consultations are taking place also on the mutual

FIGURE 2-8

Profiles: EU and U.S., 1992

The EU is the world's largest unified consumer market.

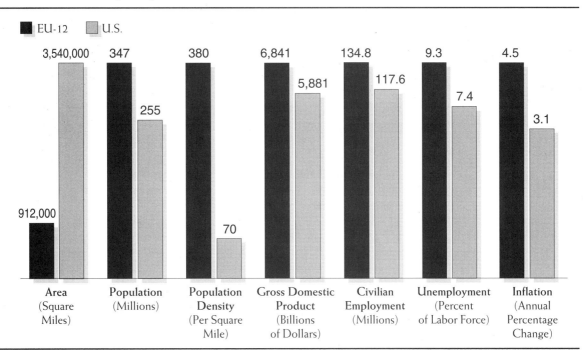

Source: EC Commission & OECD.

> "It often seems to be the case that there is a great deal of focus, understandably, on some of the trade disputes that divide us, rather than the bonds which unite us. It's useful to recall that our common ground is far, far wider than the areas of disagreement.
>
> The United States has long been a strong proponent of European unity and the importance of our transatlantic ties. Thirty-one years ago, President Kennedy made a statement that I believe holds as true today as it did then.
>
> He said we see in Europe a partner with whom we could deal on the basis of full equality in all the great and burdensome tasks of building and defending a community of free nations. That same vision guides this administration.
>
> The European Community is our largest single trade and investment partner. Our relationships with Europe are directly responsible for an inordinate number of American jobs, and if we cultivate that relationship properly and grow our trade and investment, it will mean more economic opportunities for the American people.
>
> Even more important, perhaps, is our shared commitment to our democratic values, to the protection of basic human rights, and to our collective responsibility to assess others who aspire to those values in their own society.
>
> We fully support Europe's efforts toward further integration and we will work with the European Community to achieve our common goals.
>
> We believe a strong and united European Community as a key partner in the pressing problems around the world is very much in the interest of the United States.
>
> I want our partnership to be effective in finding solutions to the problems we face together and to those few problems that continue to divide us."
>
> *President Clinton, May 7, 1993*

recognition of testing and certification procedures. Overall, uniformity of standards and procedures, with the resulting economies of scale, will reduce costs and administrative burdens for small and medium-sized companies that, until recently, have been unable to meet the requirements of twelve different markets.

THE WAY AHEAD

The European Union and the United States have a crucial role to play in shaping the new international order that is emerging from the worldwide movement towards political and economic freedom and market globalization.

The United States and the EU are working together to ensure the peaceful transition of the Eastern and Central European countries to systems based on multiparty democracy and free market economies.

The U.S. presence on the European continent, which has made a decisive contribution towards peace and stability during the last 40 years, is adapting to the end of the Cold War and the rise of new challenges to stability.

The United States and the European Union are also seeking together a more open world trading system, in particular through the GATT and its successor, the World Trade Organization (WTO), assuming ratification of the Uruguay Round Agreement.

THE TRANSATLANTIC DECLARATION

The United States of America and the European Community and its member states solemnly reaffirm their determination further to strengthen their partnership in order to:

- Support democracy, the rule of law and respect for human rights and individual liberty, and promote prosperity and social progress worldwide
- Safeguard peace and promote international security, by cooperating with other nations against aggression and coercion, by contributing to the settlement of conflicts in the world and by reinforcing the role of the United Nations and other international organizations
- Pursue policies aimed at achieving a sound world economy marked by sustained economic growth with low inflation, a high level of employment and equitable social conditions, in a framework of international stability
- Promote market principles, reject protectionism and expand, strengthen and further open the multilateral trading system
- Carry out their resolve to help developing countries by all appropriate means in their efforts towards political and economic reforms
- Provide adequate support, in cooperation with other states and organizations, to the nations of Eastern and Central Europe undertaking economic and political reforms and encourage their participation in the multilateral institutions of international trade and finance.

Principles of U.S.-EC Partnership

To achieve their common goals, the European Community and its member states and the United States of America will inform and consult each other on important matters of common interest, both political and economic, with a view to bringing their positions as close as possible without prejudice to their respective independence. In appropriate international bodies, in particular, they will seek close cooperation.

The EC-U.S. partnership will, moreover, greatly benefit from the mutual knowledge and understanding acquired through regular consultations as described in this Declaration.

Economic Cooperation

Both sides recognize the importance of strengthening the multilateral trading system. They will support further steps towards liberalization, transparency, and the implementation of GATT and OECD principles concerning both trade in goods and services and investment.

They will further develop their dialogue, which is already underway, on other matters such as technical and non-tariff barriers to industrial and agricultural trade, services, competition policy, transportation policy, standards, telecommunications, high technology and other relevant areas.

Education, Scientific and Cultural Cooperation

The partnership between the European Community and its member states on the one hand, and the United States on the other, will be based on continuous efforts to strengthen mutual cooperation in various other fields which directly affect the present and future well-being of their citizens, such as exchanges and joint projects in science

continued

continued from page 41

and technology, including, inter alia, research in medicine, environment protection, pollution, energy, space, high energy physics, and the safety of nuclear and other installations, as well as in education and culture, including academic and youth exchanges.

Transnational Challenges

The United States of America and the European Community and its member states will fulfill their responsibility to address transnational challenges, in the interest of their own peoples and of the rest of the world. In particular, they will join their efforts in the following fields:

- Combatting and preventing terrorism
- Putting an end to the illegal production, trafficking and consumption of narcotics and related criminal activities such as the laundering of money
- Cooperating in the fight against international crime
- Protecting the environment, both internationally and domestically, by integrating environmental and economic goals
- Preventing the proliferation of nuclear armaments, chemical and biological weapons, and missile technology.

Institutional Framework for Consultation

Both sides agree that a framework is required for regular and intensive consultation. They will make full use of and further strengthen existing procedures, including those established by the President of the European Council

and the President of the United States on 27th February 1990, namely:

- Bi-annual consultations to be arranged in the United States and in Europe between, on the one side, the President of the Commission, and on the other side, the President of the United States
- Bi-annual consultations between the European Community Foreign Ministers, with the Commission, and the U.S. Secretary of States, alternately on either side of the Atlantic
- Ad hoc consultations between the Presidency Foreign Minister or the Troika and the U.S. Secretary of State
- Bi-annual consultations between the Commission and the U.S. Government at Cabinet level
- Briefings, as currently exist, by the Presidency to U.S. Representatives on European Political Cooperation (EPC) meetings at the Ministerial level.

Both sides are resolved to develop and deepen these procedures for consultation so as to reflect the evolution of the European Community and of its relationship with the United States.

They welcome the actions taken by the European Parliament and the Congress of the United States in order to improve their dialogue and thereby bring closer together the peoples on both sides of the Atlantic.

The Declaration on EC-U.S. Relations was adopted by the EC and the U.S. on November 20, 1990, in Paris.

Building the Social Dimension

The European Community is rightly mindful of the rights of its citizens and its workers. The unemployed, the disabled and the elderly are entitled to its support. The fundamental right of EC citizens to live and work in the Member State of their choice is written into the Rome Treaty, the Community's founding charter. So are the commitments to improve the social protection of working people and to help the unemployed retrain for new jobs. Article 119 of the Treaty spells out women's right to equal pay for equal work. The first concrete action of the Community was to set up, in 1960, the European Social Fund (ESF) to improve job opportunities for the unemployed through retraining and the acquisition of new skills and to raise workers' living standards in general. It has been difficult over the years to ensure that the social dimension of the European Community kept pace with its economic and commercial integration. The single market program has done more for business than it has for workers. But considerable efforts have been made in recent years to strike a better balance. The Community has helped create a new platform for the dialogue between workers and employers. In 1989, 11 Member States adopted a social charter of fundamental workers' rights. Britain did not join in. As part of the Maastricht Treaty, the same 11 agreed on a series of procedures and measures for putting the Social Charter into practice.

> Our long-standing ambition has been a society accessible to all. If it can achieve this, Europe will remain faithful to its model of society and to its tradition of openness and generosity. Parliament's legitimate and constant concern matches ours. We both want the Community's social dimension to match its ideal of justice.
> —*Jacques Delors presenting the Commission's program for 1992 to the European Parliament, Strasbourg, February 12, 1992.*

MEETING THE CHALLENGE

Well before the formal start of the Community's single market in January 1993, EC leaders recognized the need for balance between its economic and social aspects. At a meeting in Rome in December 1990, Heads of State or Government declared that the establishment of the single market must result in genuine improvement in a employment and in the living and working conditions of all Community citizens. In the future, the Community will be judged by many people on the way it responds to the challenge of rising unemployment in Europe.

Part of the reason for the delays in adopting social legislation in the past has been the need for unanimous agreement among the Member States. Following the adoption by 11 Member States of the Agreement on Social Policy annexed to the Maastricht Treaty, many decisions will henceforth be taken by a qualified majority vote instead. This should speed up procedures.

The Maastricht Treaty builds on the other two pillars of Community social policy, the European Social Fund and the 1989 Community Charter of the Fundamental Social Rights of Workers.

THE EUROPEAN SOCIAL FUND

Although prospects are brighter in some areas in the medium term, there is no denying that we still face major difficulties and social hardship. Those affected must not be left to suffer alone. I am well aware that unemployment, deskilling and the difficulty of obtaining new qualifications can lead to self-doubt, loss of confidence and despair.
—*Jacques Delors, addressing a conference on Europe and German unification, Berlin, June 6, 1991.*

The Social Fund is the basic tool of Community policy. Its aim is to promote the geographical and occupational mobility of workers. With an annual budget of nearly ecu 5 billion, it directly benefits more than 2.7 million people a year. But the Social Fund is only part of what the Community spends in the inter-related fields of social, regional and rural development.

It was in 1989 that the Community took the decision to forge the three structural Funds into a single instrument of economic and social development. Taken together, spending in these three exceeded ecu 20 billion in 1993 or more than a quarter of the Community budget.

With eight million long-term unemployed and with many young people lacking the skills needed by the labour market, the Social Fund has concentrated on retraining schemes for the long-term unemployed and special programs to help the under-25s get a job. Other beneficiaries of the Fund include workers threatened with unemployment, women, migrants and workers in small and medium-sized enterprises.

In 1990, the European Commission launched three major new human resources initiatives:

Euroform which aims to develop new skills and new job opportunities for the unemployed.

NOW whose aim is to create equal access for women to jobs and professional training.

Horizon which will promote the employment of disabled people and other less-favoured groups.

Also in 1990, the EC Council of Ministers adopted a resolution for the integration of handicapped youngsters into normal education programs. Since then, the Council has adopted an action program in favor of the elderly and has declared 1993 as the Year of Older People and of Solidarity between Generations.

In addition, the **Helios** program seeks, through the exchange of experience and information, to make it possible for disabled people to live independent lives and participate fully in all aspects of life within the Community.

THE SOCIAL CHARTER

As its name implies, the Social Charter sets out the basic principles concerning workers' rights and labour relations within the European Community. Since 1989, the Community has started the task of translating these principles into practice by means of EC legislation. Progress has been achieved in several areas, but only slowly.

The 12 principles enumerated in the Social Charter are:

1. The right to work in the EC country of one's choice.
2. The freedom to choose an occupation and the right to a fair wage.
3. The right to improved living and working conditions.

4. The right to social protection under prevailing national systems.
5. The right to freedom of association and collective bargaining.
6. The right to vocational training.
7. The right of men and women to equal treatment.
8. The right of workers to information, consultation and participation.
9. The right to health protection and safety at work.
10. The protection of children and adolescents.
11. A decent standard of living for older people.
12. Improved social and professional integration for disabled people.

PROTECTION FOR WORKERS

Each member country of the European Community has developed its own system of social security and labour market legislation. Much of this diversity will remain. What the Community seeks to do is to define a minimum set of basic rules to be observed by every country. If individual EC States have already moved to higher levels of worker protection or want to go further, they are entirely free to do so.

Harmonization of social legislation is difficult in a Community where living standards in the poorest country are less than half those in the richest countries. But the Community has chosen to level upwards, raising standards in the poorer countries rather than lowering those in the most advanced countries.

The starting point for worker protection is the right for an EC citizen to live and work in another Community country under the same conditions and for the same salary and social protection as workers of that country. Additional progress has been made in the protection of the social security rights of workers and their families moving from one EC country to another (payment of pensions, sickness insurance, family benefits). Students and retired persons, although not "economically active," also have the right to live in the country of their choice.

Following the adoption of the Social Charter, initial focus was on measures to improve health and safety in the workplace. More than a dozen Directives have been adopted. A specific Directive has been agreed, extending health and safety protection to workers on temporary or fixed-term contracts.

Since then the Community has taken action in other areas in order:

- To create a new European information network for job vacancies known as **Eures** (European Employment Service);
- To oblige employers to inform workers of the conditions under which they are hired;
- To improve procedures in the event of collective redundancies;
- To promote schemes to enable workers to share in the profits of the companies they work for;
- To recommend common criteria for fixing adequate provisions in national social security systems.

Harmonization While Maintaining Improvements

Community rules may under no circumstances obstruct or dilute national rules in the social field which are particularly progressive and generous to ordinary people.

For some time social legislation will continue to be more advanced in some Member States than in others.

The Community wants to implement a social charter which affords the best possible protection to *all* workers in *all* Community countries. This means laying down minimum conditions to be observed in all the Member States.

The Community's aim is to harmonize health and safety standards and all other social conditions while maintaining improvements which have been made.

The most prosperous Member States and industries are pursuing their own development of social policy. The Community welcomes this, for the only improvements that can be maintained are those that have actually been made.

Wage levels, the right of association, the right to strike and lock-outs are all areas lying outside the Commission's competence.

EQUAL TREATMENT

Equal pay for men and women is a fundamental right embedded in the Rome Treaty. Although still not strictly enforced by Member States, its validity has been upheld on numerous occasions in cases brought before the European Court of Justice. In 1976, this principle was enlarged to cover equal treatment for both sexes in terms of access to jobs, vocational training and working conditions.

Action programs have been developed to promote equal opportunities in a variety of fields. The third equal opportunities action program, running from 1991 to 1996, aims to consolidate the legal framework for improving the position of women in society. Specific legislation has been enacted on issues like child care for working parents and better health and safety requirements in the workplace for pregnant women.

The Social Dimension of the Single Market

Most Europeans (65%) see the social dimension of the single market as a 'good thing'. Support for at least a minimum of social regulation at Community level is particularly strong in Italy (77%), Portugal (74%) and The Netherlands (73%), while the people of Luxembourg (54%), Denmark (55%) and the United Kingdom (57%) attach less importance to this kind of legislation. In Ireland 72% of people are in favor of Community rules in the social field, in Greece 71%, in Spain 70%, in Germany 63% and in Belgium and France 58%.

Source: *Eurobarometer 36*, December 1991.

Different Social Situations

	EMPLOYMENT (1991)			NET HOURLY EARNINGS IN INDUSTRY (1991) ECU	SOCIAL PROTECTION BENEFITS (1990)	
	TOTAL (1,000)	AGRICUL- TURE (%)	INDUSTRY (%)	SERVICES (%)		% OF GDP	ECU PER INHABITANT
B	3,758	2.6	27.7	69.6	8.63	26.8[3]	3,517[3]
DK	2,650	5.4	26.0	68.6	12.47	28.8	5,613
D[1]	28,886	3.2	38.6	58.2	10.65	26.9	4,836
GR	3,643	21.6	25.0	53.4	3.67	16.3[3]	710[3]
E	12,916	10.4	32.3	57.3	6.54	17.8	1,690
F	22,322	5.6	28.8	65.6	6.77	28.0	4,401
IRL	1,125	13.7	28.6	57.6	7.40	20.6	1,876
I	21,946	8.3	31.5	60.2	7.62	23.6	3,350
L	197	3.0	29.9	66.5	8.37[2]	26.7	4,619
NL	6,521	4.5	25.2	70.3	8.71	31.2	4,393
P	4,898	17.3	33.3	49.4	2.10	17.0	758
UK	26,049	2.1	27.6	68.9	8.33	20.7[3]	2,627[3]
EC	134,911	6.1	31.2	62.4		24.6[3]	3,183[3]

[1]Federal Republic of Germany as constituted prior to 3.10.1990.

[2]1990.

[3]1989.

Source: Eurostat.

In other areas, unanimous agreement will still be required. These include social security, social protection, protection of workers following the ending of an employment contract and the collective defense of interests of workers and employers. The Agreement on Social Policy does not apply to pay, the right of association, the right to strike or lock-outs.

THE SOCIAL DIALOGUE

The Maastricht Treaty introduces the possibility of concluding collective agreements between trade unions and employers' organizations at European level. This follows an initiative by representatives from the two sides of industry who asked EC governments to write into the Maastricht Treaty their right to conclude collective agreements.

These agreements may be implemented once they have been adopted by a decision of the Council of Ministers.

PART II

Completing the Internal Market: Europe 1992

Europe's Internal Market: Survey of Europe in 1992

AFTER THE FIREWORKS

There is a spring in the step of European civil servants that they have not known since the late 1960's. In February the heads of the European Community's governments managed to sweep an interminable wrangle about money to one side. The cost of Europe's farms; the spending power of the European Commission; the amount that should be spent on the infrastructure of the EEC's poorer regions; the depressing subject of Britain's contribution to the EEC budget—all were shelved for a while. Eurocrats could at last turn undistracted to the EEC's great project of the moment, a campaign to turn its 12 countries into one barrier-free market by the end of 1992.

It has taken more than two years, since the commission lit the fuse of this project, for "1992" to burst upon the world. The French, West German and British governments have mounted campaigns to raise their countrymen's eyes to it. Conference organizers are doing a brisk trade explaining it. Squads of Japanese corporate planners fly to Europe to assess it. Non-EEC European countries like Sweden, Switzerland and Austria worry about its portent for them. America eyes it warily for any unfriendly protectionist message. "1992" is the European phenomenon of the spring of 1988, and this summer will probably be remembered as the high-point of unquestioning hope for it.

What is it, and what difference will it make? Project 1992 is a clever campaign to bounce the EEC's 12 nations towards what the six original members agreed they wanted in their Treaty of Rome 30 years ago: a common market in which goods, people, services and capital could move without obstacle. Part of the power of 1992 is that it is so hard to reduce to essentials. At its simplest it is presented as "Europe without frontiers"; but to this graspable notion have been added extra after extra, all consistent with the aim of a single market but not necessarily vital to it: patent law, broadcasting standards, labelling rules, corporate structure, vocational training for young people, the pedigree of bovine animals, and so on and so on.

There is power in the diversity of this firework display. It means that there is something in 1992 for everyone. Now that most branches of European business are aware of it, 1992 has become a state of mind, a set of expectations that has political force, an obsession that amounts almost to a new reality. This survey cannot tell every reader how the big influences in his/her walk of life are responding to this display and what new business facts they are thereby creating. That would require a reference work. Instead it will burrow

The Economist (July 9, 1988).

down to the core of the project that has caused all this excitement and guess what under-lying changes will have been wrought by the middle of the next decade, when the fireworks are over.

As billed, 1992 will not be achieved this century. Equally, it is already clear that the successful parts of this project will do more for the coming together of the countries of Europe than any European initiative since the Treaty of Rome. The first reason for this success is that the designers of 1992 learnt from the mistakes of the past.

HISTORY LESSONS

Robert Schuman, a French founder of the EEC, said in 1950 that "Europe will not be made all at once or according to a single general plan. It will be built through concrete achieve-ments, which first create a de facto solidarity." Another founder, Jean Monnet, held that progress towards united Europe would be made only where clear goals and timetables were laid down. Both bits of advice were honored in the Treaty of Rome of 1957 which set a pragmatic first task and a timetable—the removal of tariffs and quotas between European countries within 12 years.

Subsequent, failed attempts to move the EEC forward showed what avenues to avoid. The Fouchet plan of 1961 envisaged a joint European foreign policy; both it and Fouchet Mark II died because they were too direct in their attempts to compromise the sovereignty of members. The Werner plan in 1970 for Economic and Monetary Union (EMU) by 1980 had a deadline going for it; but it, too, went straight for the jugular of national indepen-dence, and had the bad luck to do this on the eve of the everyman-for-himself era of float-ing exchange rates and oil crisis. EMU became the butt of hollow laughter in the late 1970's; though it found some vindication later in the founding of the European Monetary System (EMS) in 1979. A program for "European Union," presented by the Belgian prime minister, Leo Tindemans, was another ambitious Eurovision that member governments asked for and then ignored—though it too smouldered on to reappear later in the tale of 1992.

Before Mr. Jacques Delors, a former French finance minister, became president of the European Commission at the beginning of 1985, he toured the member states and tried on them four ideas to push Europe forward: closer collaboration on defense, development of the Community's system of government, another move on the monetary front, or a renewed campaign for a proper European market.

The last of these was the one that appealed to members the most, for various reasons:

- Mrs. Margaret Thatcher's government, long the black sheep of the EEC for its general stand-offishness and its maddeningly justified complaints about the European budget, wanted some pragmatic, non-airy-fairy European goal that it could advocate.
- France had lost any remaining illusions about go-it-alone economic management with a brief and painful adventure in socialist reflation in 1981-82. It was ready for less dirigisme, and more competition and interdependence.
- West Germany had a freshly installed liberal-conservative government making new, if rather empty, promises of liberal economic management.
- High unemployment right across Western Europe created a hunger for some new ini-tiative that might cure it. The Reagan administration (before its own economic come-uppance) suggested freer markets as an antidote to "Eurosclerosis."

FIGURE 4-1

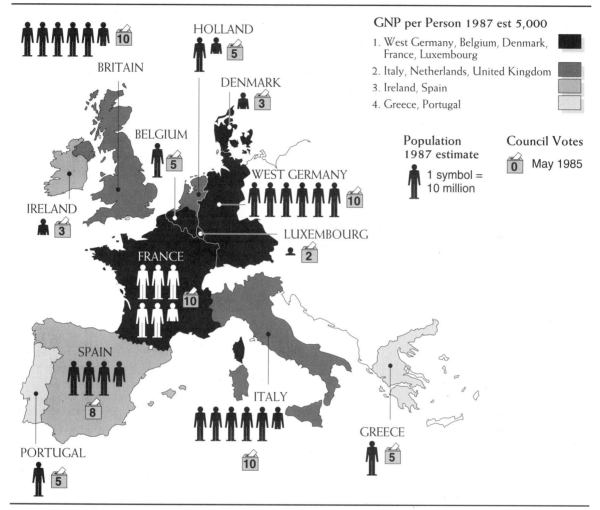

GNP per Person 1987 est 5,000

1. West Germany, Belgium, Denmark, France, Luxembourg
2. Italy, Netherlands, United Kingdom
3. Ireland, Spain
4. Greece, Portugal

Population 1987 estimate

1 symbol = 10 million

Council Votes May 1985

HOLLAND 5
BRITAIN 10
DENMARK 3
BELGIUM 5
WEST GERMANY 10
LUXEMBOURG 2
IRELAND 3
FRANCE 10
SPAIN 8
ITALY 10
GREECE 5
PORTUGAL 5

Source: OECD; EEC.

- European industrialists, notably Mr. Wisse Dekker of Philips and Mr. Jacques Solvay of Solvay, were campaigning energetically for an end to the EEC's economic divisions. They saw it as part of the answer to the challenge presented by Japan and the Asian dragons.

At Mr. Delors' bidding, Lord Cockfield, a doughty British conservative ex-businessman and tax-supremo, who had arrived in Brussels with no great fanfare as commissioner for the Internal Market, took to the task of preparing a white paper with almost alarming gusto. His tactics would have delighted Monnet and Schuman. He rapidly cobbled together a list of 300 measures that were needed for a wholly unified European market. He laid out the hectic timetable that would have to be followed to get those directives (European laws) adopted by the end of the next commission's reign, December 1992. The cleverness of the approach lay in the absence of priorities—which always favor one member-state's interests over another's—and in the strict focus on practical ends such as "no security checks at frontiers," rather than on political consequences, in other words, "this means a common immigration policy."

The magic of those 300 directives was potent—20 or more have since been quietly dropped or replaced, but the mystique of Leonidas's round number remains. After years of piecemeal fiddling, European governments were suddenly presented with the full measure of what they said they wanted. The challenge of so much lawmaking bounced those governments into passing the Single European Act, the second reason why 1992 must already be deemed a success.

ODD PARENTS, ODD NAME

The Single European Act started life as an attempt by an avid European, Altiero Spinelli, to re-ignite Tindemans's ideal of European Union by increasing the powers of the EEC institutions, and of the European Parliament in particular. As such, it probably would have died the normal death at the hands of those governments, notably Britain's, which instinctively mistrust any shift in the balance of power towards the EEC's institutions.

The pragmatic lure of the great market won the sceptics round. The act was greatly watered down before being adopted by the governments at the end of 1985; nevertheless it moved the scope and power of the Treaty of Rome forward on several fronts and, vital for 1992, ordained that most of its 300 directives would be adopted by "qualified majority voting" between ministers, rather than by unanimity.

The act was an early, irreversible triumph for the 1992 project. It took referendums in two countries—Ireland and Denmark—before it was ratified, but its precarious passage showed clearly how a practical goal could ginger EEC countries into concessions of sovereignty that would have got nowhere if presented only as woolly ideals.

The act also embodied reason number three why 1992 has already delivered something: mutual recognition, two dry words whose importance is worth a great number of frontier posts. Until the end of the 1970's the route to a common market was thought to lie through "harmonization." Frontiers would wither as the pasta, taxes, company laws, and anti-terrorist policies on either side of them were forced by the Eurocracy to conform to Euro-norms that would make the Community a seamless continuum. It was a hopeless prospect wherever countries were asked to take unanimous decisions over national quirks that were dear to them.

But in 1978 along came a West German company called Rewe Zentral AG, an unsung European hero, whose contribution to the great market should be toasted regularly in kir. This firm wanted to import Creme de Cassis, a liqueur otherwise known as Cassis de Dijon, into West Germany. It found it could not, because the elixir did not contain enough alcohol to be deemed a liqueur by West German standards. Rewe started legal proceedings which led to the European Court of Justice in Luxembourg, a body that will loom larger and larger as the 1992 story unfolds. The court looked at West Germany's claim that its liqueur norms did not discriminate between West Germans and foreigners, and ruled that it would not wash. West Germany had no right to block the import of a drink that was on sale in

France, unless it could show that it was blocked for reasons of health, fiscal supervision, fair trading or consumer protection. West Germany could not.

1 ECU=	1987 AVERAGE	MID-JUNE 1988
$	1.15	1.21
£	0.71	0.66
BFr	43.0	43.4
DKr	7.88	7.90
DM	2.07	2.08
Esc	162	171
FFr	6.93	7.01
Guilders	2.33	2.33
lire	1495	1544
Ptas	142	137
IR£	0.78	0.78

On this unlikely base was built a whole new technique for demolishing the EEC's unseen barrier—not those at frontiers but the barriers within. The technique is enshrined in the Single European Act—"the Council may decide that provisions in force in a member-state must be recognized as being equivalent to those applied by another." A new approach to industrial standards has evolved from Cassis de Dijon. Banks in one EEC country will be able to establish themselves in all. Insurance can be sold across frontiers. All benefited from this case.

More generally, the Cassis ruling means that 1992 offers the prospect of competitive lawmaking in European countries. Europe's companies and people will, in principle, be allowed to vote with their feet, or their wallets, for the member-state that offers them laws with the right blend of freedom and responsibility. Might freedom without responsibility be the unwanted victor? The scope for argument is obvious and already bedevils the attempt to apply mutual recognition more widely. But, equally, an analysis of America's internal market, later in this survey, shows that "competitive rulemaking" has not led to anarchy there.

However far this Cassis approach is ultimately taken, 1992 has here achieved a lurch towards a Europe that is alien to French or West German eyes. The extreme reluctance of Mr. Helmut Kohl's government to deregulate the West German economy shows how attached that society is to norms and standards painstakingly connected, and how unwilling it is to see them undermined by those of less fastidious nations. What would the Meistersingers say to an Italian tenor who breezed into Nuremberg claiming mutual recognition for his Venetian singing diploma unless he could be shown to be a health risk?

For France, with its long-established tradition of unchallenged dirigisme from the center, the prospect of competition in rules seems insidious in a different way. A senior French diplomat, Mr. Henri Froment-Meurice, has written one of an impressive series of studies of

FIGURE 4-2 ————————————————————————————
Who Trades Where
EEC Trade, 1987

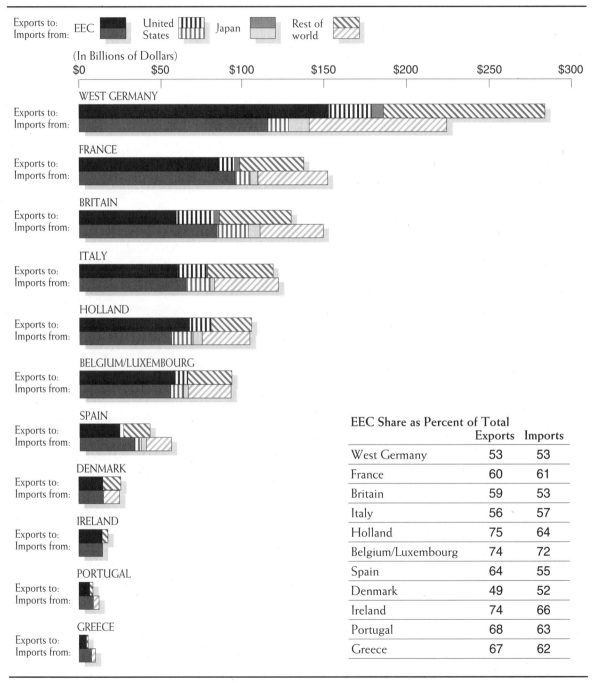

Exports to:
Imports from:

Exports to: / Imports from:	EEC	United States	Japan	Rest of world

(In Billions of Dollars)

$0 $50 $100 $150 $200 $250 $300

WEST GERMANY

FRANCE

BRITAIN

ITALY

HOLLAND

BELGIUM/LUXEMBOURG

SPAIN

DENMARK

IRELAND

PORTUGAL

GREECE

EEC Share as Percent of Total

	Exports	Imports
West Germany	53	53
France	60	61
Britain	59	53
Italy	56	57
Holland	75	64
Belgium/Luxembourg	74	72
Spain	64	55
Denmark	49	52
Ireland	74	66
Portugal	68	63
Greece	67	62

Source: OECD

1992 commissioned by the French government. In it he says that one of the dangers of the 1992 approach is that the EEC could be governed by a government of judges inadequately balanced by institutions of political power. Compare that with the evident relish with which Sir David Hannay, the British ambassador to the Community in Brussels, notes that case law is now shaping the EEC just as the evolution of common law shaped Great Britain.

In truth, this 1992 project is an adventure in deregulation: that is why Britain likes the sound of it. That, curiously, is why the French and the West Germans go along with it. Deregulation is the economic treatment of the decade—a fashionable medicine which European counties know they should swallow like good patients, even if they dislike its taste.

A practical-sounding goal; a much-trumpeted deadline; a new, deregulatory basis for drafting Community laws; a new majority-voting system to push those laws through; all playing upon a wide-spread susceptibility: these are what have given 1992 a trampoline start in bouncing the European Community towards greater unity. The technique has put off the moment when the members see the consequence of the project for their sovereignty and for the national system, phobias, principle and habits that they hold dearest. But it cannot remove those hard choices forever. The second half of the 1992 project, which starts at the end of this year, will be the half in which sovereignty fights back. Its earliest resistance is already showing in the symbolically important matter of frontier controls.

BORDER WARS

The European Commission has put about the idea of "Europe without frontiers" as the shorthand for what it is trying to achieve by the end of 1992. This has always been both a gamble and something of a fast one. Britain and Denmark still feel that the Treaty of Rome, and the Single Act's modifications of it, are for an economic community (the initials EEC used throughout this survey reflect that British viewpoint) and not the free movement of people tout court. Nevertheless, the commission is adamant that frontiers are the most potent symbol of the EEC's divisions. It insists that if frontier-posts remain for any reason at all, they will be used, willy-nilly, as a convenient place to carry out less justifiable checks.

As for the gamble, a brief review of what is needed before the EEC can become a zone without passport controls gives an idea of the odds against them: a harmonized law of gun control; police collaboration and mutual trust in guarding Europe's external frontiers against drugs and terrorists collaborations, trust and consistent laws for immigration, visas, and rights of asylum for people from outside the EEC. Small wonder that the 1992 progress report issued by the European Commission in March said bluntly that there had been no progress in such matters.

The complications are legion. West Germany has extremely strict gun controls: France has an American-like right to bear arms. Denmark insists upon maintaining a passport-free arrangement with the Nordic countries, so someone flying into London from Copenhagen could be a Dane, or a Swede, or a blonde alien let into Sweden from elsewhere. Britain, with its sea frontiers, finds it convenient to check its people only at frontier ports; it eschews identity cards. France, with unpoliceable land frontiers, cares less about border posts and monitors its people from within. Entirely different patterns of government snoopiness have developed around such facts of geography. They will not be discarded this century.

The outlook is not uniformly bleak. By the end of next year all new passports issued in Europe will be slim Euro-passports bearing the name of country beneath that of the

Community. Britain's, Holland's and West Germany's will be "machine readable" for rapid computer scrutiny, but the commission is keeping up a campaign to trim formalities for the bearers of such passes so that, wherever possible, they need do little more than wave them.

There is, moreover, the prospect of a "two-speed Europe" emerging in the matter of passport controls. In 1984 Chancellor Kohl of West Germany and President Mitterrand of France surprised their own officials by vowing to remove their mutual border controls completely. The Benelux countries, which already run a passport union, joined the other two in the Schengen agreement of 1985. Italy now wants to join as well, suggesting that the original EEC six may move ahead of the rest in letting people cross land frontiers unchecked.

Given the variety of types of port, of border and of combinations of contiguous countries that exist in the EEC, the commission should welcome such a la carte removal of immigration controls, and alter its sales-pitch for 1992 accordingly. In contrast to the trade-deadening insulation provided by customs posts, the economic benefits of a passport-free Elysium do not seem worth the trouble.

RENDER UNTO COCKFIELD

Customs posts are above all a matter of tax. There is no issue like taxation to show how the good intentions behind the 1992 project are running into the sands of sovereignty. If readers have to engage mental four-wheel-drive to plow through what follows it is because this survey will suggest, in the end, that tax is crucial to the expectations for 1992 that governments have raised among their electorates.

The contents of the battered box held up each budget day by the British chancellor of the exchecker have not yet been greatly compromised by Britain's membership of the EEC. Broadly, in choosing whether to tax people's income or what they do with it, and in deciding where for the good of society to make life cheaper or more expensive, European governments have remained their own masters.

A custom-free internal market will put an end to that. Customs controls protect one European country's indirect taxes (taxes, that is, on things not people) from relative tax bargains available in others. And they allow governments to make sure that they collect the VAT that is due to them. The prospect of 1992-as-billed is not merely of shoppers with large station-wagons taking day trips to Luxembourg to buy lightly taxed whisky and luxuries. It is of businesses buying components and capital equipment across borders and sending trucks to collect them, and of a booming trade in mail-order tax avoidance. If there is to be a Europe without customs halls, Europe's governments will have to accept heavy diversions of revenue and local business nonsenses—unless they move their rates of indirect tax close enough for such tax dodging to become uninteresting. The experience of the United States shows that contiguous states can maintain differences in sales tax of up to about five percentage points without the tax leakage becoming unbearable. Europe will, one way or another, have to achieve such an American order of tax sameness if it is to get rid of its tax-frontiers.

Of all the problems of creating an open market, the tax issue was the one on which the white paper lavished the most attention. In fact, the commission's approach here departed from the general 1992 tactic of getting members committed to a simple-sounding goal, chivvying them towards it, and letting them cope with the consequences later. Rather than opt for a fiscal version of mutual recognition—you charge your tax; I'll charge my tax; and we'll see how we manage—the commission went straight for preemptive harmonization. Why?

The commission feared that far from allowing market forces to determine what tax-differences could be sustained, as the British government proposed (from beyond a stretch of sea that would do its old duty in keeping continental forces at bay), high-taxing countries with land frontiers like Denmark, Ireland or even France would not lift their barriers to let those forces do their bit.

Europeans already have an allowance of 350 ecus-worth (roughly $400) of goods that they can take across intra-EEC frontiers without tax paperwork and payments. This amount alone has prompted Ireland and Denmark illegally to restrict their allowances to "genuine" travellers: that is, those staying outside their country for some arbitrary length of time, or those lugging suitcases but not washing-machines. The amount of tax lost was already more than these two governments were willing to shrug off. What chance of them keeping their booms open in a free-for-all?

So Lord Cockfield proposed a practical form of harmonization. He started with the American example of the spread of tax rates that seemed sustainable. Then he tried to fit such spreads as best he could around the scatter-shot pattern of European tax rates. This was a challenge, as the table shows. The standard rates of VAT range from 22% in Denmark down to 12% in Spain and Luxembourg. The Italians charge a hefty 38% on consumer gadgetry; Holland and Britain do not have a luxury rate at all. Britain does not charge any tax on a range of things including books, food and children's clothes. The commission's answer was to propose two VAT brackets—a normal rate of tax stretching between 14% and 20%

TABLE 1
VAT Rates in the EEC, %

	REDUCED RATE	STANDARD RATE	HIGH RATE
Belgium	1 and 6	19	25 and 33
Britain	0	15	None
Denmark	None	22	None
France	2.1 to 7	18.6	33.33
Greece	6	18	36
Holland	6	20	None
Ireland	2.4 and 10	25	None
Italy	2 and 9	18	38
Luxembourg	3 and 6	12	None
Portugal	8	16	30
Spain	6	12	33
West Germany	7	14	None
Commission proposal	4 to 9	14 to 20	None

and a reduced rate of 4–9% that would apply to a list of basic goods and services. Countries would choose their rates within those brackets.

Alas, the commission had to propose more than just new VAT bands. The quest for a frontier-free VAT system involves changes in the way that VAT on traded goods is levied. Although VAT is a value added tax, levied stage by stage as a product evolves, governments persist in viewing it as a sales tax. They expect to receive all the VAT on a product, even if some of its value has been added in another country: that is, they want their rate of VAT on the final sale price. Until now, such payment has been arranged by exporting countries demanding no VAT on export sales and refunding to the exporter all the VAT it has paid on the ingredients of the exports. An importing country, in contrast, levies VAT at the border on the import price and then tops this up with more VAT when the imported good is finally sold to the consumer. So border posts are vital both for tax-levying by the importing country, and for tax-policing by the exporting country, which uses the border papers to make sure that the zero-rated, exported product really did leave the country.

To get round this border-dependence, the commission proposes scrapping the zero-rating of exports. The exporting country will collect tax on the value-added up to the point of export. The importing country will apply its tax to the value added thereafter. To get all the VAT levied on traded goods into the hands of the country of final sale, the commission has thought up a clever clearing system. Countries will tot up all the VAT they have refunded to companies that have bought imports—money they want back from exporters' exchequers, and all the tax they have collected on their own export sales—which they owe to other countries. They will lodge/demand the balance at a central clearing-house. Honesty will be at a premium.

UNPLEASANT DUTIES

Whisky, cigarettes, motor fuel and other things liable to excise duties present similar problems of rates and collection, but the issue of rates is even more intractable. The differences across the EEC are large and are compounded by VAT, and most of these goods are easily transportable across frontiers. A liter of pure alcohol in Britain, for example, would carry 24.83 ecus in tax, in France 11.49 ecus, and in Dionysian Greece just 0.48 ecus. The commission felt bound to come up with a list of fixed compromises that would markedly alter the price of a tipple in some countries.

In the three years since the white paper appeared, these proposals have got nowhere. The finance ministries have had two committees study them. Both have nodded gravely at the grave problems involved; neither has been able to propose a better way of doing away with tax controls at frontiers. So the ministers have set up yet another committee.

Governments have varied reasons for finding the commission's proposals impossible. The British government regards them as bureaucratic meddling. It insists that high rates of duty on drink and tobacco be maintained for health reasons. It cannot entertain the idea of VAT on food because it promised never to impose it during the campaign for last year's general election. It wants to be left to see what rate-differences it can get away with, given its particular geographic position. Unfortunately, one country's experiment will be another's problem: Britain's Mothercare, for example, would be wonderfully set up to wage mail-order war on the continent's purveyors of children's clothing if the British zero VAT on children's clothes remained. France would then have to decide whether and how to block the advantage.

France's general attitude is shaped by such prospects. It fears that the commission's proposed tax bands are too wide and that France could not coexist openly with West Germany because both France's VAT rates and its public spending are higher. It is staring at a single-market imposed reshaping of its fiscal policy; and it knows it. The Danes face the prospect of losing 6% of GDP's worth of tax: neighboring Germany's standard VAT rate is eight percentage points lower than theirs. The clearing-house plan is generally pooh-poohed as being unworkable.

All in all, the way things are going at the moment, it is most improbable that 1992 will bring even the prospect of frontiers without tax checks. The British are already toying with a scheme to delay their removal, suggesting that another increase in the quantity of duty-free goods will somehow produce the market-driven convergence it is so keen on. (This is pure self-delusion: it is a sad fact that, however automatic the pressures, it is governments in the end that have to take the nasty political decisions.) The French, too, are talking about larger duty-free allowances and more policing of VAT away from frontiers. They are already adept at stopping the unwary smuggler in his car some way from the French border. Exit the spirit of 1992, pursued by a frontier-post-on-wheels.

AND THE WORLD BEYOND

One more knotty problem before leaving the matter of frontiers: in a customs-free Europe the only trade policy that a member-state can have towards the outside world is a Community one. Such a prospect does not square with Article 115 of the Treaty of Rome, which authorizes the commission to allow member states to take their own protective measures to shield themselves from "economic difficulties." The white paper tiptoes round the problem of Article 115. Logically it should be got rid of; but its future has barely been discussed between member governments.

Article 115 underpins a number of practical blockages that are inconsistent with project 1992.

- Some European countries, the most blatant being France and Italy, limit the number of Japanese cars imported each year by "Voluntary Restraint Agreements." They buttress these with the fact that there is no uniform "type approval" for cars in the EEC, so they can use technical quibbles to block any flow of Japanese cars via other EEC countries.
- The quantity of textile products that come to Europe under the Multi-Fibre Arrangement is divided up country by country. Frontier controls make sure that the quotas of jeans and T-shirts do not leak from one member to another.
- Britain has a number of special trading arrangements with ex-colonies. It sensibly enjoys New Zealand's cheap lamb. Frontier controls on the continent make sure that this pleasure does not spread there. On the other hand, Britain chooses to import expensive bananas from Caribbean ex-dependencies and to hold down the inflow from cheaper rivals. Frontier controls make sure that banana-running into Britain via, say, West Germany does not undermine this act of self-denial.

Commission officials admit that foreign trade is an unopened book, but assert (to *The Economist* at least) that they want the great market's trade policy towards the outside world to be a liberal one. Recent anti-dumping actions and crack-downs on Japanese "screwdriver plants" make one wonder. The French point of view is wonderfully laid out in the paper by Mr. Froment-Meurice. He considers the commission's approach to be "far too legal." He wants the commission to identify sensitive trade sectors, negotiate bilateral deals on them with countries outside the Community, and only when these are in place open up the internal market for the products involved. Here is another 1992 argument waiting to happen.

Pile together the problems of immigration control and those of tax, stir in external-trade policy, season with others not touched upon here—plant and animal-health checks, and the strange price-shifts for farm goods that must take place as they cross intra-European frontiers—and the conclusion is bleak. The European governments that are getting people excited about the prospect of a frontier-free Europe have not remotely summoned the political will to deliver what it involves.

Does this really matter? The durability of frontiers will be a blow to the 1992 campaign. If it had one identifiable target to match the disappearance of tariffs in the 1960's, the removal of the border posts was meant to be it. [It has been suggested] that the absence of internal borders is a crucial psychological feature of America's surprisingly imperfect home market. A survey by the commission found that European business men, too, place frontier delays, and the administrative and tax paperwork that takes place at frontiers, high on their list of difficulties in trading across Europe. If that is what businessmen perceive, that is what shapes their enthusiasms.

EXECUTIVE MISCELLANY

These selected bones are the only parts of the grand 1992 vision that this survey will pick out. What do they add up to for industrialists who are in the grip of the fashionable awareness that "Europe is open for business," and that they ought to do something about it fast?

First, there is no "Big Bang" in prospect for 1992—no red-letter day towards the end of that year on which some new system of trading will swing into action. There might, perhaps, have been a ceremonial burning of border posts. But, adding up all the concessions needed for such a party, one is forced to conclude that it will not happen. Borders will continue to reinforce Europe's natural divergences: different languages, different mass media, different tastes, different habits. Europe will remain a Europe of national markets that become steadily more accessible.

Second, there will not be a European equivalent to America's dollar by 1992, though the pressure for one will build up faster than most people imagine. So selling or subcontracting in the European market will still be bedevilled by transaction costs and by exchange-rate uncertainty that cannot be avoided (for it is as painful to lose a windfall profit you might have made as to suffer a windfall loss you did not cover against). The Bureau Européen des Unions de Consommateurs found recently that moving 100 ecus across an EEC frontier cost an average of 9% and took an average of five days. Price lists in foreign currencies; exchange losses that are hard to calculate; lingering customs formalities—these will suffice to stop the arbitrage-on-whim that would otherwise bring different national markets for the same products together.

Third, there will, for most managers, be no post-1992 set of Euro rules equivalent to the national ones they are used to. In principle, mutual recognition of regulations will have opened up markets; in practice, it will be up to businessmen to discover what they can get away with. It is going to take more European case law to discover what Dutch banks can do in Wiesbaden, whether tiles built to a British interpretation of a European standard can get building insurance in France, or whether Tiefbau of West Germany really has a chance of getting a public-works contract in Huddersfield.

So where is the good news? First, the cost of transport across Europe will come down. A newly introduced "Single Administrative Document" for taking goods across frontiers is a big step in the right direction; and if there is any area in which governments will be under pressure to honor the expectations they have generated for 1992, it is in trimming commercial frontier delays to an absolute minimum. Meanwhile a deregulated road-haulage business will lower its prices, and the airline industry will be under sustained pressure to cut its overpricing, too.

Frustrations will switch to transport infrastructure. Shortage of airspace, runways and motorway lanes will become the limiting factor. There will be argument over the impact of cheaper transport on the environment. (Austria, a non-member of the EEC which provides one of the main truck-routes to Italy, will figure prominently here.) Rail transport will undergo a renaissance. The construction industry will profit.

Moral for businessmen: There will be mounting competitive pressure to concentrate production in fewer plants, made flexible enough, through automation, to serve Europe's variable tastes. Unilever, for example, will make all its dishwasher powders for Europe at one plant in Lyons and all its "toilet-soap" at one plant in Port Sunlight. The distribution of consumer products will, however, remain mainly in national hands.

Second, there will be less protectionism-through-standards than there was in the past, and much less of the nonsense of working up competing national standards for new technologies before trying to reconcile them into European ones. No breakthroughs will happen here: the example of the new machinery directive shows what a slog lies ahead. But the 1992 spirit has altered the psychology with which governments and national champions are approaching this matter.

Moral for businessmen: As in finance, they need to be closely aware of and involved in the development of the industrial norms that will shape their products in the European market. In the shadow of IBM, for instance, Bull of France, ICL of Britain, Nixdorf and Siemens of West Germany, Olivetti of Italy, and Philips of Holland have all been pushing constructively for a common standard that will allow competing computers to interconnect freely. This is a campaign in a war that stretches well beyond Europe; but it helps with project 1992.

Third, there will be slow but steady progress towards greater openness in government procurement; partly because the rules will be policed more effectively, partly because the right of jinxed bidders to appeal to national courts will concentrate the minds of buyers in the public sector, and partly because of a more cost-conscious approach to public spending throughout Europe. Progress on industrial standards will help here, too: public procurers often use national standards to specify what they want. As for the customers of the traditional state enterprises—telecommunications, airlines and so forth—they will tend to shop around increasingly anyway, particularly if privatized. Even the conservative Bundespost of West Germany recently placed an order for "data-over-voice" equipment with Racal of Britain.

Moral for businessmen: Any company that relies on (non-defense) public procurement in one country for more than 25% of its sales ought to look for the custom of other governments, or spread its sales away from government.

Fourth (some businessmen will see this as bad news), the reduction of frictions and restraints in the European markets will make competition from non-European companies stiffer. Although the Community's external-trade policy, post-1992, has not yet been worked out, and despite recent campaigns against dumping and "screwdriver plants," the effect of a more open European market will be to align European trade policy with that of its more liberal members. Non-tariff barriers like voluntary restraint agreements will be tougher to organize.

Curiously, even though 1992 should make life easier for non-European multinationals, it may sap their relative advantage. They have, till now, been able to exploit big-company efficiencies against fragmented competition in a fragmented Europe: that position of relative superiority will be undermined.

Moral for businessmen: Even big, pan-European multinational companies should re-examine their structures in Europe with project 1992 in mind. IBM, for example, organizes its manufacture by continent, but its sales by country. It thinks this structure should suffice, post-1992. Will it? Perhaps customers will buy where margins and VAT rates are lowest and then freight their computers in. They might, in these software-dominated times, prefer to deal with a Europe-wide IBM specialist for their industry rather than a less-specialized salesman in their own country.

RIDING THE WAVE

None of this is in itself the stuff of panic. Project 1992 presents businessmen with a gradually expanding opportunity in a European market that has long been there; and a gradual threat to any "nice little earners" at home that have not already been spotted. Viewed in isolation, project 1992 should not force companies to do something fast, at the expense of something sensible.

Unhappily, this gentle prospect has been overlaid with a takeover wave that upsets calm reflection. Shearson Lehman Hutton, says that the number of its assignments to "find something to buy" for European companies is running at three times what it was a year ago. Project 1992 provided a pretext for Mr. Carlo De Benedetti's takeover forays into France and Belgium. It also created a political climate that has made possible deals that would have been blocked by governments five years ago. In the mid-1970's, for instance, GKN of Britain tried to strengthen its position in the European motor-components field by bidding for Sachs of West Germany. The deal was stopped by the West German Cartel Office on narrow, technical grounds. The spirit of 1992 would almost certainly have tipped the scale the other way today, just as it did recently when the French finance ministry tried unsuccessfully to block the purchase by the Financial Times of a French business newspaper, Les Echos.

So, given a sudden imperative to make more of the European market, what should a medium-sized European company do? One specific answer comes from two little-known companies, one Dutch the other French, that have just joined forces to exploit the European market for pet food.

B.V. Safari is a Dutch private company making dried foods for livestock and pets. Continentale de Conserves is a French private company that makes upmarket tinned foods and tinned pet foods. Both companies are the same size, with annual sales of something over FFr300m ($50m).

Their 1992 plan has a nice symmetry to it:

- Each will take a stake of about one-third in the other
- Each will have the exclusive right to market its own products, and the products of the other, in its own country.
- They will jointly own a marketing subsidiary which will sell the products of both firms across the rest of the European Community.
- They will jointly run and finance a research and development unit.

The virtues of the plan? There is a good fit between the products of the two companies, within a clearly identified business. Each partner will go on playing to its existing strengths in the country that it understands, but with a wider range of things to sell. The effort, emotion and cost of a takeover are avoided. Relatively little day-to-day collaboration is required. On the other hand, the cross-shareholdings make sure that both companies gain from the success of the whole adventure.

Europe must be full of companies that have a fine market or brand position at home and that want to "Europeanize" themselves rapidly without losing their independence. For them, a "twinning" formula of this sort would seem to have much going for it.

Europe's Internal Market: What Are They Building?

NICHOLAS COLCHESTER

Little more than a year ago, Europeans themselves barely realised that the 12 European Community countries had found a real resolve to turn themselves into one open market by the end of 1992. It was only after a wrangle over the EEC's budget and farm policies had been settled in February 1988 that their governments woke up to the task they had set themselves more than two years earlier. The pace of construction picked up in 1988, helped by the weight and competence of West Germany as president of the European Council during the first half of the year. But the significance of this project for the rest of the world still rated barely a passing thought among its architects.

The first survey in *The Economist* of 1992, which appeared in July 1988, reflected that European self-absorption: it laid out the blueprint of what was being built behind the hoardings, and the great scope for rows within the consortium of states that was trying to build it. This survey follows the 1992-obsession abroad, where it has spread powerfully during the past year. It will tell of the worries of the world outside, how much they are justified, what 1992 could do for the world's trading system and how it has altered perceptions of the EEC abroad. In the end it will return to the tensions within the building-site. Some of these have been suppressed: harmony now for discord later. Others have broken out in shrill tones. Underlying them all is the question that will not go away: what is the European Community really building? The answer is grander than at first seemed likely.

THE WORD IS OUT

Government officials in Washington say that more Americans are now aware of what they call "EC92" than were ever aware of the free trade agreement that was negotiated between America and Canada. Japanese corporate planners talk of little else when Europeans come to call. The governments of European countries outside the EEC devote much time to worrying about it. The project has taken off more powerfully than most of these outsiders expected. It has presented each of them with a dilemma. America is torn between the ideal of the strong, democratic Europe that it did so much to launch, and the prospect of a less

The Economist (July 8, 1989).

malleable western partner—stronger and more self-interested in its economic policies, more self-willed in its attitude to foreign policy and defense.

Japan rubs its hands at the prospect of another great market to conquer, but wrings them in the uneasy knowledge that 1992 may make the European market less conquerable. And those West Europeans outside the EEC wonder "how can we not be part of a Community that will increasingly dominate our economic lives, and which aims at what its members presume to call European union? And yet how can become more closely involved when most of us—Switzerland, Sweden, Austria, Finland—have embraced neutrality, and when the obligations of membership deepen by the hour?"

FORTRESSPHOBIA

In the late summer of 1988 a notion that the EEC was constructing a "Fortress Europe" took hold abroad. There had been no detailed statement, till then, of the external trade regime envisaged for the completed market. The best on offer was the communiqué of the European summit in Hanover, in June 1988, which ended West Germany's six-month stint as president of the Commmunity.

The internal market should not close in on itself. In conformity with the provisions of GATT, the Community should be open to third countries and must negotiate with these countries where necessary to ensure access to their market for Community exports. It will seek to preserve the balance of advantages accorded, while respecting the identity of the internal market of the Community.

This was openness, but openness with the gloves well up. Then came Mrs. Margaret Thatcher's celebrated speech in Bruges in late September 1988:

My fourth guiding principle is that Europe should not be protectionist … It would be a betrayal if, while breaking down the constraints on trade to create the single market, the Community were to erect greater external protection. We must make sure that our approach to world trade is consistent with the liberalisation we preach at home.

Here too was openness; yet this speech, which marked a breakdown of the facade of unity with which the 12 members had set about building 1992, was more about a threat to be avoided than a principle firmly enshrined.

Words or no words, worried foreign watchers saw evidence of modern protectionism— a toughening of the EEC's use if anti-dumping actions, a tightening of "rules of origin" to stop convicted dumpers side-stepping those actions, and an uncompromising demand for "reciprocity" abroad in the draft regime for pan-European banking. They heard the pleas for protection of European industrialists, such as Mr. Umberto Agnelli of FIAT. The commission was for a time reluctant to be clear about its external-trade policy. The 300 directives of the 1992 plan already contained quite enough to give vested interests inside the EEC the shivers: it seemed no time to add the threat of the outside world to their fears. So, little was said and the outside world assumed the worst.

Since last autumn that pessimism has been assuaged, and Europe's image has improved. In late October, the Brussels commission debated external-trade policy and published a much more detailed statement of the Community's trading intentions. It stressed the Community's vested interest in vigorous trade: its external exports are 20% of world exports, against America's 15% and Japan's 9%. Those external exports are equivalent to 9.0% of its own GDP, compared with 6.7% for America and 9.3% for Japan. It promised loyalty to the GATT rule on multilateral trade. For types of trade not covered by GATT, it defined, in broadly unfrightening terms, the kind of reciprocal access to other countries it would be pushing for. It said that it might, in certain cases, replace national protection (which the planned Europe-without-internal-frontiers would make unworkable) with Community-wide protection; but it promised that the overall level of protection would not go up. The overall gloss was: "Not fortress Europe, but partnership Europe."

Other developments have further brightened the EEC's image. There was a compromise between the EEC and America over farm protectionism in April, which allowed the Uruguay round of GATT negotiations to continue its quest for a world trading regime that can cope with modern realities. There was a change of commissioners when the European Commission's new four-year term began at the start of this year. Mr. Frans Andriessen, a cool and economically liberal Dutchman, became commissioner for external relations, replacing a colorful Belgian, Mr. Willy De Clerq, who had said one or two rash things that outsiders had seized upon as evidence of Euro-protectionism. Lord Cockfield, the didactic commissioner who drew up the blueprint for the internal market, was called home to Britain by Mrs. Thatcher: as with the Sydney Opera House, it was by then clear that it would take one sort of genius to design 1992, another to make it stand up.

In came one of West Germany's economic liberals, Mr. Martin Bangemann, as commissioner for industrial affairs and the internal market. In, too, came Sir Leon Brittan, from Britain, as commissioner for competition policy, where he continues the liberal campaign conducted by Mr. Peter Sutherland, and for financial services. This trio of newcomers now forms a powerful block within the commission, pushing for an open Europe.

True, the president of the commission and re-animator of the Community remains a socialist Frenchman, Mr. Jacques Delors. But as socialist Frenchmen go, Mr. Delors is no air-headed *intello*: he helped pull France out of President Mitterrand's disastrous socialist adventure in the early 1980s and he set the French economy off on a course of very unGallic deregulation. Mr. Delors has not tried to quash the new commission's free-market tendencies; instead he has sought to compensate for them by championing Europe's "social dimension" and by projecting with great vigour a vision of Europe that stretches way beyond the completion of a market.

A combination of this more liberal commission (in the non-American sense of the word), the insistence of West Germany, Britain, Denmark and Holland, and the chivvying of worried outsiders, has chipped away at the internal market's protectionist potential bit by bit, area by area. Anti-dumping actions, standards, reciprocity, voluntary-restraint agreements: this survey later examines weapons in the armoury of modern trade warfare and how the new Europe is wielding them. For the moment, one general point suffices: as they peer into the 1992 building site, outsiders now see that there is no masterplan for a fortress Europe. Some protectionism is being created in the process of building. Some people within the commission have to control their interventionist instincts, rather as Dr. Strangelove controlled his right arm. But a surprisingly open market is being improvised on the run.

This improvising cannot use familiar and tested tools of trade liberalisation. Project 1992 is pledged to provide a degree of economic interdependence between sovereign states that has never been attempted before. This makes it a pioneer in areas that GATT will later tread in its quest for a world-wide regime against non-tariff barriers, or for trade in services, or for respect of intellectual property. In all these types of commerce, protection ceases to be a matter of quotas, recalcitrant border officials, paperwork and charges at frontiers. The rules of the sovereign states are what create the protection: the standard for exhaust gases that the foreign motorcar does not meet; the banking rule that bans the service that a foreign bank wants to provide; the state favoritism that stops foreign companies building airports in Japan. So the referee of a trading system, whether a European one or a world one, must move his gaze beyond tariffs and quotas and start pronouncing on national laws. When that happens, as in Europe 1992, sovereignty fights back.

The commission then faces quandaries that the GATT may come to know. Does it precisely define and limit its powers in each area, with books of rules that look pernickety? Or does it leave the rules vague and stand accused of the fashionable sin of the age—lack of accountability? Does it get governments to face up now to the logic of what they are letting themselves in for, the better to get the political pain over with? Or does it leave the commitments vague, hoping that political resolve will still be there when market forces test them later? Does it prepare governments now for less freedom to set indirect taxes; or let new market-driven constraints crowd in on them later? Does it prepare governments now for the need to co-ordinate their monetary policies; or let them scramble for such co-ordination when newly liberated capital flees?

The danger for the EEC in the first course is of gratuitous meddling from the center. The danger in the second is of a cop-out when the crunch comes: borders that do not stay open, exchange controls that are re-imposed. Pushed in good measure by the British, the Community and its commission have opted for the second course. So progress towards a deregulatory 1992 has been encouraging. But the directives tend to be directives of intentions rather than means, with hard choices delayed till later.

ON-SITE INSPECTION

Progress in passing the European laws in the white paper itself—the program of 300 (now actually 279) directives that forms the practical heart of the internal-market project—has remained surprisingly brisk. This summer roughly half of those directives either have been adopted by the European Council or enjoy the vital "common position" within the council (see chart on the next page). It is now four years since the white paper was published, with three and a half years remaining before the end of 1992. So the project is still vaguely in touch with its own deadline.

But beware. Some of the early directives were brewing years before the 1992 white paper was written. Moreover, adoption of Euro-laws by the council is only a start. The directives have to be incorporated into national law and then put into practice. It will take years of bureaucratic adjustment and many appeals by companies and people to the European Court of Justice in Luxembourg to make those directives deliver the access to other countries' markets that they promise.

The sources of encouragement remain powerful. A combination of the enlargement of the EEC to include 12 countries and the passing in 1987 of the Single European Act—which was the enabling treaty for 1992—made a weighted form of majority voting the norm in the council for much of its 1992 directive-passing. The prospect of such voting has encouraged much more give-and-take between governments as they concede what will not hurt them in return for support where they really want it.

The private sector within and beyond Europe now believes in and acts upon the prospect of a great market to a degree that makes the business significance of 1992 all but irreversible. Toyota of Japan was heavily influenced by the prospect of a large European market, with a still unknown degree of external protection, to invest $1 billion in a car-making plant in Britain. In high-technology industries, where access to big markets and procurement contracts is vital to defray today's vast research and development costs, the prospect of 1992 has prompted mergers between European companies, and inward investment by

FIGURE 5-1

Three-Quarters Designed and Half Built

The White Paper's 300 Directives

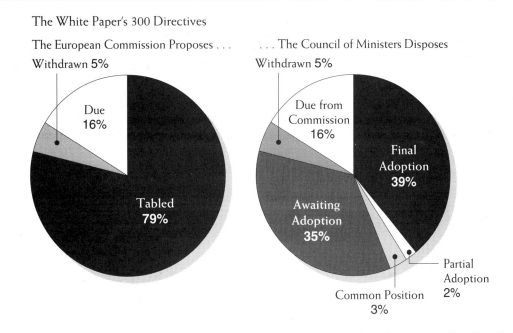

The European Commission Proposes . . .

Withdrawn 5%

Due 16%

Tabled 79%

. . . The Council of Ministers Disposes

Withdrawn 5%

Due from Commission 16%

Final Adoption 39%

Awaiting Adoption 35%

Partial Adoption 2%

Common Position 3%

Source: American Chamber of Commerce.

outsiders. The envisaged link-up between Siemens, GEC, and Plessey is an example in telecoms; ditto for that between Alsthom of France and GEC in power equipment. Northern Telecom of Canada has bought into STC in Britain. AT&T of America has bought into Italtel in Italy. Nestlé, a Swiss food company, spent more than $6 billion last year to consolidate its hold on the European food business with takeovers that included Rowntree of Britain and Buitoni of Italy. BSN of France has paid $2.5 billion for the European food businesses owned by RJR Nabisco. Argument whether such merger mania has really been spurred by 1992, or would have happened anyway, misses the point: these companies will be counting on an EEC with more open procurement and permeable internal frontiers. The 1992 white paper is going with the grain of big business.

THREE WAYS TO MARKET

The 1992 program can be divided into three parts. There is the campaign against barriers at frontiers that halt the flow of people and goods. There is the one against the "barriers within"—the national rules that stop goods being sold, capital flowing, or firms of lawyers setting up their chambers across Europe. And there are grand accompanying visions, called for in the Single European Act. These are: the "social dimension," which seeks to establish the rights of ordinary people in the great market and to help the poorer among them; moves towards economic and monetary union (EMU), including one currency and a European central bank; closer co-operation in making European foreign policy (confusingly called political co-operation); and, grandest and vaguest of all, European union.

FIGURE 5-2 ————————————————————————————

Europe by Numbers

The Number, Type, and Status of White-Paper Directives

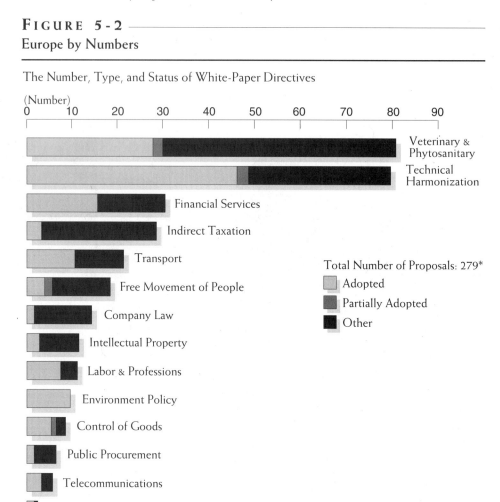

*Chart includes some duplication due to ovelapping areas and some withdrawn proposals.

Source: American Chamber of Commerce.

In the assault upon the unseen barriers the best progress has been made on industrial standards. Half the directives to stop national product regulations and safety rules blocking the free flow of goods have gone through the council. When Business International, a sister company to *The Economist*, asked European industrialists about their attitudes towards 1992, more of them mentioned progress against obstructive standards as being important to them than anything else. The commission has sidestepped man-aeons of negotiation here by insisting that EEC countries accept products made under each other's product laws, provided that these meet essential requirements for safety and against pollution that are laid down in European directives. The business of reconciling national standards to create European ones (which are there for more-or-less optional convenience) is then left to two agencies, CEN and CENELEC. The underlying idea is that governments should briskly regulate while agencies and industries methodically standardize.

The essential requirements have now been established for pressure vessels, toys, construction materials, electrical interference and machine safety. If that seems scanty, remember that the last of these covers roughly half of the output of the mechanical-engineering industry in the Community. So far, so good: but consumer-protection-through-regulations has an onion-like ability to reveal new layers of unfriendliness as each one is stripped away. There tends to be pressure for additional directives: a machine-usage directive, for example, to prevent operators injuring themselves on Euro-safe machines. There is the matter of certification, too. Britain is pushing for self-certification by manufacturers—machines declared Euro-safe would be presumed to be so unless challenged—but the Germans are fighting this: they want men in white coats and steel spectacles to scrutinise new prototypes and issue certificates.

And standards remain a trade barrier, even if voluntary. West Germany is Europe's standard-setting champion. Its Deutsche Institut für Normung (DIN) has set some 20,000 different standards, and its representatives head 40% of the EEC's committees setting European ones. West Germany's standards have an international reputation which makes DIN's leadership hard to resist as CEN and CENELEC strive for European harmony. And though following European or national standards is no longer mandatory for the European manufacturer, no one can force a private customer in Britain, say, not to demand a standard British product or imagine a West German who would not specify DIN. The only sort of business where the new approach might make a difference is government procurement, where national standards cannot be stipulated—though in practice they will often remain essential to a tenderer's chances.

THE BUSINESS OF MONEY

Last year's survey of 1992 in *The Economist* picked upon finance as the single most promising area of progress in stripping away the barriers within. A year later finance retains that title, but the going is getting tougher. The basis remains encouraging. In June 1988 the 12 EEC members agreed to remove all remaining exchange controls, both within the Community and beyond, by July 1, 1990—the exceptions being Spain and Ireland (1992), and Portugal and Greece (1995). The French agreed to do this provided the commission suggested ways to prevent tax evasion on interest income. It feared that savings acounts would migrate to Luxembourg, a member-state which charges no withholding tax on such income. The commission duly cooked something up—without much evident relish—suggesting a unified withholding tax on interest income of 15%. Britain never liked this idea. Part of London's attraction as a financial center is its lack of tax on large deposits. West Germany imposed a withholding tax of 10% early this year, but quickly found it had merely succeeded in showing its citizens the appeal of Luxembourg. It saw, too, that if Luxembourg were harmonized into line, Swiss banks would happily oblige.

So the withholding-tax idea has been pronounced as good as dead. Given that France has already got rid of the exchange controls that have any real effect on speculative outflows of money—those that stop companies holding their money where they want—and given France's enthusiasm for the idea of monetary union, the demise of this tax does not threaten the prospect of most of Europe's consumers being able to buy financial services across the EEC by late 1990. More worrying is a safeguard clause, conceded in June 1988, which allows members to reimpose exchange controls for six months, if they suffer a currency crisis.

Building upon the assumed right to move money across Europe the Community is composing its most daring variation on the 1992 theme of "mutual recognition" of rules. Broadly speaking, once essential standards for the soundness of financial firms and for the protection of their customers have been laid down in Brussels, EEC governments are to be asked to trust each other's interpretation of those rules and allow financial firms to sell in each other's markets whatever they can sell at home; and under home control. Acceptance of this broad principle has been brisk, but it is bedevilled by the details. The closer one looks at the financial services regime, the more the ifs and buts to "mutual recognition" become clear.

- In insurance, where Europe's national industries are in general highly protected, the European Court handed down a ruling in 1986 which made it clear that a lot of "harmonizing" of insurance policies and of insurance-company standards would be needed before a pan-European market in policies for the man in the street could become allowable. The commission admits that this process will last into the next century. An open market for commercial insurance will, in contrast, be legally available by mid-1990.

- Even in banking, where the 1992 directive-passing has been helped by international regulatory agreements already forged between central banks, the dread words "level playing field" threaten to extend, as in golf, to the dimples on the balls and the grooves on the clubs. It is already clear that a directive on the essential features of mortgages will be required, and perhaps another for leasing. Financial directives tend to have a clause in them that prevents the sale of financial services that might damage the "public interest" in the country of sale. Candidates include rules against interest payments on current accounts in France, or against floating-rate mortgage loans in West Germany.

- In investment services, where the commission is trying to create a pan-European regime for brokers, fund managers and investment advisers to match the banking one, there has been less international pathfinding on rules for the commission to profit from. The commission has prepared a directive, but the council has yet to consider it. An obvious problem ahead is a need for rules on capital adequacy. All financial firms, whether banks or not, should ideally underpin their securities holdings with the same requirement for capital. Certainly, if the all-important principle of home control of brokerage branches in other European countries is to apply, there have to be clear capital rules for investment services to match the banking ones. An Anglo-Saxon/continental divide in attitudes to securities risk needs to be bridged here.

Insider trading posed a problem for a time. Britain has long frowned upon it but wants it narrowly defined so that financiers do not find themselves hobbled by a vague EEC rule. West Germany and France assumed until recently that insider trading was what financial life was about. They then turned against it with the zeal of the convert and wanted to define it widely. Happily, the agreed final directive seems acceptably precise.

All in all, the (English-led) section of the commission dealing with financial services is striving to create a regime of "diversity with safety" but finds it hard to keep the genie of Euro-standardization corked up in its bottle. The commission sees that it can realistically aim only for rules that provide freedom as a principle. It must then rely on precedents and on appeals to the European Court by adventurous cross-border financiers to define what is do-able in practice.

FIGURE 5-3
Financial Services

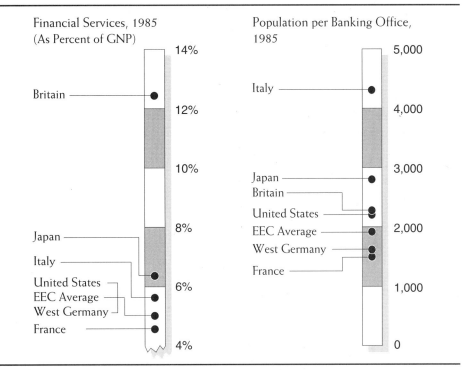

Financial Services, 1985
(As Percent of GNP)

Population per Banking Office, 1985

Source: Deutsche Bank; EEC; BIS.

WHERE NATIONALISM DIES HARD

There is another barrier-within where Project 1992 particularly shows the dangerous mix of loose regulation today that will allow cop-outs when the hard choices loom. This is in the business of procurement—the orders placed by governments and by the basic services on which modern economies depend, like telecommunications, energy, water and transport. Where last year's survey treated tax controls at frontiers as the biggest problem on the path to 1992, this one's picks the outlook for open procurement as a good test of whether 1992 is going to deliver its economic promises.

Procurement accounts for 15% of the EEC's GDP, of which about half is accounted for by those prominent services. The habit of national procurement is a particular reason for over-capacity in European industry because of the pattern of national industries that has evolved to serve it. Competition in procurement tends to be based upon factors other than price, with big-cufflink profits correspondingly well ingrained for the fortunate. Governments like to preserve a show of national competition when they place their orders, so they make sure that more suppliers keep going than even their national markets really need. What is more, government procurement tends to place orders with "strategic" industries—the ones in which countries feel that they must field national champions to hold their heads up in the modern world.

FIGURE 5-4 ─────────────────────────

Europe Underinsured?

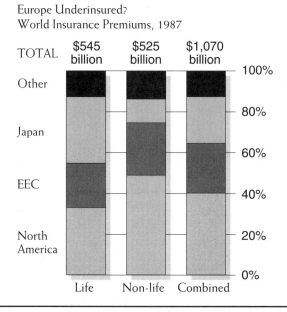

Europe Underinsured?
World Insurance Premiums, 1987

Source: "sigma," Swiss Reinsurance.

The tide in big business is flowing with the idea of breaking down this nationalism. Some of the biggest recent industrial liaisons have been inspired by the twin fears that national markets will no longer provide an adequate base for high-technology firms to compete worldwide, and that 1992 is going to put an end to such cosiness. Yet the fact remains that the commission is finding lawmaking on procurement heavy going. It had hoped to achieve more than the Community's earlier attempts to Europeanize procurement, in two ways. It wanted to stiffen the commission's own powers of refereeing procurement, knowing that national governments are unlikely to challenge their own industrial favoritism and that they have so far held the share of government contracts going to firms in other EEC countries to a miserable 2%. It also wanted to extend Euro-procurement into the lucrative services—the so-called excluded areas that have not featured in European procurement laws till now, and are not covered internationally under the GATT. This second aim is bedevilled by the fact that some of this excluded-sector purchasing is done by private companies, albeit ones with a measure of monopoly power and under varying degrees of national regulation.

BLOWING THE WHISTLE

National governments have joined forces to deny the commission powers to suspend the award of contracts that it believes are being allocated unfairly. As a result, the best that can be hoped for in the emerging "compliance directive" is some tightening of national systems of appeal against state favoritism, plus a system under which the commission will blow the whistle when it sees foul play and will ask the government in question to look into the matter. As for the directive on excluded sector, a recent study by Chatham House for the Anglo-German Foundation concludes sadly: "It is unlikely to have much effect on existing largely national patterns of purchasing, at least in the immediate future."

The idea that open procurement should extend into non-competitive, regulated realms of the private sector has been accepted: that much the commission can claim. But the ifs and buts in this matter of the excluded sectors are legion. Some governments maintain that where types of excluded sector compete—as gas vies with electricity to provide heat, for example—fair procurement should be entrusted to the rigours of such competition. Many countries have pet sectors to protect: the oil-and-gas equipment industry that Britain built to extract North Sea oil, the heavily rigged buying of coal by power stations in West Germany, the mandatory flow of orders to the Mezzogiorno in Italy. The excluded sectors' managers fear the paperwork that will be needed to show that they are buying Europe-wide: British Gas puts the cost of its compliance at £24m a year. There are as yet no proposals for refereeing this complicated, private-public game.

In short, the prospect that pan-European procurement will lead to a moment of truth for some of Europe's most famous companies is getting slimmer. It is the combination of global business ambition, spreading privatization and greater budgetary rigor that will drive Euro-procurement, not the other way round.

A TICK BESIDE TAX

In the campaign to remove frontier controls, tax collection is set to provide a nice example of how the soft-today-but-tough-tomorrow technique might keep 1992 apparently on schedule. Taxmen need frontiers for three reasons. They use them to allocate VAT between member-governments when goods cross frontiers. They need them to insulate different countries from significantly different rates of VAT next door. And they need them to do the same for excise taxes on liquor, cigarettes, etc. The commission had three answers to prepare the EEC for relatively painless removal of the frontier taxman in 1992: allocate VAT by using a clearing system, chivvy those national VAT rates towards each other; rigorously harmonize those astonishingly variable excise duties.

Taxes are what gave some national parliaments their mission. They are the purview of many nations' proudest civil servants. They involve many public-sector jobs: Britain's Customs and Excise employs 26,000 people, one-third more than the whole of the EEC's civil service. All three of the commission's original ideas offended all three interests, often in different ways in different countries. For much of 1988 it seemed that tax would remain a hopeless impasse on the road to the white paper's 300 directives. Then came the retirement of Lord Cockfield, the architect of 1992, who also happened to be a tax-zealot. A new French commissioner, Mrs. Christiane Scrivener, has brought in a more pragmatic attitude: she made small concessions to the national governments seem like big capitulations.

Where the commission once proposed two VAT bands of 14-20% and 4-9%, it now proposes a VAT floor of 15% on most goods and services, plus, in effect, a generous band of 0-9% for a list of sensitive items which different countries—Britain being the champion—have taxed more lightly or not taxed at all. The commission has abandoned its alignment of excise taxes, though it may still attempt to impose some new constraints on them. Governments will stop the worst excesses of cross-border excise tax-dodging by internal policing against commercial bootlegging, helped, perhaps, by local tax-stamps or bands on drinks and cigarettes.

So far, the commission is sticking by its VAT clearing-house scheme, but it is making every effort to get the right rate of VAT paid directly—rather than through the clearing system—to the country where intra-European exports finally end up. So, for example, Ford Motor Company will act as a sort of frontier-straddling, private, tax-free zone for the flows of its cars and components across Europe. So will big mail order firms—and the public sector in its cross-border buying.

These envisaged solutions have two effects: they stick roughly to the letter of 1992 in doing without frontier controls on the flow of goods across Europe; and they should let competitive pressures do the work of chivvying VAT rates into line, rather than pre-emptive harmonization by the commission. Fine, if governments keep the border-booms open and let those pressures do their work. Both Mr. Raymond Barre a former French prime minister, and Mr. Michel Albert, the head of Assurance Générale de France and a former French planning commissar, foresee a showdown when the moment of truth arrives. France's government faces a fiscal squeeze from every side. Its income-tax system is riddled with exemptions offered by governments in search of re-election. Its stiff taxes on savings will henceforth be dodgeable. Its 18.6% VAT rate, plus a much higher one on luxury goods, will be under pressure from West Germany and Luxembourg where the VAT rate will, presumably, be 15%.

By the end of this year, 1992's tax problem could well have been solved on paper. Wait then to see if Europe's governments face up to the reality that they have let themselves in for.

FREE MOVEMENT OF PEOPLE

A European Community within which Europeans and visitors stroll past sleeping passport officials at intra-EEC frontiers remains unlikely to emerge by 1992. Realizing that this part of his vision was in trouble, Mr. Jacques Delors appointed one of the officials who wrote the internal-market white paper, Mr. Adrian Fortescue, to try and find the common ground. He has work to do. Where Europe without internal frontiers should, in theory, mean just that, the British, the Danes, the Irish and the Greeks all want to keep checking people entering their countries from the rest of Europe to see if they are EEC nationals or not. They have four reasons for wanting to persist in this:

- **Asylum.** In a Community of free movement, the asylum-seeker could, theoretically, have 12 shots at getting accepted by a member-government—and this at a time when fewer asylum-seekers are East Europeans seeking basic freedoms and more are coming from all parts of the world in search of a better life. The members agreed in principle, in May, that asylum-seekers would be handled only by their first country-of-contact with the EEC. But jointly acceptable criteria are still lacking: the United Nations convention on asylum is too vague.
- **Immigration.** The commission tries to argue that members can police against illegal immigration within countries rather than at frontiers. Nonsense, say the resisters, either because, like Britain, they have a tradition of tight seaside frontiers and freedom within, or because it is politically and practically more painful to deport people than to exclude them in the first place.
- **Visas.** Colonial history makes trying to devise a common EEC policy on who needs a visa and who doesn't a whopping task.
- **Guns and drugs.** The commission must persuade governments to trust the vigilance at the EEC's external frontiers. It will explain that a Europe without internal-frontier controls does not stop police carrying out spot-checks for illegal things at internal frontiers, but that spot-check means spot-check—not systematic control.

Meanwhile, the prospect of a two-speed Europe in this matter has developed further. Five of the original six members of the EEC—France, West Germany, and the Benelux trio—are pushing ahead with their Schengen agreement to form a frontier-free zone. They at least have a draft text covering all the problems listed above, but they will not have ratified it by the target of January 1, 1990, that they set themselves.

Slow Fade Out

The overall prospect for the removal of Europe's internal frontier-posts remains gloomy, but less gloomy than a year ago. A consensus has developed in the past year that internal frontiers will not be used to uphold the many hundreds of national quotas that member-states apply to specific imports—the protectionism permitted under article 115 of the Rome treaty. The tax conundrum is closer to a solution than recently seemed likely.

On the other hand, the question of health checks on plants and animals has barely been addressed. Removal of the checks that hold prices for farm products at different levels across the Community depends upon the assertion that the need for the common agricultural policy's "monetary compensatory amounts" will have to go by 1993. So far there is brave talk, but not much brave action.

Above all, a helpful distinction has emerged between (a) checks at frontiers to detect criminals, and (b) checks to insulate European economies and societies from one another. True, by no longer seeking to rule out (a) project 1992 will not completely disarm governments in (b) as the commission once insisted that it should. But 1992 is creating an ever-stronger presumption that this second brand of obstructiveness will not be politically acceptable in the next decade. In the British civil service, for instance, an initial tendency to pooh-pooh 1992's too-literal promise of open frontiers has been quashed by awareness that public expectations have changed by more than at first seemed likely. As in other parts of this review, the nature of the frontier-test has shifted—from the need to agree on the principle of an open Europe to one of political will when it threatens to become reality.

Outside, Looking In

The Americans and the Japanese are learning to love 1992 in their different ways.

In the closing stages of the second world war, one French poet, Valéry, had an inkling of the forces that would drive Europe towards project 1992, 40 years later.

> History will never record anything more stupid than European competition in politics and economics, compared and contrasted as it is with European unity in matters of science.

He wrote; and much the same was said by more-obvious fathers of the EEC at the time. But the poet went on:

> Just think what will happen to Europe when, as a result of its labours, there will exist in Asia a couple of dozen Creusots or Essens, Manchesters or Roubaix, in which steel, silk, paper, chemicals, textiles, ceramics and the rest are produced in staggering quantities and at unbeatable prices by a population which is the most frugal and numerous in the world.

Postwar America woke up to the economic challenge of the East somewhat later. Today, the fear there is widespread. Mr. Paul Kennedy's "The Rise and Fall of the Great Powers" sits menacingly on many American coffee tables. In a recent film about Mr. Preston Tucker, a far-sighted American car-maker supposedly crushed by Detroit's conservatism in the late 1940s, the hero speaks straight to today's Americans when he tells a court that "if big business closes the door on the little guy with the new idea ... one day we are going to find ourselves at the bottom of the heap ... buying radios and cars from our former enemies."

In truth, both America and Europe are adjusting to a challenge from Asia. America ponders the need for industrial strategies, self-refereed "fair" trade, and government-funded product development; Europe pushes for its great market. Each professes a sustained faith in open, multilateral trade. Each sees actions by the other that belie such faith. Squaring up to the same challenge, they jostle each other and eye each other warily.

America's interest in Project 1992 has developed within one year from indifference to temporary obsession. Its awareness of and belief in the internal-market project was low until the spring of 1988 when the start of Britain's own 1992 fad impinged across the Atlantic. American businessmen became alert first, then parts of Washington's bureaucracy, and then Congress, which this year began some 1992 hearings on Capitol Hill. The new administration's attitude to the political dimension of the EEC has been affected by all this.

The dwindling of economic self-confidence that followed the ending of the Reagan "super-dollar" era in the early 1980s sensitized America to the Community's external-trade regime. This sensitivity was heightened by the EEC negotiations to admit Spain and Portugal. Americans feared that the entry of the Iberian pair would create fresh problems for their farm exports to Europe.

The trade-twitchiness was further irritated by three things: the argument between the EEC and the United States over farm subsidies in the Uruguay round of the GATT; a row over whether Europe should be able to shut out America's hormone-enhanced beef; and the news that West Germany's unstoppable export machine included the Libyan chemical-weapons industry among its clients. So late 1988 was a poor moment for America to be sanguine about the early external vagueness of project 1992. Washington's initial hunch, say State Department officials, was that the EEC would be bound to cushion the pain of European industry's adjustment to a more open internal market, and that it would do it with external protection.

Fortress Europe loomed in American minds for about four months. By this April a calmer vision; had emerged, according to Mr. William Archey of the American Chamber of Commerce, "not of a fortress but of a series of mini-forts providing selective protection." American officials realized that European trade policy was being put together on the run, with the pace forced by the internal deadline of 1992. "The worry," says a State Department official, Mrs. Anne Hollick, "is that EC92 is becoming a major actor in world trade without much capacity to think ahead. It's hard to find people in the commission with a view of the future of the world trading system. Such people exist in Washington, though what they achieve in the face of an increasingly demanding Congress is another question."

So the new watchword on 1992 in Washington, from Mrs. Carla Hills, President Bush's trade representative, is "optimism tempered with vigilance." The vigilance is focused upon:

- **Standards.** America fears that as Europe develops its "new approach" to regulations and standards, the rules will be drafted in obscurity and in a way that hurts American exports. America has: asked, in the words of its commerce secretary, Mr. Robert Mosbacher, for a "seat at the table." Officials in Washington say that they are denied observer status at CEN and CENELEC and that talking with them is "like trying to grab jello." The American National Standards Instituter they claim, is open to its

European counterparts. Washington also wants American laboratories to certify the Euro-worthiness of American exports. Europe has said yes in principle, but it could take many years for American labs to qualify.

- **Rules of origin.** America does not want to be forced to set up plants in Europe. Senator Lloyd Bentsen, the Democratic chairman of the Senate finance committee, has said darkly that he is "senator for all Americans, not just for multinational companies." Mr. Archey mentions particularly the recent "diffusion rule" under which integrated circuits must be "diffused" in Europe to count as European. "Motorola can comply," he says, "but two other companies reckon that they are going to have to invest $100m each in Europe to compete." America is sensitive, too, about European officials deciding whether a Japanese product made in America is American or Japanese.

- **Reciprocity.** Last year it seemed likely that the EEC would ask for more than "national treatment" for European banks in the United States as its price for admitting American firms into Europe. This prompted a stiff reaction from the American Treasury. Officials in Washington consider that this pressure helped force the EEC commission to tone down its reciprocity formula. Meanwhile they remain curiously silent about reciprocity in procurement in the excluded sectors. "Buy American" pressure in the Congress has been mounting of late. The EEC's ambitious scheme to impose open procurement upon private-sector utility companies could sound dauntingly virtuous down at the American country club.

- **Discriminating taste.** Not the usual variety, but the ploy whereby the EEC decides, for example, that it does not want to admit beef laced with hormones whether dangerous or not, and no matter whence it comes. America wants European consumers to decide for themselves, not Brussels or Strasbourg to do it for them. It fears that Japan could use the European example to justify many discriminating tastes of its own. The hormone-beef argument remains tense and unresolved.

That is the somewhat predictable list of economic concerns. The real news is the way 1992 has helped change America's political attitude towards Europe. There has been much discussion in Washington about whether the American government is properly set up to cope with the deeper consequences of Europe's relaunch. President Bush has established a senior inter-agency task force on the matter. The State Department has called home one of its most competent diplomats, Mr. Raymond Seitz, to lead and reorganize its bureau for European affairs. He calls 1992 a "psychological benchmark in European history," no less.

For years America has been ambivalent about a stronger and more cohesive Europe. Mr. Henry Kissinger's instinct as Secretary of State to Presidents Nixon and Ford was that America could achieve more by dealing with 14 small NATO allies separately than with one large one. It is not hard to see ways in which more European cohesion could still lead to friction. Starting in 1980 with its Venice declaration on the Middle East, the Community's developing joint foreign policy has been apt to veer away from the American line. According to Senator William Roth, a protectionist Community would play into the hands of those in Congress who want America to become more isolationist. The mere completion of the single market of 320m people and a GDP of $4.7 trillion prompts louder calls for burden-sharing within NATO. There is a fatalistic acceptance that—fortress or no fortress—the drive for co-operation within the European defense industry means that big European orders for American weapons systems are a thing of the past.

But these concerns do not set the new political tone. Mr. Seitz rejects the idea of influence over Europe through divide and rule because this "utterly contradicts what we have

FIGURE 5-5

America Buys in Europe/Creaking Open

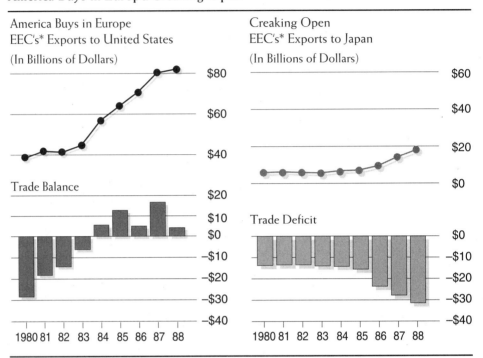

America Buys in Europe
EEC's* Exports to United States
(In Billions of Dollars)

Creaking Open
EEC's* Exports to Japan
(In Billions of Dollars)

Trade Balance

Trade Deficit

1980 81 82 83 84 85 86 87 88

*Current Membership.

Source: OECD

been urging Europe to achieve over the past 40 years." Europe's 1992 program is, he thinks, "pivotal" to the West's reaction to Mr. Gorbachev's efforts at reform. A strong EEC economy will help East European countries towards the wealth that communism did not deliver. And a strong EEC political identity will help make sure that any German move towards reunification happens under conditions in which the "old instabilities do not arise again." The Bush administration is now more interested in progress towards European union than Mrs. Thatcher is.

What of the Japanese? They have followed the Americans through a period of exaggerated fear about 1992 to one of rather more cautious optimism. They have a different economic perspective on it. They welcome 1992 with due courtesy but know that they are welcoming something aimed partly at them. Mr. Michiko Kunihiro, the deputy foreign minister, even cites fears that the EEC and the United States will somehow join forces to confront Japan.

So officials in Tokyo are quick to insist that project 1992 must not undermine the multilateral trading system refereed by the GATT. This system is Japan's best guarantee that it will not be singled out as the butt of protectionist measures. They see, in the words of Mr. Kunihiro, "a strong trend towards unilateralism or bilateralism in the United States particularly in Congress," and this impression has been strengthened by the "Super 301" procedure that the Bush administration has recently unleashed against Japan. Foreign-ministry

FIGURE 5-6

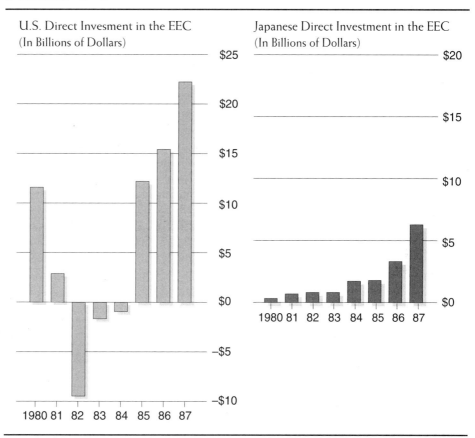

U.S. Direct Invesment in the EEC
(In Billions of Dollars)

Japanese Direct Investment in the EEC
(In Billions of Dollars)

Source: U.S. Department of Commerce; Japanese Ministry of Finance.

officials now think that Japan must become more of a champion of the GATT. Till recently, they say, Japan has been GATT-shy, mainly because its own trade practices, particularly in agriculture, have not encouraged it to ask for GATT scrutiny.

Japanese officials certainly complain about the recent toughness of European anti-dumping actions, and echo the concerns about reciprocity and standards set out above. But the nuances are instructive: the Japanese are less anxious than the Americans to fight pressure for inward investment into Europe. Japanese businessmen such as Toyota's president, Mr. Soichiro Toyoda, now see themselves as natural foreign investors: the high yen dictates it, protectionism dictates it, project 1992 demands it. The Japanese investment diaspora is viewed as the next phase of the rise and rise of Japan as an economic power. So they talk constantly of becoming "good corporate Europeans."

What worries the Japanese more is that the ECC will distort their foreign direct investment with local-content rules. They want to preserve the quality of their products. They do not want to be barred effectively, from less-developed Community countries, like Spain or Portugal, where local industry is simply not up to providing components of adequate quality. And, groping around for other arguments, they say they do not want Europe to send the wrong message about local-content to the third world.

Behind all this virtuous talk of unhindered trade, the nub of the Japanese concern is access. The Japanese rub their eyes when told that no Fortress Europe is arising: Japan is an old hand at fortress-building itself. The important thing for Japan is that, when and if Europe's walls go up, Japan's global companies should qualify as insiders.

FOR FORTRESS, READ TRADE-LABORATORY

If the great French fortress-builder, Sebastian le Prestre de Vauban, could return and work unhampered behind the sheets that shroud building-site 1992, he would find much good material to hand. He would fill the moat of his protectionist stronghold with subsidized European farm products. For his foundations he would use the Community's external tariff that averages around 5% but rises as high as 22% for some goods. Then he would take 700-odd different national quantitative restrictions (QRs) on imports into various member countries—allowed under article 115 of the Treaty of Rome, but soon to become unenforceable in an open internal market—and move them, suitably averaged, to form the Community's ramparts. For his cannon he would install the commission's latest refinements in anti-dumping technique, backed by increasingly complex local-content rules to prevent targeted importers scurrying for cover in other countries or infiltrating the Community itself.

So much for the outworks: Vauban-Europe would have strength in depth, too. The industrial standards required of imports would match Japan's for opacity and fiddliness. There would be "Community preference" in procurement and in broadcasting. The business of finance would be open only to those foreigners whose governments matched the new freedoms of Europe's financial system. There would be an industrial policy under which European consortia would enjoy exemption from European competition policy. They would be backed by a blend of central and state subsidies, and would develop new European system-standards, confident of a loyal flow of orders from member-governments. Hugely corrupt and overfed commissioners would strut about the central keep in Brussels. The head of the British prime minister would be seen on a pike above the gates.

Vauban has not been given the job. If he had been, he would find himself frustrated by the powerful free-trade lobby in the commission mentioned at the start of this survey. The Vauban vision will not stand up. The common agricultural policy (CAP) remains an inefficient and trade-distorting way of helping farmers, but at least its guaranteed prices are under constant downward pressure from within the EEC, and the whole rigged system of world agriculture is now up for GATT-reform. The CAP predates project 1992 and is not part of it. So far, it does not seem to have infected it.

The clear presumption in Brussels is that most of the national QRs on imports will be scrapped. The exceptions most often cited are shoes, textiles, televisions, motor cars and fresh bananas. The outlook for these items is uncertain. There has been no decision on how the national quotas of textiles allowed into the EEC under the Multi-Fibre Arrangement will be shared out in a frontierless Europe. The banana problem remains unpeeled. At one extreme, Greece has a total ban on imports to protect its Cretan banana economy. At the other, West Germany is (believe it or not) given the freedom of the world banana crop in a protocol to the Treaty of Rome.

Cars remain the great test case. Five countries have more or less voluntary quotas limiting the inflow of Japanese cars to a proportion of their car markets: France (3%), Italy (in effect 0%), Britain (11%), Spain and Portugal. Mr. Martin Bangemann, vice-president of the commission and responsible for the industrial dossier, says that existing national restrictions for the import of cars will be abolished by the end of 1992. Use of rules on local content to justify trade restrictions within the Community will not be permitted. The EEC members will "jointly monitor" the trend in Japanese imports for a "transitional period" to avoid serious disruption of markets. But a "firm will" remains to liberalize the European car market completely as soon as possible after 1992. Saving all this at the beginning of June, Mr. Bangemann called his words "more than a hope and less than a decision." The actual outcome will set the tone for Community's whole attitude to protectionism in physical goods.

There is no formal debate about creating a Community industrial policy to match the CAP. Nor is there much chance that Sir Leon Brittan, the competition commissioner, would go along with one. He is currently engaged in a tough battle of wills with France to limit the amount of subsidy that Renault, a French car-maker, receives from the French government. Whatever industrial policy the EEC has will evolve in a typically piecemeal fashion through such arguments over the ingrained habit of national subsidy, and through specific ventures like the Airbus project or the plan to develop a European standard for high-definition television.

True, the standards issue features on the list of American complaints—and is among the worries of the non-EEC Europeans. But the 1992 program should, if anything, reduce the scope of member-states to use standards to block imports. The American fear is of inadequate involvement in setting Euro-rules, rather than of explicit non-tariff protectionism. The EEC does have a New Commercial Policy Instrument (NIPC, in the Euro-vernacular) against unfair trade practices, such as abuses of intellectual property, but it has not been used much. The French suggested that this should be strengthened for a Europe in which they will no longer be able to route all video-recorder imports through Poitiers. The last commission said no.

Things could still tilt Vauban's way—particularly if recession strikes, and when the shake-out in Europe's heavy and high-technology industries begins. But another force nudges the evolving EEC away from protectionism: the GATT and its Uruguay round. The Community stresses that it is completing its internal market in conformity with the GATT. Any Community-wide import quotas would have to be negotiated with GATT, and compensation offered, for they would in effect introduce quotas in those EEC countries that currently have none.

GATTMANSHIP

The relationship between 1992 and the GATT's Uruguay round hovers like a vague cloud in many people's minds. They hear that 1992 is supposed to be an exercise in economic liberalism. They hear Brussels's constant assertion that it is loyal to the GATT. Yet they also hear of the danger of a world of trading blocks in which trade is managed between Europe, Japan and North America. Is 1992 good for world trade or bad for it?

First, accept a disclaimer: the future of Europe's common agricultural policy is crucial to the fate of the Uruguay round. But 1992 and the CAP have little to do with one another (an open internal market will actually make today's compartmentalized CAP that much more difficult to sustain). The America-Japan-Europe row over farm trade is a vast topic that this survey will dodge to remain readable: what follows is hard to digest, even without it.

Farming aside, the completion of Europe's market and the evolution of the GATT affect each other in two distinct ways. The emerging rules for trade within the Community in new activities such as intellectual property, financial services and government procurement are an example to GATT of how trade in such things can work given a framework of essential rules that sovereign states accept as binding. In the fixing of their rules for trade in intellectual property (patents, copyrights, computer software), for example, the internal market and the GATT have fed upon each other very usefully.

Second way: in its behaviour on trade with the rest of the world, the EEC is exploring—or negotiating—how such trade might be ordered, given GATT rules involving a lesser pooling of sovereignty. So, for competition policy within the EEC, the external equivalent is anti-dumping policy where a rough set of international rules—the GATT anti-dumping code—already exists. Matching the new financial-services regime within the EEC, there are contentious suggestions on financial reciprocity beyond it where no international rules yet hold. For surrender of national preference in procurement (within the EEC), there are demands for reciprocity backed by a degree of Community-preference (beyond it) in areas of procurement outside GATT rules.

Take financial services, an area in which the Uruguay round could shortly start to evolve rules for international trade. What are the precedents being set by the internal regime of project 1992? First, the regime is sectoral, which is against the tradition of the GATT. In GATT's negotiations on trade in goods, the idea of "overall reciprocity" holds sway: there is an agreement to lower import barriers generally, not to negotiate them down industry by industry. This approach is harder if the true barriers to trade are national laws and regulations. Overall reciprocity then becomes tantamount to: "He can flout my laws on insurance, provided I can flout his laws on banking." The European regime on banking is self-contained, as is that on insurance, or on television. The message for the Uruguay round on services is obvious: common principles may be worked out by the end of the round in 1990, but to make any real difference these will have to be applied and negotiated sector by sector—a process that could last more than a decade.

Next, the European financial-services regime breaks new ground in its mutual concessions between sovereign states. The America-Canada free-trade agreement, another exercise in regional block-building, restricts itself to "national treatment" (see box) in financial services. But the Community decided that such national treatment would have led to an uninspiring European internal market in services. It would have prevented good ideas in one European country being offered in the market of an another, and it would have limited the types of service that could be sold directly across frontiers.

So the Community opted for mutual recognition of rules. This corresponds to a much more demanding form of reciprocity—"equivalent access." If British banks were to ask for it in America, they would be asking for the right to do more there than America allows its own banks to do. Mutual recognition forces regulatory systems to compete and ultimately to declare a winner. It is only feasible if, before such competition starts, the governments agree that their different rules apply the same essential standards in different ways.

The EEC's early thoughts on banking reciprocity vis-a-vis the outside world were worryingly tough, both for outsiders and for those, particularly the British, who want to run international financial centers within the Community. The early formula would have demanded prior clearance by the commission before foreigners could set up new banks within the Community. It would have left the Community too little flexibility in deciding how to react. And it was seen by some as demanding equivalent access: the exact words were the rather vague "reciprocal treatment."

The implications of equivalent access were not lost on Washington, which reacted sharply and demanded that Europe stick to national treatment. So did free-traders within

> ## RECIGLOSSARY
>
> Reciprocity is a vogue word in trade parlance, and needs qualifying to mean much. The basic concept is: "Your firms can sell on my market only if my firms can sell on your market." But it comes in various brands:
>
> **Overall reciprocity** is GATT wisdom. All countries open up a little in different ways, but without matching them sector for sector, or country for country.
>
> **Sectoral reciprocity**: "You can sell widgets on my market only if I can sell widgets on your market."
>
> **National-treatment reciprocity**: "Your firms will be treated in my market like my own, provided that my firms will be treated like locals in yours."
>
> **National treatment with effective access**: "Your national entry-criteria are horribly restrictive. Get my firms in, and I'll offer my national treatment to yours."
>
> **Equivalent treatment**: "I will offer you national treatment, provided that you bend your business rules to give my firms equivalent opportunities."
>
> **Mirror-image, or identical, reciprocity**: "Your firms can do in my market only what my firms can do in your market." This means that mutual restrictions will remain until the regulatory systems are the same; which is no way to run a lively banking center.
>
> **Reciprocity on level of trade**: "You can sell to me only as much as you buy from me." Crazy. Imagine saying this to your butcher.

the EEC. In the event, after much discussion, the commission has preserved a right to push for "national treatment that gives effective access." It argues that, for instance, pure national treatment in the tightly regulated South Korean insurance market would be tantamount to an acceptance of protectionism.

A demand for effective access remains a demand for a bending of local rules in favor of foreigners—and thus applies some pressure to liberalize local rules. This idea is incorporated in the guidelines, agreed on in Montreal last winter, for the GATT negotiations on trade in services. The text expressly calls for "effective marker access" and says that the aim is "a progressively higher level of liberalization taking due account of the level of development of individual signatories." It is also worth noting that even a demand for equivalent access in financial services would not be as cheeky as it might seem. Finance has an insidious way of undermining national rules. In the matter of securities, for example, America, Canada and Britain are already discussing mutual recognition of disclosure rules. The effect could be that America would accept a British share prospectus in America that would technically be illegal there. Why? One way or an other, the shares tend to get there anyhow.

NO TRUCK WITH DUMPERS

Before coming to conclusions about the internal market and GATT, the reader must bear one more dose of the jargon of modern trade diplomacy. This is that of anti-dumping action-an area where behaviour in Brussels is at its most suspect, and foreigners are at their most suspicious.

The temptation for the Community to use anti-dumping actions is great. Here is a weapon whose use is legal under GATT, yet which can be aimed at a particular country or company. If the commission can show that a European company is being injured by Asian competition—and show, too, that the Asian competitor is selling his wares in Europe at below the price he is charging at home (or even elsewhere), it can GATT-legally force him to pay import duties or to raise his prices in Europe. The EEC and the United States have few grounds to insult each other about anti-dumping actions; each is adept in making use of them against communist or newly industrialized countries. Their mounting problem is that, as the trend towards foreign direct investment continues, they find the enemy operating out of forward bases in each other's territory.

Project 1992 has not directly affected the number of anti-dumping actions being launched by the European Commission, although there has been an uptick of late. But some recent developments in the EEC's use of the weapon have stoked foreign sensitivities:

FIGURE 5-7
Anti-Dumping Actions

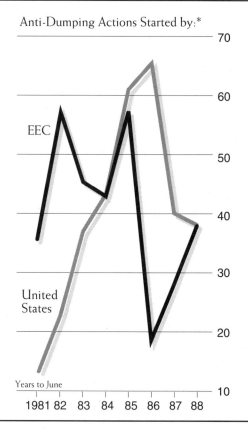

Anti-Dumping Actions Started by:*

EEC

United States

Years to June
1981 82   83   84   85   86   87   88

*Including those against non-members.
Source: GATT.

- Since 1987 the EEC has cracked down on Asian companies, notably Japanese producers of office equipment, supposedly dodging existing anti-dumping duties on completed products by setting up "screwdriver plants" in Europe.
- The EEC has extended this technique to America, forcing Ricoh of Japan to add more value to its copiers in California if the EEC is to regard them as being of American origin.
- It has extended use of the anti-dumping weapon into services by challenging the pricing of Hyundai Merchant Marine of South Korea.
- It is prepared to pile additional duties on convicted dumpers whose prices in Europe do not move after being hit with a first round of duties. (Its remorseless logic is that absorption of anti-dumping duties merely makes the earlier degree of dumping worse.)
- It has launched eight anti-dumping investigations against Hongkong in the past 18 months. These have been particularly contentious because of the extreme openness of the Hongkong economy and the lack of financial clout of many of its firms, and suspect because of Hongkong's reluctance to bow to protectionist pressure with "voluntary" restraint of its own exports.

Foreigners need to know two things in assessing whether Europe's anti-dumping cannons are likely to swing in their direction. How fairly are the GATT's anti-dumping rules being applied? And what "rules of origin" must be met to stay out of the line of fire?

On the first point, the commission has been under attack in the past year for rigging its price calculations in a way that makes the discovery of dumping more probable. The argument, pursued at length in the *Financial Times*, has been intricate and has shown how much scope the GATT rules leave for protectionist artistry wherever trade involves complex international marketing arrangements, complicated products that quickly become obsolete, and volatile exchange rates. The argument has not and cannot be settled one way or another, but commission officials admit that it has prompted them to be less rigid in their approach.

The officials insist, however, that they pursue no systematic anti-dumping strategy of protection. They receive about 100 complaints a year from hard-pressed sections of European industry. They investigate roughly 50 of them. They find dumping in about 30. They impose duties in about 15 cases, and demand commitments to higher prices in the rest—with both penalties lasting five years. An inquisitive team of British officials, chivvied into action by the campaign in the *Financial Times*, left Brussels satisfied that the commission was not systematically using dumping as a convenient form of protectionism.

RULES OF ORIGIN

The second point—exemption from anti-dumping action—leads straight into the next vault of the armory of modern protection, the one devoted to "rules of origin" and "local-content regulations." Rules of origin are needed wherever a degree of preference, or a non-tariff barrier, creeps into trade. If there is a quota or an anti-dumping duty on cars from Japan, then there has to be a rule describing when a car is Japanese. If the EEC wants to preserve "Community preference" in its new, open procurement market, it must define what goods or services are of EEC origin. This is sad but inescapable.

The EEC's basic definition of origin remains the one that was internationally accepted in 1968: goods originate where they undergo their "last substantial transformation." EEC history has however overlaid this simple and liberal definition with a mounting number of more precise ones, sometimes involving stipulations of "local content":

- For the purposes of the article 115 restrictions, radios, televisions and ball-bearings are deemed by the commission to be European when 35-45% of their value is added in the EEC. A rule for VCRs is in the works, too.
- To qualify for low-tariff access as EFTA products, cars must have 60% EFTA content.
- The commission has said that, whenever a product from a particular country has been found to be dumped, the same product made in the dumper's plants elsewhere must have at least 40% of its value added outside the dumping country.
- The commission has recently developed a precise rule for integrated circuits. They must be "diffused" in Europe to be regarded as European. This was a pre-emptive answer to an unresolved anti-dumping complaint against Japanese memory chips and also part of its campaign against "screwdriver plants."
- The commission has used negative definitions—for example, "assembly is not enough to give origin"—in its highly sensitive move to stop American-assembled Ricoh copiers from dodging an anti-dumping ruling.
- The commission has opposed the use of local-content rules to give cars EEC origin. This followed argument between member states over what local content Nissan cars made-in Britain should have to count as European. Figures as high as 90% were bandied about.

All in all, it is not surprising that confusion reigns abroad, which cannot be assuaged by the commission's sincere invitation to "send us your inquiry and we will give you an answer." Even if the commission is merely wrestling with problems that various forms of trade distortion logically throw up, the message for outsiders is clear: it is safer to manufacture inside the Community than to do it where business sense might otherwise dictate.

The pressure for GATT to take a new and harder look at its anti-dumping code and at rules of origin is justifiably mounting. The outcome of the Japanese appeal to GATT over the European screwdriver case will be watched with interest, but the paragraph in the GATT code that defines dumping is pitifully thin. As the world's economies become more interdependent, the need grows not for a trade referee but for a global competition policy applied by a supranational body. Perhaps, in time, the principles being hammered out by the EEC commission's competition directorate will emerge as pioneering work for world trade, too.

In discussing the impact of 1992 upon the multilateral trading system, there are those who argue that any free-trade area, whether GATT-legal or not, will distort the law of comparative advantage that should drive an efficient world economy. The nervousness of the EFTA countries about 1992 is partly based upon this premise. Yet, overall, the world probably has worse things to worry about.

The two examples of finance and dumping give different slants on the trading virtue of 1992. The first now seems forward-looking and liberalizing: in this sector, if 1992 succeeds, America, not Europe, will be left looking sclerotic. Through the forging of such Euro rules, world trade is made less uniformly multilateral, but freer overall and with experiments underway on how that freedom might best be extended. The European experiment already suggests how, to move towards open trade in services, the sovereignty of independent countries must be compromised not just by market forces but by supranational referees.

The second is the backwards slant. Anti-dumping action is a trade-weapon ripe for arms-control: one that would be ridiculed if used within the EEC ("What do you mean dumping?

Sainsbury drives a hard bargain"). The search for fairness in trade is not to be sneered at: a capitalist economy does not allocate resources properly if it must cope with variously sub-sidized competition. But the anti-dumping action, even when used without malice, confuses what is methodically cross-subsidized with what is horribly competitive. It is a crude device which throws up a need for rules of origin and thus encourages all good companies to get inside Europe's walls. Anti-dumping badly needs to be GATT-refined and GATT-moni-tored.

OTHER EUROPEANS

Nothing will get your dinner-guests heading for the door faster than the subject of EFTA-EEC relations. Why is this worthy theme such a conversation-stopper? Partly because none of the six members of the European Free Trade Association—Austria, Finland, Iceland, Sweden, Switzerland and Norway—is arrestingly unreasonable. Partly because any talk of the way an Association might relate to a Community is bound to be bloodless. But mainly because EFTA's identity is negative—its members are chiefly not-in-the-EEC—and any attempt to make non-members of a club feel more like members is an attempt to square a circle. The topic becomes more interesting when it turns to particular EFTA countries and asks: what is it that prevents Austria or Sweden or Norway from joining the Community?

Once upon a time, in the 1950s and 1960s, EFTA had a stronger identity: it was a rival view of a European Community, one that eschewed supranational institutions where the EEC from the start embraced them. That vision lost out. Members defected to the EEC—first Britain, then Denmark and Ireland, then almost Norway but not quite, and most recently Portugal. Nevertheless, in the 1970s, EFTA membership retained its attractions. It allowed its geopolitically neutral members (Sweden, Austria, Finland and Switzerland) to remain uncompromised. It had helpful EFTA old-boys within the EEC in the shape of Britain and Denmark. It still had work to do in removing the remaining tariffs and restric-tions on trade with the Community. It could watch the EEC going through a dispiriting phase in the wake of the oil shock, and count itself lucky to be out of the squabbles about farm prices and money.

From the mid-1980s onwards those comforts ebbed away, as Mr. Thomas Pedersen has explained with clarity in a recent paper for Chatham House. The ex-EFTA members of the EEC became less supportive. The comfortable assumption that the EEC would develop haltingly became less tenable. By 1984 the EFTA-EEC tariff-free zone had been achieved. So what next? In Luxembourg that year, the French foreign minister, Mr. Claude Cheysson, speaking as president of the EEC Council of Ministers, suggested that EFTA and the EEC work towards a "European Economic Space"—a vaporous concept said to embrace, among other things, a truly free internal market. But within a year, Mr. Jacques Delors had launched the EEC's own internal-marker project, whose full measure made it clear what an unEFTAlike pooling of sovereignty a truly free internal market entails.

Suddenly, EEC club-membership has become both harder to eschew and harder to contemplate. The EFTA countries share most of the fears already listed for America and Japan. But their stake is far higher because 65% of their non-mutual exports go to the EEC, equivalent to 14% of their joint GDP. In addition, they fear trade-diversion. Where Sweden and West Germany, say, are now equally placed to sell to, say, France, the Germans will soon have an inside track. The EFTA countries will be in the grip of EEC laws and

FIGURE 5-8
The EEC's Greatest Market

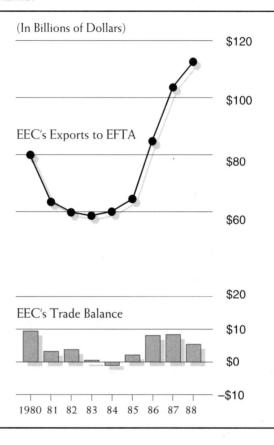

(In Billions of Dollars)

$120

$100

EEC's Exports to EFTA

$80

$60

$20

EEC's Trade Balance

$10

$0

−$10

1980 81 82 83 84 85 86 87 88

*Current membership.
Source: OECD.

product regulations without being able to affect their framing. All good reasons to join fast: but Austria, Sweden, Switzerland and Finland know that the mounting foreign-policy co-operation between EEC members is becoming ever less compatible with their neutrality.

The Community is now playing hard-to-get, too. The commission has expressly stated that "internal development takes a priority over enlargement." In January Mr. Jacques Delors offered EFTA another road to satisfaction—"a new more structured partnership with common decision-making and administrative institutions . . . to highlight the political dimension of our co-operation." At a summit in Oslo in March, the EFTA six nervously agreed to forge such a partnership in a joint declaration. But even as they announced it, Austria made it clear that it might lodge an application to join the EEC, and Switzerland stressed its opposition to any sort of supranational EFTA.

Mr. Delors's offer was not an expanded European vision: it was chiefly a bid to prevent the dilution of his existing one. But there is a good chance that Mr. Delors's halfway house will offer most of EFTA too little in return for too much. This survey has contained many examples that show how a really open market and the preservation of full sovereignty are incompatible. The members of a proper "internal market" have to be subject to the same laws, respect the same trade embargoes, honor the same competition policy, accept the same basic standards, co-ordinate their monetary policies, and so on, inescapably.

The program to flesh out the idea of a European Economic Space will go on: much work is being done in such areas as standards, rules of origin, procurement, frontier documents and technical collaboration. This will temper the discomfort of non-membership of the EEC for determinedly neutral Switzerland and precariously poised Finland. For the rest of the EFTA six, starting with Austria and Norway, a snowballing bid for membership seems probable. And this must affect the ultimate goal of the Europe-builders.

DIFFERENT VISIONS

There is an uneasy truce about the style of the open market, but not about what lies beyond it.

"You cannot fall in love with a single market," Mr. Jacques Delors has said several times since the 1992 fever took hold. There are many Europhiles who wince at the unexpected success of this unlovable project. Like the friends of a magnificently mismanaged museum that has been rudely privatized and is thriving, they fear that a grand ideal has been hijacked by economic pragmatists. Listen to Mr. Delors, in a speech to the European Parliament in January:

> History is knocking at the door. Are we going to pretend that we cannot hear? ... It will not be enough to create a large frontier-free market, nor, as implied by the Single European Act, a vast economic and social area. It is for us, in advance of 1993, to put some flesh on the Community's bones and give it a little more soul.

He went on to say with a hint of glee:

> Now that the demands of the Single Act have really struck home, there is much more resistance ... I am tempted to echo the remark of a French politician who declared that at long last the problems are starting.

Last year's survey of 1992 told how the internal-market project drew strength from Europe's pre-occupations in the 1980s—a phase of enthusiasm for free markets, the challenge from Asia, the unstoppability of trade—and how it had bounced the EEC's members into surrenders of sovereignty and national habit that they would never have countenanced in pursuit of an abstract ideal. Those pragmatic surrenders have since been sustained—though at some price of woolliness. Argument over the immediate project has been avoided. It has flared over the vision beyond. Bottled-up frustrations have started to pop out: some in pursuit of more of the European ideal, others in fear of it.

Mr. Delors has been forcing the pace towards his grander vision of Europe. He warned last summer that "in ten years' time 80% of economic, and perhaps social and tax, legislation will be of Community origin." He pushed for a European system of social rights to counterbalance the rigors of the open market. He moved on towards economic and monetary union by calling for the setting up of the Delors committee to study how it might be achieved. This year he has raised the stakes still further with his appeal for a pan-EEC foreign and security policy on East-West relations, for a new political relationship with the

EFTA countries, and for "providing the Community with the dimension needed to tackle the problems of education, culture and society." With an impressively rounded vision of the Europe he wants, Mr. Delors is riding his 1992 wave for all it is worth.

Mrs. Thatcher had pent-up frustrations of exactly the opposite sort. With her speech in Bruges last September, she gave vent to them. The speech gave her view both of the goal of the EEC and of the style in which it should be run. Of the first she said:

> Willing and active co-operation between sovereign states is the best way to build a successful European community. To try to suppress nationhood and concentrate power at the center of a European conglomerate would be highly damaging ... It would be folly to fit [EEC countries] into some sort of identical European personality.

And of the style she said:

> We have not successfully rolled back the frontiers of the state in Britain only to see them reimposed at a European level ... The Treaty of Rome was intended as a charter for economic liberty ... Our aim should not be more and more derailed regulation from the center: it should be to deregulate, to remove the constraints on trade and to open up.

In the setting up of the internal market, Mrs. Thatcher has been getting her own way on style, though not by enough to get her to crack a smile. Both protectionism and interventionist bureaucracy have been held in check. France and West Germany have different approaches to economic intervention, and these have cancelled each other out in the commission and council. The French have tended to side with the British in eroding the West German penchant for perfectionist internal standards and rules. The West Germans have tended to side with the British in resisting the French penchant for protectionism—as in the continuing debate on car imports—and for fiscal harmonization where France was particularly stung when West Germany abandoned its withholding tax on savings rather than incorporate it into France's desired pan-European one.

A senior French civil servant, Mr. Guy Carron de la Carrière, has observed that Britain and France are building two different internal markets: the British are building one for consumers, the French, for producers. Yet the fact remains that the showdown between these two visions has not yet occurred, and that, if stated intentions are any guide, the consumer has so far got his own way. The commission's competition directorate, under first Mr. Sutherland and now Sir Leon Brittan, has been particularly powerful in making sure that France's Europe for producers is a Europe of a pretty testing sort. The reaction against this climate could yet come, if general directives spawn more detailed ones, as in finance; or if promises to open up markets are simply not kept when the home-market share of, say, the cosseted Italian car industry starts to tumble.

THE STYLE

For the moment, the battlefield for style, which is fundamentally a struggle about ideology as much as about the future of Europe, is the "social dimension" of the Community. Some of this is not contentious: structural funds to help the poorer regions of Europe, or a gradual harmonizing of rules on hygiene and safety at work. The rallying points for Brussels's retreating interventionists are the European social charter and the European company statute.

The social charter is vital to all those who believe that the abrasive competition promised by 1992 must be offset by a social safety net for employees. Mr. Delors is committed to it, and the West Germans have backed him, fearful that their highly developed standards for wages, working hours and worker-participation in management will be under-cut by the EEC's poorer members.

As drafted, the social charter would not be binding but would certainly create a political obligation. It would establish a maximum working week and a minimum working age. It would demand that individual countries establish a "fair wage." It would stipulate the rights of workers to vocational training through their careers, to join a union and to bargain collectively for pay. Much of the charter calls for self-evidently desirable things; but, for its opponents, that is not the point. For them the charter is a symbol of central bossiness that is not necessary to the existence of an open market—standards that can and should be set at national level. Their gloom is heightened by the prospect that the charter will be the forerunner of laws, and will be used to help the encroachment of majority voting in the European Council into social legislation.

Another contentious aspect of social Europe is the proposed European company statute; here, something of obvious practical worth has had social strings attached to it. At the moment a European company has to be incorporated under the laws of an EEC country; if it has subsidiaries in other European countries they must be incorporated there and conform to their local reporting, tax and labor laws. Since 1970 the commission has envisaged a statute that would allow a company to incorporate itself in Europe, rather than in a country, and be subject to one European set of rules.

There is certainly some appetite among managers for this convenience, although according to the European employers' federation, UNICE, they do not regard it as crucial to Europe's single market. Ford of Europe told the *Financial Times* that it would be keen to simplify its current complex structure by setting up as a single European entity.

Two problems have long bedevilled the prospect: tax, and rules on worker participation in management. Governments remain predictably reluctant to allow parts of a European company operating on their territory to be taxed as though they were part of the parent company in the state where it is domiciled. So, though it would offer some tax advantages, the draft company statute would not free pan-European companies from preparing different accounts in different countries.

West Germany has always demanded that any company statute should insist upon some form of worker participation in management, fearing that without this clause some German companies would Europeanize themselves and thus dodge the country's elaborate system of *Mitbestimmung*. The British government is strongly opposed to anything that will allow unions to re-establish their influence in British companies. It has fastened upon the company statute as a symbol of social engineering by Brussels that must be resisted. The commission has bent itself almost double in trying to compromise between the two views. Incorporation under the law would be a voluntary convenience. There would be three options for worker participation; a West German model; a French model, or any other model agreed between management and workforce. The tax advantages might even be available to companies that chose not to Europeanize themselves. To no avail: British conservatives continue to vibrate at the prospect.

THE GOAL

If the social dimension is the battlefield for the style of the single market, economic and monetary union (EMU) is the battlefield for Europe's goal. Here Mrs. Thatcher is losing.

The Single European Act, which she accepted in 1985 and the British parliament later ratified as the enabling treaty for project 1992, actually committed Britain to much more than the completion of a market. Among other things, it called upon EEC members "jointly to implement a European foreign policy"; it agreed "to transform relations as a whole amongst [the EEC] states into a European union," and it reminded them that they had agreed to the "progressive realization of economic and monetary union." The European summit in Hanover in the summer of 1988 picked up on the last point and set up a committee to report within a year on how EMU might be achieved.

The report that the Delors committee of monetary experts and central bankers produced envisaged a far greater surrender of sovereignty than anything implicit in the single market: national monetary policies completely in the hands of a European central bank; the European Council of Ministers having powers over national fiscal policies; and, to ensure no backsliding, insistence that "to enter upon the first stage should be a decision to embark upon the entire process."

The report laid out three stages through which the EEC would pass to reach a Europe with one currency and a centrally run system of central banks. Stage one, starting in July 1990, would essentially be the European Monetary System (EMS) as it operates today, but with all the current absentees from the exchange-rate regime—Britain, Portugal and Greece—participating, and with economic policies more tightly co-ordinated to offset the fact that capital would be sloshing freely about Europe.

Stage two would require an amendment to the Treaty of Rome; it would create a European system of central banks—analogous to America's Federal Reserve System—which would gradually impose itself upon national monetary policies. The movements of currencies allowed within the EMS would be narrowed, and the exchange-rate bands would be changed only in exceptional circumstances. The Council of Ministers would establish, by majority vote, guidelines for the macroeconomic policy of individual members. This stage would essentially be a period of practice for stage three, when exchange rates would be locked together and the key thrown away. Central monetary and budgetary control would be binding. A single currency would emerge.

Here was a true test of what different members of the EEC were really ready to accept in pursuit of the vague grail of European union. Britain said no, outright. Its chancellor of the exchecker, Mr. Nigel Lawson, explained in January, "It is clear that EMU implies nothing less than European government—albeit a federal one—and political union: the United States of Europe. That is simply not on the agenda now, nor will be for the foreseeable future." The Bank of England, whose governor, Mr. Robin Leigh-Pemberton, had sat on the Delors committee, explained defensively that "if the government did not like the answer, it shouldn't have asked the question."

Contrast that British response with that of Mr. Hans-Dietrich Genscher, West Germany's foreign minister. In a speech in early May he was positively gung-ho for the committee's suggested course. He said that there was basic agreement in the West German parliament on this matter and he even suggested that EMU could be complete by 1995—a view that the Bundesbank would probably dispute. Mr. Genscher is West Germany's political weather-vane: his views on EMU probably reflect his country's.

In France, too, the report went down well. Mrs. Edith Cresson, the minister for European affairs, told parliament that the Delors report was a "satisfying compromise." Her government wants to push the matter forward under the French presidency of the Community in the second part of the year, so that the Paris summit could set up an inter-governmental conference to prepare the amendment of the Treaty of Rome.

These reactions are worth detailing because they are not Euro-oratory that sounds grand but signifies little: they tell of a readiness to pool a lot of sovereignty in a specific way. They suggest that, far from speaking plainly of a nationalism that other Europeans feel but camouflage, Mrs. Thatcher is frankly out of touch with the depth of pro-Community sentiment on the continent, clinging to the ideal of a strong and independent Britain rather as her hero, Sir Winston Churchill, clung to the vision of empire. Project 1992 has done more than overcome national reluctance to do something pragmatic and probably painful. With the signing of the Single European Act it has reawoken an urge among the EEC's original members to move towards something closer to a political union.

Certainly there are forces at work here that are grander than a desire to shape up economically against hyper productive Asians. Mr. Peter Ludlow, the director of the Center for European Policy Studies in Brussels, wears his European enthusiasms on his sleeve, but it is hard to counter his argument that since the mid-1970s the EEC has been slowly evolving ways of dealing with problems which, till then, had been the preserve of America. The founding of the EMS was the EEC's bid to find an alternative to the wobbling hegemony of the dollar. European political co-operation thrived because of a growing feeling that, in non-NATO matters, European countries had joint priorities that diverged from those of America. The need for a European "pillar" to co-determine NATO strategy with America became steadily clearer. All these shifts imply a surrender of sovereignty—the polite word is a "pooling"—to the Community that goes beyond what is required for an open market.

As America's aura has dimmed, 1992 has unlocked political enthusiasms for closer union within the EEC. France clings determinedly to its special relationship with West Germany, aware that Mr. Mikhail Gorbachev is creating rival attractions for West Germany to its east. West Germany, too, clings to what Mr. Genscher calls "the most advanced form of association and co-operation existing between two sovereign states," precisely because that loyalty anchors West Germany in the West and preserves its legitimacy as it feels its way towards a new relationship with East Germany.

Meanwhile, the EEC's new members, Spain and Portugal, have breezed into the Community with a newcomer's enthusiasm for social Europe, the EMS, and European union. America has noted these tendencies and decided to embrace them, rather than stand aloof from them. None of these sentiments proves that Mrs. Thatcher's attitude to Europe is wrong: they merely create facts that she will find hard to ignore.

Yet there are other, more Bruges-friendly, forces at work. Europeans do not feel European in the way Americans feel American. They feel Dutch, French, Scottish, Bavarian. Language divides them powerfully. There is no European equivalent of the networked TV soap opera that defines American life for all Americans. As Europeans get wealthier they seem to attach more, not less, importance to their regional specialness: the touchiness of the West German länder, both about the Brussels law that affects them, and about Bonn shaping that law, is striking. Such forces do not help the emergence of a European superstate run by supermandarins in Brussels, though they might lead to greater local indifference as between national and European government.

Then there is EFTA and Eastern Europe. If EFTA countries apply to join the EEC—as seems likely—it is going to be hard to tell them that they must remain on hold while the 12 continue their quest for European union undistracted. Equally, it will be odd to establish a close-knit European union of Western European countries just when there is hope that some East European countries may move towards self-determination. The EEC's unpleasantly tidy frontier to the east is going to become steadily more permeable.

So, pulled this way and that, what is Europe building? The EEC launched a project to complete a long-promised common market. Tapping pent-up enthusiasm among governments, the public and business, the project took off more abruptly than most Europeans and outsiders had expected. The prospect of it prompted irreversible changes in the EEC's supranational institutions—more areas of influence for the commission, more majority voting between the national governments, more influence for the European Parliament. Where, in another decade, that market might have been a planned, harmonized and protected market, in the 1980s it is not, so far, taking shape that way: market principles hold sway, national systems compete, the external ramparts are being levelled down, not levelled up.

The goal is not remotely achieved. Brave principles have yet to be turned into brave practice. But the argument has already moved on, beyond the immediate goal towards a particularly rigorous and supranational approach to economic and monetary union. The continent's enthusiasm for this shows how 1992 has refreshed its appetite for political union. There are forces in the other direction, too—British reluctance, the coming pressure for enlargement of the EEC. And there is an old danger: the Euro-rhetoric which, as in the 1970s, outstrips reality and comes back to haunt and discredit the orators. What sits under the wraps is not as much as a United States of Europe, nor as little as Mrs. Thatcher's "willing and active co-operation beween sovereign states." It is a demonstration of the central laws, central institutions and political sacrifices needed when modern countries bravely decide that they are really going to open their economies to each other.

European Community: An Expanding Universe

CHARLES GRANT

A POWER IN ITS OWN RIGHT

During the second half of the 1980s the European Community's impressive progress was driven largely by its own internal development, centered on the single-market program. But over the past year the world outside—especially Eastern Europe and American—has propelled the EC forwards. The goals are undefined, but the direction is clear. Slowly but surely, the Community is becoming rather less a collection of nation states and rather more a coherent entity which the rest of the world recognizes as a power in itself.

The decision in 1985 to aim for a single market by the end of 1992—with a program of 279 measures—was the spark that relaunched the Community after ten years of rancorous stagnation. The EC could never have approached such an ambitious project without the Single European Act of 1986, which endowed its institutions with the means to take decisions more quickly.

And so it has. With 2 1/2 years to go, 60% of the 1992 measures have seen agreed. The program has made businesses inside and outside the Community change their behavior. In industries as diverse as electronic engineering, packaged food and insurance, companies have rethought strategies and leap into cross-border alliances in anticipation of the post 1992 world. The chart on the next page shows that the market is already more single: trade between EC members as a percentage of their total trade has grown.

The 1992 program has restored *elan* to the Community and given it the confidence to tackle more ambitious projects. The attack on internal barriers led to thoughts of scrapping the ultimate obstacle to a truly single market, 11 national currencies. A year ago the Madrid summit adopted the goal of economic and monetary union (EMU), which meant that an inter-governmental conference would be needed to write a new treaty. And that set people thinking about another round of political reform.

The Economist (July 7, 1990).

The brio of 1992 has changed the way outsiders see the EC. The six countries in the European Free Trade Association (EFTA) decided that if they were not going to join the club they should at least make sure that their voice was listened to. So they started talks with the EC about the creation of a European Economic Space. America and Japan began to respect the EX as an economic power and decided to upgrade relations with it rather than rely exclusively on bilateral links with the 12 members. And even before Eastern Europe was swept by a wave of revolutions in the second half of last year, some of its countries were turning to the EC in the hope of closer trade relations. As early as May 1989 President George Bush recognized that a "resurgent Western Europe is an economic magnet, drawing Eastern Europe closer, toward the commonwealth of free nations."

For the past year the EC has gained momentum from its relations with other powers and its response to the upheavals in Eastern Europe. In July 1989 President Bush nudged the European Commission into the role of coordinator of the West's economic aid for Eastern Europe. Then in December, America called for new institutional links with the Community. Both these initiatives prompted the EC to rethink the way it runs foreign policy. The need to act quickly in Eastern Europe forced a blurring of the traditional separation between economic policy, which is Community business, and the rest, which is supposed to be left to the members.

The collapse of communism in East Germany last November set off a chain reaction leading towards German unity. This has transformed the way most Germans and many other Europeans view the Community. They think German unity will be more palatable inside a more united Europe. Recent European summits have reflected the feeling that European integration should speed up: the one in Strasbourg last December set December 1990 for the start of the EMU conference, while the one in Dublin last month agreed that a second conference on "political union," should start at the same time.

The Community has never had more on its plate—the Uruguay round the GATT talks, the rescue mission in Eastern Europe, the deal with EFTA, EMU and political union. And now it has decided to absorb East Germany as quickly as possible. With such an overloaded agenda, some—like Mrs. Margaret Thatcher—fret that the EC might take its eye off the single market. So far, however, the march towards 1992 has not slackened. Since last December ministers have agreed on several of the program's most difficult measures, including the opening-up of public procurement in telecoms, water, energy and transport, and a new regulation to vet cross-border mergers worth more than 5 billion ecus.

The one part of 1992 that promised to make a big difference to ordinary people, the abolition of frontier controls, has also been the one part that threatened not to happen. But the signing last month by France, Germany and the three Benelux countries of an agreement to scrap all controls on people at their mutual borders makes it feasible that most, if not all, of their fellow members will make the same commitment in time for 1993. The Community's inability to agree on a new system of collecting VAT also threatened to keep up frontiers, because VAT on inter-EC trade is controlled by form filling at borders. But the governments have at last agreed on a system which should make border controls on VAT unnecessary: importers and exporters will instead report their VAT liabilities to their national tax authorities.

For all the importance of 1992 this survey will not dwell on the single market. The biggest changes in the Community are now responses to events beyond it rather than inside it. The survey looks at how the Community's influence is extending east-wards into the

FIGURE 6-1 ————————————————
The Single Market Works

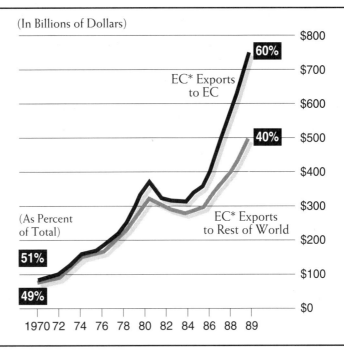

(In Billions of Dollars)

EC* Exports
to EC

60%

40%

(As Percent
of Total)

EC* Exports
to Rest of World

51%

49%

$800
$700
$600
$500
$400
$300
$200
$100
$0

1970 72 74 76 78 80 82 84 86 88 89

*Takes account of changing membership.
Source: OECD.

EFTA countries and Eastern Europe, before picking up the stories of EMU and constitutional reform. But first, since foreign relations have become a crucial influence on the evolution of the Community, it is necessary to turn to Washington.

NORTH ATLANTIC TRYST

When future historians come to write about the European Community's surge towards greater integration in the late 1980s and early 1990s, they will look for a "second generation" of founding fathers to set beside the first generation of Robert Schuman and Jean Monnet. Two Americans may get a mention: President George Bush and his Secretary of State, James Baker.

In the spring of 1989 America reassessed its policy on Europe. The worst fears of a Fortress Europe had been calmed by the liberal tenor of the EC's banking legislation. The review concluded that, since the European states were in any case moving more closely together, it would be in America's interests to look benignly upon, and even gently encourage, the changes.

Mr. Bush said at Boston University in May 1989:

> The United States welcomes the emergence of Europe as a partner in world leadership. We are ready to develop—with the EC and its member states—new mechanisms of consultation and co-operation on political and global issues, from strengthening the forces of democracy in the third world, to managing regional tensions, to putting an end to the division of Europe.

America would like both Japan and the EC to play an international role more suited to their economic strength. So it was natural for Mr. Bush to suggest at the Paris seven-nation summit in July 1989 that the European Commission should coordinate the West's relief for Poland and Hungary.

"We think the Community has a tendency to be insular," says a senior official in the Bush administration. "We thought this new role would make the EC more aware of its external responsibilities." It certainly made EC question the division between the economic side of its foreign policy, which is Community business, and the political side, which is supposed to be left to European Political Co-operation (EPC), a network of the 12 foreign ministries. In Eastern Europe the commission had the resources to get things done quickly, so it took a political lead.

Last December Mr. Baker gave the Community a second, mild push towards developing a more solid political identity. In a speech in Berlin he proposed new institutional links between the EC and America. Mr. Baker did so because his one big worry about a more integrated Europe is that it might take decisions on foreign policy without consulting America. In human-rights talks last year under the Conference on Security and Co-operation in Europe (CSCE), EPC took a common line and presented it to the rest of the NATO causes as non-negotiable. The administration was also piqued this January, when EC foreign ministers suggested a CSCE summit without consulting America. "It seems they only want to talk to us when they feel like it," says one official. "We want to commit them to come to the table." To which, the French sometimes retort, why should America have a seat at Europe's table?

The state department is content with the Community's eventual response to the Baker proposal. There will be twice-yearly meetings between the presidents of America and the European Commission: twice-yearly meetings between the American president and the current president of the European Council (as EC summits are know); and twice-yearly meetings between the American secretary of state and EC foreign ministers.

A third prod came last May, when Mr. Baker proposed a relief operation for Central America and the Caribbean similar to that in Eastern Europe. America would act as the chief coordinator, with the European Commission as deputy. This initiative may push the EC into developing a common foreign policy for this region. These three initiatives do not mean that the Bush administration would prefer to deal with Brussels to the exclusion of bilateral links with Europe's capitals. It thinks the best way to maximize influence is to talk both at national and supranational levels as much as possible.

Nevertheless, some American officials admit to feeling frustrated with Europe's Byzantine way of organizing foreign policy. It is not always clear whether they should deal with officials from the commission, the council or an individual country. And every six months a different country assumes the presidency of the council and of EPC. Political Co-operation is a particularly slow animal to deal with, since it cannot take a position until 12 foreign ministries have reached a consensus.

Take the Baker proposal of last December for new links with the EC. No one responded. It was not clear whose job it was to do so. Not until this spring did the new system of biannual contacts emerge. Similarly with Mr. Baker's initiative on Central America and the Caribbean in May; the European reaction so far has been little more than "how interesting."

Not everyone in Washington thinks it is wise to promote a stronger Europe. After all, its political influence could one day rival America's and oppose American policy in, say, the Middle East. The State Department response is that there is no alternative. A grudging attitude towards European integration would be counterproductive. And the risk of the EC becoming a Frankenstein that turns against its sponsor is slight, given that America and Europe share so many values in common. As for the Middle East, the State Department doubts that the EC has much leverage there. It also thinks that a common European foreign policy could help America, by constraining, for instance, an EC member which tried to close American military bases. And America knows that it will not get help in sorting out the world's woes unless the EC becomes more active in international affairs.

Two clouds—one in the foreground, the other still on the horizon—could dim the Bush administration's Europhilia. The immediate problem is the EC's refusal to talk about reducing its subsidies on agricultural exports. America is no mean protector of its own agriculture, but its trade negotiators claim that the EC's export subsidies are particularly pernicious because they distort markers in the rest of the world. If the Community continues its line of no compromise, the Uruguay round of GATT talks will remain blocked and American anger could spill over into the State Department and the White House.

The distant cloud is the possibility that an EC security policy could stretch to defense and undermine NATO. There is some ambiguity on this subject in Washington. Mr. Baker has repeated the long-standing American policy that there should be a strong, European pillar within NATO. The EC or, possibly, the Western European Union (which groups most of the EC's NATO members) are the obvious candidates to become such a pillar. But America would not like it if the Community became a substitute for NATO. Even if the EC limited its defense ambitions to acting as NATO's European wing, America would still be unhappy if the wing failed to consult it on important decisions.

And who would control the nuclear weapons? Mrs. Rosanne Ridgway, who recently retired as assistant secretary in the State Department, argues that if America was kept out of a European sub-group within NATO it could hesitate about providing a nuclear umbrella: "Europe would be saying we'll defend ourselves, but then if we fail please come in with your nukes."

Current American policy, however, is essentially optimistic. In the long term the European Community is likely to take on a larger role in security and even defense. On existing trends, America's response is likely to be that since it cannot stop the process it will accept it graciously—while doing all it can to wedge open the European door so that its voice can be heard.

TWELVE OR TWENTY-FOUR?

Chez Jacques is the Brussels club that everyone in the neighborhood aspires to join. But, like all the best clubs, Chez Jacques imposes a waiting list of several years and is most particular about whom it admits. Turkey sent in a membership form with good references from its North Atlantic friends in 1987, and received a reply (sent second class) two years later: "Come back in another decade." Now the queues outside the strangely ugly clubhouse, called the Berlaymont, have grown longer. Mediterranean and East European faces have come because they want to learn some decent, democratic manners from club members. Many Nordic and Alpine faces are animated by the sounds coming from behind the firmly-shut steel gates: the chink-chink of a game in which all players are piling up more and more coins.

From time to time the faces in the queue turn glum. For the gruff proprietor steps outside, sniffs impatiently as those in the line, and, with a *"Fichez-moi-la-paix"* (which can be translated liberally as "Beat it"), returns to his rich and happy friends at the gaming table.

Rebuffed though they are, those in the queue will not disperse. Many businesses from neighboring countries do not want to be excluded from Community rules, such as those of fair-play on bidding for public contracts, or those for setting industrial standards. Unlike their EC based rivals, these companies cannot influence the Community's decision-making process; yet to compete in the single market of 340m people they have to follow its laws.

Austria applied to join last year. This year Malta and Cyprus may follow suit. Norway is thinking about reapplying (it decided not to join after a referendum in 1972), while public opinion in Sweden, Finland and Switzerland has become more favorable to Community membership. All the new democracies in Eastern Europe say membership is their long-term goal.

The commission president, Mr. Jacques Delors is unmoved. The policy of the commission and of the council is that the EC's hands are full until 1993, and that no membership talks should start before then. The Berlaymont ideology is that further widening of the Community would endanger "deepening"—the process of 12 countries moving towards greater political union. Those outside the gates retort that previous rounds of widening have helped rather than hindered deepening after Britain, Ireland and Denmark joined in 1972 the EC set up its first regional funds, and the arrival of Greece (in 1981), Spain and Portugal (both in 1986) influenced the Single European Act's principle of majority voting on some EC laws.

Hoping to ease the mounting pressure for full membership in some EFTA countries, Mr. Delors launched a plan in January 1989 for the creation of a "European Economic Space" (EES). Starting in January 1993, this would link the EC to the six nations of EFTA—Switzerland, Austria, Norway, Swenden, Finland and Iceland. EFTA would have a say in "decision-shaping," but not decision-making on laws affecting the EES. After 18 months of preparatory work the two sides have now begun formal negotiations. They have already agreed on some outlines for the Economic Space.

Each side will maintain autonomy over its decisions. That means that if they cannot reach a consensus on a law for the EES, the EC will go ahead with its own which EFTA need not apply. EFTA countries say that provided they are consulted properly while the laws are being hatched, such fractures in the Economic Space would be few and far between. They point out that they will be under a lot of pressure not to be awkward. At the highest level joint meetings of ministers will link the two bodies. EFTA judges will sit with those from the European Court of Justice to resolve disputes about the EES.

Yet the differences remain profound, and a cloud of pessimism now hangs over the talks. The commission no longer speaks of an EFTA role in "decision-shaping" or even "consultation." It talks rather of "exchanges of information" between the two sides before the EC takes a decision. Some commissioners believe that EFTA is being offered so little that the talks are likely to fail.

The commission line has toughened because it now fears that if EFTA was consulted on every law, Community decision-making would slow right down. The European Parliament, which would have to approve an EES treaty, has also put the commission on its guard. The parliament worries that if the Council of Ministers and EFTA agreed on a law it would in practice be unable to amend it.

Mr. Delors now says EFTA must give ground on three points. First, it is asking for too great a role in decision-making. The EFTA members want some meetings of 19 countries (Liechtenstein will count as an honorary, seventh member of EFTA) so that they can speak before EC ministers take a final decision among themselves. But the commission insists that EFTA countries should not participate in meetings of the EC Council; rather, the commission should act as a go-between, conveying EFTA's opinions to the member states. Otherwise EFTA might make a tactical alliance in the council with, say, Denmark, and so gain a real say in decisions. The commission also wants the joint ministerial body to deal with broad policy rather than decisions; EFTA wants it to ratify laws that both sides have agreed on.

Second, Mr. Delors demands that EFTA should form a harder organization which would allow it to speak with one voice. EFTA works by consensus, and its skimpy secretariat in Geneva cannot take initiatives. Mr. Delors wants a body with enough teeth to enforce, for instance, EC competition rules. Who could discipline the Swedish government if it gave unjustified subsidies to Volvo?

Third, Mr. Delors says EFTA is asking for too many exceptions to the *acquis communautair*, the body of 1,000-odd regulations and directives that EFTA would have to take on board. The commission is sensibly prepared to let the EFTA countries off its agriculture and trade policies. But it does not like Iceland's refusal to let EC ships touch its fish, Finland's ownership, or Switzerland's refusal to allow EC citizens residency rights.

Sweden and Norway say they will not lower environmental and health standards to EC norms. The problem of standards could darken the Economic Space with any number of black holes. Suppose that EFTA rejected new EC rules on car exhaust emissions so that is could keep its own higher standards. Community cars would be cut out of the EFTA market, but Saabs and Volvos would still sell it in the EC. Sweden hopes that EFTA could "buy" the Community into tolerating such asymmetries, by for instance, topping up the EC's regional funds or making agricultural concessions to Mediterranean countries. Unacceptable, says the commission.

The EFTA countries have so far spoken with one voice. But their common line may not hold because they have very different approaches. The Swedes and Norwegians are so keen on the EES that they would accept a tougher organization to please the Community, yet the Swiss run away from the idea of an EFTA "pillar." The four Nordic countries and Switzerland are all more or less determined to clinch some sort of deal with the EC. Even an EES which left EFTA little role in decision-shaping would be better than nothing for companies like Asea-Brown Boveri, Nokia and Norskhydro. But these five countries have doubts about Austria's commitment.

On its own admission, Austria's priority is full EC membership as soon as possible. But Austria says it wants the EES to work because if a lot of the labor of swallowing the EC's law book can be got out of the way now, eventual membership talks will be much quicker. Norwegians keen on membership also view the Economic Space as a useful antechamber on the way to the inner sanctum.

WIDER OR DEEPER?

Community policy, to Austria or any other applicant, remains firm: it is too busy with EMU, political union and the single market to contemplate any membership talks until after 1993.

FIGURE 6-2

Three into One?

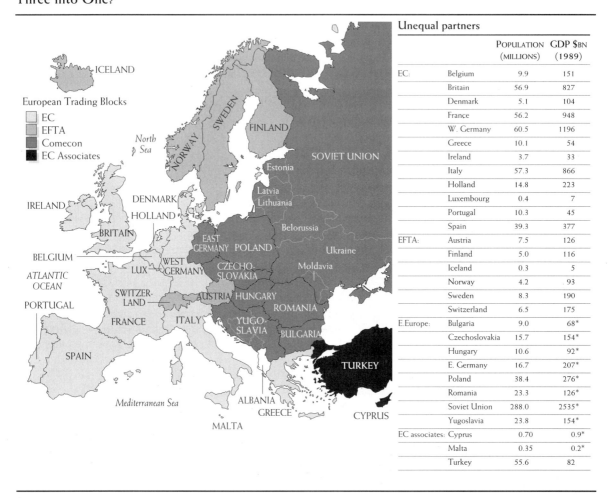

		POPULATION (MILLIONS)	GDP $BN (1989)
EC:	Belgium	9.9	151
	Britain	56.9	827
	Denmark	5.1	104
	France	56.2	948
	W. Germany	60.5	1196
	Greece	10.1	54
	Ireland	3.7	33
	Italy	57.3	866
	Holland	14.8	223
	Luxembourg	0.4	7
	Portugal	10.3	45
	Spain	39.3	377
EFTA:	Austria	7.5	126
	Finland	5.0	116
	Iceland	0.3	5
	Norway	4.2	93
	Sweden	8.3	190
	Switzerland	6.5	175
E.Europe:	Bulgaria	9.0	68*
	Czechoslovakia	15.7	154*
	Hungary	10.6	92*
	E. Germany	16.7	207*
	Poland	38.4	276*
	Romania	23.3	126*
	Soviet Union	288.0	2535*
	Yugoslavia	23.8	154*
EC associates:	Cyprus	0.70	0.9*
	Malta	0.35	0.2*
	Turkey	55.6	82

Unequal partners

European Trading Blocks
- EC
- EFTA
- Comecon
- EC Associates

*1988

Source: UN; OECD; IMF; CIA.

As for the East Europeans, the argument once used in favor of Greek, Spanish and Portuguese membership—that it would help "cement democracy" after years of dictorship—has been laid aside. The new association agreements that the Community plans for Poland, Czechoslovakia, Hungary, Bulgaria, Yugoslavia and (perhaps) Romania will not mention the prospect of membership—although those signed with Greece, Turkey, Malta and Cyprus in the 1960s did just that. Many East Europeans would welcome the words "eventual membership" as a sign that they could aspire to a wider heritage.

The commission points out the East European states are a long way from being politically or economically mature enough for membership. Not one of their economies could stand up to free trade. The commission says there is no need for the association agreements to mention membership, since the EC treaties make it clear that any democratic country with a market economy can apply. But in reality the commission does not want the East Europeans to think of membership as an option for the foreseeable future.

Although the Community's gates are firmly shut, the tremors set off by the fall of the Berlin Wall could nudge them open sooner than Mr. Delors wants. The decision to let in East Germany as a special case has changed perceptions of the Austrian application. Belgium once opposed it, but now argues that it is unfair to keep Austria out if East Germany is coming in—especially since 70% of Austria's trade is with the Community. Because of their historical and cultural ties with Austria, West Germany and Italy are sympathetic to this line. Denmark wants all the EFTA countries to be let in as fast as possible. And the commission is no longer solidly behind Mr. Delors; four members favor Austrian membership sooner rather than later.

Since last November the commission's old argument that neutrality is incompatible with membership has lost its force. In the post Cold War world, neutrality matters less to some people. The governments of Switzerland, Sweden and Finland still make a fuss about theirs, but Austria says its neutrality would not prevent it from joining in any future EC foreign and security policy.

Surely it is up to any applicant to worry about whether its neutrality is compatible with Community membership? Not for Mr. Delors and his advisers, who remain hostile to neutral members and say that Ireland is a special case since its neutrality is so flexible. In private they are even less enthusiastic about opening the club doors than the official line suggests. At one commission meeting Mr. Delors argued that it could take 15 - 20 years of planning before East European countries were ready for membership. And it is said that talks with Austria should not begin until the Community has had several years of experience with the EES.

Mr. Pascal Lamy, Mr. Delor's chief adviser on strategy, cites three reasons for the reserved attitude towards widening. First, the experience of new members has been that the rest of the EC has to devote a lot of time and energy to the difficulties of digestion. More new members would mean less energy available for the substance of deepening.

Second, a more integrated Community has to take more decisions more quickly. Yet swelling the numbers at council and commission meetings would inevitably make it harder to reach decisions. Mr. Lamy thinks the existing constriction could just about tolerate 14 - 15 members, but no more. He thinks it will be many years before the members of the EC are ready to create the sort of constitution—with lots of majority voting and fewer than one commissioner per country—that would allow a Community of 24 to work smoothly.

Mr. Lamy's third point is that neutrality still matters. A neutral member might *de facto* brake the EC's progress towards a common security policy, and prevent the EC from becoming the European pillar of NATO. The real drawback, says Mr. Lamy, is that "the more integrated the Community becomes, the harder it is to let in new members. We have to favor integration." This policy seems unfair on those European countries which, by accident of history, were not lucky enough to be among the current 12.

The rest of the world is now reassured that the EC's economic policy—agriculture apart—will not be that of a Fortress Europe. In the 1990s the complaint of outsiders may be more political, that the Community has fallen victim to a Little Europeanism. The Community seems set to become a powerful core surrounded by concentric circles—EFTA, Eastern Europe, perhaps the Maghreb—which economically are integrated or becoming integrated but politically are second-class citizens.

"Why should Europe remain divided into seniors and juniors, deciders and receivers?" asks Mrs. Ridgway, now director of the Atlantic Council, a Washington think-tank. She believes the EC can widen and deepen at the same time. "The EC will be a better partner for America if in the long run it can represent all Europe. And an EC of 12 will be too small a base for Germany's political role."

As Mr. Delors is so fond of saying, history is accelerating. Sooner or later the Community may find its existing policy on enlargement morally untenable in the eyes of its many international partners. If, by early next year, the EFTA talks are seen to have failed. Norway is likely to follow Austria in applying for membership. Even people as adroit as Mr. Delors and Mr. Lamy will not be able to find good arguments against NATO member Norway joining. A failure to achieve the EES would push the rest of EFTA in the same direction, while if the Economic Space does take shape, it is unlikely to be on terms which give the EFTA members much political satisfaction. In the long run, most of them will probably conclude that they are better off inside the EC where they are able to influence the decisions which affect their economics.

Czechoslovakia, Hungary and Poland look set to lodge applications by the mid 1990s. If the six EFTA countries, Malta, Cyprus and say, Slovenia also joined by the turn of the century the EC could stretch to two dozen members. In the very long run the other Yugoslav republics, Bulgaria, Romania, the Baltic states and Turkey could be candidates, taking membership to well over 30.

BRUSSELS'S NEW EMPIRE

The collapse of Soviet power in Eastern Europe has left the European Community, by default, the dominant power in the region. America realized this sooner than Western Europe's own leaders and in July 1989 suggested that the commission should coordinate 24 rich countries' aid to the two new democracies of Poland and Hungary. This became known as the G-24 or Phare program (after the French word for lighthouse), and is now being extended to East Germany, Czechoslovakia, Bulgaria, Yugoslavia and—if it treats its opposition more gently—Romania.

Mr. Delors knew that if the commission fluffed its lines in Eastern Europe it would not get another chance to strut across the international stage. So he and Mr. Frans Andriessen, the foreign affairs commissioner, took no chances and put 20 of the commission's best staff onto the Phare program. One year later they have been rewarded by the judgement of the Bush administration, which is that the commission has managed the operation efficiently.

The Community is also building up bilateral links with the East European countries. Having completed trade and cooperation agreements with each of them, it now plans a series of "association agreements." These will offer free trade into the EC while allowing a transitional period of protection for the East Europeans. The agreements will cover joint projects—in areas such as banking, research and development, the environment and telecommunications—which should encourage the transfer of western expertise. They will also include offers of EC money and loans from the European Investment Bank. The part of "associate" status that most excites the East Europeans is "political cooperation," which will mean formal, frequent and high-level meetings to discuss bilateral problems or anything else such as regional conflicts.

The commission would like these countries to form a regional association, for that might help to postpone their eventual applications for membership. The countries concerned, however, seem more interested in links with the EC than each other. A more likely prospect is that a series of bilateral channels will extend eastwards from Brussels. The EC's aid for

Eastern Europe—quite apart from its coordinating role in Phare—is steadily deepening these channels. This year Poland and Hungary will receive 300m ecus ($370m) of EC money, and the other countries joining Phare a further 200m ecus. The EC plans 850m ecus of help for the region in 1991 and 1 billion ecus the year after—not to mention several billion ecus from the European Investment Bank.

Emergency food aid (worth 140m ecus) has been sold on the Polish market, and the proceeds put into a rural infrastructure fund which is managed jointly by the commission and the Polish government. The fund has already invested in about 100 schemes—some small, such as the piping of water to villages, and some ambitious, such as a rural telephone project. In this the fund provides engineers and 25% of the cost of connecting a village to the telephone network, while villagers pay the rest—mainly through local labor and materials.

TEMPUS is one of the Community's more ambitious projects in the region. It encourages firms and universities in the West to help upgrade university departments in Eastern Europe. If say, a Polish university is setting up a business studies department, TEMPUS will arrange for French companies to help and for Polish staff to attend a British business school. The program has 107m ecus to spend on Poland and Hungary in the next three academic years—about half on projects in universities and the rest on exchanging staff and students. In the first year, starting this autumn, 650 Polish students will go to the West. Poland and Hungary have asked for help with the teaching of business studies, languages and applied science—but Czechoslovakia stresses that its arts faculties need pepping up.

The commission has found it much more difficult to conduct an orchestra of 24 individualistic players than to perform on its own solo projects. Its staff have travelled throughout Eastern Europe, seeking to identify projects and define priorities for Phare. Back in Brussels they have chaired groups of delegates from the G-24 countries and drawn up lists of things that need doing. The idea is that countries come forward with offers to match, while the commission tries to prevent overlaps and to ensure that the most needy gaps are filled.

In practice each donor country has tended to do what it would have done anyway. Most of them prefer to indulge in spectacular bursts of generosity—which get the right headlines at home—rather than study seriously where help is most needed. Few countries have been willing to take part in joint projects, and a lot of the aid is tied to being spent in the donor country.

Take the example of training aid, which is so far doing little to help Eastern Europe to develop its own training capacity. France and Britain have paid for a lot of Poles and Hungarians to come to courses in France and Britain. Among the schemes to be financed by Britain's "Know how Fund" in Poland are a seminar for Polish members of parliament on "British parliamentary concepts" and a course at Leicester Polytechnic for local government councilors and officials. Commission officials estimate that, on average, three times as many people would be trained if a set sum of money was spent on sending trainers to Poland rather than Poles to trainers.

Yet for all the bilateralism, the conductor has made the orchestra play better than it would have done on its own. Countries have swapped information about what they are up to. Silly overlaps have so far been avoided. East Europeans have a forum to which they can bring their request. And priorities have been set, which is particularly helpful for small countries that may lack the resources to organize and finance whole projects on their own. Thus Ireland learned from the commission that the Warsaw center which coordinates training aid lacked office equipment. So the Irish obliged by sending personal computers, fax machines and photocopiers.

The commission has recently managed to stitch up some joint projects:

- The EC, the World Bank and America are jointly trying to clean up Poland's Mazurian Lakes.
- The EC will contribute money to the environmental agency that America is setting up in Hungary.
- The International Finance Corporation (part of the World Bank) thought up and will manage a Polish privatization agency. The EC will finance it and its members are expected to contribute financial skills such as merchant banking and accountancy.

Eastern Europe will need Phare until all its economies are fit for full Community membership. Phare's achievements have already ranged from billion-ecu credits for Poland and Hungary to the European Bank for Reconstruction and Development (BERD), which, powered by 10 billion ecus of capital will start lending to the region next year. Although a founder member of BERD, Russia will at first not be allowed to borrow more than its paid-in capital. Like its absence from Phare, this reflects the fear that Russia's hugh thirst for cash would leave the rest of Eastern Europe dry.

But at last month's Dublin summit, EC leaders took a deep breath and decided that they would help the Soviet economy—but only after detailed studies of its needs had been carried out. The summit mandated the commission to produce two plans: one on how to help the Soviet Union's short-term credit needs and the other on longer-term structural reforms. If, as expected, the European Council approves these plans in October, other G-24 countries are likely to join the EC's efforts. President Bush is happy for the EC to organize relief for the Soviet economy, partly because America itself does not want to contribute any money.

Like everything the EC has done in Eastern Europe, help for the Soviet Union will be conditional on its progress towards a marker economy and democracy. The EC refused to sign a trade treaty with Romania last month after its government treated the opposition thuggishly. And the commission declined to invite Romania to a meeting of the G-24 donors. Community governments accept that, since politics and economics cannot be kept apart in Eastern Europe, the commission should take political initiatives.

POWER TO THE CENTER

Those strange beasts the ECU and the EMU have been rather overlooked during the excitement of the hunt for political union. Yet economic and monetary union (EMU) is likely to change the Community more profoundly that another round of institutional reforms. As well as transferring monetary sovereignty from national governments to a new European central bank, dubbed "Eurofed," EMU promises to increase the powers of the commission. It will also simplify life for tourists.

The Community's preparatory work on EMU has reached an advanced stage. The committee of EC central-bank governors, under the chairmanship of Mr. Karl Otto Pohl, the president of West Germany's Bundesbank, is working on a set of Eurofed statutes which will be ready in time for the inter-governmental conference on EMU which starts in December. That conference will draw up a new treaty for economic and monetary union. In Dublin last April the heads of state—Mrs. Thatcher included—agreed that the treaty should be ratified by the national parliaments before the end of 1992.

Mr. David Mulford, under secretary in America's Treasury, welcomes the prospect of EMU. He tries to achieve some coordination of currency policies among the Group of Seven (America, Japan, Germany, France, Britain, Italy and Canada). "Having only three main currencies—the yen, the dollar and the ecu—could allow progress towards improving the world monetary system," he says. At the moment, when America deals with an EC currency it has to take into account the knock-on effects inside the European Monetary System (EMS). "The simplicity of one European currency would give us a chance to strengthen policy coordination and discipline," Mr. Mulford says.

Europe's partners now assume that EMU will happen, because there is a consensus among 11 countries—Britain being the odd one out—on what its main traits should be. Fears that the gap between financially orthodox Germans and supposedly profligate Latins would be unbridgeable appear—on current evidence—not to have been justified.

On the broad outlines of EMU, the Germans will get more or less what they want. An independent Eurofed will set Europe's interest rates. The objective of monetary policy will be price stability. Banking supervision will be left to national authorities. There will be no direct link between EMU and a beefing-up of the EC's regional funds, but these are in any case doubling over the period 1988-93, after which they will be reviewed. There would be no guarantee of a bail-out if a member of the currency union went bankrupt, but the EC might lend it money with conditions attached.

The commission recently produced a paper on the institutional arrangements for EMU which most EC governments find broadly acceptable. It envisages a Eurofed council made up of the 12 central bank governors and a full-time board of four. Council members would be obliged to act independently. The European Council would consult the European Parliament before appointing a board member as chairman for a five-year term.

To reduce the risk of economic and monetary policy pulling in different directions, the president of Ecofin (as the council of finance ministers is known and a member of the commission would have the right to attend, though not vote at, meetings for the Eurofed council. The commission could make "observations" to Eurofed on "the consistency of monetary and economic policy." As for accountability, the parliament would receive an annual report from the Eurofed and have the right to question the chairman.

Some countries are unhappy that, for the sake of pleasing Germany, neither council, commission nor parliament will be able to order changes in interest rates. But they know that Germany will not sign up unless it gets a bank which it regards as politician proof and therefore tough on inflation. Most members would prefer a German influenced EMU to the existing EMS in which they have to follow every interest rate whim of the Bundesbank. They see EMU as a way of increasing sovereignty, since it would hand interest rate decisions to a body which included their own countrymen.

Even though 11 countries have reached a rough accord on the sort of EMU they want to aim for, there are still thorny issues to settle. For instance, it is agreed that exchange rate policy should be set by Ecofin but carried out by Eurofed. That formula leaves room for dispute because interest rate policy, supposedly the domain of Eurofed, is a main instrument of exchange rate policy. Another sticking point could be the plan for all members to deposit a proportion of their foreign currency reserves with Eurofed. The central bank would manage these reserves, but if it lost, say, Irish money while intervening, who would bear the cost?

Germany will take some convincing before it accepts that the Eurofed will be genuinely independent. It fears that a national government could ignore the statutory independence of Eurofed council members and bully its central bank governor to vote a certain way. Germany wants all the national central banks to be made as independent as its own. There is little chance of that. The commission argues that independence will seep down from the Eurofed to the national central banks, and that in practice no government would dare to sack a governor for ignoring its advice on how to vote.

FRANKFURT FRETS

Germany is at the center of two other big arguments that need to be resolved. Does EMU mean that 11 Community currencies would be permanently glued at set exchange rates, or that the ecu would replace national currencies? Their strong emotional attachment to the D-mark makes German people antagonistic to the commission preference that everyone should use ecus. For equally symbolic reasons, most other countries back the commission; otherwise, they fear, that ensign of Germany supremacy, the D-mark, would become the currency that people wanted to use. Symbols apart, the commission plan has some economics on its side: while separate currencies persist, markets could speculate against the union lasting and provoke higher interest rates in the weaker economies. Sir Leon Brittan, the competition commissioner, proposes a compromise that would reassure markets of the union's durability: one side of a banknote would be denominated in ecus, the other in D-marks, drachmas or whatever.

The second big argument is whether EMU requires central control of budget deficits. Britain, with some support from France, argues that EMU could work with each state setting its own budget. Germany, supported by Holland, wants binding centrally set rules on members' budgets. Germans do not explain in public why they are so keen on strong controls. "We worry about the Italians, Spanish, Greeks and Portugese," says a Bonn official in private. "Italy might over borrow and then demand a bail-out. If we could leave those four out of EMU it would help to reassure doubters in the Bundesbank." Mr. Pohl has suggested that "advanced" members could leave the rest behind on EMU, but most governments find the idea anathema: the EC's philosophy is that everyone should move forward together.

The commission has now come up with a clever formula which seems to satisfy both the Germans and the British. Instead of binding rules, there would be "binding procedures." Each government would submit its budget to Ecofin. If the proposed level of borrowing was so irresponsible that it would push up interest rates elsewhere in the EC, the ministers could, on a majority vote, order a change. If the sinner did not mend his ways and peer group pressure had no effect the Community would apply sanctions—like the withholding of regional funds. The commission claims these binding procedures are less rigid than binding rules since compulsion would be applied only against the real basket cases like Greece (see Figure 6-3).

With the goals more or less defined, the debate is shifting to how to reach them. Last year's Delors report mapped out three phases, the first of which—involving free capital movements and more monetary and economic cooperation—has already begun. In phase two the Eurofed would be up and running; but national authorities would retain ultimate authority for monetary policy, and occasional currency realignments would be possible.

The Bundesbank argues that phase two should be skipped, since shared monetary authority could make the not-quite-fixed EMS unstable. If an external shock struck an economy, the markets could expect a realignment and, by speculation, force one to come about.

FIGURE 6-3 ————————————
The Good, the Bad, and the Ugly

General Government Budget Balances
(As Percentage of GDP)

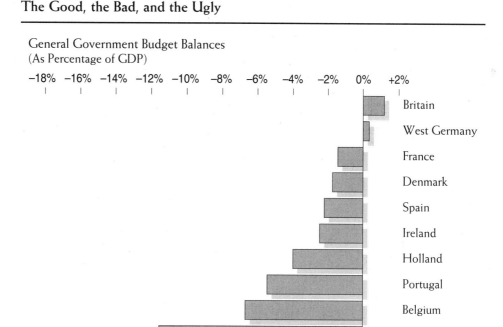

Source: BIS.

There would be no central authority to hold the system together. The commission is sympathetic to these arguments and is now prepared for a phase two lasting only a few months. But it maintains that an interim phase is still needed in order to give the new bank a chance to run itself in. A commission official predicts that although member governments would retain monetary authority in phase two, "Once Mr. Pohl is sitting in his chairman's office and the pictures have been hung in practice they'll do what he says."

By contrast Britain's new plan for a phase two aims to make it last as long as possible—and is thus "permanent purgatory" for one commission official. Britain suggests that a European Monetary Fund should issue ecu banknotes and manage a "hard" ecu—one that could never be devalued against other EC currencies. Many governments favor greater use of the ecu, but because Britain still opposes "phase three"—fixed exchange rates and Eurofed setting interest rates—they tend to view the plan as a cynical tactic to divert them from EMU.

Many British officials now concede that the inter-governmental conference of EMU is likely to be over by next spring. They, if not their prime minister, are resigned to EMU happening. They know that if Britain tried to wield its veto the others could go ahead with a new treaty among 11 states.

Don't Forget the E in EMU

The argument about binding rules on budgets is the tip of an iceberg that is often ignored: economic union. It could have a big impact on the balance of power between the Community and its members. Last spring Mr. Delors proposed that the EC should coordinate national economic policies in order to "fine tune" the continental economy. The finance ministers squashed the idea of demand management, but not the concept of an EC economic policy. Such a policy should, according to the commission's recent institutional paper, be "based on the coordination of member states' economic policies and on the implementation of the different common policies, in particular competition and structural."

In phase one of EMU Ecofin makes annual recommendations on economic policy for each member, based on reports drawn up by the commission. The commission paper envisages that in phase three the council should adopt, after a proposal from the commission and an opinion from the parliament, three-year policy guidelines for the EC and for each country. The country guidelines would deal with budgets, costs, savings and investment, and sometimes include policy recommendations. If a recommendation was ignored and the council failed to take action, the commission would publicize the recommendation.

The commission's unspoken philosophy is that it should become an embryo economic executive to balance Eurofed. The paper argues:

> It is difficult to see how powers assigned by treaty to the commission in terms of initiative and control can be shared with bodies that will not be subject to control by the European Parliament [that is, the council]. . .the commission will be accountable to parliament, whether in respect of the preparation of annual reports on the economic situation in member states, the formulation of annual recommendations and multi-annual guidelines, the surveillance of their implementation by member states, or relations with Eurofed.

The EC's governments are not resisting these ideas. After all, while some of them think the commission should keep its nose out of foreign policy, its right to manage and take initiatives in the economic domain is seldom challenged. What is new is that EMU increases the size and scope of the economic domain.

The powers of the Community's "federal" institutions—the commission and the parliament—have often grown by what is known as the "spillover theory." In this case, countries debated monetary union and decided that it was a good idea. Only much later are they coming to realize that monetary union spills over into economic policy coordination, and that that means—hey presto! — an enlarged role for the commission and the parliament.

TIME FOR A NEW CONSTITUTION

As recently as a year ago, when EC leaders committed themselves in Madrid to economic and monetary union, the idea that they would also embark on another round of constitutional reform carried little credibility. The parliament hoped for little more than one or two new powers to be tagged on to the EMU treaty. Yet constitutional reform was the principal subject of last April's Dublin summit, while at that held in June all 12 members agreed to rewrite the Community's constitution.

The subject has always excited federalists, but last year a wider audience took an interest:

- Many countries became concerned about a "democratic deficit": national parliaments have little influence over EC legislation, while the Strasbourg assembly has only feeble powers of amendment.
- Debates on EMU provoked thoughts about the constitution. How would the EC's economic and monetary policies be made accountable?
- The Community had to face the prospect of more members. A larger EC would slow decision-taking unless the institutions were revamped.
- Some of the partners and most of the practitioners of EC foreign policy thought its organization was creaking under the weight of new challenges.

Though the democratization of East Germany was the yeast which set this brew in motion, Mr. Delors stirred things skillfully. Last autumn it became clear (in Bonn, Brussels and Washington, though not in Paris or London) that the two Germanies would unite within a few years. In a speech that he delivered in Bruges in October, Mr. Delors asserted that "history is speeding up, so must we." He said that the EC should respond to events in Eastern Europe by accelerating moves to EMU and by strengthening its institutions.

By the Strasbourg summit in December, the inevitability of German reunification was evident to all. This shifted perceptions about the future of the EC. Both West Germany and its continental neighbors felt that German unity would somehow be safer and more acceptable if at the same time Europe became more united. So the Scrasbourg summit decided that the inter-governmental conference on EMU should start in December 1990. Early this year Mr. Delors threw out some ideas on constitutional reform before suggesting that the subject merited its own inter-governmental conference.

This idea won backing from Mr. Helmut Kohl, the West German chancellor, and Mr. Francois Mitterrand, the French president, who issued a joint appeal in April for "European Union." Their aims were "to reinforce the union's democratic legitimacy, to make its institutions more efficient, to ensure economic, monetary and political cohension and to define and set in motion a common foreign and security policy." They wanted "political union" to enter into force in January 1993, at the same time as the single market and EMU. The two Dublin summits which followed this appeal decided that the constitutional conference should start, like that on EMU, in December.

The views of France and Germany carry the most weight in the constitutional debate: France, because of its traditional influence in the Community and its ability to persuade neighbors to follow its lead; West Germany, because of its economic muscle and its special role in splicing East Germany into the EC. When this pair renew the marriage vows of their long-standing but often strained alliance, they are an unstoppable force in EC politics. But soon after their appeal for "political union" they started to discuss what is actually meant, and it became clear that they had different ideas.

France had been exasperated last year with West Germany's reluctance to set a date for the EMU inter-governmental conference. But this year, convinced that nothing will prevent German unity, West Germany has bounded beyond France in its Euro-enthusiasm. Many Germans realize that it would not have been so easy to move towards unification without a strong EC to reassure those who were uneasy about the prospect. A senior official in the Bonn government explained Germany's shifting view of the Community: "In the past, we worried that too much European unity could cut us off from East Germany. But achieving reunification means that there is no longer any need for us not to be pro-European. We now feel freer to move quicker."

Mr. Kohl is most concerned to prove that German unity is not slowing down European integration (as some had thought it would). This may explain the relish with which he calls for a big transfer of power to the European Parliament and the commission. Mr. Kohl is inspired by the memory of his hero Konrad Adenauer, one of the Community's founders. Mr. Kohl (no less than Mr. Mitterrand and Mr. Delors) worries about his own role in the history books. He wants to be seen as the forger of two unions, Germany's and Europe's.

Germany and Belguim, this year's most ardent champions of a more federal Europe, are the only two EC members with federal governments of their own. Partly-federal Italy and Spain seem more or less at ease with the concept of a federal Europe. It is those ancient, centralized and proud nation states, Britain and France, which agonize the most about loss of national sovereignty.

If Germany marks one pole of the debate on political union, France marks the other. The French approach is to achieve the goals of the Kohl-Mitterrand appeal while retaining as large a role as possible for the nation state. One French emphasis is to elevate the role of the European Council. "If you want to go for something ambitious in foreign and security policy, what else can give coherence and orientation?" asks a senior diplomat. Heads of government would meet more often and take the big decisions on foreign policy.

France would scrap the system whereby the presidency of the council rotates every six months. To achieve more continuity and focus. French officials talk of either a single person or a large country holding the presidency for several years. In the latter case, small countries would hold six monthly vice-presidencies. Either way, there would be a rival authority to the commission.

The third French priority is that national parliaments should play a role in plugging the democratic deficit. "We'll do a lot for the European Parliament, but democratic legitimacy does not come only from Strasbourg," says a government official "Public opinion is not yet ready for national parliaments to delegate more [to the European Parliament]." France has therefore floated the idea of a second Strasbourg chamber, or "senate," made up of national MPs. While Durosceptics think it would be another tier of bureaucracy, most federalists dislike the idea since they hope the Council of Ministers, representing member governments, will ultimately evolve into a (weak) second chamber. Holland is a rare supporter. It suggests that if each country had an equal number of senators, small countries would lost their reluctance to cede powers to a parliament which is dominated by MEPs from big countries.

The commission in Brussels worries about France's seeming disregard for the federalist agenda. It fears that Mr. Mitterrand could hark back to General de Graulle's idea in the early 1960s of a parallel body, outside the Community, which would discuss high politics and take decisions by unanimity. The fear is probably misplaced. There are Gaullises in the French foreign ministry, but Mr. Mitterrand is as committed a European as Mr. Kohl. When the French and the Germans get down to the details of their blueprints, the differences may be not be huge.

Mr. Mitterrand is more constrained than Mr. Kohl by domestic politics. In West Germany the three main political groupings all support a more federal Europe. But in France the National Front, the Communists, many of the Gaullists and even one minority faction of the Socialist party—led by Mr. Jean-Pierre Chevenement—oppose moves towards further political integration. The government's stress may be intended to win acquiescence from Mr. Jacques Chirac's Gaullists.

The Gaullists like the idea of a European Senate and of a beefed-up European Council. But some of their rhetoric veers closer to Mrs. Margaret Thatcher than to Mr. Mitterrand. "Mr. Delors is wrong to think you can solve the German problem by emptying nations of sovereignty," says Mr. Pierre Lellouche, Mr. Chirac's adviser on foreign policy. He believes the Community's priorities should be 1992 and EMU. "It is a mistake to try and move towards political and military union before the status of Germany has been settled, for that will determine the nature of the EC," he adds. He sees a parallel with the mid-1950s: it was only after West Germany was allowed an army of its own and to enter NATO that the EC could take off.

IN NEED OF A FACE-LIFT

In the coming arguments on constitutional reform, the one that really matters will be on foreign policy. The fundamental French interest in political union is the desire to tie down Germany. Some Germans believe that it is in their country's fundamental interest to be tied down. For those who worry about the possible dangers of a resurgent Germany, tying down means constraining its foreign policy—so that, for instance, Germany would find it harder to make provocative comments on the permanence of its Polish border.

Leaving aside such emotions, most EC members believe that their method of coordinating foreign policy needs attention. European Political Cooperation began in 1970, and received statutory backing from the Single European Act of 1986. Political Cooperation has had its successes: in about three-quarters of votes in the United Nations, EC countries take a common line. But it can rarely agree on joint action: since the Venice Declaration of 1980, which implied that Palestinians should be involved in the Middle East peace process, EPC has taken no initiative in the region.

Every six months the presidency of EPC (as of the Community) passes to a different country. It can be a strain for a small country with few embassies to represent the 12 around the world, and policy can suffer from a lack of continuity. When EPC decides that it should take a stance, a five-man secretariat in Brussels sets to work on coordinating the views of national foreign ministries, and eventually publishes a common, usually bland statement. Some Japanese and American diplomats complain that EPC is ineffectual. The problem is not only that it works by consensus, but that the officials who run it come from national foreign ministries and therefore have little inclination or incentive to consider what is the Community interest. There is no equivalent of the commission to promote that interest or to take initiatives.

Japan would welcome dealing with a more solid body, since it finds its twice-yearly meetings with EC foreign ministers (wearing EPC hats) unsatisfactory. The EPC side can do little more than read out a common position and is not free to respond to Japanese suggestions. Japan would like its relations with the Community to be as tight as its relations with America. So in May it sent a team of ministers to Brussels to discuss more formal links with the commission. Japan hopes that a more full-bodied relationship with the EC would raise its own profile on the international stage. Commission trade officials suggest, for instance, that Japan might be tempted to remove barriers to EC exports such as shoes and processed food, if in return the Community pushed it to play a greater role in the Cambodian peace talks.

F I G U R E   6 - 4
Community Commerce

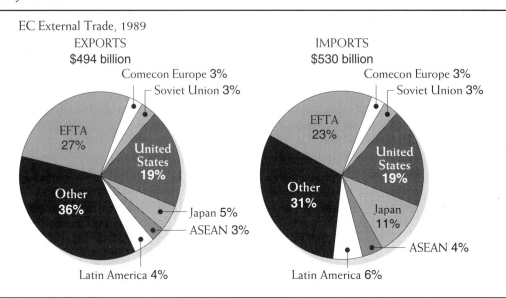

EC External Trade, 1989

EXPORTS
$494 billion

Comecon Europe 3%
Soviet Union 3%
EFTA 27%
United States 19%
Other 36%
Japan 5%
ASEAN 3%
Latin America 4%

IMPORTS
$530 billion

Comecon Europe 3%
Soviet Union 3%
EFTA 23%
United States 19%
Other 31%
Japan 11%
ASEAN 4%
Latin America 6%

Source: OECD.

The need to coordinate economic and political strategies for Eastern Europe has led to a blurring of the EC-EPC distinction. Normally the officials from national capitals who run EPC would seldom meet the officials that countries keep in Brussels to manage EC business. But over the past year the two groups have met frequently to talk about Eastern Europe. Britain cites this example to argue that the current system works well so long as the EC and EPC collaborate.

"The machinery that produces policy is unimportant compared to the policy itself," says a senior British diplomat who sees no need for big structural changes. Instead he suggests three modest reforms: a bigger EPC secretariat, a more prominent secretary general who could explain EPC positions to third countries, and more meetings between officials from national foreign ministries and ambassadors to the EC. Such reforms would allow the Community to run a common foreign policy in areas where all members agreed that they should work together. The diplomat plays down the significance of EPC's inability to take initiatives: "Foreign policy is 75% reactive and 25% proactive—while for economic legislation the proportions are reversed.

But Britain's gradualism will satisfy few of its partners, who insist that if policy is to be made more quickly it needs some Community input. They argue that, since policy sometimes has to be backed by action such as sanctions, trade treaties or aid, it makes sense to involve the commission. And the British approach scarcely addresses either the problem of external identity—other countries would like to be clearer about who they should talk to—or the desire of some members for a big, symbolic change.

Most EC countries agree that there should be a common authority to deal with third parties and define and pursue common interests. But they do not agree on how this should be achieved. The French idea that a strong council president should lead foreign policy incites jealousy among most member states and the commission. The federalist alternative is to treat foreign policy as normal EC business and let the commission run it. Although the parliament likes it, this idea is no more popular with the member states than the French or British proposals.

A compromise approach, backed by Germany, several other countries and Mr. Delors, stands a much better chance. This would give EC members a larger role in foreign policy than in normal Community business, but loosen the hold of national foreign ministries. Political Cooperation would merge with the council secretariat, an efficient machine which helps the Council of Ministers to take decisions smoothly. National officials based in Brussels rather than home-based civil servants, would prepare policy.

At the highest level the European Council and the council of foreign ministers would take decisions. They would produce policies for areas where everyone agreed that it made sense to take a common line, such as Eastern Europe and America. Some of those backing this plan would like to soften the principle of unanimity so that one or two states could not block a policy: but such an attack on individual members sovereignty is unlikely to win the support of many countries.

The commission would attend meetings and take initiatives. But individual countries could also make proposals, which they cannot do for normal EC business. The commission and the diplomats of EC governments would share the implementation of policy—and could pool some of their overseas embassies. Two faces would represent the EC jointly to the outside world: the president of the commission and the current president of the European Council.

Such a compromise would disappoint many of those who were excited by the grand talk of political union. But Mr. Peter Ludlow, director of the Center of European Policy Studies, argues that making the national diplomats in Brussels responsible for foreign policy would lead to subtle but far reaching changes. "The council is an increasingly autonomous organization which works closely with the commission. When ambassadors to the EC meet in the council, it is very hard for one member state to block all the others, even on subjects which need unanimity, for they are used to thinking about the EC interest."

UP IN ARMS

Should a common security policy extend to military matters? Many argue that the EC should not discuss defense before Germany's security status has been settled. "To talk about it now could make the Americans concerned about NATO's future, and it could perturb the Russians," says a senior Bonn official. "Let's leave it undefined until they say their troops are leaving East Germany."

It is not just this worry about timing that turns many Germans off the idea of an EC defense force. Germans tend to favor the EC broadening into Eastern Europe and Scandinavia, where they are naturally influential, and they worry that a Euro-army could make it more difficult for neutral countries to join the club. Prospective members who are neutral would like to know whether, in the long term, the Community intends to play a role in defense.

It will be hard to keep this subject off the agenda of the coming inter-governmental conference. A lot of taboos are vanishing along with the Russian threat, and politicians are talking about the future of NATO. The commission will certainly push for defense industries to be given the single market treatment. In 1985 NATO estimated that if the EC countries opened up their defense-procurement markets, they would save one-fifth of the 30 billion ecus that they spend every year on weapons.

Sir Leon Britain has proposed that a European Security Community (ESC) should become the European pillar of NATO. This would not have exactly the same members as the EC, since Ireland (and later perhaps Austria) might not want to join while Turkey, Norway and Iceland (NATO members not in the EC) would participate. Ministerial decisions in the Security Community would be unanimous and the commission would act as a civil service. The ESC would concern itself with military R&D, joint training, military collaboration and defense procurement. It might even manage the nuclear deterrent as an equal partner with America.

These ideas are probably more suitable for the inter-governmental conferences of the coming century than the one which starts in December. But the long-term trend is for defense policy to become less concerned with military affairs and much closer to foreign policy. There may be a gradual process of foreign ministers talking about NATO business more often at EC council meetings. At some distant point America might want to discuss a new NATO treaty, and the EC could formally be stamped as NATO's European pillar.

From their offices on the top floor of the Berlaymont, the EC commissioners gaze towards NATO's headquarters on the edge of Brussels. The commission's federalists are determined to grab defense policy one day, if it takes them a dozen inter-governmental conferences. The commission is therefore most concerned that however the Conference on Security and Cooperation in Europe (CSCE) develops, it should remain a lightweight, inter-governmental organization with a small secretariat. The strong CSCE that the Russians and some East Europeans demand could turn into a pan-European security club, and block the Community's own ambitions in that direction.

DEMOCRACY VERSUS EFFICIENCY

Once the constitutional conference has sorted out foreign policy, two other big questions will have to be tackled. How can the Community's institutions be made more efficient? And how can the democratic deficit be reduced?

Britain and France worry the most about the lack of involvement of national parliaments in EC legislation. While France favors a European senate of national parliamentarians, Sir Leon Brittan suggests a committee of national MPs that would act as a bridge between the Council of Ministers. The merit of the idea is to recognize that the council represents national governments rather than parliaments. But some reckon that the consultative status of Sir Leon's committee would render it too feeble to hold the council truly accountable, and others view it merely as another tier of bureaucracy.

Mr. Bruce Millan, also a British commissioner, proposes that national parliaments should receive a draft of every EC law and the date that the European Parliament would consider it. Each would then send a member to the relevant committee of the European parliament, to argue but not to vote. This idea could prove popular, but most governments consider that tinkering with national parliaments is a side issue. They believe that EC legislation can be made accountable only at EC level. This argument is particularly strong when the council of ministers makes law by majority vote, for it is then impossible for a national parliament to block a law.

Thus German officials argue that the answer to the democratic deficit is more clout for Strasbourg. They would give it the right to elect the commission president and to sack individual commissioners, so that the commission felt more responsible to it. And they would increase Strasbourg's legislative sway by allowing it to propose laws (as long as the commission agreed) and to wield a veto.

This is music to the parliament's ears. But the report written by Mr. David Martin, the parliament's institutional spokesman, does not call for a pure veto. It proposes, if the council and parliament cannot agree on a law, a "conciliation procedure." This already happens for the annual budget, and involves both sides having to work out a compromise.

The constitutional conference will thin down many of the parliament's demands. So far it can be sure of strong support only from the Germans, Belgians, Italians and Greeks. Many countries are uncommitted, while Ireland, Portugal and—especially—Britain lack enthusiasm for boosting the parliament's powers. But even Britain suggests that the parliament's budget committee should have more clout to hold the commission to account for the money it spends. Britain would probably not resist a few other sops to Strasbourg. The parliament has a good chance of getting at least three of its demands into the new treaty: an extension to all legislation of the "cooperation procedure," which allows it to amend laws so long as the commission agrees and the council is not unanimously opposed; the right to approve all constitutional and foreign treaties; and the election of the commission president on a proposal by the European Council.

The inter-governmental conference will talk about the fashionable term, "subsidiarity," the idea that decisions should be taken at the lowest practicable level. Britain will cite the principle in arguing against any new powers shifting from national governments to the Community. But subsidiarity can also justify devolving power even lower, from national to regional level. Over much of Europe there is a slow but noticeable trend for people to identify with regional entities, and this is now touching the debate on the EC's institutions.

Bavaria wants the regions to be represented in a European senate. Mr. Millan, the regional commissioner and a Scotsman, proposes a consultative assembly made up of regional representatives. He would also make the main Strasbourg assembly more regionally conscious. Most countries elect MEPs on national lists, so those who win have no contact with, and take little interest in, any particular region. The result is that 80% of the letters that the commission receives from MEPs on regional policy are from the British and the Irish. Britain and Ireland are the only EC countries with constituencies based on small geographical units. Mr. Millan suggests that the new treaty should require the use of regional rather than national lists in European elections. He would also let regional delegates into the Council of Ministers, with the right to speak but not to vote. The German Länder are already allowed in to watch.

THE BIG STICK

When the inter-governmental conference comes to discuss efficiency, the debate will shift from the parliament to the European Court of Justice, the commission and the council. One fetter on the progress of the single market is the inability of the court to enforce its decisions. At the start of this year there were 43 outstanding cases of a government ignoring a court ruling on the non-implementation of a directive, or on an abuse of the single market. Italy had ignored 23 judgments, followed by Greece (eight), Belgium (six) and Germany (five).

Mr. Peter Sutherland, an Irishman who was once competition commissioner, suggests that national courts should help. "If a government ignores a European Court ruling, national courts should enforce it," says Mr. Sutherland. "People generally accept their authority. Then if a government still flouts the law, the commission should be able to mete out punishments." Britain wants the European Court to be able to fine countries for contempt. Fines could be most easily enforced if the commission withheld regional or agricultural funds from the guilty countries. But that would be hard on the innocent individuals who lost out, so a system of straight fines is more likely to win approval. When it comes to protecting its cherished single market, Britain is always game for a bit of supranationality.

The "efficiency" of the Council of Ministers, defined as speed of decision, depends on the ministers voting by majority. Efficiency happens to transfer power from governments to the council. Federalist therefore favor "efficiency," but non-federalists have to admit that the Community would never have been able to tackle the 1992 program without the use of majority voting for many of its measures. It leads not only to quicker law making, but also to fewer of the fudged compromises that the need for unanimity inspires.

The new treaty will allow more majority voting, because all countries, including Britain, think it makes sense for environmental laws. And all countries except Britain and possibly Germany want some social laws to be voted on by majority. Many countries will resist giving up unanimity on indirect tax. But when ministers take into account the number of new members and therefore new national vetoes that could join the club, and then recall the five years it has taken to harmonize VAT rates (without, so far, success), they might ponder majority voting on the details if not the design of indirect tax.

The prospect of new admissions will also color the debate on the commission's efficiency. There are now 17 commissioners, two from each big country and one from each small one. Already, there are not enough substantial portfolios to share out, and the full commission is an unwieldy body. The members of the Community might agree to one commissioner each, but Mr. Delors thinks even that would be too many if more countries were to join. The minnows will resist the idea that they should take turns to have a commissioner.

The second question that must be settled about the commission is the use of agencies. Some suggest that the enforcement of competition policy should be transferred to an independent agency, so that commission rulings on mergers and state aids would not be influenced by the political wheeler-dealing that has been evident in recent cases, such as that of illegal French aid to Renault.

The Italian commissioner for research, Mr. Filippo Maria Pandolfi, goes further, suggesting that many of the commission's administrative departments should be hired off into agencies. These would be supervised by the commission but managed by boards appointed by governments. The benefit, says Mr. Pandolfi, is that the agencies would be free of the inflexibilities that plague the management of the commission—such as rigid rules on pay, a slow system of promotion, the difficulty of recruiting outsiders and the near impossibility of sacking bad staff.

Mr. Pandolfi reckons that most of the departments dealing with agriculture, the environment, regional aid, development, the single market and research could be turned into agencies. He would let the commission keep six or eight large departments to work on strategy and legislation. The Berlaymont's seasoned bureaucrats are predictably skeptical about the efficiency of agencies. They argue that agencies have a tendency to build empires and would be even worse than commission departments at following their own wishes without regard to anyone else. And could they be managed more flexibly? When considering the statutes of the new environmental agency, ministers opted for the same (inflexible) staff rules that apply to the commission.

EUROPE À LA CARTE

The Community does not exist to serve the ambitions of its mandarins, nor the particular interests of its member governments, but to enhance the material and political welfare of its people. Many of the changes described in this survey are remote from the concerns of most Europeans. Over the coming decade the argument will run between those who say that it "makes sense" for more things to be managed at EC level, and those who resist the tendency for decisions to move ever higher and further away from ordinary voters.

The EC's continuing economic development will work in favor of greater political integration. The commission will find more to do in managing and policing the single market, and in helping to coordinate the economic policies of national governments. This will lead to more demands for the commission to be run like an efficient business and to become more accountable to the European Parliament. The world beyond, of America, Japan, Eastern Europe and elsewhere, will continue to press the EC into establishing a more solid identity as a negotiating partner. Here EC governments will hold on to a greater independence than in economic policy, but they will find that they can achieve more by agreeing on common policies towards some parts of the world.

Public opinion may resist these centralizing tendencies. But the growing-together of Europe's economies and greater personal travel will, slowly, nudge Europeans into tolerating rather more Community involvement in, say, training, labor law and public health.

As several East European countries become eligible for membership, the pressure on the EC to let in new members will grow. Sooner or later the EC's politicians will have to devise constitutional forms which allow neutral countries to join without threatening others' ambitions to give the Community a role in defense. An idea such as the "European Security Community," with a membership that did not exactly match, could permit the EC both to widen its membership and to deepen its integration.

The Community's philosophy that all members should subscribe to all parts of it has already broken down with the abolition of frontier controls: the "Schengen five"—France, Germany and the Benelux countries—have temporarily left the rest behind. There will be latecomers for EMU as there were for the EMS. Why not let each country pick its à-la-carte Community?

There would have to be a core, compulsory menu covering the basics of the single market and economic and foreign policy, or else decision-making would become too complicated. But France, Germany and the Benelux countries, say, might want to merge their education systems. They would be free to do so while Britain would be free to maintain its own system. Decisions in these "optional communities" would be taken by ministers, MEPs and MPs from the relevant countries. The commission would be civil service to all communities.

Hard-line federalists shy away from this idea, for a patchwork Europe would probably never become a United States of Europe. They dream of the American model, with all states subject to a uniform system of government and defense. But to pursue such homogeneity would mean turning away any countries from EFTA and Eastern Europe that cared strongly about their neutrality—and would risk chasing out those current members which do not want to hand over a lot more sovereignty.

Most Europeans still identify mainly with the nation (and in some countries, with their own region). Europe's constitution should therefore respect real differences of national feeling. If the Swiss wanted to maintain, inside a greater EC, their tradition of part-time service in the army and freedom from military alliances, let them. If a Europe Health Community aimed to introduce the French system of compulsory private health insurance, and the British remained attached to their system of free healthcare, let them stay out. Multiple community could satisfy such national feelings, and they would inevitably stop the European state becoming too centralized.

Many people are not just nationalists. In varying degrees they also feel European. But such sentiments are in no way limited to the current, 12-nation EC. Any European federation that is not to be the mere plaything of politicians and bureaucrats must correspond to a cultural reality. It is preposterous to imagine that a united Europe could exclude the country of Mozart and Mahler, or the land of Kafka and Kundera.

Business in Europe: Second Thoughts

MARTIN GILES

ON THE DEFENSIVE

The Gulf crisis, a heated debate on a common European foreign policy and a gaggle of conferences about EC political and monetary union have conspired to keep Project 1992 out of the headlines. Now the plan to create a single European market is edging its way back into the news. With fewer than 600 days to go before January 1st 1993, when the market is supposed to be ready, the project is falling behind schedule. Worse, a backlash against 1992 is growing. The resistance comes from the very people who were supposed to be the single market's firmest friends: captains of European industry.

That seems odd given that 1992 looked tailormade for business. Wisse Dekker, chairman of Philips, even helped to draft the European Commission's 1985 white paper, which laid out its plans to abolish EC frontier controls, harmonize product standards and prize open the markets for public procurement (the buying of goods and services by governments and utilities). Other industrialists, such as Jacques Solvay, head of Belgium's biggest chemicals company, and Giovanni Agnelli, boss of Italy's FIAT, also lobbied hard for the single market.

One reason for their enthusiasm was that Project 1992 appeared an ideal antidote to Eurosclerosis, a nasty European disease whose symptoms included relatively low levels of investment and rapidly rising labour costs (see Figure 7-1). This was blamed for Europe's lack of clout in fast-growing industries such as electronics. But there was another reason, one which held the seeds of today's discontent. Many such business leaders assumed that European mega-projects in research and development and infrastructure would form part of the project. Few assumed that Europe's internal openness would be matched by openness to competitors from outside.

Jean-Jacques Servan-Schreiber, a French journalist, publisher and radical politician, had called for a European market that was both whole and supportive in his book "Le Défi Américain" (The American Challenge), published in 1967. At the time, Europe was being

The Economist (June 8, 1991).

FIGURE 7-1

The Sickness that Started It

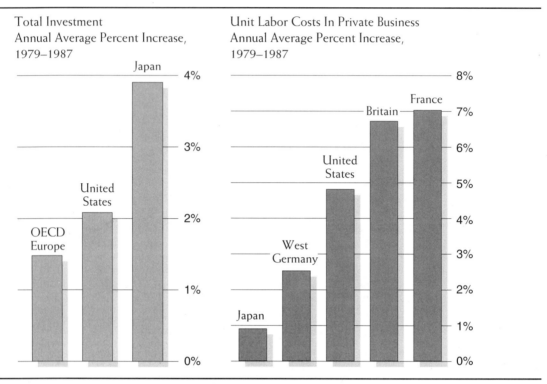

Total Investment
Annual Average Percent Increase,
1979–1987

Unit Labor Costs In Private Business
Annual Average Percent Increase,
1979–1987

Source: OECD.

invaded by American multinationals like Ford and IBM. In Mr. Servan-Schreiber's view, this invasion was a sign of Europe's industrial weakness, not the cause of it. To repel the invaders, he recommended the creation of a common market and pan-European companies big enough to take on the Americans.

The Cecchini report, published in 1988, promised that a single market would be a liberal bonanza for business. Coordinated by Paolo Cecchini, a senior EC official, the study examined the costs of Europe's fragmented markets. Among its tantalizing (if somewhat dubious) estimates, the report calculated that sweeping away red tape at EC border posts would create one-off savings for companies of some 8 billion ecus in administrative costs and customs delays; generate up to 15 billion ecus-worth of new business as a result; and save businesses billions of ecus more by getting EC states to accept one another's product standards.

Lured by the prospect of such rewards, European companies have been getting ready for the market. Some have refocused their businesses, selling off their stakes in marginal activities. Others have expanded at home and abroad. In some of the biggest cross-border deals, Siemens of Germany and Britain's GEC jointly acquired Plessey; Carnaud of France and Britain's Metal Box merged to form CMB Packaging; and FIAT and France's Alcatel-Alsthom (formerly CGE) announced plans to swap shares and some businesses.

Exchange Rate

per dollar	1990 AVERAGE	1991 MID-MAY
Ecu	0.79	0.82
D-mark	1.62	1.70
FFr	5.45	5.76

This wheeling and dealing was the easy part of 1992. Now they have signed on the dotted line, businessmen face the task of closing plants, axing jobs and cutting costs. That is hard to do at the best of times; slower economic growth and falling sales will make it harder now. So will stiff competition. "Europe is still a pretty cosy place in many industries," says Richard Giordano, the boss of Britain's BOC, an industrial gases company. Not for much longer. If Project 1992 overturns barriers according to plan, European businessmen are in for a shock.

David Ernst of McKinsey, a management consultancy, reckons that America's airline industry experienced a foretaste of what is to come in Europe. After the American market was flung open to competition in the 1970s, over 200 new carriers piled into it. Of these, less than a third are still flying. Airlines that were already operating before deregulation suffered too, as ticket prices plunged and the cost of advertising skyrocketed. Less than half of them survived the following decade; the rest either went bust or were taken over by other carriers.

DEEP DIVISIONS

Project 1992 will make this shakeout look like a pyjama party. After decades of cosseting, many European companies have grown fat and lazy. That will make them vulnerable to new firms whose costs and prices are a fraction of their own. Moreover, whereas American deregulation was largely a domestic affair, the European version promises to be an international free-for-all. Powerful American and Japanese firms like Philip Morris, IBM, Fujitsu and NEC are already limbering up to do battle.

With chilly new draughts of competition wafting through boardrooms across the EC, some European companies wonder wistfully about the cosier other half of Project 1992. They are as keen as ever about the nuts and bolts of the single market, harmonised standards, open procurement markets and suchlike. But a growing number want the Community to reconsider its liberal position on key issues closely linked with 1992, like competition, industrial policy and trade. Their lobbying shows, that European business has yet to cure itself of a craving for subsidies and support; if these cannot come from a national government, firms want them from Brussels.

Governments are divided over how to respond. Broadly speaking, those of France and Italy incline a sympathetic ear to companies' cries for help, whereas the German and British governments are usually deaf to special pleading. The European Commission is split, too. A group of free-marketeers, including Sir Leon Brittan, the EC's British competition commissioner, and Martin Bangemann, a German in charge of industrial matters, think that the market should determine the fates of firms. Ranged against the hard men is a shifting alliance of French, Italian and other commissioners and Eurocrats who favor intervention.

The battle between the two camps swings back and forth, but over the past few months the free-marketeers have been on the defensive. Some companies have frustrated the EC's attempts to cut state aid to industry. In April, for example, Groupe Bull, an ailing French state-owned computer-maker, won the promise of a FFr4 billion hand-out after losing nearly FFr7 billion last year.

Pressure is also mounting for an interventionist industrial policy to support Europe's biggest electronics companies. Some firms argue that Europe needs to copy Japan and America, both of which have nurtured their high-technology industries with huge public orders. And they say that it is up to the commission to think up (and help pay for) ambitious European projects.

Europe's commitment to free trade is also being tested by car-makers and semiconductor manufacturers. The car companies have lobbied for continued restrictions on Japanese imports for at least another six years. That is the breathing space they claim they need to get themselves ready for battle. Some chip-makers want higher tariffs.

All of these industries claim they are special cases deserving exemption from the rigors of the single market. This survey weighs up their claims. But first it looks at the commission's progress on the nuts and bolts of 1992—or at the lack of it.

MARKET FAILURE

Jacques Delors, the president of the European Commission, once said that it was hard to fall in love with a single market. He had a point. After all, detailed directives for pressure vessels, gas cookers and toys are dull. Yet after the publication of the commission's 1985 white paper, thousands of businessmen set their hearts on such things. Some of them are already disappointed. Although the January 1st 1993 deadline is flexible, they think that the EC has not moved fast enough to open up public-purchasing markets or fix product standards.

There are still some areas where business gives the architects of 1992 the thumbs-up. They include:

- **Customs controls**. At the end of next year, the "Single Administrative Document," a straightforward questionnaire that has already replaced reams of frontier-bumf, will be scrapped. From then on, companies will be able to ship goods anywhere in the EC with minimal delay. That is bad news for Europe's small army of customs officers, but good news for firms like Marks & Spencer and BMW that run pan-European distribution systems.
- **Freight transport**. Restrictions on *cabotage*—the right of foreign hauliers to pick up and deliver goods within another member state's borders—should be abolished by the end of 1992. That could reduce the cost of haulage within the EC by 10-15%.
- **Exchange controls**. Most countries have lifted restrictions on foreign-exchange transactions on or ahead of the schedule laid down by the Community. Only Portugal, Ireland and Greece still have exchange controls in place.

In other matters, though, businessmen feel cheated. Take value-added tax. Firms grumble about the commission's decision to put off devising a VAT system that treats the

FIGURE 7-2
Overrated

Vat Rates, March 1991

	STANDARD %	LUXURY/HIGHER %
Ireland	23.0	
Denmark	22.0	
Italy	19.0	38.0
Belgium	19.0	25.0
France	18.6	22.0
Holland	18.5	
Greece	18.0	36.0
Britain	17.5	
Portugal	17.0	30.0
Germany	14.0	
Spain	12.0	33.0
Luxembourg	12.0	

Source: UK Treasury

Community as a single market until at least 1996. Instead, countries will continue to collect VAT on the full price of an item bought inside their borders. To make matters worse, widely varying tax rates in Europe are still causing headaches for firms (see Figure 7-2). FIAT says that its Alfa Romeo subsidiary has to produce two different versions of one model simply to avoid getting caught in luxury VAT bands.

Companies also feel that progress in opening up public procurement has been slow. Worth perhaps 15% of the EC's combined GDP—4.7 trillion ecus in 1990—procurement markets are often closed to companies from other member states, thanks to a combination of chauvinism, political pressure and cosy relationships between contractors and bureaucrats. Only 2% of big public-sector contracts flow across EC frontiers.

In the 1970s several directives were adopted by the EC in an attempt to prize open procurement markets in the fields of public works (construction) and public supplies (investment goods and equipment). But these had several handicaps. First, there was no effective means of ensuring that purchasers played by the rules. Second, key industries like telecommunications, energy, water and transport were excluded from the regime. Lastly, public authorities used all sorts of wheezes to ensure they could still favor local firms. These included splitting contracts to keep them small enough to escape the directives, and specifying national rather than European product standards in tenders.

To put a stop to these shenanigans, the commission has revamped the old directives and produced some new ones. The revised versions already in force cover supplies and works for public authorities. They insist that information about tenders be widely publicized and that standards stipulated be, where possible, European ones. A supplies and works directive covering the previously excluded industries will come into effect at the start of 1993 (a bit later for Spain, Portugal and Greece). The snag with all of these is that they still leave plenty of scope for favoritism. Buyers are required to accept the "most economically advantageous bid." That means decisions could be made on the basis of price, delivery dates, after-sales service or any other variable that favors national bidders.

In order to ensure fair play, the commission has drawn up two compliance directives: one which is due to come into effect in December, covering purchasing by public authorities, and another covering utilities, which is still in the legislative pipeline. These will establish uniform complaint procedures for companies that suspect discrimination Though the commission will not be able to freeze disputed contracts, it will be able to notify member states of clear cases of rulebreaking. If governments ignore its warnings, the commission could then take them to the European Court of Justice.

This is no empty threat. Take the case of a big Danish bridgebuilding contract awarded in 1989. Convinced it was the victim of discrimination, Bouygues, a French construction firm that was one of the bidders, complained to the commission. The commission then took the case to the European Court, demanding that construction work be stopped and tenders re-opened. Faced with legal action, the Danes admitted they had broken the rules and allowed unsuccessful bidders to seek damages in Danish courts.

In spite of this episode, most businessmen reckon that procurement will remain almost exclusively a national affair. That is one reason why engineering companies have been spinning pan-European webs of alliances. In two of the biggest deals, Sweden's ASEA merged with Brown Boveri, a Swiss engineering firm, and GEC and France's Alsthom put together their power and railway businesses. By passing themselves off as insiders in as many EC states as possible, these companies hope to sidestep remaining barriers to cross-border procurement.

Other bidders will have to put their faith in the compliance directives. Companies are skeptical about whether these will have much effect. Some claim that it is unrealistic to expect them to launch legal action against potential clients. They think the commission should have the power to suspend contracts on its own initiative. Others, like Germany's Siemens, which relies on procurement for a third of its sales, say that until local politicians are prevented from awarding contracts, the temptation to give them to national firms in return for political favors will be irresistible. And there are other barriers to open procurement: one of the biggest is still a dearth of European standards.

LOWERING ITS STANDARDS

Sweeping away different national product standards and replacing them with a set of Euro-norms would be a Herculean task: Germany alone has some 20,000 standards, France 18,000 and Britain 12,000. Instead, the Community is using the principle of "mutual recognition." According to this, a standard developed in one European country should be accepted in another providing it meets certain basic requirements in matters such as health and safety. These are laid down in EC legislation. So far the Community has agreed several directives on minimum standards for products like toys, pressure vessels and gas cookers.

For some products, national standards are so diverse that European ones are clearly required. These are being thrashed out by Europe's two big standard-making institutes, CEN and CENELEC, which include representatives from national standards bodies. CEN and CENELEC published 293 standards in 1990. But many more may be needed. John

Farnell, who heads the commission's standards office, reckons that another 1,000 Euro-norms—an average of about two a day until the end of 1992—are required to create a fully-fledged single market.

Businessmen are doubtful. Dr. Peter-Michael Asam of Siemens complains that the commission is wasting time on unimportant standards—like those for medical systems, which should be set by health authorities. He reckons Eurocrats need to listen more carefully to industry's advice about what is needed and what is a waste of effort. Mr. Giorgio Bodo, the head of economics at FIAT, has another gripe. He argues that by taking years to come up with standards, the commission makes it hard for European companies to plan ahead. One example: car firms that spent large sums developing "leanburn" engines subsequently discovered that the EC was working on an environmental standard that such engines cannot meet.

The commission has listened to its critics. In a document published last October, it outlined proposals to speed up standard-setting. These include:

- the creation of European standards in their own right. At present, Euro-norms have to be translated into national ones before they can be used—a process that can take more than six months;
- the creation of a single European conformity mark; and
- shorter public enquiries to mull over draft standards.

Top of the list was a strong recommendation that European businesses become more involved in standard-setting. Some companies, it seems, are reluctant to provide experts to advise the standards bodies. Why? Probably because they fear that harmonized European standards will make it easier for foreign rivals to attack their home markets. The longer the invaders are delayed, the better.

UNSOCIAL EUROPE

Another bone of contention between businessmen and Eurocrats is the EC's Social Charter, which outlines basic rights for European workers. The Charter itself is nonbinding, but the commission is preparing a set of 47 directives which, if enacted, would add up to a comprehensive system of panEuropean industrial relations, courtesy of Brussels. Among the measures—which were added after the 1985 white paper was published—are ones that would restrict night work, give part-time and temporary workers the same rights as normal staff, and force EC companies to consult workers about decisions like plant closures and the sale of businesses.

These proposed directives have met with a storm of protest. "If they are enacted, they will ruin Europe's companies," says Zygmunt Tyszkiewic the head of UNICE, the European employers' Federation. Jean-Louis Beffa, the chief executive of Saint-Gobain, a French conglomerate, agrees. He complains that the texts are "excessively rigid" because they have been drafted by lawyers not bosses. They are right to complain. One key to competitive advantage is a flexible labor force; the commission's plan could put companies in a straitjacket.

Fortunately for business, progress on these social measures has been slow. In most other areas of the single-market program, firms moan about delays. Yet much of the blame lies with some national governments that are painfully slow at translating Community directives into national law. At the end of March 1991, member states were supposed to have implemented 122 EC measures. Italy the worst offender, had managed just 45. This is not the only problem that the commission has with unruly governments. Another is the battle to stop them propping up their national industrial champions.

WHAT, US COMPETE?

Frightened by the prospect of what the Cecchini report called "a new and pervasive competitive climate" in Europe, businessmen have thrown themselves into one merger or strategic alliance after another. These, they say, will help create the giant companies needed to look Japanese and American rivals in the eye. But some of the link-ups seem destined to create sluggish national giants with larger and more vested interests than before.

Not all mergers are pernicious. Many EC industries are still more fragmented than, say, American ones (see Figure 7-3). That leaves European companies in businesses such as white goods at a competitive disadvantage to huge rivals that can reap economies of scale.

FIGURE 7-3
Small Fry

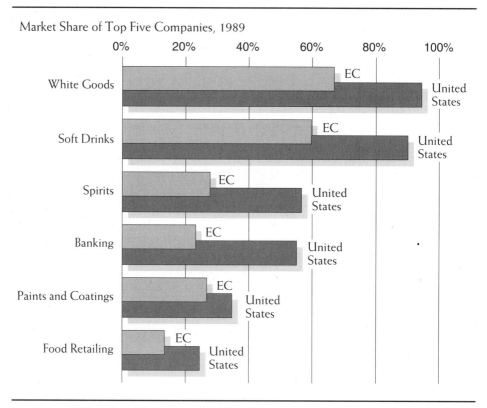

Market Share of Top Five Companies, 1989

Source: Booz Allen & Hamilton.

So to beef themselves up, European firms have been on a shopping spree. According to the most recent set of statistics from the European Commission, the number of mergers and acquisitions made by Europe's 1,000 leading firms—either within a member state, across EC frontiers or internationally—leapt from 227 in 1986-87 to 492 in 1988-89. The size of deals has grown rapidly, too. In 1986-87, about 70% of mergers involved firms with combined sales of over 1 billion ecus; in 1988-89, that figure was over 90%.

Most of the deals recorded by the commission were purely national ones (see Figure 7-4). That does not necessarily mean that companies are bent on dominating domestic markets. They may prefer to buy at home because differences in language and culture make cross-border acquisitions tough to manage. Or they may want to buy abroad, but have been frustrated by barriers to hostile takeover bids. These barriers include the relatively small number of publicly traded companies in continental Europe, legal restrictions on voting

FIGURE 7-4
Home Shopping

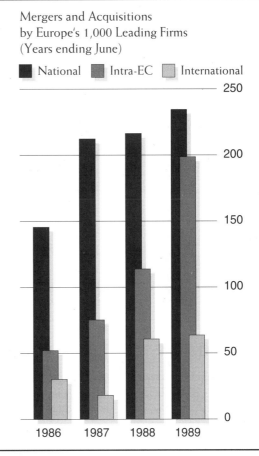

Mergers and Acquisitions
by Europe's 1,000 Leading Firms
(Years ending June)

■ National ■ Intra-EC □ International

Source: European Commission.

rights, and shareholding structures that are dominated by banks (in Germany) or families (in Italy).

But in some industries, domestic deals have been deliberately designed to create flag-carrying champions. Look at the rash of national mergers between airlines in Britain and France. Look, too, at Daimler-Benz's merger with MBB. This was cleared by the German government even though the country's cartel office had objected to it.

Though such mergers threaten to crush competition, the commission has found it difficult to block them. Sir Leon Brittan, the EC's competition commissioner, has already brewed one storm in a coffee cup by trying to unwind a merger signed in 1988 between Douwe Egberts and Van Nelle, two Dutch coffee companies. He argued that the merger was an abuse of the two companies' competitive position because it gave them 70% of the Benelux coffee market. Last November the commission gave its stamp of approval to the deal after Frans Andriessen, the Dutch commissioner, and Karel Van Miert, the Belgian one, both objected to Sir Leon's proposal. They argued that it was up to the authorities in Belgium and Holland to decide whether the deal should go through or not.

In future, companies will find it harder to corner markets in Europe with the connivance of politicians. Since September 1990 the commission has had the authority to vet and, if necessary, veto all deals involving firms with a combined turnover of more than 5 billion ecus—providing that at least 250m ecus-worth of these sales are in the EC The only exceptions to this rule are mergers involving companies that derive two-thirds of their business from the same EC state. Such deals are policed by the country's national merger authorities.

In the first six months of operation, the commission's 40-man merger watchdog handled over 20 cases, clearing all but three within one month. That reassured companies which thought the commission would drag its heels when reviewing bids. But its investigation into a deal involving Italy's FIAT and Alcatel-Alsthom, a French conglomerate, has aroused other fears. Last October the two companies announced they would swap shares and several businesses. After reviewing plans to give Alcatel control of Telettra, FIAT's telecommunications subsidiary, the commission decided that this would give the combined unit an 80% stake in the Spanish transmission equipment market. So it agreed to clear the deal only if Alcatel and Telettra severed their shareholding links with Telefonica Spain's telephone company.

That has not pleased Alcatel, which is furious that Telefonica will be allowed to keep stakes in Sweden's Ericsson and AT&T, two of Alcatel's rivals. Nor has it pleased companies which were hoping that the commission would smile benevolently on pan-European link-ups. That is a sure sign the regime is working well. But it has yet to pass its biggest test. When the commission vetoes a large deal designed to create yet another national champion, the political heat generated will be intense.

CRACKING THE COMBINATION

Sparks are already flying between the commission and some of Europe's biggest companies over another issue: cartels. As deregulation strips companies of the rules and regulations that used to protect them, the danger is that they will try secretly to fix prices amongst themselves to keep profits up. So, as a warning, the commission's trustbusters have been waging war on cartels.

Last December the commission fined two chemicals companies, ICL and Belgium's Solvay, a record 47m ecus for running a soda-ash cartel. Then, in January, officials raided the offices of four steel makers in search of evidence of a suspected cartel that had fixed the price of steel for the construction market. If they are found guilty, the company involved, which include British Steel and France's Usinor Sacilor, could face fines of up to 10% of the annual sales.

Private companies are not alone in the commission's sights. State monopolies are under fire too. In April the commission threatened to take legal action against ten governments (only Belgium and Germany escaped) if they did not take steps to create a single market in electricity and gas. If they refuse, the commission may try to use its power under Article 90 of the Treaty of Rome, the EC's founding charter, to force them to loosen their energy monopolies. That will be yet another nail in the coffin of state-owned businesses in Europe, many of which are utilities. One more nail will be needed before they are finally laid to rest.

THE AID PLAGUE

"A level playing field where individual talent, effort and comparative advantage lead to victory, rather than an inclined pitch with moving goalposts, a biased referee and an opposing team full of steroids." That is how Peter Sutherland a rugby-playing Irishman and a former EC competition commissioner, described his view of the new Europe. By slowly dismantling protectionist devices like procurement regimes and national standards, the commission is levelling the pitch. Now Sir Leon Brittan, Mr. Sutherland's successor, is stepping up the number of state-aid dope tests too.

Since the start of the year, Sir Leon and his team of sleuths have launched more than 15 aid investigations. They include inquiries into:

- France's decision to pump almost FFr6 billion into Groupe Bull, a state-owned computer-maker, and Thomson, a state defense and electronics group;
- a 287 billion lire ($230m) plan from the Italian government to revamp Italy's trucking industry;
- Belgium's BFr35 billion ($1 billion) plan to recapitalize Sabena, its state-owned airline; and
- the use of six big French state-owned companies to channel aid to firms in poor regions.

These subsidies are just the tip of an iceberg. In its most recent survey of state aid in the Community, the commission noted that the average level of subsidies in Europe had fallen in the 1980s—but not by much. According to its figures, aid dropped from an average of about 89 billion ecus a year in 1981-86 for the then ten members of the Community, to about 82 billion ecus a year in 1986-88. Of that, agriculture took an average of 11 billion ecus year, coal 13 billion and railways 26 billion; industry accounted for the rest.

Cutting the industrial-subsidy mountain is a daunting task, but it is one that is vital to the success of Project 1992. If governments coddle national champions, those firms, whether they are public or private, will have an unfair advantage in an open European market. That is why Sir Leon and his colleagues are attacking some of the most profligate governments. Italy is top of their list. In spite of an enormous budget deficit, the Italian government still spent an average of 9.6 billion ecus a year on industrial aid in 1986-88, more than any other

FIGURE 7-5
High on Subsidies

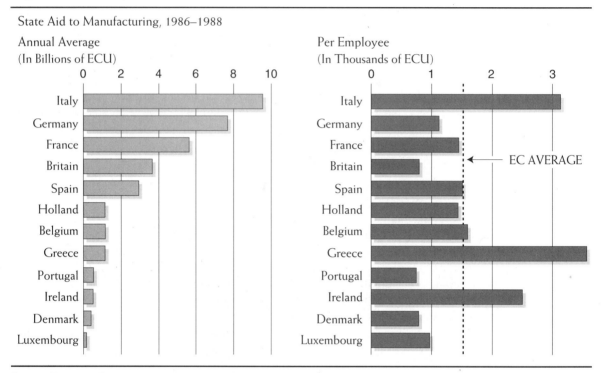

State Aid to Manufacturing, 1986–1988

Source: European Commission.

EC state (see Figure 7-5). This works out at a average subsidy per employee of 3,136 ecus, second only to Greece's 3,545 ecus. France is also in Sir Leon's sights. It paid out 5.7 billion ecus of aid in 1986-88, mainly to finance the restructuring of its chemicals industry. Since then, it has handed out one subsidy after another to troubled state firms.

The challenge for the commission is to distinguish which of these subsidies are legal and which are not. Digging into their copy of the Treaty of Rome, the commission's aid policemen point to Article 92, which forbids "any aid granted by a member state in any form whatsoever which distorts or threatens to distort competition by favoring certain undertakings or the protection of certain goods" insofar as this affects trade between EC members. For those out of breath, Sir Leon has come up with his own, mercifully shorter, version It says that an illegal subsidy is almost any action in which the state, as owner, acts differently from a private investor. Such actions may include cash payments, debt write-offs and any case in which governments:

- accept a rate of return below the market rate on investments in nationalized companies;
- implicitly guarantee their borrowings,
- inject additional equity capital into them when a private investor clearly would not; or
- waive dividend payments.

To help it track down wrongdoers, the commission insists that member states keep information on their financial dealings with companies for four years and hand this over when asked. But that means that illicit aid payments are often spotted several years after they have been paid out, by which time it is hard to get them back. To speed up investigations, the commission wants to force state-owned manufacturers to file annual statements with it, just as private firms publish their accounts for shareholders. The competition directorate wants this scheme to apply initially to manufacturing companies with sales of more than 200m ecus, but to be extended later to other state businesses. It is due to publish a paper with its proposals soon.

TAMING LEVIATHAN

Neither the Italian nor the French government likes the sound of this. Both complain that Sir Leon has declared war on the mixed economy when the Treaty of Rome neither outlaws nor discourages state ownership. However, the commission's position is clear. The question is not one of ownership—aid to private companies can be pernicious tool—but of the effect of subsidies on competition. The single market simply requires that all companies operate on the same basis: that is, according to market forces.

This means that governments can no longer run state industries for social and political rather than economic ends. Therein lies the rub. What is the point of state ownership if the state must run its firms as if they were private ones? Rather than face this question, governments have turned aid cases into political footballs. Take the Renault affair. In March 1988 the commission let France write off FFr12 billion of the debts of Renault, a state car-maker. In return, the firm agreed to cut capacity and abandon its status as a *régie*—a legal entity that cannot go bust. But when the French delayed action, Sir Leon ordered Renault to repay FFr8.4 billion of the loans. It refused, so he threatened to take the case to the European Court of Justice. Arm-twisting in Brussels by Michel Rocard, the former French prime minister, won the French enough support among the 16 other commissioners to force a compromise. In May 1990 Renault agreed to pay back just FFr6 billion.

The feisty Sir Leon has also crossed swords with the British government. In June 1990 he ordered British Aerospace to repay £44m it had received from the state as part of its purchase of the Rover Group, a nationalized car-maker. British Aerospace is challenging the ruling in court. As 1992 gets nearer, the determination of other governments and companies to defy Brussels will grow. That is why some countries, like Germany, fear that unless the commission sets up an independent cartel office, its attempts to police state-aid will be dogged by more political in-fighting. Others say the present system works given a tough competition commissioner, but that it will crumble if Sir Leon's successor is a wimp.

Still, the commission does have powerful allies. European businessmen who are fed up with competing against—or having to operate alongside—a bloated public sector wish it well. Carlo De Benedetti, an Italian industrialist, complains that Italy "is in the second tier of Europe" thanks to its heavy-handed state. Raul Gardini, another of Italy's leading businessmen, would no doubt agree. In February, he quit the presidency of Ferruzzi, a chemicals and agribusiness group, in protest at the Italian government's decision to nationalize Enimont, a large chemicals joint venture between Ferruzzi's Montedison and ENI, a state holding company.

British companies and government officials have also backed Sir Leon. ICL, a computer-maker, has complained bitterly about the aid given to Groupe Bull. It reckons that this will help the French firm to pinch more of the British computer market by allowing it to put in cheap bids for public contracts. Peter Lilley, Britain's industry minister, has already referred several deals involving foreign state-owned companies to Britain's Monopolies and Mergers Commission on the grounds that the companies involved have access to cheap finance that may distort competition. And the British government has publicly warned France, Germany and Italy not to subsidize plans by Deutsche Aerospace, a subsidiary of Daimler-Benz, to develop a 130-seat airliner together with France's Aerospatiale and Italy's Alenia, two state-owned aerospace groups.

International pressure will also force EC governments to be more stingy with aid. Take the case of Airbus Industrie, a European aircraft-making consortium. Daimler-Benz, one of the consortium's members, has received big subsidies from the German government under the terms of a 1989 agreement to cover the company's exchange-rate losses on Airbus work. Airbus's American rivals claim that these are equivalent to an export subsidy of about $2.5m for every aircraft that Airbus sold last year. America has already taken this case to the General Agreement on Tariffs and Trade (GATT) and is planning another complaint about the $26 billion in direct subsidies that it says Airbus has also received from EC governments.

SELLING THE SILVER

The anti-state-aid brigade will also be helped by economics. Heavy social-security payments and the cost of the Gulf war have made it hard for governments to balance their budgets. That will make them reluctant to hand over huge sums to ailing companies. France has already cut the budget for the state sector from FFr23 billion in 1986 to FFr5 billion last year (though the aid promised to Bull and Thomson may push it up again this year). Italy, which risks seeing its sovereign debt-rating downgraded because of its bloated budget deficit, has also squeezed aid to industry.

Some countries are already selling a raft of state businesses. Following Britain's lead, both Spain and Portugal have put "for sale" signs on some of their biggest nationalized industries. Even France has softened its position. It has agreed to allow private investors to take a stake of up to 49% in state businesses, provided they meet certain conditions. But governments are not going to drop their national champions just like that. Instead, as the French decision to pump money into Bull and Thomson shows, they are hoping to provoke the commission into producing a pan-European industrial policy to help struggling firms.

OVER TO BRUSSELS

Publicly, the European commission insists that it will not interfere in the management of European industry. But the debate between those who are in favor of an interventionist industrial policy and those who prefer a hands-off approach has only just begun. As the restructuring of European business continues, the temptation to lend a hand to troubled firms will grow. The EC's electronics industry will provide an important test of the commission's free-market credentials.

Nobody disputes the fact that Europe has a high-tech headache. The EC's trade deficit in electronics has doubled over the past four years to 31 billion ecus in 1990. Computer firms and chipmakers blame their dire performance on a crisis similar to the one which hit Europe's steel industry in the 1980s. Overcapacity in the world semiconductor business has forced down prices. At the same time, the cost of developing new generations of microchips has soared. European firms have been caught napping. As a result, they now control barely one-tenth of the world market for semiconductors, while fast-moving Japanese firms control nearly half of it. European computer-makers are also in a fix. Sales have plunged and profits have followed suit. Though American and Japanese companies have suffered too, European manufacturers have been the hardest hit (see Figure 7-6). Now they say that unless they get help from the community, many of them may not survive.

The case for a rescue package runs something like this. First, if Europe allows itself to fall behind in one area of high-technology, it will struggle in others too. Those who believe this domino theory point out that America's semiconductor companies ran into trouble after competition from Japanese firms had destroyed its consumer electronics industry. Second, if Europe does not nurture its high-tech companies, it will end up as little more than a subcontractor of Japan Inc. Third, that would have a knock-on effect on other European industries. Michel Carpentier, the director-general of the commission's information-technology directorate, points out that by the end of the century, some 17% of the value of a car will lie in its electronics. So if Europe does not have its own high-tech champions, he says, its car-makers could lose business to Japanese competitors too.

FIGURE 7-6
Europe Unplugged

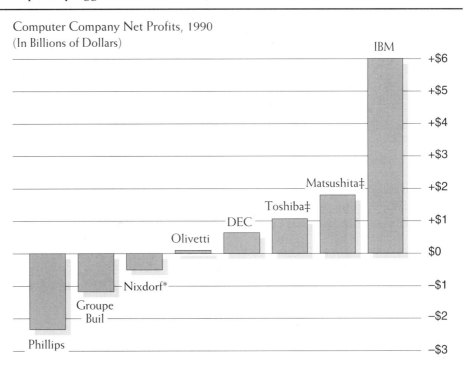

Computer Company Net Profits, 1990
(In Billions of Dollars)

*Nine-month financial period.

‡Years ending March 1990.

Source: Morgan Stanley Capital Int.; company reports.

But other officials argue that Mr. Carpentier and his colleagues are too sympathetic to the industry. They reckon its problems are caused not by overcapacity but by inefficiency. Europe's computer firms, for example, have grown fat on exclusive procurement contracts and government subsidies. As a result, many of them have been slow to spot developments in private-sector markets. These include the shift away from minicomputers towards PCS and the move from proprietary to "open systems" that let users hook up different brands of equipment. Only a few companies, like ICL and Italy's Olivetti, reacted fast enough to limit the damage.

European companies have also hurt themselves by charging high prices for their products. A PC, for example, costs half as much again in Europe as in America. This is doubly damaging. Expensive products deter potential customers. That is why about twice as many Americans have PCS on their desks as Europeans. And because demand is sluggish, European companies have little incentive to come up with bright ideas for new products. When they do, they are frequently inept at marketing them. Why should Brussels help these firms, say the critics, if they will not help themselves?

NANNY OUGHT TO LEAVE . . .

This division of opinion is reflected in the commission's policy-making process. In a paper published in October 1990, Martin Bangemann, the German industry commissioner, warned businessmen that there would be no more nannying by the Community. "In future," the paper says, "the main responsibility for industrial competitiveness must lie with firms themselves." The role of public authorities is to act as "a catalyst and a pioneer for innovation." Though the liberal tone of the paper was hailed as a victory for free-marketeers like Mr. Bangemann and Sir Leon Brittan, the commission's interventionist bent had been curbed, not cured.

It surfaced again in February in the first draft of a policy paper produced by the commission's information-technology directorate. This argued that because of the "strategic importance," of Europe's electronics firms, they should have "if not self-sufficiency in all areas, at least the capacity to control this sector's progress at the most advanced level and to put together strategic alliances which guarantee security of supply and mastery of technology." Such language raised the spectre of a return to the controversial system of centralized planning and control used by Etienne Davignon, a former industry commissioner, to deal with the steel industry's problems in the 1980s.

After several changes, the final document published in March was less dirigiste in tone. But it still failed to acknowledge that European electronics firms are their own worst enemy. Instead, it blamed the industry's problems on a lack of cheap capital and an inability to integrate several businesses into single firms. To help put European companies back on their feet, the paper suggested that the Community should step up its efforts to harmonize standards and improve training in electronics. And it called for the Community to boost demand for high-technology products by investing in a "European Nervous System" (ENS). Designed to promote a single market, the ENS is supposed to link together different national computer networks such as those carrying VAT, social security and customs data.

Even this modest attempt at intervention may backfire. Though governments account for 15% of computer sales, the other 85% of spending comes from non-government consumers. There is no guarantee that the majority of the computer firms' customers will be keen on products developed for state bureaucracies. Computer companies are also unimpressed. The ENS "is too little, too late," says Dr. Asam of Siemens. The German company and other EC firms say Europe needs much bigger development projects along the lines of the ones run by Japan's Ministry of International Trade and Industry in the 1960s, or those directed by America's defense department. To press the point, in April the heads of some of Europe's biggest computer-makers met privately with Jacques Delors and other commission officials to lobby for more help.

Afraid that the dirigiste dinosaurs in Brussels may try to cobble together an industrial policy for electronics, some countries have insisted that the commission conduct a study of the sector's problems before taking any action. Attention will focus on the Community's high-technology research programs. These include JESSI, for advanced microchips; RACE, for telecommunications; and ESPRIT for information technology. Together, they are supposed to encourage pre-competitive research among European electronics firms. They are not cheap. In 1990-94, these and similar programs will receive 5.7 billion ecus from Community coffers, plus extra money from EC states and companies. Yet the high-tech fraternity says this is not enough. What more does it want?

CRITICAL MESS

The answer begins with a criticism of JESSI from Alain Gomez, the boss of Thomson, a French stateowned defense and electronics company. He reckons that while EC support for research is a good idea, it is managed in the wrong way. Instead of dividing the funds for JESSI among scores of big and small companies in various EC states, he argues that the money should be put directly into a handful of industrial goliath—including Thomson, of course. That way the Community would get the critical mass among semiconductor companies that is needed to compete with the Japanese.

Other firms' criticisms are less self-interested. One is that JESSI and its counterparts still spread their resources too thinly by financing a large number of projects. Another is that at times there seems to be little co-ordination between the various research programs. A third is that work plans can take up to three years to prepare. That means some of the projects still on the drawing board may already be obsolete. Lastly, some companies complain that the programs support areas in which Europe is weak, like hardware and semiconductors, rather than reinforcing strengths in fast-growing businesses, like software and systems integration, where European firms are ahead of the pack.

To answer these criticisms, the March paper proposes a "second generation" of research projects that would be more ambitious than their predecessors, and better targeted. The computermakers want Brussels to go even further, arguing that as product life-cycles get shorter by the day, it is no longer sensible to separate pre-competitive research from development and commercialization. The implication is that Brussels should help fund the lot. But that would take the commission well beyond its role as a "catalyst" of innovation, and into a fully-fledged industrial policy for the high-tech sector. Will it go that far? All Mr. Carpentier will say is that the EC must look at what the Japanese and Americans do for their companies.

In consumer electronics, at least, the EC seems determined to promote European champions. At a meeting which is due to take place after this survey goes to press, the commission is expected to promote D2MAC, a broadcasting standard pioneered by Philips and

Thomson. This will pave the way for high-definition television broadcasts in Europe. Some broadcasters using other systems are reluctant to switch. To encourage them to do so, the commission has hinted that it would help to pay for the changeover.

In computing and chip-making, however, it is hard to single out "European" champions. Crossborder links between American, Japanese and European firms are common. Siemens and IBM are working on a new generation of microchips together, Olivetti buys mainframe computers from Hitachi, and Bull is negotiating with Japan's NEC which may take a stake in the French company. These international liaisons, and Fujitsu's purchase of an 80% stake in ICL last year, make the notion of a European industrial policy look ridiculous anyway. After all, what is the definition of a "European" firm? Mr. Carpentier has a stab. He says that a company should qualify for EC funding for pre-competitive R&D if(a) it has laboratories in Europe that are able to present (b) a project together with other European firms that (c) brings some added value to the Community. But as well as getting caught up in a logical circle—what makes the other firms European?—Mr. Carpentier's definition raises the subjective question of what does or does not add value.

This word game may seem petty, but it has serious consequences. Take the ICL case. After its takeover by Fujitsu, the company was thrown out of a European computer industry's trade group. Then in March it was forced to leave three of the five JESSI projects in which it was participating because its other partners refused to let it stay. Yet IBM is participating in two JESSI projects. How come? Because, some EC firms say, IBM is an "honorary European."

This high-tech jingoism is the inevitable product of industrial policy. Once they have plowed millions of ecus into projects designed to nurture European champions, governments are unlikely to take kindly to foreigners who try to walk off with the results. Worse, they are unlikely to let other companies walk in and steal European markets. That plays into the hands of the protectionists still lurking in Europe's boardrooms.

Pulling Up the Drawbridge

When Europe is finally open for business will it be open to foreign companies as well as EC ones? Given the free-market philosophy of Project 1992, the answer should be yes. But Europe's stubborn refusal to compromise in a row with America over farm subsidies has revived the spectre of a Fortress Europe. A fudged decision on Japanese car imports and calls for protection from Europe's electronics industry are signs that some businessmen want moats and drawbridges too.

So far, the EC's record on trade has been mixed. A report published in April by the GATT dismisses claims of a Fortress Europe. Yet some of the GATTS criticisms of the Community suggest its verdict may be a trifle optimistic. It accuses the EC of striking bilateral trade deals which delay restructuring in European industry. It notes that the commission has been unhealthily fond of anti-dumping actions, implementing some 256 of them between 1980 and 1989. And it warns that the EC's institutions are not strong enough to resist demands from member states for protection of their pet industries.

This last criticism is particularly worrying. Now that European companies are closing plants and cutting jobs, the commission is under increasing pressure to protect them. French and Italian firms are shouting loudest for help. That is hardly surprising. The GATT report notes that both Italy and France still have a wide range of national quotas on products. But the single market program means that these must be dismantled. So Italian and French companies that have grown fat and lazy thanks to coddling at home, now want the EC to protect them instead.

The British, German and Dutch government are skeptical. But the French government, which is unhappy with the anti-dirigiste bent of the commission, backs its companies' demands. Edith Cresson, France's new prime minister, has already criticized the EC for being soft in trade talks. That has encouraged bosses who hope she will fight hard to stop the EC becoming what Roger Fauroux, France's former industry minister, called "a land that is open to all the winds."

The wind that bothers politicians and businessmen most blows from the East. Europe's trade deficit with Japan now runs at about $25 billion a year. That makes Japanese firms the targets both of barbed comments and many of the Community's anti-dumping actions. But these have had the opposite effect to the one intended. Instead of discouraging Japanese companies from doing business in the Community, the anti-dumping measures encouraged many of them to set up factories in Europe in the hope that they will be treated as locals. One sign of this trend: the stock of Japanese direct investment in the Community rose from $6.6 billion at the end of March 1987 to $42 billion at the end of March 1990.

CAR WARS

Much of this money has been used to set up "transplants" producing Japanese cars in Europe. For European car-makers, that is a worrying prospect. Although some transplants are not yet up and running, Japanese producers already control 10% of the European market and their exports to the EC have been rising fast (see Figure 7-7). They would have risen even faster were it not for restrictions on Japanese imports, limiting these to about 4% of the French market and 2% in Spain and Italy. In unfettered European markets like Ireland, the Japanese account for about two-fifths of sales.

Faced with this threat, some of Europe's biggest car companies have been fighting a rearguard action. Though German firms like BMW and Mercedes Benz, which export cars to Japan, were in favor of opening up Europe's market quickly to Japanese imports, others like FIAT wanted a longer "breathing space." Jacques Calvet, the forceful chairman of Peugeot, a French car firm, wanted Japanese imports blocked altogether. But last November, his European counterparts isolated him by forming a new industry lobby. Its demands for controls limiting Japanese firms' share of the European market to 15% until 1999 still looked extreme. Yet in April the commission proposed a scheme that met most of them. Starting from 1993, those EC countries that still have quotas on Japanese car imports will lift them gradually until the end of 1998. Meanwhile, Japanese producers will voluntarily restrain sales so that by the end of the century they control no more than about 17% of the European market. After that, all barriers are supposed to come down.

This is the worst kind of Euro-fudge. First, it sets the stage for another battle between the commission and the car lobby at the end of the century, when the protectionists may again try to wriggle out of the agreement. Second, if it includes the output of Japanese transplants in its calculations, the commission will discourage Japanese firms from investing in Europe. And it could get into a row with America over the thorny problem of how to treat Japanese cars made in American transplants and then shipped to Europe. Third, by buying the agreement of European car-makers with a promise of more cash for R&D, the

FIGURE 7-7
Drive-Ins

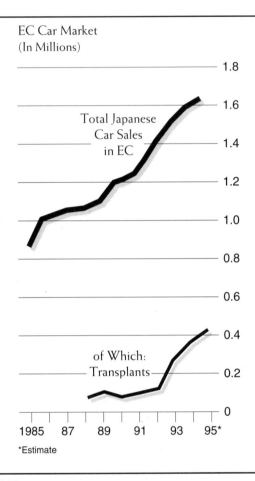

EC Car Market
(In Millions)

1.8

1.6

Total Japanese
Car Sales
in EC

1.4

1.2

1.0

0.8

0.6

0.4

of Which:
Transplants

0.2

0

1985   87   89   91   93   95*

*Estimate

Source: DRI/McGraw-Hill.

commission has set a dangerous precedent that other industries will remember when they ask for help.

Japanese car-makers do not like the EC's plan. However, perversely, they may benefit from it. To see why, look at America's experience with voluntary restraint agreements (VRAS). After more than a decade of similar protection, America's big three car companies—Ford, General Motors and Chrysler—are still bleeding red ink. Instead of using the time to achieve Japanese-style efficiency, they have stayed that much more complacent. At the same time, Japanese car-makers have been minting money. For the daftest thing of all about such schemes is that by restraining the sale of a product consumers want, they push up prices and profits. This money then floods back to Tokyo, making the Japanese even more formidable competitors.

Another reason for not coddling Europe's carmakers is that they have already had plenty of time to restructure. The competitive threat posed by the Japanese has been around for years, yet many European companies are as weak as ever. Some are still too small. Of the region's car-makers, only Volkswagen has more than 15% of the European market. And while

FIGURE 7-8
Staying Small, and at Home

EC Car Market, 1990

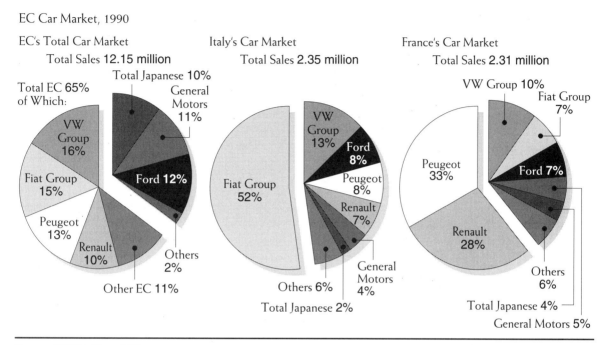

EC's Total Car Market
Total Sales **12.15 million**

Total EC 65% of Which:
VW Group 16%
Fiat Group 15%
Peugeot 13%
Renault 10%
Total Japanese 10%
General Motors 11%
Ford 12%
Others 2%
Other EC 11%

Italy's Car Market
Total Sales **2.35 million**

Fiat Group 52%
VW Group 13%
Ford 8%
Peugeot 8%
Renault 7%
General Motors 4%
Others 6%
Total Japanese 2%

France's Car Market
Total Sales **2.31 million**

VW Group 10%
Fiat Group 7%
Peugeot 33%
Ford 7%
Renault 28%
Others 6%
Total Japanese 4%
General Motors 5%

Source: DRI/McGraw-Hill.

American firms like Ford and GM went multinational decades ago, many European ones like FIAT and Renault remain dangerously wedded to their home markets (see Figure 7-8).

Worse, European firms still lag far behind Japanese ones in productivity. According to "The Machine that Changed the World," a study of the world car industry by the Massachusetts Institute of Technology, Japanese plants can, on average, assemble cars in less than half the man-hours of a European plant.* The Japanese also build cars with fewer defects than the Europeans and can put new models into production faster. Other recent studies have shown that European car manufacturers still have too many suppliers, and that many of these have yet to master the technique of just-in-time production that is one of the keys to Japan's competitive advantage. By shielding European companies with quotas, the, commission will help them to paper over these weaknesses rather than correct them.

CHIPS AND BLOCKS

Though European car-makers are still many countries' largest employers and a source of national pride, the strength of national electronics industries has become the new test of

---

The Machine that Changed the World. James P. Womack, Daniel T. Jones and Daniel Roos. Rawson Associates. 323 pages, $22.50.

industrial virility. Nowhere is this high-tech jingoism easier to see than in the semiconductor business. Dominated by three companies—Philips, the Italian-French SGS-Thomson and Germany's Siemens—the European industry is struggling. True, its share of world sales rose from 9.5% in 1989 to 10.5% last year thanks to football's World Cup, which boosted demand in Europe for television sets and video recorders. But this was a mere blip. Big Japanese firms like NEC and Toshiba, and American ones like Motorola and Intel, have been pinching business from EC firms left, right and center. Philips, the hardest hit, has already cut back its commitment to European semiconductor research.

To stop the rot, some European businessmen want the commission to raise semiconductor tariffs. At present the Community has a common 14.9% tariff on all chip imports. Alain Gomez, the head of Thomson, thinks this is not high enough. He wants tariffs for semiconductors and consumer electronics alike lifted to between 30% and 50% for a limited period of five years, to give the European industry time to recover. "If we lower our guard now," he says, "the result will be zero industry."

However, if the EC raised tariffs on semiconductors it would simply hurt itself. Remember that the biggest customers of Europe's chip-makers are European computer companies like ICL, Olivetti and Bull. If tariffs force up the price of European chips, these companies will have to raise the price of their computers. That in turn will lead to fewer sales and, consequently, even less demand for locally-produced chips. Computer firms are worried by the prospect. "We want a world class European chip industry so we can pit it against our American and Japanese suppliers," says one ICL executive, "but we are not ready to pay 50 cents more per chip to get one."

If they cannot have higher tariffs, Europe's chip-makers would like the commission to insist that other countries, notably Japan, open up their markets to European chips. At present, EC firms control just over a third of the European market, while Japanese chip companies dominate nearly 90% of theirs. Calls for reciprocity have been echoed in Brussels. Michel Carpentier, of the commission's information-technology directorate, says that there should be "mutual access to opportunity" for EC firms in foreign markets. In plain English, this means that European firms should be given access to foreign markets, and should get the same treatment as national firms.

Reciprocity sounds reasonable. But in practice, it is often a protectionist ploy. Some commission officials point out that in public procurement there is a Buy American Act and what they call unwritten Buy Japanese Act too. So, they say, the question of whether there should be a Buy European Act for projects like the European Nervous System is a legitimate topic for discussion.

Such talk is worrying given the present fragile state of the international trading system. Europe, whose share of world exports is greater than America's and Japan's, has most to lose in any tussle over a trade. So the Community should think hard before it gives in to the demands of a small but noisy group of businessmen that has yet to learn that protectionism does not pay.

No Pain, No Gain

The remarkable thing about business's flirt with the single market is that it lasted so long. From the moment it was launched, Project 1992 spelled trouble for thousands of feeble European firms. Most businessmen seemed to think that their companies would not be among the casualties. Now some are not so sure. Worried that the treatment of

Eurosclerosis will be more painful than the disease, they want bigger state subsidies, higher tariffs on imports and other protectionist painkillers.

The European Commission is dithering. Though it has cracked down on illegal subsidies, it has proved a soft touch on trade, letting Europe's car industry twist its arm over protection against Japanese imports. Now it is agonising over what to do about Europe's troubled electronics companies when the answer should be clear: let the market decide their fate. But in the battle between dirigistes and free-marketeers in the Community, dirigistes now seem to have the upper hand.

The next skirmish between the two sides will probably be fought over the semiconductor industry Europe's three chip-makers are discussing closer collaboration. This could be the prelude to precisely the type of pan-European merger that Jean-Jacques Servan-Schreiber would approve of. If the troika were to, say, jointly fund research and development, supporters of a link-up reckon the companies would form a unit big enough to compete successfully against huge Japanese rivals.

Maybe, but: two buts in fact. First, as Michael Porter of Harvard Business School argues in his book "The Competitive Advantage of Nations," successful national industries tend to be ones like the Italian clothing business where intensely competitive rivals push each other to excel.* The same is true of Japan's semiconductor industry. Japanese companies co-operate on basic research, and then spend a fortune developing the same techniques on their own. By agreeing to a deal that limits competition in its own chip industry, the EC would deprive it of this incentive to innovate.

Second, if it approved a deal creating a European champion, the commission would then feel obliged to support it if it ran into trouble. That would mean getting involved in the type of centralized planning that has gone out of fashion even in Eastern Europe. And it would mean repeating the mistakes made by national planners on a pan-European scale. Worse, if the health of its electronics industry continued to deteriorate, Europe might be tempted to raise tariffs on high-tech imports. Given the tension that already exists between America and Japan over the issue of semiconductor imports, such a move could spark off a global trade row that would make the EC-American spat over agricultural subsidies look tame in comparison.

Better, then, for the Community to ignore pleas from its industries for special treatment. Better still, it should heed the message of this survey: that European business needs more competition, not less. That means, among other things, devoting extra resources to completing the single market as fast as possible. Once it is complete, there will be no barriers left behind which companies can hide.

The EC must also resolve not to sacrifice long-term gains to ease short-term pain. Martin Waldenstrom of Booz Allen & Hamilton, a consultancy, warns that 1992 will mean the end of entire national industries as countries focus on those businesses in which they have a competitive edge. As a result, unemployment will rise rapidly. But the Cecchini report predicts that Europe's supply-side revolution will add 2% to the EC's combined GDP in the medium-term, creating as many as a million new jobs. Even if its estimates are halved, the ultimate rewards are still impressive.

Europe will also have to remind itself that companies are often big because they are successful, not vice-versa. That is why the EC needs a tough competition policy which

---

*The Competetive Advantage of Nations. Michael E. Porter. The Free Press, 855 pages, $35.

stops firms swapping national oligopolies for pan-European ones. The problem is that governments cannot resist interfering in a cases involving their national champions. Given that all 17 commissioners vote on competition issues, opportunity to apply political pressure is great. So to insulate trustbusters from lobbying, the community needs an independent cartel commission.

LE DÉFI JAPONAIS

Businessmen who want more protection should also be ignored. Such demands are dangerous because they revive fears of a Fortress Europe at a time when the international trading system is already looking fragile. And they worry Eastern Europe which is counting on exports to the EC of steel, textiles and other products to help haul it out of poverty and misery. They are also misguided because by raising tariffs to shield domestic firms, they would end up protecting "good Europeans" like America's Motorola, Intel and IBM, and Japan's Toshiba and Fujitsu which already have, or are building, plants in Europe.

True, the EC can count the output of these factories in quotas as it did in the case of Japanese car imports. But that is self-defeating. It will simply drive Japanese investment to other countries, depriving the Community of jobs. It will also slow the pace of change in Europe. For in the absence of hyperactive corporate raiders and a well-developed takeover market in continental Europe, Japanese companies operating in the Community with leading-edge technology and management methods are the best incentive that European companies have to restructure their businesses.

Though he was wrong on mergers, Mr. Servan-Schreiber was surely right when he wrote that:

> No matter how determined we are that Europe be the mistress of her destiny, we ought not to forget what Alexander Hamilton said in 1791 about foreign investment in the United States: "Rather than treating the foreign investor as a rival, we should consider him a valuable helper, for he increases our production and the efficiency of our businesses."

That is something reluctant European businessmen should keep in mind as they walk up the aisle towards 1992.

READING 8

The European Community: Into the Void

NICHOLAS COLCHESTER

ALTERED STATES

This is the decade the European Community was invented for. Back in 1957 the motive for "laying the foundations of an ever closer union of the peoples of Europe" was that the result would make war between European nations obsolete. For 32 years the EC was built without being much tested by this mission. National maneuvering was gripped within two great alliances at loggerheads and within a band of neutral states that ran between them. Now those constraints have gone. Nationalism in both its opposite guises the Bismarckian state-maker and the ethnic state-breaker—can breathe again.

Will the Community curb that double-headed nationalism, or will it collapse because the ambition of its institutions has leapt beyond the enthusiasm of its peoples? The recent No in the Danish referendum on Maastricht's Treaty on European Union launched what will be seven lean years for the Community, after seven years fat with Europromises. The pain will lie in keeping those promises, and in dealing with the main topic of this survey, the enlargement of the Community to absorb an unprecedented number of would-be members. But, in the end, what was once dubbed the Unidentified Political Object will fly on, challenging the nation-state as the dominant institution in European politics.

THE POT PLANT

The EC's post-cold-war trial got off to an impressive start. It is easy to forget how, when the Berlin Wall ruptured in 1989, there were fears that Germany would drift into no-man's land in its search for national unity, watering down its commitment to the EC and to NATO. Even Hans-Dietrich Genscher, a high priest of federal Europe and until recently Germany's foreign minister, wobbled briefly when he mused whether the EC ought to stick to economics to make pan-German membership of it less provocative for the Soviet Union. The question in those distant days was: "Will we Brusselize them, or will they Finlandize us?"

The Economist (July 11, 1992).

The answer for the moment is clear. Eastern Germany is being rebuilt within the Community. The Finns, like the Swedes and Austrians, have applied to be Brusselized, fast. Poland, Hungary and Czechoslovakia (at least the Czech part of it) would like to join the Community yesterday. Even the persnickety Swiss are steeling themselves to abandon hundreds of years of profitable aloofness. The question has changed: "Will we Brusselize them, or will they Balkanize us?"

The fate of EFTA is instructive. The European Free Trade Association was founded in 1960 as a different way to European economic integration—free trade without sovereignty-sapping central institutions. Some members have already defected to the Community, and the seven that remain have just negotiated a form of junior membership of the EC—a club known as the European Economic Area (EEA)—in which they agree to obey Community law without having much say in making it. The appetite for national independence in Europe—*pace* Denmark—is clearly waning.

The Community exercises such a pull partly because it has been through a glitzy phase of late. After the expensive oil of the 1970s halted the EC's development, economic growth powered by the cheap oil of the 1980s tempered national selfishness and allowed grand designs to be dusted off again. Internal protectionism crumbled, and the single-market (1992) project took off after 1986 when the Single European Act destroyed the principle of national veto that had long paralyzed the Community's rulemaking.

Making best use of the new momentum, the president of the European Commission, Jacques Delors, pushed on towards the dream of a Community with one currency and one central bank. Then, in 1990, the coming-apart of Eastern Europe prematurely boosted the coming-together of the western part. First Helmut Kohl, the German chancellor, then Francois Mitterrand, the French president, were seized by an urge to swaddle Germany in European obligations before the reunited country could develop other instincts. They hijacked Mr. Delors's monetary-union project and turned it into a pair of inter-governmental conferences on not just monetary but also political union.

The result, at least in terms of words on paper, was astonishing. The arguments before and after the Maastricht Treaty last December were so prolonged and arcane that the European public was never properly informed of what a profound change to the Treaty of Rome (which set up the Community) was being prepared. Whereas the Single European Act allowed the Treaty of Rome to work, the Maastricht treaty grandly sought to redefine what the Community involved. Maastricht marked the culmination of the growth of the Community in its cold-war hot-house.

THE WAITING FROSTS

The Community must now live with what it has boldly promised, both in its single-market program and at Maastricht. It must do it on a continent in flux. And it must do it with the great facilitator, economic growth, weakened.

Some grim and traditional Community tiffs will sour the atmosphere before the new adventures can begin. The Community's five-year budget must be settled this year before any negotiations with new members can start—that is written into the Maastricht Treaty. The budget brought the Community to deadlock in the early 1980s mainly because of the unending canker of a special rebate to Britain (which, because its farming is slim and efficient, gains particularly little from EC spending programs). Now Mr. Delors's request for the spending power of the EC to increase from 1.2% of its GDP to 1.37% by 1997, coupled

FIGURE 8-1
European Trading Blocks

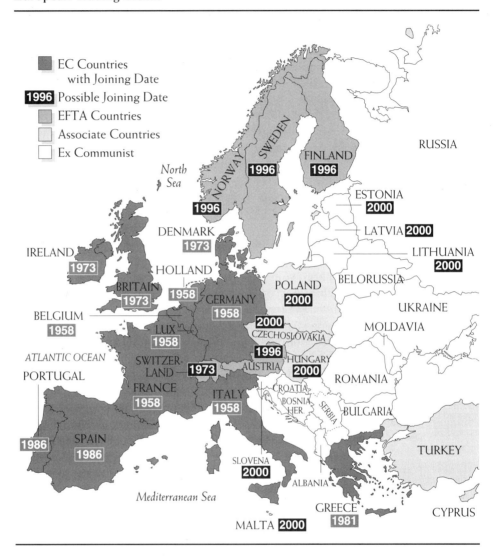

with the British problem, will make for another period of haggling—and this time with Germany, the EC's traditional sugardaddy, badly stretched for cash.

Farm policy is another old faithful. It used to be just a matter of the cost of the common agricultural policy (CAP). Now the policy has become the most obvious example of the protection of a special European interest group at the expense of trade and development in the world beyond. The Community has made an encouraging start at reforming the CAP, but it is not yet out of the dock. The GATT round of international trade talks will demand still more reform, and so, in time, will the inclusion of Poland and Hungary, which find the EC perniciously restrictive in just the business in which they are competitive.

These matters are nothing, however, compared with the grander arguments launched with the Danish referendum. The Maastricht Treaty was put together on the run under special circumstances. It is no surprise that Britain was the only big member to have argued out its pros and cons in advance—a discussion prompted by a split over the issue in its ruling Conservative Party. France and Germany had particular reasons to be bent upon strengthening their ties without looking too hard at what they would involve; and their governments were undividedly pro-European.

Now, when and if they ratify Maastricht, the EC's members will find themselves bound to a timetable under which they will submit their budgets to increasingly centralized control in order to prove themselves fit, by the end of the century, to abandon their right to issue their own money. That alone would promise a good decade's work. But, no, they will also set about making a European foreign police—and try to lay the basis for a European defense policy—in a new European landscape in which all the old assumptions no longer hold.

The Gulf war, and the civil war in Yugoslavia were both warnings of what post-cold-war challenges the EC will have to cope with. The impression left by both tests was nicely dubbed as one of "chain-gang diplomacy." The 12 break into an impressive clinking run when they happen to agree, but jangle in immobility when they don't. Perhaps this jangling is better than the competitive diplomacy of the 19th century, in which regional flareups became the stuff of larger rivalries; but it makes for a tame superpower.

The prospect of new members clashes with Maastricht's ambitions. Given that the four most probable next entrants—Sweden, Switzerland, Finland and Austria—are all neutral countries, imagine their impact on a forceful foreign police decided by unanimity. The chains will clank indeed. Or, with the world's champion and deputy-champion farm-subsidizers among them (Switzerland and Finland), imagine their contribution to the EC's trade talks with the less-subsidized Americans.

Taken together, these struggles before Maastricht, for Maastricht, and after Maastricht promise a testing time for the European Community. Arguments about budgets, butter mountains and protectionism—the stuff of the 1970s and 1980s—were merely dispiriting. Arguments about coinage, foreign policy, immigrants and armies are often explosive. The Eurosceptics have plenty to point to. The biggest reason for thinking that they will be confounded is that the EC is, amazing to relate, bound together by market forces, rather than in defiance of them.

BECAUSE IT WORKS

An economic imperative glues today's ambitious European structure together. Much of the authority surrendered by national governments to the EC has gone there not out of idealism, but because that authority no longer works at home. What was the point of France retaining exchange controls when electronic financial markets had overwhelmed them? What is the point of Switzerland priding itself on secretive banking laws, when the big Swiss banks, now multinational, have to reveal all in countries where the rules are different?

The chart on this page shows how intimately EC members trade with each other. The greater such intimacy, the more meaningless it becomes to distinguish trade with neighbors from commerce at home, and the less feasible it becomes to regulate commerce nationally. For good or for ill, the technology of moving goods, services, people and money around has ousted the European nation as the convenient unit of economic administration.

One historian, E.J. Hobsbawm, points out that the building of 19th-century nation-states was due not to some prehistoric urge, but to the increasing role of governments within nations, and the democratic involvement of people in them.* Nation-states were the right administrative units for their time, though loyalty to them was certainly bolstered through the media, jingoism and even sport. The bringing of smaller regions and peoples into greater nations was seen in the 19th century as natural progress for the human race. The process prompted much debate that finds echoes in discussion of the European Community today. What set the limits of a nation? Was it language, religion, common historical memories or territorial integrity? The answer then was: none, or all, of these. A nation was what worked. The same answer shapes the EC today.

This is not to claim that Europe's great market is so natural as to be unbreakable. Trade did not preserve ancient Rome's version of it, nor did a monster-system of planning, specialization and interdependence prop up Comecon, or the Soviet Union. It took vision in the mid-1950s for six European states to commit themselves to the removal of all the tariffs and quotas between them. It took more vision for ten (later 12) countries to see in the mid-1980s that Europe's market remained divided by national commercial laws doing double-duty as protectionist fixes. They disarmed themselves by agreeing to accept each other's commercial rules as adequate, and by framing more common commercial laws by majority vote. Those break throughs, the essence of the Single European Act of 1986, demolished a lingering British pretence that the creation of a European common market could somehow be kept separate from ideas of political union.

More than a desire for free trade drove that change. It also involved a consensus between governments that industrial policy did not work. In the 1970s, another historian, Alastair Buchan, could lament; "There is as yet no sign of a European computer consortium to retain the 40% of the Community market not yet captured by American firms." Single-market building in those days meant replacing national champions with European champions. That in turn involved an impossible wrangle between jealous national bureaucracies.

Abandonment of that route was a precondition for dismantling the protectionist scaffolding within which national champions were being built. Today the EC has more or less ruled the notion out. The competition directorate under Sir Leon Brittan has made state aid to industry much more difficult and is in the process of stopping state ownership of industry from being a means of industrial favoritism.

Whatever its proportions of statesmanship and necessity, the market remains a powerful glue. Its stickiness has drawn the countries of EFTA into a regime of national surrender even more humbling than the EC's—the European Economic Area. However depressed, self-obsessed and divided Europe's nations may become during the 1990s, the commercial ties that now bind them to the EC's main institutions are going to take some breaking.

The European project called 1992 has become so hackneyed that many must wonder what was real in the project and what was hype. Yet sceptics thinking back a decade must admit that things have really changed. At the beginning of 1983, the European Commission was investigating 770 different cases of protectionist blocking of the flow of goods between

---

*"Nations and Nationalism since 1780," by E.J. Hobsbawm, Cambridge University Press.

FIGURE 8-2

Almost a Home Market

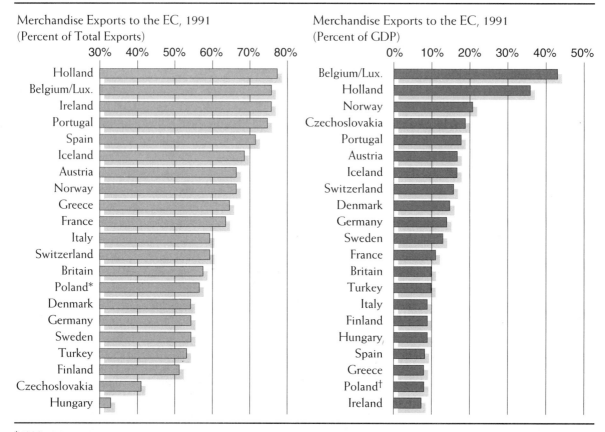

Merchandise Exports to the EC, 1991
(Percent of Total Exports)

Merchandise Exports to the EC, 1991
(Percent of GDP)

*1990.

‡1990 as % of NMP.

Source: OECD; IMF, EIU.

EC countries—within the common market, not from the world beyond. During that year the federation of German chambers of commerce asked that tariffs be reintroduced between members: it thought them preferable to the jungle of red tape that had replaced them.

Here is a sampler of how the "four freedoms" promised for the European market will look, ten years on, in January 1993.

- **Goods.** From the beginning of next year, trucks carrying goods across EC frontiers will not have to present any papers at all. An entire industry of customs-paper-processing agents will have been shredded. There will be no technical excuses left for blocking the sale of the vast majority of goods right across the Community. Even cars will need to conform to only a single set of European regulations.

The collection of indirect taxes, whether value-added or excise, was the biggest reason for the existence of customs controls at intra-European frontiers. With much heartburn a frontierless system of national tax collection has been devised that will go into effect at the start of next year. The man in the street will be able to buy all that he could reasonably need—with the glaring exception of motor cars—anywhere in Europe, paying the local taxes and duties and carrying his buys across frontiers with no more ado. The resulting threat of tax competition—people shopping where taxes are lowest—has obliged the governments to agree to a minimum VAT rate across the Community of 15%, though with exceptions galore.

- **Services.** In most service industries, January 1, 1993, will be celebrated more for a process underway than for a job done. Two laudable exceptions are banking and road transport. On that date any bank anywhere in the Community will be able to open up branches in any other member-country, with their soundness being supervised only by the supervisors of the parent. This, in light of the traumas of depositors in BCCI, is quite an act of faith, and one that goes well beyond anything achieved in America. The road-haulage industry has been deeply altered by the single market, too. Eight years ago the industry was smothered in national permits and, quotas. By the start of next year any truck will be able to haul any load across the Community.

FIGURE 8-3
Brussels Defies Brussels

State of Implementation of White Paper Measures, April 30, 1992

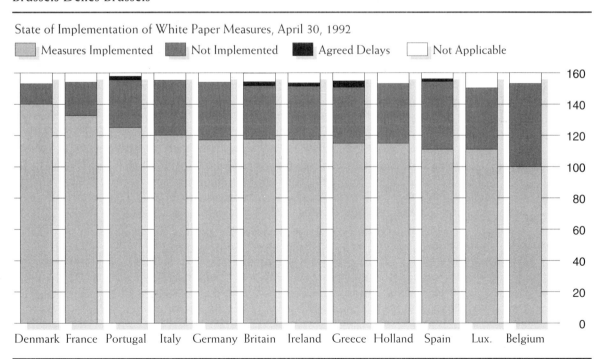

Single market entails 197 measures of which 158 need national approval and 39 apply directly.

Source: European Commission.

Much remains to be done in services. The insurance industry is being opened up steadily, but only commercial insurance policies will be sellable right across the EC by the start of next year. The securities business remains prey to the competitive ambitions of different financial centers. Air transport will not be properly freed until 1997. National telephone companies are fighting a rearguard action against competition from beyond their frontiers.

- **People**. Given the recent sensitivity about immigration and political extremism in Europe, it is not surprising that the "area without internal frontiers" against people, promised for the end of this year in the Single European Act, has been slow to take shape. The EC's members have not yet signed, let alone ratified, an external-frontiers convention, which lays down what border checks must take place at the EC's rim so as to make an EC without internal checks possible. Meanwhile Britain, Ireland and Denmark dispute their obligation under the Single European Act to allow people to cross their frontiers unchecked.

  Eight of the 12 members have pushed ahead with plans for a passport-free zone within the EC and Greece has applied for membership. But only France and Portugal have ratified the Schengen agreement that launched this idea. Here, too, the systems are not yet in place to make the ideal a reality. A police computer, designed to make up for lack of border controls by telling police forces across this "Schengenland" who is wanted for what, is still not running. Yet despite these delays the inspection of passports within the EC is becoming ever more cursory.

- **Capital**. Ten years ago, exchange controls were still commonplace within the EC. One of Project 1992's earliest achievements was to nudge the EC's members to agree to do away with such controls. Today, only Greece and Portugal retain them, with a promise to abandon them by 1995. The Maastricht Treaty would formally prohibit European exchange controls, not just within the EC, but on payments to the world beyond as well. Thus in the matter of capital, "fortress Europe" has been designed out of existence.

  This renouncing of exchange controls has had an impact beyond the building of a European financial market. One of the basic assertions of the Delors report of 1989, which devised the approach to the EC's goal of economic and monetary union, was that national monetary policies were doomed by the free flow of capital. This conclusion of the central bankers propelled the Community down the road to Maastricht, where the governments pushed their union-building to a degree never before attempted.

ESSENCE OF MAASTRICHT

It takes a masochist to piece together the constitution that the European Community had promised itself until a Danish referendum put the future of the Treaty on European Union in doubt. The 250-page Maastricht Treaty is a mass of amendments and additions to the three founding treaties—most significantly the Treaty of Rome of 1957—that are already peppered with amendments from the Single European Act of 1986.

The Single European Act, which propelled the EC out of its post-oil-shock doldrums, was easy to underestimate. Its name and rather technical amendments seemed a far cry from the European idealism that had first inspired it. The Maastricht Treaty is not so coy. After a "Treaty on European Union," what might the next European treaty be called? Spiritual Union?

Four points stand out. First, the Maastricht agreement strives for a big increase in the scope of what the European Community is about. The new treaty formally redubs the EC the European Community; it was the European Economic Community before. It no longer restricts itself to the Treaty of Rome's ten activities, which were mainly economic and designed to promote "closer relations between the states." It cites, in one way or another, just about every goal and policy with which a modern national government could concern itself. A joint foreign and security policy is created. A common defense policy becomes an aim. Health, education, the environment, industrial policy and consumer protection are all to be part of the EC's established activities. Co-operation on immigration policy is formally set in train. There is an agreement to forge common law on the treatment of workers (the social chapter which Britain opted out of). A form of European citizenship is created.

The second striking feature is the Community's new macro-economic clout. The most obvious elements are the blueprint, timetable and conditions for a move before the end of the century to one European currency and one central bank. Economic and monetary union (EMU) is this treaty's equivalent of the white paper for a single market that gave the Single European Act of 1986 so much to work on. The steps to monetary union are set down, and the charter of the future European central bank fully worked out. This is no 1970s-style expression of a grand monetary whim; it is a set of railway lines.

What is less well known is that the Community's say in all aspects of national economic policy is being increased. The United States would not enjoy life in the post-Maastricht EC. After ratification, the European Commission and Council will be continuously assessing the economic policy of each member to see if it is progressing towards the virtue required for EMU—a budget deficit of less than 3% of GDP, total government debt that is no more than 60% of GDP and an inflation rate close to the EC's best. As the year 2000 approaches, the Community's powers to enforce its views will get ever stronger, moving through public criticism, direct command, withholding of EC benefits, to eventual fines for disobedience.

The third striking feature of the Maastricht Treaty concerns the nature of the Community that is getting this new influence. Despite being freed of the word "economic," the European Community is demoted to being but part of a grander "union." The making of joint foreign policy, and co-operation in policing and border controls, form part of this union but are kept outside the original Community. The effect of this finessing is to promote the Council of Ministers—the conclave of ministers of national governments—and its secretariat, as the power center of the union. The commission's right to initiate policy and lawmaking, which it possesses in all the Community's activities, does not extend into the new areas.

Maastricht therefore nudges the Community (for which read "union," but the old name will doubtless stick and is used throughout this survey) away from central government answering to a parliament of the European people, towards what Peter Ludlow, the director of the Center for European Policy Studies, calls "government of the member-states, by the member-states, for the member-states" answering to a forum of their ministers. Despite its much-broadened activities, the commission is touchy about this demotion, but the fact remains that the heart of the Community lies not in the small print of its treaties but in the web of practical contacts that bind together the council, the commission, the European Parliament in Strasbourg and the European Court of Justice in Luxembourg. The commission may not be taking the lead in making EC foreign policy, but Brussels will be—through the secretariat of the council and a commission that is newly entitled to be "fully involved" in the process.

So government of states by states is promoted. What is that government supposed to do, and not do, in its many areas of interest? The fourth point about Maastricht is that the treaty makes the EC's first proper attempt to limit the ambitions of European central government. "In areas which do not fall within its exclusive competence the Community shall take action ... only if and in so far as the objectives of the proposed action cannot be sufficiently achieved by the member-states and can therefore, by reason of the scale or effects of the proposed action, be better achieved by the Community."

This is the principle of "subsidiarity." It is going to come increasingly to the fore as the EC's membership becomes larger and more diverse and, potentially, more expensive. The true worth of the principle will be known only once some busybody directive has been challenged in the European Court and the judges have ruled on where Brussels stops and nations are to be left alone.

As this survey goes to press, the fate of these great changes to the Community remains uncertain. It is a measure of the Europhoria of the late 1980s and early 1990s that the Danish peoples' No came as such a bombshell to all EC governments—that a process that seemed so strongly established should turn out to be so vulnerable. When one glances back at the Single European Act, and reflects that that modest document increased the grip of the Community to the limit of what was politically feasible at the time, it is not surprising that the Maastricht Treaty should be faced with a rougher ride.

The Danish derailment threatens a prolonged phase of introversion in the EC, delaying its attempt to face up to the next great imperative—the absorption of a swathe of countries freed to apply for membership by the ending of the division of Europe.

ON THE WAY TO THE FORUM

An enlarged Community will not be able to operate effectively without major institutional change. This will, in particular, affect the commission, council and parliament. The only realistic path for the Community is towards a federal Europe." Thus wrote the commission, in a typical blend of logic and the true faith, in a recent internal analysis of the onrush of new members.

In the past, whenever the European Community got bigger there were worries that it would enfeeble itself. But enlargement always led in the end to commission, council and parliament getting more power to govern than they had had before: not automatically, but because growth brought problems that could be sorted out only by streamlining the way the Community ran itself. Thus the arrival in the early 1970s of Britain, Ireland and Denmark led to the EC getting a right to its own financial resources. The entry of Spain and Portugal in the mid-1980s promoted the idea of more majority voting in the council, which was later enshrined in the Single European Act. That made the singlemarket program possible, and that, in turn, paved the way to Maastricht.

History may be about to be repeated, but the scale of the gamble is of a different order this time. It is not hard to list 20 potential applicants, either freed by the ending of cold-war geopolitics or caught up in the general urge to merge, which could have completed their EC entry-forms by the end of the decade. They are of unprecedented diversity in size, wealth and religion.

Article 237 of the Treaty of Rome says that any European state may apply to become a member of the Community." So far, six applications are pending: Austria, Sweden and Finland; Malta, Cyprus and Turkey. Switzerland's government has recently become a seventh.

It is already clear that the EFTA applicants—including Norway, if it makes up its mind in time—will constitute the next wave of newcomers.

Britain, which now has the presidency of the EC for six months, is in favor of starting talks with the EFTA aspirants early in 1993 and getting them in by 1995–96—at any rate before Son of Maastricht, the next treaty-revising conference, already scheduled for 1996. France's instinct is to slow the process down, starting talks next year, but giving the existing 12 members time to live with Maastricht's changes and build their experience into Europe's constitution in 1996 before opening the doors.

The enthusiasts for enlargement in the commission point to the way that rich Eftans coming in could help both with the quest for economic and monetary union and the mounting argument over the Community's budget. Henning Christopherson, a commissioner, points out that all members of the first wave would be rich enough to be net contributors to the EC's budget, and rigorously managed enough to qualify early for EMU. Their entry would thus help the Community along. Budget refuseniks, such as Britain, will see that they must agree on the budget before the Eftans can join. The southern members, which are counting on the EC providing more regional aid, will know that they are more likely to get it if they let the rich Eftans in.

The purists within the commission want to systematize enlargement now. They want to establish rules for the future on such things as voting power in the Council of Ministers, seats in the parliament, the rotation of the EC presidency, and so forth, so that future members can come in on a formula.

"Delaying tactics!," cry the pragmatists, "let us face these problems as they occur." The pragmatists will probably carry the day, but they could well rue it later. The key problems in the EC's voting structure date back to two basic considerations for the original six members: first, that Germany should not outweigh France in its voting-power in the council; and second, that the EC should act as a leveller between sovereign members, whatever their size. Tiny Luxembourg was thus given whopping votes relative to those of France and Germany in both council and parliament, and also a disproportionate right to a commissioner. Germany has ten votes in the council, or one vote for every 7.8m people. Then the numbers descend until they reach Luxembourg's two votes, which is equivalent to one vote for every 188,000 people.

As the number of smaller members multiplies, the effect of this nationhood premium is going to become harder to accept. The handicap in being a large country will become absurd, particularly as more and more sovereignty-crushing decisions are taken with a qualified-majority vote that requires roughly 70% of votes to pass a piece of European law. At the moment a sort of "security-council effect" operates within the council: it takes just two big countries and one small one to block Euro-legislation. But as more two-vote and three-vote states become members, the Lilliputians will increasingly over whelm the Gullivers.

Also, small states will run the presidency of the Community for more and more of the time. Latvia, Lithuania and Luxembourg will form the "troika" (of council president, plus immediate predecessor and next in the chair) at one point, while Britain and France wait for a chance that comes round but once a decade. The number of commissioners will multiply and become even more of an absurdity of nationality over talent.

The price of putting this right is bound to be a cut in the rights of small nationhood. It was Jacques Delors's musing along these lines that enraged the Danes. It is mainly because Malta is roughly the size of Luxembourg that Malta's membership is delayed, for must Malta really have a commissioner? The purists are right that the time to sort out this problem is now. The greater the number of small members, the more impossible it will be to achieve

Waiting in the Wings

Country	Population in 1990 M	Employment in agriculture, % 1989/1990	Problems	Possible Council Votes	Possible Entry Date
EFTA					
Austria	7.7	7.9	Popular doubts, neutrality	3	1996
Switzerland	6.8	5.6	Popular doubts, neutrality, farms	3	1996?
Norway	4.2	6.5	Popular doubts, farms	3	1996?
Sweden	8.6	3.3	Neutrality	5	1996
Iceland	0.3	5.7	Little to gain; fish dependent	2?	?
Finland	5.0	8.4	Neutrality, farms	3	1996
Central Europe					
Poland	38.2	26.4	Reforms, farms, bigness	8	c2000
Hungary	10.6	19.6	Economic reform, farms	5	c2000
Czechslovakia	15.7	11.5	Fissiparous, economic reform	5	c2000
Slovenia	2.0	na	Reforms, Yugoslavia	2	c2000
Romania	23.2	27.9	Economic and political reform	5	?
Bulgaria	8.8	19.2	Economic and political reform	5	?
Albania	3.3	55.9	Economic and political reform	3	?
Baltic states	8.0	16.9	Economic and political reform	–	c2000
Mediterranean					
Cyprus	0.7	13.7	Division of island, smallness	2?	?
Malta	0.4	2.5	Smallness, proximity to Libya	2?	c2000
Turkey	56.1	47.8	Islam, human rights, cost	10?	?

Sources: European Commission, OECD, national statistics.

a unanimous vote on the matter. The applicants need the bad news before they join, even if the bad news leaves Luxembourg uniquely privileged. The *ad hoc* approach could have the perverse effect that the countries that most need the perspective of membership, the ex-Comecon escapees, will be delayed in the late 1990s by a bitter defense of Austria's or Switzerland's newly won rights.

For beyond the EFTA nations lies an immense swathe of EC wannabees, headed by the Central European trio of Poland, Hungary and Czechoslovakia. There are small statelets which have broken out of their cold-war predicaments and would clearly relish an EC framework in which to start afresh: Lithuania, Latvia, Estonia, Slovenia and Croatia. There are Balkan countries with a long way to go before they can hope to cope with the EC's obligations: Bulgaria, Romania, Albania and what remains of Yugoslavia. Then there are applicants and would-be applicants who are on the EC's collective conscience:

Turkey, so big, so poor, so Muslim; Cyprus, which is divided between Greece and Turkey; and tiny Malta.

The logistical difficulties alone of coping with such a diverse Community are daunting:

- **Languages.** Bringing in the Eftans and the central European trio would create a 16-language EC, requiring 54 interpreters at every meeting. In fact, the commission reckons that if the EC's present approach to languages were sustained in a 20-strong Community, translation would come to account for one-fifth of the EC's total budget. It will probably be necessary to limit Community business to German, French and English.
- **Budget.** If the criteria used by the Community in paying out 7.4 billion ecus ($9.2 billion) of regional aid (the "structural funds") to the 12 members in 1991, were applied to Poland, Czechoslovakia and Hungary, they would merit an extra 6.5 billion ecus. Turkey by itself would get 5.4 billion ecus. The sums paid out for agriculture, which today consumes 36 billion ecus, or 53.4% of the Community budget, will rise steeply if the EFTA applicants and the Central European trio were to join.
- **Council meetings.** A 20-member Community would have to abandon the right of each member to say its bit at Council meetings. Such a *tour de table*, plus the commission's intervention and the president's summing-up, could last four hours. Mounting numbers would, in effect, turn the council into more of a senate and less of a negotiation between governments. This prospect of the council being a parliament of nations where the vote's the thing is hard to deny. But it remains anathema to most ministers attending it.

As would-be members apply, they will be faced with the two basic EC criteria (both always described in French, perhaps for the extra mystery thus conferred): do they swear to accept both the *acquis communautaire* and the *finalité politique*? In other words, do they accept all the obligations that the EC already imposes upon members, and do they accept that the EC's goal is political union? Broadly speaking, the Eftans will have no trouble accepting the *acquis* but will be more reserved about the *finalité*, where the newcomers from central Europe will have precisely the opposite reaction. It is the sight of the Swiss practicing such promises in their shaving-mirrors that brings the depth of Europe's transformation home.

NEUTRAL AGAINST WHOM

Blend together the ambition of the Maastricht Treaty and the Swiss government's recent decision to apply to join the EC and you have as good a proof as any that the role of the European nation-state is changing. For more than 500 years Switzerland's neutrality has been basic to its national identity. That neutrality is, or was, a thing apart from any other practiced in Europe.

Most of Europe's neutral zone involved a decision not to take military sides in the cold war. Switzerland's permanent armed neutrality is, in contrast, a strategy that has been continuously refined since the country was invaded by the French at the end of the 18th century. It demands that Switzerland be demonstrably vulnerable to nobody, dependent upon nobody and answerable to nobody. Such visible independence is what makes permanent neutrality credible.

This, coupled with an ever-present calculation of how wealth is best enhanced, is what swung the Swiss to vote against membership of the United Nations in 1986. In the late 1980s the reasons cited by the Swiss government for not joining the European Community still formed quite a list. Membership would endanger neutrality, Swiss direct democracy (referendums), Swiss federalism, the parliament's authority, the supreme court's competence, farm aid, immigration control and the government's treaty-making powers.

It seems incredible that the Swiss public would abandon these endangered habits as fast as their government has done—as unthinkable as all the other unthinkable things that have happened in Europe since 1989. The best guide as to whether the Swiss will take this plunge will come later this year when they vote on whether to form part of a European Economic Area (EEA) linking the European Free Trade Association (EFTA) to the EC.

In moving from EFTA through EEA to EC, these countries are experiencing the various stages of trade freedom—and of national surrender that are involved in the building of trading blocks. The basic free-trade area is a tariff- and quota-free zone. Its members have no mutual tariffs or quotas, but they retain differing tariffs against the outside world, and they use their mutual border controls to sustain those external inconsistencies. Should they wish to escape that need for mutual controls they must create a customs union, such as the European Community was till recently, with a common external tariff and a common external-trade policy.

A customs union, however, removes only one need for mutual customs-posts. Others remain, such as differing rates of value-added or excise taxes, differing regimes of farm support and differing commercial laws. To get rid of these reasons for frontier-posts requires a move towards a single market, either by harmonizing commercial standards or by agreeing to accept some leakage between regimes. Such an area aims to achieve the EC's "four freedoms" (of people, goods, services and money) across its internal frontiers. It requires a centralized authority to enforce the common rules that make them possible.

The EFTA countries have come from being a basic free-trade area, when EFTA was first set up in 1960, to something close to a single market. The EEA, which should come into force at the beginning of next year, links EFTA and the EC in all the four freedoms provided by the EC's 1992 program. So a Portugese bank will be able to set up a branch in Switzerland and have it regulated from Portugal, and a Greek worker will be able to settle in Sweden, provided he has a job to go to. This commitment has involved the EFTA countries in bowing to large chunks of the EC regime that makes the four freedoms possible within the Community, including environment rules, competition rules, and bans on state aid for industry.

The exceptions, which will prevent the EEA from being a frontier-free market, are that the EEA is not a customs union, does not have free trade in farm products and does not attempt to harmonize its rates of indirect tax. In fact, its attempt to have both internal-trade freedom and varying trade policies vis-a-vis the outside world involves a vast protocol of rules of origin which define what makes a good freely movable within the EEA.

This unwieldy EEA agreement will give the average EFTA state a good foretaste of unsovereign life in the court of Brussels. Community rules will apply, and unlike in EFTA, the commitments will be enforced through a (somewhat fudged) system of courts. The Eftans have also agreed to pay contributions to the Community's "cohesion fund," which is designed to help the EC's poorer members.

Austria, for example, calculates that it will pay ASch5 billion ($450m) a year to be in the EEA compared with a net cost of about ASch14 billion if it joined the EC. The Swedish government reckons that it has already settled between one-half and two-thirds of the negotiations needed to take it into the Community.

Of the seven EFTA countries, only Norway, Iceland and Liechtenstein are still balking at applying to the Community. What is moving the rest of the Eftans to leave their free-trade area?

First, there is the gravitational pull of a powerful trading block and rule-system, and the sense of discrimination in being outside it.

Second is the dwindling desire in some of these countries to protect their own economic ways. In Finland's case the reason is obvious: the collapse of the Soviet Union meant that only 5% of Finnish exports went there last year, compared with 25% in the early 1980s. The EEA countries now account for almost two-thirds of Finnish trade. Finland was long a prosperous trading oddity. No more.

As for Sweden the point is well made by the prime minister, Carl Bildt: "In the 1960s we used to think we represented a superior sort of society; that we should not mingle with dubious Catholics and reactionaries down on the continent. Why join Europe, when Europe was going to join Sweden? In the 1970s the Social Democrats went through a radical phase: capitalism was a dirty word and the ideologues said it was a choice between membership of the EC and socialism, and, anyway, Europe was not so attractive at the time. Then came the concept of the third way—of offering something between the raw capitalism of the West and the planned economies of the East. That concept has now collapsed; you can't be half-way between a success and a failure."

The equation of the EC with economic liberalism is a factor in Switzerland's new interest, too. There is today much worry within Switzerland that its closely regulated and cartelised economy is not prospering as it used to—that its economy needs to be ventilated by being opened up to the EC.

The third driving-force is impatience with the half-way house of the EEA, particularly in Austria, which applied for membership of the Community back in 1989. Andreas Khol, the director of the political academy of the Austrian People's Party, explains: "A cynic would say that Mr. Delors and his commission have never wanted new members. That is why they invented the EEA. Now they want to keep us in it like well-fed slaves."

The last and strongest factor is the eastern revolution. As Europe's confrontation has faded, so the feeling has grown that the EFTA neutrals no longer have anyone to be neutral against. This does not prompt them to take up arms and join military alliances, however: their appetite is, instead, for collective systems of security.

Mr. Bildt puts it this way: "Swedes have retracted into neutrality whenever great power conflicts have loomed in northern Europe. But whenever there has been a chance of establishing a wider system of security, we have been in the forefront of it." Austria, Sweden and Finland are keen to get involved in an EC foreign policy that works as another powerful forum for the fostering of reasonableness. Even Switzerland seems to be moving in this direction and away from its hedgehog pose of well-defended non-involvement.

The Eftans will not accept the idea of a Community defense policy, however. All their governments heaved a sigh of relief when the 12 at Maastricht stopped short of common defense, which the treaty mentioned only as an aim, not as a commitment. This allows the neutrals to assert with straight faces that they can accept the Europe that the Maastricht Treaty enshrines. As for the future, they ask, why should we be expected to be more committed to common defense than are some existing members? Mr. Khol in Vienna is more robust. Austria, he says, needs time to get its people used to the idea of a defense Community: if one were to emerge, Austria would be part of it.

So the Austrians and Vikings will reinforce Maastricht's emphasis on a Community of sovereign states. They will not want to undermine the role of NATO. They will be particularly keen on subsidiarity: "as little Brussels as possible, as much Brussels as is necessary." They will probably advance the cause of EMU, because they are bored with the speculative buffeting of their currencies. The Swedes have already asked if they can join the European monetary system. The Nordic group will be happy to be part of the Schengen area of the Community in which people can move without border controls: they already run a passport union which includes Denmark.

Will the Eftans really join? This remains less certain than the governments would lead one to believe. The Danish cliff-hanger of a referendum on Maastricht gives a foretaste of popular suspicion that Nordic habits solitariness, but with mutual support; intense respect for nature; a belief in conciliation; self-denying ordinances to rein in their love of alcohol—will be undermined by southern rule. Austrians have come to regard neutrality as a magic provider of prosperity. The Swiss, however rattled, will cling to the endless logic and consultation that make them Swiss. And in all of them the business that most enshrines their apartness is that of farming.

FARMERS AND PARK-KEEPERS

The combination of the single market and the ambitions of Maastricht have buried an old lie that Europe's common agricultural policy (CAP) is the heart of the Community, or the "only common policy that Europe's got." Its demotion is timely, for the CAP is going to be more battered in the decade of the 1990s than any other habit of the cosy, coldwar EC. The battering started because of its cost, was taken up by the Uruguay round of trade talks, and continued with the recent MacSharry plan to reform the policy. Next comes enlargement. This will make the CAP do the splits between some of the EFTA newcomers who consider the CAP too rigorous, and the three Central European would-be members, which have just gone through a farming reform that makes the MacSharry regime seem like a kindergarten.

The EFTA and EC countries share an attitude to farmers. They are a protected species, kept comfortable by societies rich enough, through their industry and services, to pay generously for their protection. This attitude was laid down in the Treaty of Rome, which promised to raise the standard of living of farmers.

Modern governments have been ingenious in devising means of helping farmers. And recently much effort has gone into comparing those approaches so that rules on trade can be devised. The table opposite provides a graspable way of seeing how different OECD countries have gone about it. The first column shows the total subsidy each country sends its farms. The last three columns are the most helpful. They show how much each person in each country is sending farms, both by way of taxes and by paying more for food than is necessary.

The average EC citizen is now paying over $400 a year, or over $1,000 per household, to farmers. The greater part of that is transferred through rigged prices. Americans pay about three-quarters as much, with the emphasis being on taxes. The average Swiss, Norwegian or Finn, on the other hand, is paying around $1,000 a year for the rural idyll.

The average Australian and New Zealander pays almost nothing—but he, conveniently, for Europe, is at the other end of the earth. Right next door, Poland, Czechoslovakia and

Hungary have been through such an economic upheaval of late that no comparable figures yet exist. But America's Department of Agriculture's best current guess is that farming in all three is now unsubsidized, overall: in fact Central European subsidies are probably negative at the moment because of a recent collapse of purchasing power and farm prices in these economies.

THE RIGGING REDESIGNED

The balance between the consumer element and taxpayer element in farm aid plays a big part in the story of the reform of the CAP, and will do so again in negotiating membership for some of the EFTA countries. When the CAP was set up, the EC was not self-sufficient in most foods and therefore a net importer of them. So Brussels adopted an elegant way of helping farmers. It set a minimum EC price for each commodity and defended that price against cheaper imports by imposing a variable levy on them. For as long as a hungry Europe was net importer of food, this worked smoothly. The consumer helped farmers directly, and such aid did not have to be haggled over in any budgets.

As soon as European farming started to produce surpluses, the elegance vanished. Between 1973 and 1988 the volume of EC farm output grew at 2% a year, while consumption went up by only 0.5%. Today the EC produces 25% more than it consumes, which would be fine were it not being produced for sale at rigged prices. These mounting surpluses have to be bought by government and either stored (3.7 billion ecus' worth in 1991) or dumped onto the world market at whatever loss it takes to sell them.

In the late 1970s and early 1980s the main argument was about the effect of this on the EC budget. The main answer was recourse to bureaucratic ways of rationing output. This can be done either through quotas, which work well with milk because milk does not keep

Transfers to Agriculture, 1991

	TOTAL	TAXPAYERS	CONSUMERS	TOTAL
	$BN		$ PER HEAD	
Austria	4.1	143	381	524
EC	**142**	**168**	**241**	**409**
Finland	5.9	460	677	1,137
Sweden	3.6	100	316	416
Norway	4.2	493	494	987
Switzerland	6.4	236	689	925
United States	81	200	1,189	318
Australia	1.2	41	29	70
Japan	63.2	16	494	510

Source: OECD.

and is hard to smuggle to other farms; or by making farmers "set aside" acreage unsown; or by fining farmers for producing bumper crops.

After 1986, however, farming became part of the GATT negotiations, and this strengthened the argument for a complete rethink of the EC's way of helping farmers. The laudable mission of Ray MacSharry, the Irishman who took over as farm commissioner in 1989, was to bring EC prices much closer to world ones, and to help farmers, instead, with direct income aid aimed at the smaller farms.

It took Mr. MacSharry almost 18 months to overcome widespread resistance to this logic. The deadlock in the GATT talks over farming shamed Europes governments into seeing things his way. The price of their acceptance was some dilution. First, the price cuts were reduced a bit. The present EC intervention price for wheat of 155 ecus a ton is to be slashed not to 100 ecus, as Mr. MacSharry wanted, but to 110: the current world price is around 75 ecus. The compensating direct aid to farmers is to be biased less sharply towards small farms. But a vital principle has survived. While the total amount of farm support may not decrease that much, the balance in our table will shift firmly towards the taxpayer.

Tell that to the Finns. The table shows how they are the farm-subsidy champions of Europe, raising almost three times as much for their farmers through price-rigging as the average EC country does. The farm-gate price for milk in Finland is 60% higher than the EC price. The cereal price is currently double the EC's, and now the EC price is set to drop sharply.

Of all the current applicants for membership, Finland has the most intractable farming predicament. The entire country lies north of the line at which Sweden finds that farming becomes problematic. The government knows that the income differential across its border with Russia is one of the biggest in the world and that this 1,200 kilometer frontier—longer than the distance between the Baltic and Black seas—is unpoliceable. It therefore claims a special need to keep its frontier-country populated.

Finland's farm negotiations could imperil its entry into the EC. Could but probably won't, because—in contrast to Norwegians, with their energy wealth—the average Finn accepts that his country's industrial interests must outweigh its farming ones. In any case, the country faces a daunting task in adapting its farms to the criteria that will form the basis of any GATT deal. The Finnish government actually welcomes the MacSharry reforms of the CAP. They stress direct help for needy farmers, and Finland feels that its chilly north qualifies as a new category of disadvantaged farmland to match the hill farms of Europe to the south. Transitional arrangements will not help Finland: it does not feel that any transition to a depopulated landscape is bearable. Norway thinks the same.

Switzerland and Austria have problems of a different kind that beg for different solutions. They, too, beat the EC in farm support, with Switzerland hitting the consumer harder than any other country in Europe. But on top of fondness for the look of their landscapes, there is a hardheaded awareness that the cowbell-clonking cow and the dirndl-wearing farmer's wife are a potent part of the two countries' attraction for tourists. Both countries are following MacSharry down the road towards income support in place of production subsidy. Both are wrestling with the widespread problem that farmers want to be thought of as food producers rather than park keepers. But park-keeping will not go away. Already, in parts of Austria, farmers are paid to take their cows up to mountain pastures rather than fatten them more cheaply in sheds in the valley. The hikers are waiting up there with Nikons at the ready.

Austria's farm regime is easier to align with the EC's than Switzerland's. But Austria is a neighbor of Hungary, and this closeness to the most effective ex-communist economy offers a daunting prospect for its farmers. "Where they compete with us, we can't let more than a purely symbolic amount of their produce in without ruining our own agriculture," says Hans Reisch of the Austrian agriculture ministry. "They want to sell us 11,000 hectoliters of wine per year. We are ready to accept 100 hectoliters. They say 500 tons of salami. We say 100. The gap is vast. We would prefer that they be given money to sell their products to the former Soviet Union."

Here is a nice example of nostalgia for Comecon *perdu*. It introduces the second great challenge of Europe's enlargement: the integration of Poland, Hungary, and Czechoslovakia.

GUILT BY ASSOCIATION

Wherever the European Community spreads, a horde of acronyms moves before it. Welcome to the CEECS (the Central and Eastern European Countries), the PECOS (*Pays d'Europe Centrale et Orientale*), or the delicately named Partners in Transition—yes, the PITS—which means Poland, Czechoslovakia and Hungary. There is a revealing passage about them in the internal paper on enlargement prepared late last year by the European Commission. "Basically," it says, "there is a contradiction between the trade liberalization policies undertaken by the PECOS and their wish to join an economic community. This contradiction arises in areas such as textiles, steel and coal as well as agriculture, but the CAP is its most spectacular manifestation."

The Central European trio are, indeed, poor fortress-building material. Czechoslovakia and Poland (but not Hungary) now run import regimes that out-liberalize those of many OECD countries. Poland and Hungary have applied market medicine to their farmers in doses that would be unthinkable in Western Europe. In 1991 Hungary cut its agricultural-export subsidies by 50% in one year, having already cut them sharply the previous year. The OECD estimates that Poland subsidized its farms barely at all in 1991, corroborating the hunch of the American Department of Agriculture cited earlier. This rigor was sustained despite a 36% fall in Polish farm incomes between the last half of 1990 and the first half of 1991.

The trio can scarcely be called homogeneous, ranging from the almost Austrian efficiency of Budapest to the third-world disorder that reigns in the anterooms of Warsaw. But they are united in their enthusiasm for membership of the Community, and are marching towards it in locked step, thanks to a pact made between them in Visegrad, Hungary, in February 1991. Their joint aims will confound almost everybody. Those secretly hoping that widening the Community eastwards will halt its "deepening" must accept that these would be members want the whole federal dream—or so their leaders say. Those who count upon Comecon escapees to cherish their independence will hear them explain that "national identity is something that does not depend upon sovereignty." Those who feel that the EC must assert itself against America will be piqued: the trio want NATO membership quite as much as European defense.

Their links with Brussels have had to be developed at tremendous speed. It was not until 1988 that Moscow would concede that the European Community represented the trade policies abroad of its members. In July 1989 the commission won the job of co-ordinating all western aid to Eastern Europe and of monitoring the Eastern European countries' worthiness to receive it. This was seen by a delighted commission as a nice symbol of the EC's emerging role in Europe, and of America's recognition of it. In practice, western countries preferred to go on giving aid on their own terms, so the commission remained mainly a clearing-house for ideas.

As soon as Moscow softened. the EC signed trade and co-operation agreements with the former communist countries. These gave them the trading terms they could have had as members of Comecon had Moscow permitted it. In particular, they replaced hundreds of national import quotas with EC-wide protection. The association agreements—now called

FIGURE 8-4
GDP per Head, 1990

"Europe agreements"—that then followed were originally seen by the Community as a surrogate for membership. The ex-communist countries would commit themselves to good democratic government; their reward would be membership of a sort of third tier of the Community beyond the European Economic Area. The commission wanted to avoid the prospect of membership raised in the Greek and Turkish association agreements—and the embarrassment that the undertakings to Turkey subsequently caused.

The Visegrad trio fought hard against such tiering. In return for agreeing that multiparty democracy, human rights, the rule of law, a market economy and social justice are "the basis for this association," they won a clause in the preamble accepting that the final objective of Hungary or Poland or Czechoslovakia is to become a member of the community and that this association, in view of the parties, will help to achieve this objective." The EC, note, did not express enthusiasm.

The essence of the Europe agreements is that they will "gradually" establish a free-trade area between the EC and the trio over a transition period lasting not more than a decade; and that this mutual opening of markets will be asymmetric—the EC will do more in the first five years, the trio in the second. Not bad on the face of it; but sadly these agreements are deeply ungenerous. The commitment does not hold for farm products, which, in Hungary's case, currently account for one-quarter of its exports to the EC. Here the initial gestures are pitiful. Hungary, for example, will be permitted in the first year to sell just 5,000 tons of beef to the Community. This annual allowance will rise to 6,600 tons over five years. In the mid-1970s Hungary was selling a smaller EC some 100,000 tons of beef a year, paying whatever levies the EC was charging to bring imported beef up to the CAP price.

Turning to non-farm products, roughly 40% of Hungary's exports to the EC have, under the agreement, been duty- and quota-free since March, when the trade pan of the pact took effect. A more generous gesture? Not really—most of those goods had been traded freely since 1990. Textiles and clothing (15% of Hungarian exports to the EC) remain subject to quotas whose removal has yet to be negotiated. Steel (5%) will be quota-free but with duties declining over six years. Industrial goods accounting for the remaining 15% are divided into no fewer than 93 "sensitive" product lines, each of which will sport its own gradually loosening import regime.

These percentages, remember, reflect Hungary's current, highly distorted trade: they do not say anything about the country's areas of natural comparative advantage, in which agriculture and textiles would feature more strongly. Nor does this crude impression of Hungary's trade deal capture the complexity of the safeguard clauses, and rules of origin that the EC has insisted upon: nor, to be fair, the mysteries of Hungary's own regime against goods from the EC. To talk to the trade officials who negotiated Hungary's deal is to sense that a whole cadre of clever state planners has been offered new employment by the intricacies of managed trade with the EC.

Indeed, in all three countries unemployment among trade negotiators must be low. The European agreements required not only deals with the EC, but deals with EFTA (country by country for agriculture), and talks within the Visegrad trio on their own trade-zone-to-be. Building mutual consistency into such interlocking trade blocks must rival four-dimensional chess.

It all amounts to a trade labyrinth barely worth entering, were it not for the glimmer of trade freedom that supposedly lies at the end of it. The central European trio have a joint GDP that some think is equal to that of Austria. Is their potential to harm parts of EC industry so great that protection of such complexity is required? Sariusz Wolski, Poland's chief negotiator with the EC, is scathing about the mixed signals that Poland is getting from the West. The IMF insists that its inflation be got under control, but western European protectionism makes the cost of doing this harder to bear. The West urges market economics on the trio, yet also makes sure that their trade and therefore industry remains thoroughly bureaucratized. The West is stingy with aid unlike Greece and Turkey, the trio got no "financial protocols" in their European agreements—but stingy, too, with the trade that would make such aid less important. He dismisses Poland's European agreement as "the right to knock on windows."

"It is frankly amazing," says Mr. Wolksi, "that the EC should feel it has such a problem adjusting to us. The Community now accounts for 57% of our trade. We account for about 1% of its trade. We think that the threat posed by our textiles and food has not been properly assessed. Look what has happened as a result of visa-less travel. There has been no flood of people. The same truth will be revealed when the market is opened to our goods." The chaotic administrative state of Poland suggests, first, that he is right; and, second, that Poland's struggling entrepreneurs need all the western encouragement they can get.

Where the EFTA countries are, to European enthusiasts, economically sound but politically suspect, the Visegrad trio are exactly the opposite. Janos Martonyi of the Hungarian foreign ministry talks of "our unlimited commitment to the *finalité polique.*" Certainly the perceived richness of the EC countries is a lure to the trio. Spain is often mentioned as a newcomer that somehow rocketed from backwardness to wealth, simply by joining the EC. But the strongest reason why they want to join remains political, not economic. They are looking for something to cling to in a crumbling part of the world, and that leads straight to the question of European defense.

UNITED IN RIVALRY

While the problems of Maastricht and enlargement will grind on, the matters that could really buffet the European Community over the rest of this decade will be foreign policy, security and defense. This is because what the late Andrew Schonfield called the EC's "illusion of privacy within the international system, of living in a charmed circle bounded entirely by its own problems and preoccupations" can no longer hold.

The continent of Europe is today one of the least stable on earth, but without the prospect of a "monstrous tyranny" or a "new dark age" to make sure that America watches over it while Brussels gets on with lawn-mower directives. Europe's instabilities particularly touch Europe's would-be members to the east. They look to Western Europe for security, and America expects Western Europe to provide them with it.

The ugly phrase "collective security" is in vogue. It comes into its own when big threats recede. Such security consists of forums of nations, which enshrine certain standards of behaviour, and promote them with diplomatic action or, at the limit, with peace- keeping forces. It seems apt when the continent's main source of violence is the break-up of multi-ethnic states, rather than any overt aggressor that only armies can cope with. Collective security is like group therapy: useful when neighbors quarrel, but, when they resort to armed robbery, no substitute for the police.

The coming enlargement will bring in countries with lots of enthusiasm for collective security. Rudolph Joo of the Hungarian defense ministry points out that Hungary has been given three new neighbors within the past six months: Slovenia, Ukraine and Croatia. The war in Yugoslavia threatens Hungarian minorities there and has sent 50,000 refugees to Hungary. So Hungary has an intense interest in any persuasion that can be applied to damp down that war and protect the rights of its minorities abroad. The central Europeans also share the big unstated desire of the existing EC members and America to contain united Germany. Like France, they have bitter memories of Germany on the loose, and talk a lot of the need to protect Germany from "temptation."

The EC with its associates form a natural temptation-damper, upholding the right values, deeply involving the members, and, whenever they can reach agreement, expressing disapproval abroad with collective force. Switzerland apart, the ex-EFTA members want to play their part in this: Sweden is a practiced provider of peace-keeping forces. The club complements Europe's other security-enhancers, the 24-member Council of Europe with its Court of Human Rights, and the CSCE, which embraces the former Soviet Union and North America and is an accepted referee on arms control, elections and human and minority rights.

So far, so good. The trouble is that the nice distinction between therapy and police work is blurring, and with it the convenient distinction between the Community's foreign and security policy, as ordained at Maastricht, and its defense policy, as merely envisaged there. The civil war in Yugoslavia is pushing the West ever closer to using its soldiers as peacemakers rather than peacekeepers. The CSCE may soon be inviting NATO troops or troops of the WEU, the Western European Union, to intervene forcefully in such conflicts. What will the Swedes or Germans make of that?

When it comes to using force, European morale is sapped by a never-ending argument between the Euro-centrics and the Atlanticists. NATO remains unable to broaden its mandate to deal with threats to America's and Europe's joint interests outside the NATO area. The French resist such a broadening, and Germany's constitution makes it hard for it to send troops abroad anyway. Nor can NATO easily extend its military shield to include the Central European countries: American public opinion would not accept a Ukrainian foray into Poland as an attack on America, and the mere fact of extending the shield would cast Ukraine as the foe beyond the pale. Lacking a clear opponent or a fresh military strategy, NATO, too, has gone into the therapy business. Its North Atlantic Co-operation Council is duplicating the CSCE as a vast forum of nations. Now it is exploring how it might provide peacekeeping forces at the behest of the CSCE.

As for the EC, it has set about forging common foreign, security and defense policies in a singular way. When they first created themselves, the United States and the former Austro-Hungarian empire put these big policies into the central pot first and sorted out commercial wrinkles later. The Community, however, is being built from the bottom up, using sovereign states as bricks and commerce as mortar. Independent armed forces remain the guarantors of members' sovereignty; any member can still walk out of the EC without a red army stopping it. This desire for military independence is not something that can be lightly signed away. It is a given that will fade only with time spent living under Brussels law, and only if real threats unite Europe rather than divide it.

The Maastricht Treaty asks the till-now moribund Western European Union to "elaborate and implement decisions and actions of the union which have defense implications."

The WEU is to move to Brussels, set up a planning cell, and invite all non-WEU-members within the EC (Greece, Denmark, Ireland) to join it, and all non-EC-members within NATO (Turkey, Norway, Iceland) to become associate members.

Is this WEU a pillar of NATO, a complement to NATO or a rival to NATO? Well might you ask. In a mission statement last December, the WEU governments agreed that it would be developed "as the defense component of the European Union and as the means to strengthen the European pillar of the Atlantic alliance." That sounded straight forward enough. But WEU's planners already talk of restricting NATO to its current role so as to "leave the WEU a job to do." The Maastricht Treaty's commitments on foreign policy are, moreover, studded with clauses that promise incoherence in Europe's common defense. These commitments shall "not prejudice the specific character of the security and defense policy of certain member-states—that means individualistic France and neutral Ireland. They shall "not prevent development of closer co-operation between two or more member-states on a bi lateral level"—that means the newly created Franco-German corps.

This 35,000 strong corps symbolizes the current tension over the future defense of Europe. For the French it is the kernel of a European army free of American influence, which is exactly why the British and Americans detest it. The Germans do the splits between the two sides, claiming that the corps will tie the French armed forces more closely to NATO. The WEU secretariat is also doing the splits. It sees its future troops being provided by two rival schemes: the Franco-German corps (all new members welcome); and a British plan to put British troops at the disposal of WEU (other EC members please follow suit).

This dilemma has been there since the EC was created, but has become acute with the passing of the cold war. America's military commitment to Europe is now wobbling. Europe's military commitment to Europe still barely exists. Any attempt to build the second shakes the first.

WHITE HELMETS

How to proceed? By building WEU with extreme caution, given the materials available. Effective defense depends upon decisiveness. The Community is still a long way from being naturally decisive in foreign policy, let alone defense. As Niels Ersbol, the secretary-general of the Council of Ministers, says: "These are areas where members are simply not ready to accept the Community model."

If that suggests lack of vision, consider the problem of conscripts. The Gulf war made it suddenly clear to France that it was hard to send national conscripts to join a supranational force. Defense of the nation by conscripts was fine, but not sending them to face distant risk in a common cause. The EC's newly created citizens need more time before they will allow their conscripted sons to march off in a WEU expeditionary force.

As new members stream into the EC, the problem of indecision will, if anything, mount. Gradually the EC's military extroverts, Britain and France, will be submerged among well-meaning countries that do not have the instinct to project military power. Germany will not fight the trend. Neutral countries will not join the EC; the EC will join the neutrals. That is one big reason why this survey ends with a plea: let the enlarged Europe be a more flexible one—a Community in which things done jointly can also be things done well.

DREAMING SPIRES

Peter Balazs, secretary of state in the Hungarian trade ministry, ponders the "Comecon-isation of the European Community." He recalls the ingredients of Comecon's failure. It was held together by coercion. It was centralized. It was planned. It was introverted. It was inflexible. This provides a check-list to help judge the EC's chances of shaping Europe into the next century.

Coerced? No: members still retain a sovereign right to apply to join the EC or to quit it, without a centralized armed force threatening to stop them. But there are worrying tendencies. The mounting power of the EC trade block gives nearby countries an ever smaller option but to be subject to its rules, whether they help frame them or not. The growing significance in world trade of foreign direct investment raises the economic price of remaining outside. The dash towards union has featured politicians running too far ahead of their electorates, as the Danish referendum made clear. As soon as coercion is felt, the Community becomes a useless defuser of nationalism. Nation-states and ethnic regions are tempted to express their identity against the Community, rather than through it.

The antidotes to coercion are an open trading regime with the outside world, the greatest possible degree of Maastricht's promised "subsidiarity" and democratic openness in the way the EC is built and run. The last of these is tricky. National parliamentarians—particularly British ones—who growl about "unelected officials" in Brussels growl still louder if told that these faceless ones will be, given democratic credibility by the European Parliament in Strasbourg. The evolution of pan-European democracy will have to remain a careful blend of directly elected MPS and an indirectly elected conclave of governments, which becomes more like a senate and more open to outside scrutiny than it is today.

Centralized and planned? This survey has explained how the single market was pulled together by members renouncing state *dirigisme* and the notion that national rules had always to be replaced with Brussels ones. Nevertheless, both habits retain a powerful appeal. The commission itself, while small by the standards of national bureaucracies, has an instinct to regulate and control anything which can be remotely accused of being an impediment to trade.

National ministers often misuse the commission and council to concoct laws. Why? Because they find they are stronger in the council of their fellow ministers in Brussels than they are in their cabinets at home. Recently the 12 governments asked the commission to draft a directive on health and nutrition. Mr. Delors–convinced of late that the Community should do fewer things, better, rather than dabble in everything poorly—refused. He explained that guidance on healthy eating, and suchlike, could and should remain a matter for individual countries. The other commissioners backed him (just) in renouncing this right to prescribe the European adult's minimum daily intake of Community law.

As the EC expands, it will become ever more vital that it permits competition between systems of government, rather than attempts to harmonize them. Those who argue that labor laws or industrial policy must be levelled to remove unfairness within the European market are implicitly suggesting that the result must be shielded against "unfair" competition from the world outside. The best check of the virtue of any national system of, say, apprentice-training is that its results beat those of European countries that do things differently.

Introverted? The EC was built introvertedly during the cold-war era. It seemed good enough that the nation-states of Europe could be extrovert towards each other. The question

FIGURE 8-5

The Start of á la Carte

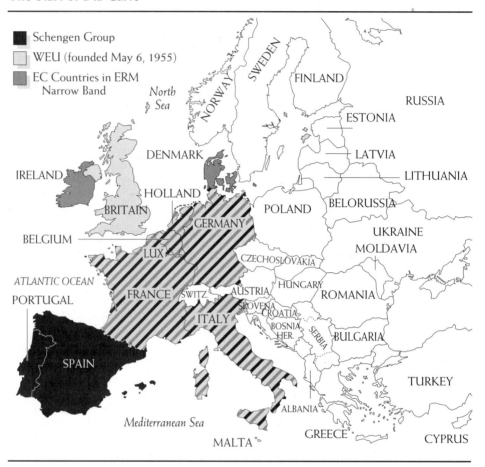

of their joint attitude towards the outside world did not arise—and barely needed to. Maastricht was the last feast of introversion, and now, alas, rescuing that treaty could make the feast a long one.

For the external obligations are crowding in. The queue of would-be members is one of them. The sight of Yugoslavia at war with itself is another. The pressure from the Uruguay round on European protectionism in farming and textiles is a third. The need of Eastern Europe for free trade and wise aid is a fourth. The fact that the EC can no longer blithely count on America to defend it is probably the biggest.

This survey has touched upon many of those, and painted a mixed picture. The threat of a Fortress Europe against imports has dwindled. By and large the ramparts are being levelled down rather than up. Even the EC's keep, the common agricultural policy, is being dismantled, though with a reluctance that still helps to block improvements in the GATT. The sheer variety of the new members-in- waiting makes a fortress ever harder to imagine.

On the other hand the "Europe agreements" with the central European countries are unimaginatively selfish.

As for foreign policy and defense, it would be rash for the world to count on much leadership from a united Europe soon. Maastricht proved that the members are still not ready to have a Community foreign policy based upon anything more constraining than their ability to reach unanimous agreement on a given problem. And in the matter of defense, the combination of a wobbling NATO pillar and competing plans for a European one is not impressive—but then neither, thank goodness, is the threat. Those impatient with this state of affairs must remember the Danish lesson on Maastricht— pan-European will-power cannot be signed into existence by far-sighted statesmen.

Inflexible? The basic challenge for the EC in the post-cold-war world is to accept that a unitary federal republic of Europe is no longer a sensible dream. The diversity of the existing, let alone the new, members is so great that the price of one regime for all will be mediocrity, plus that fatal feeling of coercion. This principle needs to be the starting-point in thinking about the wider Community that has become so suddenly possible. To this day it remains a heresy against the true faith.

The examples of such heresy multiply. The architecture of Maastricht's union, with its pillars for foreign and judicial policy outside the Community, is one. The Schengen passport-free zone, featuring eight members, is another. The process of qualifying for economic and monetary union is another. The decision of 11 members to go ahead and create social law, without Britain, is a fourth. The Franco-German corps is a stab at yet another. And it is possible that the Danes will be reconciled with Maastricht by a sixth— inviting them to be part of Maastricht's union but not of all of it.

Now look ahead to an enlarged Europe. Is it credible to work towards a common foreign and security policy—which is getting ever harder to disentangle from defense— that embraces countries with a tradition of neutrality? It is surely a recipe for impotence. Is it credible to imagine Turkey, with its 60m people, rising to 83.7m by 2020, having full freedom of movement of people within Europe, let alone providing the external frontier of a passport-free zone? Is it sensible to insist that island members, such as Britain, apply the same approach to people-control as landlocked members? Is it sensible, even, to make one agricultural regime embrace arctic herdsmen and the struggling banana plantations of Crete?

Accepting that the answer is No—and in some case No, never—will not weaken the EC: it will strengthen it. But the change needs to be more than just accepted. It needs to be planned for, and the EC's system of government adapted to cope. The basis of Community membership could be the single market and its obligations, which would, for practical reasons, have to remain a powerful all-or-nothing affair. Those obligations would have, of necessity, to include a single trade and economic sanctions policy. Beyond that there would be different realms of joint policy—monetary, social, home affairs, foreign affairs and defense, and immigration for which there would be entry criteria. Members would not merely have the right to opt out of them: they could be kept out of them.

For a unitary state, or anything aiming to become one, having such flexibility in government would be a nightmare. But with the EC's singular construction it need not be. The EC's councils of ministers meet topic by topic, so it should be possible to devise rules whereby attendance, or voting, was limited to those who were bound by the joint policy in question. In the parliament the same principle would apply to an MP's right to vote.

When Western Europe was cleanly bound by sea and barbed wire, and the scope of its policies was less demanding, it could think of itself as a flat-topped Acropolis, with a degree of integration common to all. But today the EC is much wider in its possible reach, while aspiring more loftily in its common government. The architecture must change to that of a Community with many pillars or spires. The right image from now on is of a Mont St. Michel—with Jacques Delors and his successors preaching from the top-most pulpit.

The European Community:
A Rude Awakening

DANIEL FRANKLIN

BACK TO THE DRAWING BOARD

If you believe in the cyclical theory, then the European Community is merely in one of its periodic spells of gloom. EC cycles, so the theory goes, closely match economic fortunes: periods of strong growth go with the intense bouts of Eurobuilding, to be followed by lean years and talk of Eurosclerosis. No surprise, then, the long economic advance of 1984–91 produced a sustained push for European integration (the drive for a frontier-free market, the plans for a single currency.) And no surprise that the current recession comes with a sharp revival of skepticism. In due course, seasoned observers of the European scene are convinced, the impetus for integration will return.

Maybe it will. But this is not just an ordinary Euro-cycle, for two reasons. First, Europe's economies face a deeper-than-usual adjustment if they are to resume their rises in living standards, reduce unemployment and compete internationally. Unless economic decline is halted, you can forget about any constitutional innovations and plans for monetary union; the old demons of protectionism and nationalism will haunt the continent. Second, the European scene has changed—fundamentally—with the collapse of the Berlin Wall.

The Community grew up as a cozy West European club with the avowed ambition, as its founding Rome treaty put it, of "every closer union." Suddenly, at the age of 35, it finds itself with one uncozily enlarged member (united Germany) and all of Eastern Europe clamoring to get in. This has plunged the Community into an identity crisis of a scale that is only just beginning to become clear to its members. For the EC's leaders, tackling it is all the harder because their first response to the end of the cold war was to press ahead with the old agenda for integration.

Future historians will no doubt puzzle over the Community's debilitating, two-year distraction from its real problems. Why, for example, with ethnic cleansing taking place just across their borders, have EC leaders spent much of their time fussing over the theology of "European union"? Why have they persisted with plans to cope with Germany's new-found strength when it has become obvious that the immediate threat is Germany's

The Economist (July 3, 1993).

new-found weakness? The answer goes back to their decision to clamber aboard a federal express that took on a momentum all of its own.

Jacques Delors, the president of the European Commission, had stoked the engine with his blueprint for monetary union and his 1988 prediction that within ten years "80% of economic legislation, perhaps even of tax and social legislation," would come from Brussels. President Francois Mitterrand, in a panic over German unification, pressed on the throttle. Chancellor Helmut Kohl, convinced that a united Europe was the only safe destination for a united Germany, was an enthusiastic co-driver. And though John Major pulled on the brakes, he stayed on board for fear of being left behind. Thus in December 1991, they all hurtled on to the Dutch city of Maastricht.

It might as well have been Mars, so far as millions of ordinary Europeans were concerned. The Maastricht Treaty of European Union has since seemed an almost insulting irrelevance, given the televised Balkan horror-show and the growing worries over jobs. Martians had surely drafted the text or so it read, with its combination of the absurd ("A common foreign and security policy is hereby established") and the impenetrable (suggested reading: Article 189b, paragraph 6). The treaty seemed a conspiracy by technocrats against citizens.

The citizens took their revenge. Just over half the Danish voters rejected Maastricht last June, and just under half of the French voted *Non* in September. In between, turmoil on Europe's foreign-exchange markets all but destroyed the credibility of the core of the treaty, its program for economic and monetary union (EMU). Germans, it became clear, did not want to give up the D-mark: 60% of those surveyed in March-April 1993 said they were against the EMU project and only 29% were in favor. According to the same Eurobarometer poll, only two out of five Europeans are positively in favor of Maastricht, and support for the EC among its citizens has fallen sharply (see Figure 9-1).

All this has left Maastricht, and the politicians who designed it, badly battered. Mr. Delors has disappeared into a long sulk. The phrase "United States of Europe," which had crept into Mr. Kohl's speeches, has tiptoed out again. Mr. Mitterrand no longer talks of Europe's "federal vocation." Mr. Major has been through a year of parliamentary hell.

Yet the treaty survives. However unloved, Maastricht was the only route-map Europeans had. On second thoughts (and with opt-outs gálore), the Danes voted Yes in May. The last stages of British parliamentary approval and a challenge in the German Constitutional Court are now all that stand in the way of final ratification. That still leaves scope for the ultimate crisis—a German *Nein*—but the best guess is that the treaty will be in force by the autumn. If so, EC leaders can wearily lift their eyes to the real world, and decide what to do next.

THE WAY AHEAD

The questions they face have changed. Not "How shall we huddle into ever-closer union?," but "How shall we cope with a wider Europe and a weakening economy?" The radical answer would be a total rethink. Europe's governments are too tired and divided for that. So they will try to trundle along the Maastricht track.

The next main stop is a review conference scheduled for 1996. Pre-programming that conference was a way of finessing German demands for more federalism last time round. The review will be premature—there will hardly have been time to see what the original treaty means in practice—yet a postponement looks unlikely. Too many governments will have a wish-list of reforms.

FIGURE 9-1
Not Impressed

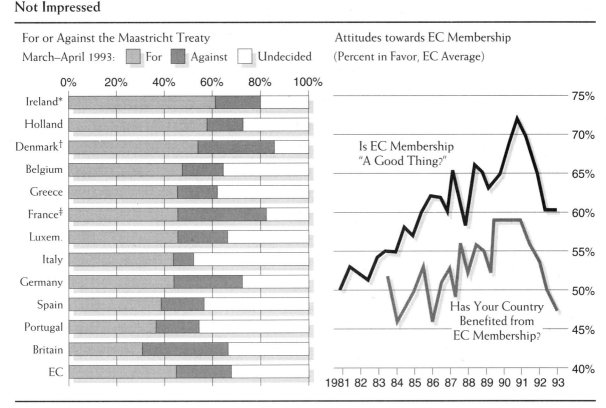

For or Against the Maastricht Treaty
March–April 1993: ▢ For ▢ Against ▢ Undecided

Attitudes towards EC Membership
(Percent in Favor, EC Average)

*69% voted for in June 1992.

†49% voted for in June 1992; 57% voted for in May 1993.

‡51% voted for in September 1992.

Source: Eurobarometer.

Hence a daunting prospect: before long, EC governments could find themselves once again plunged into an exhausting round of negotiations over where they are heading— towards a superstate, a glorified free-trade area, or whatever. Maastricht itself, a jumble of compromises, settled nothing. The main players in the Community are far apart in their interpretations of Maastricht, and in their perceptions of what lies ahead.

But there is one point on which all the large EC members are starting to agree: as the Community expands it will be increasingly absurd for everyone to attempt to do everything together. Enter "variable geometry"—Eurospeak for the idea that subgroups of countries might co-operate on certain subjects even if others cannot follow. The idea is already enshrined in the Maastricht treaty, in the British and Danish opt-outs. A still more flexible version of variable geometry would work from the bottom up, through coalitions of consenting partners: opt-ins rather than opt-outs.

Such flexibility is essential. The mistake of the Maastricht mentality was the idea that it was possible to fix the European future at a time when the continent was in its biggest state of flux since 1945. It is still in flux.

This survey argues that Europe has even now not properly woken up to the scale of the changes needed to adjust to an undivided continent and a restlessly competitive world. The rich countries of Europe can no longer take the privileged assumptions of the post-war years (America's protective embrace, expanding welfare systems, a cozy Community) for granted. So Europeans should hold on for a bumpy ride. If it is any consolation, they might remember on the way that one of their toughest challenges—dealing with all the countries wanting to join them—is a tribute to the extraordinary success of the EC adventure so far.

SHAKEN AND STIRRED

In the center of Brussels, the berlaymont stands eerily empty, poisoned by asbestos and so abandoned by the European Commission. Opposite, another tall building is going up, the future home of the EC governments' Council of Ministers. The symbolism is exquisite. The 1980s belonged to the commission, the 1990s will belong to governments.

Even at Maastricht, governments arranged to keep foreign policy and internal security for themselves, establishing for the first time since Monnet that Europe could progress in a way that was not strictly *communautaire*. Post-Maastricht, the commission has lost its way. Governments are now determined to exercise more control.

But they have difficulties of their own. The Maastricht backlash showed them to be out of touch with their voters. Elections and scandals have inflicted further punishment. In all the five big EC countries, an entire political class is on the defensive (or, in Italy's case, under investigation).

This is more than an ordinary swing of the political pendulum. It is part of a tumult in western politics that seems to be following the revolution in Easter Europe. The old left-right divide matters less, leaving greater room for "issue politics": greenery, regionalism, xenophobia, Europe. In the arguments over Maastricht, strange alliances formed. The pros tended to occupy the middle ground, backed by the richer regions and the professional classes. The antis came from the fringes of left and right, with supporters in depressed regions and among the "little people" (as Lady Thatcher likes to call them) who mistrust grand schemes. The politicians have now seen that while they were designing a baroque constitutional cathedral, the ground was trembling beneath them. European architecture will not be quite the same again.

First, the politicians' minds are going to be elsewhere. They are turning inwards. Their main concern will be to address the worries of voters back home. And right now the voters are much more worried about jobs, immigrants and crime than about constitutional conceptions for Europe.

Second, when they do get around to such niceties, the politicians will need to pay more attention to their voters. "The argument for the next steps of integration will have to be much more political than for Maastricht," says an adviser to Mr. Kohl. In France, thanks to the Maastricht precedent, politicians will be aware while negotiating any future treaty changes that they will probably face a referendum on the outcome.

The voters' rebellion is also bringing a different bunch to power. The EC's leaders formed a remarkably stable club during the 1980s. No longer. Italy will go to the polls once it has a new electoral law; who will then run the country and what they will think of Europe is anybody's guess. Germany's bumper election year in 1994 (including one for the Bundestag) could bring a change of government; and any successor to Mr. Kohl is almost bound to be less misty-eyed about Europe. In 1995 France is due to elect a new president. He might be Jacques Chirac, who is lukewarm on Europe.

Already France's new conservative government has shown how policy can change. The top people in the cabinet are still staunch Europhiles, but they rely on a parliamentary majority whose biggest component, Mr. Chirac's neo-Gaullist party, has a large and unignorable anti-Maastricht clan.

French policy on Europe is becoming choosier: *à la carte* than *table d'hôte*. The government has postponed the so-called Schengen arrangement under which nine EC countries had hoped to press ahead with the lifting of passport controls at their mutual borders; the arrangements for controlling drugs, immigrants and criminals remained inadequate. Other examples of a more nuanced French approach include the return to respectability of Gaullist talk of a "Europe of nations," and a new toughness about the arrangements for letting the next batch of countries into the Community (about which more later).

So any Maastricht II will be a very different affair from Maastricht I. But note that, in France and elsewhere, the reservations about what the EC's politicians have been up to should not be misconstrued as "anti-Europeanism." It is mainly anti-Maastrichtism. The idea of Europe is still widely popular. The question is, what type of Europe?

SCUSI, SPRECHEN SIE EUROPEAN, MON AMIGO?

A concise phrasebook could tell you almost everything you need to know about current thinking across the Community. Pick a key expression from each of the five main languages, and the outlines of the great European debate become clear. Here is a selection from the 1993 version.

English: *Wider still and wider.* Britain wants new members in fast, for a wider, looser Community. Mr. Major thinks Britain is "in a better position than at any stage of our membership to start influencing the Community to go in the direction we, the British, would like to see it moving." He has always sold Maastricht as a dam against federalism. Subsequent events, the governments believes, mean that the argument is "moving our way." "I feel in my bones very confident that Europe is moving in the direction of [Margaret Thatcher's 1988] Bruges speech," says Sir Charles Powell, who drafted that famous anti-federalist manifesto.

German: *Das Gesamtkonzept* (the total concept). German policy-makers, as they themselves explain, like to have a plan, a clear idea of the eventual shape of the whole European enterprise. Their *Gesamtkonzept* was, and remains, that of a federal Europe. Maastricht was seen at the time as just a step on the way. True, since then there have been setbacks, and ordinary Germans may see things differently. But the policy-makers' concept is still the same. Federalism has worked for Germany' it must work for Europe. A senior diplomat describes Britain's preference for inter-governmentalism as "outrageous, short-sighted in the extreme."

French: *La préférence européenne* (preference for Europe). This is now many politicians' favorite phrase. It is a polite expression for protectionism. It described the Community's protectionist farm regime. Now the French want more *préférence* for industry, as a defense against imports from countries without rules against sweatshop labor. "Whether you like it or not," says a top government official, "given the state of the economy, importing T-shirts made by children in Thailand or political prisoners in China won't do any more."

Spanish: *La cohesion.* The EC's euphemism for aid to poorer members. Spain sees a role for itself in bargaining hard on behalf of the poorer bunch.

Italian: *Risotto milanese e cassata siciliana.* In other words, when it comes to thinking about Europe, Italians are out to lunch. They are tied up with the chaos of home. Meanwhile, government from Brussels is better than non-government in Rome.

Note that, strange as it may seem all these views have one thing in common: a perception that "more Europe," not less, is the answer. The tussle will be over whose idea of Europe wins though.

The French-German axis has always driven the Community. By now the relationship has become thoroughly institutionalized. There are stresses, of course: over Yugoslavia, over the GATT trade talks and even, believe it or not, over bananas (the Germans, big banana-eaters, are furious about French and British insistence on protecting expensive Caribbean producers). But the relationship can survive many a banana-skin. It will remain the most powerful force in the Community.

Less powerful than it was, though. One reason is that Germany, though bigger, is in some ways also more constrained than before. Its 16 *Länder* (regional states) have insisted on a greater say on European affairs. And whereas in the past Germany could afford to throw D-marks at EC problems, it is now strapped for cash like everyone else.

OLD GAME, NEW RULES

The other reason is that the influence of the French-German partnership is bound to be somewhat diluted as the Community grows. Alain Juppé, France's foreign minister, says that in a bigger club Europeans will have to think of "solidarities by themes." France and Britain are already moving closer on defense.

The more countries join the club, the greater the scope for alliance-building. The Community may well be moving towards a system of shifting alliances, similar to those in 19th-century balance-of-power politics, but with the late-20th-century difference that all the countries remain bound tightly together through increasingly shared economic decision-taking. To prevent the arrangement from falling apart, the presumption would be that a oneway system operated: once countries have opted in to a particular area of joint decision-taking, they try very hard to stay in.

If so, the net result will be a hybrid unlike anything the various members now expect. The Community will be too 19th-century and inter-governmental to match the *Gesamtkonzept.* The British will find that, even as the EC widens, there will be a tightening not a loosening of its core structure, the economic Community. Spain will press an increasingly tight-fisted Germany for more *cohesion,* only to find itself on the tight-fisted side of the argument once the poorer East Europeans enter the club.

What about *préférence européenne?* It will be the earliest test of the Community's balance of power. It is also, given the precarious state of the European economy, the most important.

DELORSISM OR DARWINISM?

"The situation has never before been so serious," proclaimed the headline in the weekly *Die Zeit,* above a doomsday analysis of a Germany threatening to go into economic decline. Scaremongering by a paper that takes pleasure in criticizing the government? Not this time: within weeks the government had come round to much the same view. Soon Theo Waigel, the finance minister, was talking about "the sharpest economic crisis" in the federal republic's history. Such panic is the most encouraging sign yet that Germany is starting to get serious about its problems.

The German economy stopped growing last summer and will shrink by perhaps 2% this year. France is in recession too. Among the main EC economies, only Britain's is growing—and that only after the longest recession since the 1930s. The Community will have about 19m jobless by the end of this year, 11% of its workforce (see Figure 9-2).

These woes would be less worrying if they were just a result of the normal business cycle. Alas, a lot of the trouble seems to run deeper.

German unification has been the immediate shock. The financing of unity brought high interest rates (spread across the Community, courtesy of its exchange-rate mechanism), depressing growth just when EC governments were aiming to bring public finances into line with Maastricht's convergence rules in time for monetary union by the late 1990s. Now, with revenue falling and spending on unemployment rising, government deficits and debts are proving extremely hard to control. This is compelling EC governments to think hard about how they can live within their means.

Still more disturbing is evidence that European competitiveness has been continuing to slip. The Community's share of world exports in manufactures has fallen by a fifth since

FIGURE 9-2
Miserable Times

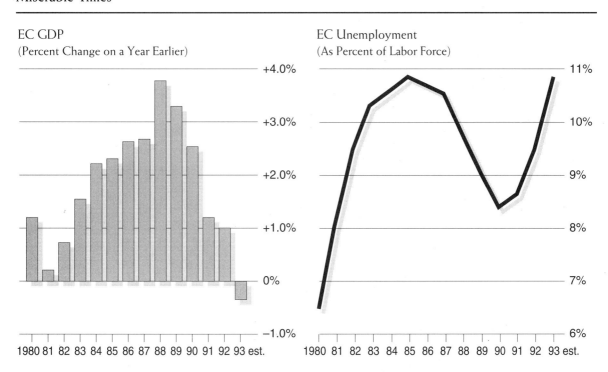

EC GDP
(Percent Change on a Year Earlier)

EC Unemployment
(As Percent of Labor Force)

Source: Datastream; European Commission.

1980. It has a widening deficit in trade in high technology: a study by the commission showed that, between 1982 and 1990, the volume of EC high-tech exports to the rest of the world grew by only 2% a year, while high-tech imports grew by 7.7% a year.

Improvement in manufacturing productivity in the EC has been sluggish. Between 1979 and 1990, according to the Confederation of British Industry, value-added per person employed in manufacturing rose by 4.6% a year in Japan and 3.5% in America, but by only 2.5% a year in the Community. Persistently high West European unemployment—the EC's 10%-plus compares with 7% in America and just 2.3% in Japan—reflects labor-market rigidities that are especially damaging at a time when businesses are looking for more and more flexible ways of organizing production and when investment capital moves freely round the world in search of cheap, efficient labor.

EC labor is hardly cheap. Not only are wages high, but so are non-wage costs (such as social-security payments and fringe benefits). In Italy, the European champion at this non-wage costs make up half the total labor costs in manufacturing (see Figure 9-3). West Europeans are pricing themselves out of jobs compared with Americans and Japanese, let alone Indians and Chinese.

Back to Germany. its labor costs are the highest in the world. Right next door, in the Czech Republic, is a skilled workforce that costs one-sixth as much. More German companies are discovering that they can make German-quality goods more cheaply outside Germany. Take the car industry, Germany's pride. Volkswagen is investing massively in the Czech Republic, is a skilled workforce that costs one-sixth as much. More German companies are discovering that they can make German-quality goods more cheaply outside Germany. Take the care industry, Germany's pride. Volkswagen is investing massively in the Czech Republic. BMW is building a new plant in South Carolina; Mercedes also plans an American plant, where labor costs per car will be about one-third of what they are back home.

RICH MAN'S BURDEN

Add the fact that two out of five working Germans are employed in manufacturing—a far higher proportion that in any other western country of Japan—and it is easy to see why some Germans are getting scared about the possible shake-up ahead. The government money that could have helped western Germany adjust with minimum pain is now flooding into the impoverished east: transfer payments amounted to some DM130 billion ($80 billion) last year. From a record current-account surplus of DM108 billion in 1989, it swung to a deficit of DM40 billion last year. Once a big net exporter of capital, it has turned into a net importer.

No wonder so many Germans preferred to pretend that nothing had changed, that life could go on being as *gemütlich* as before. But a theater of the absurd this spring seems to have made more people look at harsh realities: workers in the east went on strike to demand big pay rises, despite low productivity that already made them 60% more expensive per unit of output than workers in the west. That seems to have sounded some alarm bells. Germans are beginning to wake up to their new world.

Other West Europeans face a similar awakening. Cherished policies which may be contributing to loss of competitiveness will come under scrutiny: the generosity of the welfare system, the retirement age, the minimum wage (where one exists). Such scrutiny may be an economic necessity, but it is political dynamite nonetheless. The European attachment to welfare runs deep, supported by a formidable alliance of socialists and Christian Democrats.

Mr. Delors, whose success at the commission has had a lot to do with his talent as a theme-spotter, is looking into the causes of unemployment in the Community (possibly as a last flourish before an early return to Paris). He wants to consider the effect of the national welfare system on jobs. He will also have to explain how his quest to get Europe back to work squares with his championship of the EC's "social dimension," which critics call a recipe for unemployment.

PROTECTION RACKET?

A bitter argument is looming in the Community about how to adjust. Should free trade and fierce competition force the changes? Or should the EC throw up barriers to give industries time to adapt?

Préférence européenne if French shorthand for the second option. Officials explain that this is not protectionism, but a question of opening "intelligently," of arranging transition periods, of using leverage to open others' markets and increase social protection *chez eux.*

FIGURE 9-3
Pricing Themselves Out of Markets

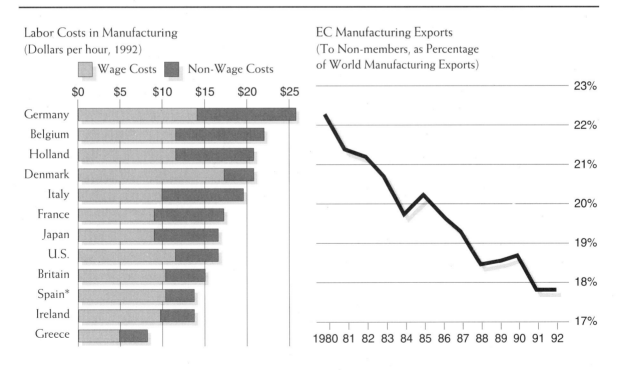

Labor Costs in Manufacturing
(Dollars per hour, 1992)

EC Manufacturing Exports
(To Non-members, as Percentage of World Manufacturing Exports)

*Split between wage costs and non-wage costs not available.

Source: Swedish Employers' Confederation: Eurostat.

"Building Europe is to defend our type of social organization," says a top businessman. The same sort of thing was once said about building the Soviet Union, which deployed 100% protection from foreign competition in order to have a long transition period to Utopia.

If France yields to this protectionist urge, it would have several potential allies. Spain could be one, Italy another. Italy's industry minister, Paolo Savona, explains in one breath the virtues of openness—productivity growth in the 70% of the Italian economy that is exposed to competition is six times as great as in the 30% that is not—while in the next explaining how Italy needs time to liberalize, especially in the south.

Germany could tilt the balance. The French reckon that the scale of its restructuring problems will make a bit more protectionism seem like a nice idea. At the moment, it still stands firmly, with Britain, in the free-trade camp.

Will it therefore lean heavily on France to accept a GATT agreement? France was alone among EC countries in denouncing the Blair House farm deal with America that would form part of a GATT package. Farmers have a powerful place in French minds and in French politics, to put it mildly. The new government made campaign promises to tear up the Blair House deal; it would dearly love to reverse the reforms of the Community's common agricultural policy. At the same time, however, it is also promising a policy of "movement" in the GATT talks.

The French government will probably wait until it sees what the entire package looks like. It will try to exact as big a pay-off as possible for its farmers. It will then decide whether the deal is sellable at home. The G7 summit in Tokyo this month could be decisive.

A GATT deal would not end the protectionist pressures in the EC. But a GATT breakdown would almost guarantee that *préférence européenne* became rampant.

SINGLE-MINDED

Getting less competitive. Losing out to Japan and America. In danger of terminal decline. Hasn't Western Europe heard it all before? And hadn't it already come up with the solution?

It had. The solution was called the single-market program, designed to bring free movement of people, goods, capital and services in an EC stripped of internal frontiers by January 1, 1993. This would give the Europeans the big "home" base they needed to take on the world. The 1988 Checchini report for the European Commission estimated that the result would swell the Community's GDP by some 5% and boost employment. Other analysts predicted even greater dynamic benefits, such as a rise of half a percentage point in the EC's long-term annual growth rate.

Yet 1993 has arrived, and Europe has a recession, appalling unemployment and a need for more restructuring. This does not exactly help to foster a popular belief that all the effort at integration has been worthwhile. What has gone wrong?

Three answers. First, momentum from the single-market project probably did contribute to the EC's surge of growth in the late 1980s; more businesses are in part a sign that the single market is starting to work. And third, the single market is in reality a process, not a deadline. Much still remains to be done. It may take another decade or more of hard work and acclimatization before the great market is really in full swing.

A lot has been achieved. The legal infrastructure is largely in place; some 95% of the 280-odd laws planned back in 1985 are through. People can now take a car-load of goods for their personal use across EC borders without paying duty, trucks cross frontiers without customs checks, public contracts must be advertised Community-wide, banks with a license in one country can operate anywhere in the EC. All controls on the movement of capital have gone, except (until 1995) in Greece and Portugal.

Yet the idea that the single market is more or less "complete," as they say in Brussels, is true only in the narrowest bureaucratic sense. In the real world, the list of inadequacies is long. It includes:

- **Omissions.** Two big industries were left out of the original legislative program because they were too sensitive: telecommunications and energy. Telecoms liberalization is now only a question of (ample) time. Energy liberalization is a pious official goal but remains deeply controversial. Most countries except Britain, which has liberalized its own energy, are resisting even the cautious attempts by the commission to tamper with their national monopolies.
- **Delays.** Passport checks remain despite the end-1992 deadline. Britain, for one, is determined to keep them as a defense against terrorists, drugs, and rabies. Even "Schengenland," the would-be fast track to frontier-free travel by nine countries, is in trouble. Decisions on intellectual-property protection are also late.
- **Transitions.** There are many examples. The value-added-tax system that allows customs-free transport for goods is only a temporary fix (which does not anyway apply to the distorted market for cars), due for review in 1996. Full liberalization of air transport is scheduled for 1997. Foreign banks will not gain direct access to stock exchanges in Spain, Portugal and Greece until 1999.
- **Missing standards.** The rules on technical harmonization are in place, but many of the detailed industrial standards needed to make them work are not. So, for example, a British manufacturer of smoke alarms complains that the French and German markets are in effect closed to it until about 1996, when the new Euro-standard is expected.
- **State aid.** This continues to distort markets. Take steel. A lot of Italian capacity, and probably the entire steel industry in Spain's Basque Country, survives only thanks to government subsidies, which deprive efficient French and British producers of business. Politics makes it hard for the commission, which has responsibility for policing fair competition, to get the subsidies down. As one government official puts it, "You can't just shut down the Basque Country."
- **National bias.** This applies particularly to the huge public-procurement market—worth, on one estimate, over 10% of Community-wide GDP. Nobody believes that the mere invitation of bids ensures open access to contracts. Both the French and the British think they are more open than others. When, say, Italy's public authorities start buying cars and buses made by somebody other than Fiat, skepticism over the openness of public procurement might subside.

In short, making the single market happen is a vast enterprise. It is a wonder that the Community has got as far as it has. The various single-market tensions that have surfaced this year are all in their way proof that the thing is for real.

The British drinks industry, for example, says sales of beer through off-licenses and supermarkets are suffering because of the amount of lower-taxed booze coming into the country duty-free, some of it for (illegal) resale. In January Holland and Germany abolished some 6,500 national quotas on goods from outside the Community (the very idea of national quotas is incompatible with a single market). This brought howls of protest from southern EC members who wanted to keep their own quotas until tougher, Community-wide protection was in place. The French complain about the difficulty of policing imports such as textiles and shoes from outside the Community now that these can cross the EC's internal borders unchecked.

There was an uproar in France earlier this year over Hoover's decision to close a factory in Dijon and concentrate its vacuum-cleaner production at a plant near Glasgow where the workforce was prepared to accept new working practices. This was decried as "social dumping" by Britain, which with its opt-out from Maastricht's social chapter would increasingly poach jobs from its neighbors.

Behind many of the teething troubles is a lack of mutual trust. A committee chaired by Peter Sutherland, a former EC commissioner and the GATT's new director-general, concluded last October that the single market had to be more transparent. Information should be improved, laws made more user-friendly (there are 38 directives on tractors), cooperation organized more systematically to enforce the rules.

This is easier said than done. Attitudes to rules vary: pedestrians in Bonn wait patiently for the little red man to turn to green before crossing the road, even when there is not a car in sight; motorcyclist in Rome routinely zoom through red lights. In the single market, Northerners such as the British complain that: "We enforce the rules while southerners cheat." Yet the British themselves are rule zealots who insert the maximum amount of red tape when turning EC directives into national law.

The single-market process probably has enough momentum to survive these tensions. What it might not survive, however, is further bad bouts of turbulence in the foreign-exchange markets. If you are French, in a recession, and you suddenly see three of your main trading partners appear to steal at least a 10% competitive advantage through currency devaluations, it would be amazing if your protectionist nerves did not start to twitch. Pretty soon, the stress can lead to competitive devaluations, to the restoration of capital controls even to new trade barriers.

A minimum of exchange-rate stability is needed for the single market to work. Some believe that a maximum of stability is needed—that in the long run the single market must have a single money. The creation of such a thing is the Community's most ambitious project.

BETTER LATE THAN NEVER

The only country that currently almost passes Maastricht's macroeconomic test for single-currency suitability is Luxembourg, with 0.1% of the Community's population. Germany, the key to the plan for economic and monetary union and the country that insisted on such strict rules so that EMU would not undermine its financial rectitude, now has the highest inflation rate among G7 countries plus a budget deficit that will probably not get back under the Maastricht maximum for years. France, still tied into approximate currency parity with Germany, languishes in recession while Britain and Italy have broken free and enjoyed an economic boost. Surely the whole idea of a single currency has become a bad joke?

It is still deadly serious. Cynics, mainly but not only in Britain, underestimate the determination of most governments to press ahead with the plan, as a means of living more comfortably with Germany, as well as for economic reasons. The economic prize remains big: freedom from the strains on the single market from currency fluctuations, freedom from the currency risk in investment decisions, freedom from the transaction costs of changing money.

What has changed, however, more than many EMU-boosters care to admit, is the credibility of the Maastricht plan for getting there. The treaty followed the glide-path approach recommended by Mr. Delors: countries would travel gently towards monetary union, virtually on auto-pilot. Safe arrival under a definite timetable seemed almost guaranteed, at least for some countries. No longer. The turbulence over the past year (see Figure 9-4) very nearly caused a crash.

There is now widespread agreement about what went wrong. Circumstances, as they often are when-accidents happen, were exceptional: very high interest rates in Western Europe because of German unity; very low rates in America because of its recession; sudden jitters in the air because of the Maastricht referendums. All this led to intense speculative pressures. Plus there was pilot error. Those in charge of the guidance system, the Community's exchange-rate mechanism (ERM), had forgotten that they could still twiddle the controls (there had been no adjustments since 1987). Instead, they treated the ERM as virtually fixed already. A timely realignment might just have held things steady.

As it was, the system found its own way of adjusting. The British pound and the Italian lira were ejected from the ERM and depreciated outside it. The Spanish peseta and other weak currencies had to devalue within it. The French franc came under enormous pressure. Yet it—and the ERM—just managed to survive.

FIGURE 9-4 ——————————————————————

Things That Go Bump Overnight

Currencies against the D-mark
(End 1986=100, Inverted Scale)

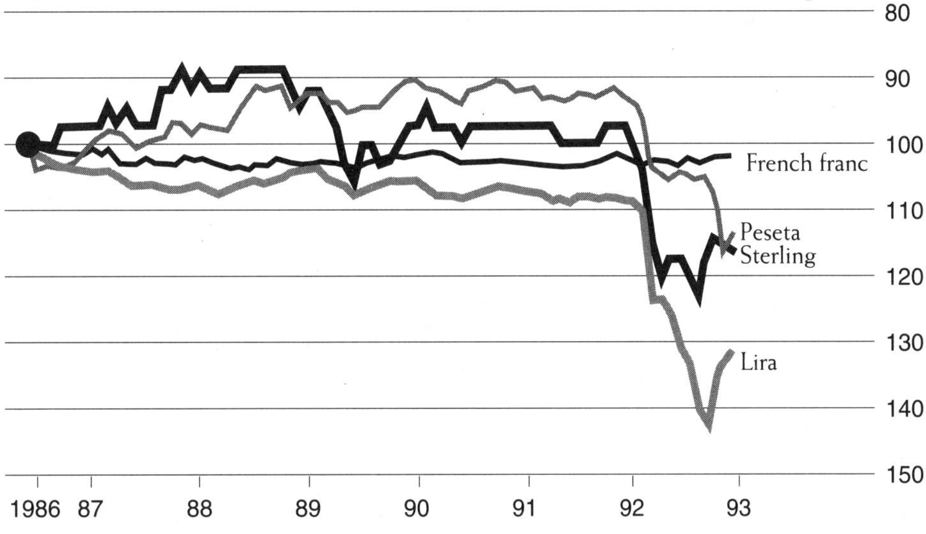

Source: Datastream.

Official inquests concluded that there were no design flaws, despite the British government's claims of "fault-lines" in the ERM. The system just needed to be operated more flexibly, rather than as a *de facto* monetary union. The quasi-fixing of currencies was meant to happen only as fast as the convergence of economies allowed, not regardless of differing rates of inflation. Henceforth, realignments should be both more routine (as has indeed been happening in the case of the peseta) and less politicized. There should be more discreet consultation between finance ministers and central bankers, on the basis of an agreed set of statistics, to make sure that they see potential trouble early.

Optimists hope that with such fine-tuning the ERM and hence the plan for monetary union, is now safe. Conditions have improved, with German interest rates lower and Maastricht nearly ratified. Currency calm will return. Italy wants to be back in the ERM once things have settled down at home, possibly some time next year. Even Britain, where the ERM is associated only with disaster, will eventually want to rejoin.

NOT SO FAST

That is too complacent by half. The ERM will be very lucky to avoid another set of "exceptional circumstances" in the 1990s. Indeed, it is stuck with the exceptional circumstance of German unification; even the mighty D-mark could one day become a target for speculators. A lingering recession in France could put the franc under renewed strain. Any amount of timely adjustment might prove inadequate in the face of a currency market with a turnover of $1 trillion a day. It would therefore be prudent to adjust the rules to allow still more flexibility, such as the possibility of temporarily moving out of the normal 24% fluctuation band when there are unusual pressures—say, during elections.

As for EMU, the Maastricht model now looks in need of adjustment. The present timing seems over-optimistic (see Figure 9-5). The schedule runs as follows. In 1996 governments decide which countries are fit for EMU (according to the Maastricht guidelines on such items as inflation, public debt and budget deficits), and if a majority of countries are ready they can decide to go ahead. Otherwise, monetary union will start at the latest in 1999, assuming more than one country is reckoned to be ready.

The first deadline can already be ruled out, since neither France nor Germany will be ready in time. It is far from certain that both will be ready by 1999, and without one or other of them monetary union would not be worth having. Might the convergence criteria be softened to make EMU entry easier? Only over the Budesbank's dead body. To admit in public that the timetable is slipping is tricky (though France's prime minister recently did so), since several governments have been trying to set their entire budgetary strategy according to the Maastricht deadlines.

Whenever it comes, the final descent on the glide to monetary union now looks fraught with danger. To qualify, says the treaty, a currency has to have had no devaluation for two years. That is hard to square with the new-found realization that the ERM must work more flexibly. It sounds like an invitation to speculators.

Those future two years of exchange-rate stability look especially ambitious now that the worries surrounding an eventual move to EMU have emerged more clearly. Most Germans dislike the idea; it means giving up the D-mark, the closet thing they have to a symbol of national pride. They are terrified that the Italians will be let in, and think that even the French still have a lot to prove. One thing they do trust is the Bundesbank. Will they be willing to see responsibility for their money switch overnight to a European Central

FIGURE 9-5

Hmm...   ...oops...   ...aarghh

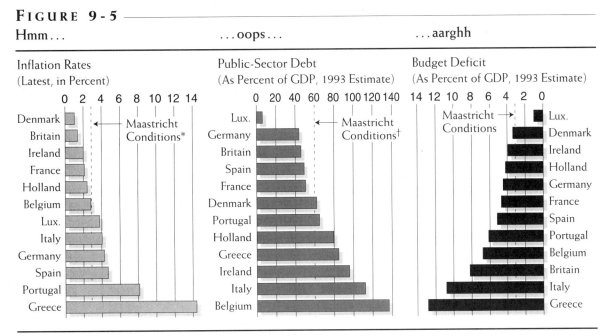

| Inflation Rates (Latest, in Percent) | Public-Sector Debt (As Percent of GDP, 1993 Estimate) | Budget Deficit (As Percent of GDP, 1993 Estimate) |

*Applying the treaty arithmetic to current figures.

†Levels laid down in the treaty.

Source: National statistics; OECD; European Commission; Swiss Bank Corporation.

Bank which, under the Maastricht design, has no change to build up a proper track record beforehand?

The German government has consistently said that the counterpart of monetary union must be greater political union, and that the political side of Maastricht was inadequate. Its assumption was that it would make up for the inadequacy at the 1996 review conference. That now seems much less likely. Would the government then face a revolt against the idea of sacrificing something big (the D-mark) in return for nothing much at all?

Germany's own unification-induced currency union has served as a laboratory for EMU, with mind-concentrating results. Without separate currencies, there are three ways of adjusting to big disparities of wealth: wage flexibility, mass migration or transfer payments. In Germany, wage flexibility has turned out to be zero, mass migration was reckoned to be intolerable, so transfer payments have been crippling. Conclusion: the Community (which, as the map shows, has large regional variations in wealth) ought to be preparing for great flexibility on wages. Instead it has saddled itself with "social Europe."

MID-FLIGHT CORRECTION

It would be wrong to deduce from all this that the Europeans on board for EMU are about to reach for their parachutes. There is too much at stake, politically as well as economically.

French leaders see monetary union as a way of regaining a share of the monetary sovereignty they have ceded to the Bundesbank. For Spaniards it is a matter both of "dissolving German predominance" and of proving their own European *machísmo*. Top Italians are also worried about German monetary "hegemony," and they like much about the Maastricht design, even if at first other countries proceed without them (something they accept as not merely likely, given Italy's outsized public debt, but desirable too). In Italian eyes, the beauty of Maastricht is that it reserves an eventual place for them, and prevents a cabal of countries rushing into an exclusive mini-EMU of their own.

The institutional preparations continue. France is pressing ahead with legislation to make its central bank independent. If and when the Maastricht treaty is finally ratified, plans can proceed to set up the European Monetary Institute, the embryo of the future European Central Bank. It is due to be established at the beginning of next year, probably in Germany (anywhere other than Frankfurt would be "ridiculous," say German officials).

Some adjustment to the Maastricht model will almost certainly be necessary. The timing of monetary union may have to be rescheduled. The final transition to it must be made safer. One suggestion is to bolster the credibility of the European Monetary Institute by giving it some real power, beyond mere analysis, in advance of monetary union. If the Bundesbank comes round to accepting that idea, it will be a sign that monetary union really is on the way.

With luck, some time early next century it might not prove impossible to persuade ordinary Germans to accept a monetary union with a select group of proven partners—say, France, the Benelux three and Austria. The financial markets have helpfully demonstrated that this will not happen without real economic convergence. They have also shown that, monetary union or not, such convergence is needed anyway for a reasonable stable ERM, and thus to avoid an outbreak of economic strife, with all the dangers that could bring. The height of folly would be to see disintegration in the West added to the disintegration in the East.

THE SHAME OF IT

"War is the usual condition of Europe," said Peter Kropotkin, a Russian anarchist, in 1884. "A 30 years supply of the causes of war is always to hand." After the interruption of the East-West stand-off, parts of Europe have returned to the usual condition.

The war in ex-Yogoslavia broke just as the European Community was developing ambitions in foreign policy and defense. "This is the hour of Europe," proclaimed Jacques Poos, who as foreign minister of tiny Luxembourg found himself talking for the Community at the time. The Americans were happy to let the Europeans handle this one for themselves. But what enthusiasts hoped would be a proof of new-found European power has turned into a demonstration of European impotence. It has been, as one of the enthusiasts puts it ruefully, "an enormous setback for the European idea."

Wimps, bunglers, insouciant, appeasers. Those are some of the kinder descriptions of the Europeans' record in the Balkans. Bosnia has been generally judged a bad example of limp. uncoordinated, lowest-common-denominator policy.

The final verdict on the Europeans' record may turn out to be a bit more nuanced. They did at least stick together (despite bitter disagreements), thus avoiding the rival side-taking that in 1914 turned a Balkan spat into a world war. As President Bill Clinton soon discovered, it is one thing to be outraged by the Yogoslav tragedy, quite another to agree on a policy to stop it. Even with 20:20 hindsight, it is far from obvious what the Europeans

FIGURE 9-6

Patchwork Prosperity
GDP per head in EC regions, 1990 (PPP basis) EC=100*

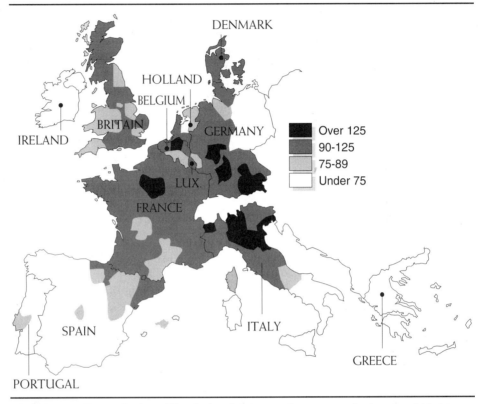

■	Over 125
▓	90-125
▒	75-89
□	Under 75

*Excludes new German *Länder* and East Berlin, the overseas departments, the Azores and Madeira.
Source: Eurostat.

should have done. It is not true to say they did nothing. They provided mediators and monitors, imposed sanctions, sent several thousand troops to distribute humanitarian aid. Tragically, none of this remotely matched the scale of events.

The experience has punctured some overblown Euro-rhetoric and brought a number of lessons in post-cold-war reality. First, any big military action still needs the Americans. A common European defense is a long way off. The Europeans have neither the military structure nor the unity of purpose for such a thing. "There is nothing more serious than deciding who gets killed," says a senior American diplomat. "Europe is not mature enough yet."

Second, the German giant remains a defense dwarf, and no tinkering with supposed constitutional inhibitions on taking part in non-NATO operations will change that in a hurry. Post-1945 reeducation has worked, argues one who experienced it: "We Germans do things thoroughly—total war or total peace." Other Europeans may secretly prefer it that way. What they saw as German near-hysteria over Croatia warmed up some old doubts about the reliability of their neighbor.

Hence the third lesson: France and Britain have a lot in common when it comes to instincts and capabilities in foreign policy and defense. They were the only two serious western players in Bosnia. This has led to a significant rapprochement.

The British note that France is moving discreetly closer to NATO—not all the way into the alliance's military structure, but to a relationship like Spain's with participation in the defense and military-planning committees. In planning for Bosnia, France has been flexible in finding politically correct formulae that would allow French troops to take part in actions commanded by NATO generals. French paranoia over NATO is diminishing with the size of the American forces in Europe. It is keen to keep an American presence, not least to avoid being left alone with Germany, and it has hopes of a "more balanced" alliance, with a stronger European voice.

The French, for their part, note that as Britain realizes France has no wish to break NATO it will be readier to develop a European defense structure through the Western European Union. The British, say policy-makers in Paris, must have learnt from Bosnia that there is no longer anything automatic about American involvement in Europe's conflicts; so the Europeans need a capacity to act on their own if necessary. The British themselves admit to being "slightly warmer" about the idea of a European defense identity, so long as this does not reduce the American presence. In short, thinking on both sides of the Channel in evolving. The basis for a stronger Franco-British alliance is there.

That would not amount to a strong Europe. Yugoslavia has shown that, willy-nilly, the Community will be drawn in to the game of foreign policy, and possibly defense too. How is it to become more effective? Majority-voting might work on minor issues, but not on the really sensitive ones. How would Germany have responded to being outvoted on Croatia? Until they can find realistic answers to such questions, the Europeans had better hope that the Americans stay around.

Maybe Yugoslavia was an unfair test. The EC was not designed to cope with such a crisis. But on the other big test on the security front—the integration of ex-communist Europe—the Community has the wherewithal to rise to the occasion. As its leaders half-recognized at their Copenhagen summit last month, it has so far failed to do so.

WELCOME TO CAPITALISM

The best way to underpin democracy in Eastern Europe (discounting ill-defined French proposals for a pan-European "initiative") is to offer open trade and the prospect of EC membership. On trade, there is a great gap between the Community's rhetoric and what it is offering. On membership, it has preferred to set conditions than talk about dates.

The principle behind the Community's approach to trade with East European countries—enshrined in a series of bilateral treaties known as Europe Agreements—is that liberalization should be asymmetrical. The rich West Europeans (who do only 3% of their trade with those easterners) should open their markets more rapidly than the East Europeans (who rely on the Community for more than half their trade). In practice, asymmetry has not been enough to prevent roughly balanced trade in 1990 turning into a surplus of 2.5 billion ecus ($3.2 billion) last year.

The Europe Agreements, which some EC countries have yet to ratify, set out a timetable for phasing in free trade in industrial goods. The trouble is that the agreements are toughest where the East Europeans are most competitive. Trade in steel and textiles is subject to "safeguard measures" to protect EC producers against surges in imports. The agreements restrain the growth of EC farm imports.

The Community, bowing to pressure from its producers lobbies, has not been slow to deploy its protectionist arsenal of special quotas, tariffs, anti-dumping duties and health regulations. When the Czechs and Slovaks became too successful at selling steel, the EC clamped down. In April it slapped a month-long ban on the import of meat and dairy products because of an outbreak of foot-and-mouth disease in ex-Yugoslavia, which is not involved in the Europe Agreements; there were no proven cases of the disease in the relevant East European countries (but there was one in Italy).

To their credit, EC politicians have now accepted proposals by the commission for a slightly more rapid opening. But that is only a small step in the right direction. Especially in a recession, everyone has worries about going faster: the French on food imports, the Spanish on steel, the Portuguese on textiles. Even countries with loud free-trade rhetoric (such as Germany) play the protectionist game when it comes to details (such as steel).

The irony is that it is in the Community's own interest to open up. Yes, some of its industries would suffer. Opening up to Polish and Hungarian agriculture would bust the common agricultural policy. But consumers would benefit from cheaper prices and overall the effect would be to hasten a necessary restructuring of production throughout Europe. The best thing the Community could do, according to an expert at the commission, would be to drop controls on sensitive products and give aid for restructuring to EC areas hardest hit by the new competition. Jacques Attali, the president of the European Bank for Reconstruction and Development, advocates a treaty for a continent-wide common market, a sort of European version of the North American Free Trade Agreement (with the Community as the United States, EFTA as Canada and Eastern Europe as Mexico).

Politically, the EC's interest in opening up is even greater. The young democracies in the East are still fragile. They look to the West for security—from Russia, from their local Milosevics, from the effects of an economic transition which makes the EC's recession look like a luxury (the East Europeans' GDP has shrunk by about a fifth over the past two years). As disillusionment with the West grows, so does the risk of yet more instability on the Community's doorstep.

It is not enough to tell East European governments, as the Community has done, that they really must meet more often. A clear timetable for eventual EC membership is needed. The Community could have opted to offer the East Europeans "transition in": that is, early membership with an adjustment period stretching over many years. Instead it has opted for "transition out": adjustment first, membership later ("decades" later, if it was up to President Miterrand).

The cautious approach comes not only from worries about the economic implications (the Czech Republic and Slovenia might slot in easily, but poorer, 40m-strong Poland is another matter). Caution also comes from worries about the institutional implications. How will a much-enlarged Community work? If France has its way, the current entry negotiations with Austria, Finland, Norway and Sweden will provide some answers.

UPSIZING

Here is an unstaggering prediction: the current entry negotiations with four EFTA countries will take longer than scheduled. The talks, which began in February, are meant to be finished this year, to be followed by ratification (after referendums) in 1994 and the entry of the new members in 1995. That timetable is almost bound to slip. What could cause more of a surprise is the possible length and bitterness of the delay.

This batch of applicants should in theory be easier to bring in than any previous (or future) lot. They are rich and fairly small, with a combined population of 26m, so they pose no special trade or financial problems for the Community's existing 345m people. They have already accepted most of the *acquis communautaire,* the body of Community law, through the previous negotiation of a European Economic Area (EEA).

Yet even some of the subjects covered by the EEA are proving sticky. Austria had 12 years to adjust to EC laws on the transit of trucks; should it have so long once it becomes a member? Some sensitive matters have to be sorted out: Norway's right on fish and oil, the Nordic alcohol monopolies, farm subsidies. The question of budget contributions, which the commission estimates might total 3 billion ecus ($3.6 billion) net for all four, is always delicate. Talks about the Maastricht additions can begin only when that treaty is ratified; the four newcomers are supposed to accept a version free of opt-outs. Their voters may object.

The eventual referendums will be no pushover. Norway got that close once before, in 1972, only to vote No. Opinion polls this time are again running against membership.

However, the biggest hitch could come before that. The formal position is that this round of enlargement can take place without any reform of the Community's institutions; there would merely be technical adjustments to allow for more commissioners, Euro-MPS and the extra votes in the Council of Ministers. Bigger changes will wait until the 1996 inter-governmental conference. Mr. Major is keen on this arrangement, because he believes, rightly or wrongly, that the more members are in, the merrier Britain will find the next round of reforms. He says it is "pivotal" to the way he sees the EC's future to have the newcomers in "before any further consideration is given to institutional change in the Community."

The French government thinks it is pivotal to consider institutional change first. Its position has hardened on this. The French will not necessarily insist on formal changes before the EFTA countries come in, but they want at least a clear idea in advance of how, say, a 20-member Community would work. They say they have "no reason to accelerate negotiations."

On the surface, this toughness is about ensuring that a larger Community continues to function effectively. Underneath, it is all about power. France wants to make sure that in a Community with more members it keeps a maximum amount of clout.

And it knows it has the maximum amount of leverage before the EFTA lot come in. The queue beyond includes Malta, Cyprus, Turkey and (technically, though its application is on hold) Switzerland, apart from the East Europeans who have yet to apply formally. The worry for big countries—including Britain, if Mr. Major thinks harder about it—is that they will lose out badly if such applicants get in without a reform of the existing rules.

1996 AND ALL THAT

The later stages of the current negotiations could therefore turn into a warm-up for the review conference scheduled (assuming Maastricht is ratified) for 1996. The plot for that conference turns on two conflicts: one between big countries and small, the other between supranationalists and inter-governmentalists. Governments hoping to influence the outcome ought to be sorting out their ideas well in advance on the main issues. These are:

- **The Council of Ministers.** The current voting arrangements give disproportionate weight to small countries (see the table entitled "Ins and Outs"). Germany has ten votes, one for every 8m people; Luxembourg has two votes, one for every 190,000 people. If

Ins and Outs

In the Club			In the Queu†			In the Distance		
	PEOPLE M	COUNCIL VOTES*		PEOPLE M	POTENTIAL VOTES‡		PEOPLE M	POTENTIAL VOTES
Germany	79.8	10	Austria	7.8	5	Albania	3.1	3
Britain	57.6	10	Finland	5.0	5	Bulgaria**	8.6	5
Italy	57.1	10	Norway	4.3	3	Czech Rep**	10.4	5
France	57.1	10	Sweden	8.6	5	Estonia	1.6	3
Spain	39.0	8	Switzerland	6.8	5	Hungary**	10.3	5
Holland	15.1	5	Cyprus	0.7	2	Latvia	2.7	3
Greece	10.3	5	Malta	0.4	2	Lithuania	3.7	3
Belgium	10.0	5	Turkey	57.7	10	Poland**	38.3	8
Portugal	9.8	5				Romania**	23.2	6
Denmark	5.2	3				Slovakia**	5.2	3
Ireland	3.5	3				Slovenia	2.0	3
Luxembourg	0.4	2						

*It currently takes 54 votes out of 76 to pass a law by "qualified majority."

†Applied to join the Community.

‡Estimated, under extension of existing rules.

**Countries with "Europe agreements" with the EC.

votes continued to be distributed along the same principles, then in a 20-member Community coutries with a fifth of the population could have half the votes. One possible solution might be a "double majority" rule: a decision would pass only if it was supported by a majority of members and it those members represented a majority of the EC's population.

Something will also have to be done about the council's rotating presidency. Otherwise a future Yugoslav-scale crisis could find the Community in the middle of an alphabetical succession of minnows (...Kypros, Latvija, Liechtenstein, Lietuva, Luxembourg, Magyarorszag, Malta...). If small countries took turns with one of the big five, then there would always be a big country on the *troika* of previous, current and next presidents.

- **The European Commission**. It is already too big, with 17 members when there are real jobs for only about ten. Countries will have to abandon the automatic right to a commissioner (or to two commissioners, in the case of the big countries).

  Small countries want to defend the commission's power. Big countries want to check it, though they disagree over how. Federalist Germany wants the European Parliament to do that job; inter-governmentalist France and Britain prefer to rely on the Council of Ministers.

- **Democracy**. Everyone agrees there is not enough of it about. But how to narrow the deficit?

  Because of the Maastricht backlash, France, Germany and others are improving their national parliaments' (hitherto cursory) scrutiny of proposed EC laws. Next, several countries want to clarify the relationship between national parliaments and the European Parliament. The European Parliament was a winner at Maasricht, gaining the right to vote on the appointment of the commission, as well as veto powers over some laws.

Federalists like Germany think the answer to the democratic deficit lies with granting the European Parliament much more power. Britain and France think true legitimacy rests with elected governments, acting through the Council of Ministers. If this survey is right that more "variable geometry" is on the way, that is bad news for the parliament. As Britain's opt-out from Maastricht's social chapter has shown, opt-out territory is awkward for a parliament containing deputies from all EC countries. "Variable geometry" thus favors the council, which can adapt to it more easily.

The trouble is that ordinary citizens know little about the council. Despite the occasional recent intrusion of television cameras, it works largely behind closed doors, aided by the "secret government of Europe," as a member calls the Committee of Permanent Representatives (alias Coreper) in Brussels. Open sessions of the council, acting like an upper chamber of parliament, would be an answer, if governments could only be persuaded to give up the secrecy they like so much.

- **Foreign and security policy.** More effectiveness here is a priority for both France and Germany—a formidable alliance if they can agree on the means. In the Maastricht treaty, foreign policy is an inter-governmental show. Germany would like it to be more *communautaire.* Its ideas include: a commissioner elected by the European Parliament to be the EC's foreign-policy spokesman; any foreign-policy action to be voted on, just as there is voting on economic matters; a small EC military force (say, 20,000-30,000 men), financed from the Community's budget, for use by the United Nations.

France may prefer to keep things strictly inter-governmental. Britain certainly will.

- **Immigration, drugs, crime.** Another inter-governmental area under Maastricht, with decisions taken unanimously. Another German priority for majority voting.
- **Subsidiarity.** This is the idea that the Community should get involved in rule-making only when strictly necessary. Since Maastricht, proposed laws have had to be accompanied by an explanation of why legislation is necessary at the EC level. That condition seems to have had something of a deterrent effect. Even the commission, which is usually blamed for petty EC interference, is keen on subsidiarity. It says that it wants to concentrate on doing a few important things effectively (and blames governments for lobbying for a lot of the petty rules, to protect special interests). Several governments would like to be more specific about subsidiarity than Maastricht's murky form of words.
- **Languages.** The Community uses nine at the moment, which is already costly and unwieldy. With enlargement, the need to rationlize down to three or four becomes overwhelming.

At the end of all amending and adjusting, what sort of creature will governments have created? Will it work? Will it remotely correspond to the needs of the sort of place Europe is becoming?

INSTITUTIONAL OVERSTRETCH

"We hope to see a Europe where men of every country will think as much of being European as of belonging to their native land." Thus Winston Churchill in 1947.

A lot has happened in the half-century since then to move Europeans at least a few steps in that direction. Their economies have become more and more integrated, they travel far more to each other's countries, they have similar social trends that throw up problems common to all (such as an ageing population and a rise in single mothers). The development of the European Community itself has led to an intensive circulation of elites—including perhaps 10,000 assorted EC meetings a year—and a focus for the idea of Europeanism.

Today Churchill would see widespread use of the European flag—at least if he travelled to the continent, using his European Community passport—and observe diplomats mediating on behalf of all the European Community in ex-Yugoslavia. This summer he could even root for Europe against America in Ryder Cup golf. He would no doubt marvel at the changing perceptions of his own countrymen: back in 1969, 21% told MORI's pollsters that Europe was most important to Britain, compared with 34% saying America and another 34% the Commonwealth; in 1993, 57% said Europe.

What he would not find, however, is many people who had transferred to Europe their principal sense of identity, be that French, British, Bavarian, Basque, Scottish, Walloon or whatever. Nationalism remains potent in Europe's West as well as in the East. "Put crudely," wrote Kelvin MacKenzie, the editor of the tabloid Sun and flagwaver for the British version of fundamentalist nationalism, "the British have nothing in common with the Greeks, just as the Portuguese have nothing in common with the Danes." Hardly Churchillian, but he presumably reflects the views of many of his 10m readers. The sense of Europeanness, not just in Britain, is weak. Only two out of five people in the Community, says a recent Eurobarometer poll, would be "very sorry" (as opposed to indifferent or relieved) if the EC were scrapped.

Maastricht has shown that there is no such thing as "the European debate." There were 12 European debates, conducted in the national political framework that still dominates the newspapers Europeans read or the television they watch. The Gulf war and then, more painfully, Bosnia have proved how hard it remains to come up with a definition of "the European national interest."

In the absence of a developed sense of "European nationalism," the idea that the Community could in the foreseeable future become a United States of Europe is far-fetched. It is nonetheless a force in the world: with a bigger population and economy, and more people in uniform than the United States (see Figure 9-7). It acts collectively on trade, albeit with internal arguments. But in foreign affairs and defense, despite huge potential collective clout (not least from the British and French nuclear arsenals), the sum of the Community's effectiveness can seem smaller than that of some of its parts. Add together its economic, political and military weight, and you have at best three-quarters of a superpower.

A troubled one, too. If powerful nations can suffer from "imperial overstretch," the Community is in danger of suffering from something just as serious: institutional overstretch.

Tugging at the Community's structures is the prospect of extending them to more countries. Pushing towards more and more supranationalism are growing demands in politics and increasing interdependence in economics, maybe leading all the way to a single currency. Pulling in an opposite direction are great differences in how the various members perceive the European venture.

In responding to this, the Community is becoming a bit more flexible (hence "variable geometry") and inexorably more complicated (hence the Maastlicht Treaty). Too much rigidity, and for some members at least, the disadvantages of togetherness in the Community may start to outweigh the advantages. Too much flexibility, and the coherence of the club could be destroyed.

The Community's great strength up to now has been its ability to find a way of living with such conflicting pressures. It has built block by block on the Treaty of Rome, through innumerable compromises and the retention of enough ambiguity to allow all members to

FIGURE 9-7

Supereurope?

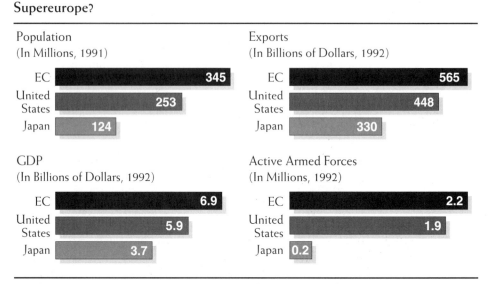

Population
(In Millions, 1991)

EC 345
United States 253
Japan 124

Exports
(In Billions of Dollars, 1992)

EC 565
United States 448
Japan 330

GDP
(In Billions of Dollars, 1992)

EC 6.9
United States 5.9
Japan 3.7

Active Armed Forces
(In Millions, 1992)

EC 2.2
United States 1.9
Japan 0.2

*Exports to the rest of the world.

Source: OECD; International Institute for Strategic Studies; Eurostat.

keep the construction work going while having wildly different ideas about what its eventual shape might be. The question for the 1990s is whether this incremental approach will remain viable—whether institutions originally designed for a six-member group in a divided Europe might not collapse under the weight of new additions and new demands.

Maybe the Community's original design is so ingenious that it proves almost infinitely adaptable. The likelihood is, though, that the jumble of law called the *acquis communautaire* needs at the very least a drastic simplification, to become more comprehensible to ordinary Europeans. Even that may prove insufficient. If so, the Community will need a complete redesign. It would be time to replace the existing treaty with a new constitution.

The European Union: Family Frictions

JOHN ANDREWS

It is easy to caricature the European Union: a dozen countries squabbling over subsidies, 18,000 Brussels bureaucrats quarreling over perks and 567 Strasbourg parliamentarians moaning about their relative lack of power and fame. Meanwhile, even as economies switch from recession to recovery, a tenth of the EU's workers remain without jobs. No wonder that in June's elections for the European Parliament, the turn-out (despite compulsory voting in three EU countries) was barely 56%. An opinion poll this summer suggested that only one in two Europeans thought their countries had benefited from EU membership. A cynic might well ask: if this union did not exist, would anyone bother to invent it?

Actually, yes. There are perfectly sound reasons for Europe's nations to join together. As a Belgian prime minister, Théo Lefévre, once pointed out in a cutting reference to fading imperial powers: "In Western Europe there are now only small countries—those that know it and those that don't know it yet." Some 31 years later that argument for collective strength applies just as much to the countries of Central and Eastern Europe, freed from communism and now queuing up to join the EU.

Why, then, the caricature? One reason is cultural: the free-trading British and some others mistrust the expensive interventionism of the agricultural and regional policies of the European Union (as the European Community declared itself to be when members signed the Maastricht Treaty in 1992). A union in which some contribute much more than others, and receive much less in return, seems wrong to them. A second reason is popular bewilderment. If politicians stumble over the arithmetic of "qualified-majority voting" and the "blocking minority," and if Eurocrats have trouble working out the minutiae of the common agricultural policy, what chance has the man on the Paris metro? It is easier to lampoon than to understand.

But the biggest reason is that Europe's leaders promised what they could not deliver. The "single market," with the economy-boosting free flow of capital, goods, people and services, opened on January 1 last year, only to coincide with the worst recession since the 1930s. The "common foreign and security policy," launched by the Maastricht Treaty, was mocked

The Economist (October 22, 1994).

by Bosnian blood shed on the EU's doorstep. And the Maastricht journey towards "economic and monetary union" (EMU, in the EU's acronymic jargon for the achievement of a single European currency) was abruptly sidetracked—not least by high German interest rates, which-made Europe's economic troubles worse. Add the painful process by which the German parliament, the last to act among the 12 national parliaments, ratified the Maastricht Treaty in October last year, and even the most gung-ho Euro-enthusiasts feel somewhat abashed.

Perhaps that is why the quarrels over Europe's post-Maastricht future are becoming so ugly, two years ahead of a special intergovernmental conference on the subject. There is talk of a two-tier European Union, of "concentric circles" of commitment, of multi-tracks and multi-speeds, of some countries "being more equal than others." Is this grand endeavor doomed to disintegrate under the strains of its own diverging ambitions?

Such questions would be less troubling if Europe felt more confident. After the dismal recession of the early 1990s, most EU economies are rebounding. France and Germany, for example, are having to double the cautious growth predictions for 1994 that they made in January. Yet still the gloom lingers. The main reason for this is that recovery is shortening dole queues by barely a smidgen (see Figure 10-1); and half of the queues consist of people jobless for more than a year.

When that dismal record is compared with the job-creating records of America and Japan, even the most arrogant Eurocrat or government minister must worry about the future. Last December the European Commission (the EU's executive) issued a special report on growth, competitiveness and employment. This quickly provoked responses from virtually every government and industrial lobby. But there is no miracle cure for Europe's joblessness short of thinning the welfare cushion that makes unemployment preferable to many sorts of work. The unemployed might then price themselves into some

FIGURE 10-1

Doleful: EU Unemployment Rate

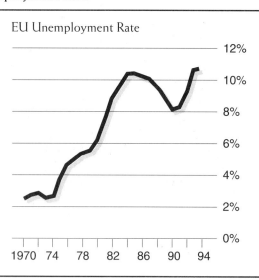

Source: OECD.

kind of job. And even this hard-headed logic can work only up to a point. Already, Europe's big cities are scarred by ghettoes of the unemployed, uneducated and disaffected—an "underclass-in-waiting," the politicians fear, if Europe deflates the welfare cushion too far and too fast.

Just as there is no miracle cure, perhaps there is no painless one either. Europeans take for granted a quality of life that many others might envy (see Figure 10-2). GDP per head is generally higher in America and Japan, but few Europeans believe that America's extra purchasing power makes up for its horrendous murder rate, or that Japan's is adequate compensation for what Sir Roy Denman, a now-retired Eurocrat, once described as "living in rabbit hutches." What sensible Parisian or Roman office worker would envy his job-insecure counterpart in crime-ridden Washington, DC, or the exhausted *sarariman* making his daily two-hour commute to central Tokyo?

The question is how to sustain Europe's quality of life. Unfortunately for the German car worker, with his six weeks' holiday a year, or the disabled Belgian who receives benefits equal to 97% of the average industrial wage, many trends in productivity, unemployment, debt and demography are working against their interests.

A JOB-DESTROYING MACHINE

Margaret Thatcher will never find a place in a pantheon of the EU's champions. That will be reserved for "true Europeans," such as Messrs Monnet, Adenauer, De Gasperi, Delors, Kohl and Mitterrand. The Iron Lady may have impressed with her intelligence (Jacques Delors, president of the European Commission, admits his admiration for Britain's prime minister of the 1980s), but she dismayed with her handbag-waving pursuit of narrowly defined national interests. If she is happy to be rid of Brussels (the derisive shorthand for the EU's affairs and institutions), the feeling is reciprocated.

Even so, future historians may yet place Lady Thatcher on an EU honor roll. After all, it was she who insisted on counting every ecu that went into and out of the community's budget, so highlighting which countries were net contributors and which net beneficiaries.

FIGURE 10-2

Indicators of Quality of Life, Latest

	EU	UNITED STATES	JAPAN
GDP per head, $	17,978	24,601	33,908
Total education expenditure, as % of GDP	5.3	7.0	5.0
Working hours per year	1,771	1,945	2,017
Unemployment benefits, as % of government spending	3.3	1.5	0.7
Life expectancy, years	76.3	75.6	78.6
TVs, per 100 people	44	81	62
Homicides, by males, per 100,000 males	1.6	12.4	0.9

Source: UN; IMD; World Economic Forum.

Moreover, it was her Micawberish determination to balance Britain's own books and lessen the role of the state that spawned privatization programs across the whole of the union and beyond. Even the dirigiste French now sometimes praise market forces and the reduction of government spending as though they mean it. Much of the Thatcherite message has become Europe's conventional wisdom.

But in the end Europe would have got the message even without Mrs. Thatcher. The countries of Europe are, quite simply, living beyond their means. Social benefits, from family allowances and unemployment assistance to sickness pay and old age pensions, are paid for by taxation and corporate earnings. If tax rates are too high, corporate earnings could fall and workers be laid off, meaning that tax revenues would flag or even fall—so tax rates would have to rise even higher. Individuals can try to escape from this vicious circle through the black economy: let no taxman benefit from bargains struck between willing householders and willing window-cleaners. Employers can seek refuge by laying off workers or moving their businesses to a friendlier country.

The escape route of governments, however, is to borrow, and this produces a second vicious circle of tax revenues being used to service the public debt instead of to build roads, hospitals and schools. When the Maastricht Treaty set out the route towards a single currency, one of the signposts was that a country's gross public debt should not exceed 60% of its GDP. Belgium's level last year was almost 150%; Greece's almost 110%; Italy's almost 120%. Those numbers are signs not so much of recent recession but of prolonged irresponsibility. The governments of all three countries are having to make annual interest payments on their debt equivalent to at least a tenth of their GDP (see Figure 10-3).

To escape through borrowing is a mere illusion and the longer it is indulged the more damaging it becomes. Any Cassandra can see that over time a country's interest rates will have to rise, its infrastructure will deteriorate—and its quality of life will gradually decline. Is that to be Europe's fate?

The real escape would be to find ways of helping Europe's jobless back to work. As the social costs of unemployment fell, tax revenues would rise and tax rates could fall, and happy employers would make bigger profits and so bigger investments. That virtuous circle, however, is hard to create.

TO THWART CASSANDRA

One reason is that governments have to live with the mistakes of their predecessors. In Italy those predecessors—a succession of venal, Christian Democrat-dominated coalitions—handed out state pension-rights like confetti. Italy's pensioners (almost a quarter of them claiming disability pensions) now soak up two-fifths of government spending. If the government of Silvio Berlusconi is to fulfill its promise to cut both debt and tax, it must reduce spending on pensions and on other aspects of a generous welfare state. Yet Mr. Berlusconi was told in June by the Constitutional Court that he could not renege on $19 billion-worth of unpaid state pensions. And because Italy has the world's lowest fertility rate, the number of pensioners will grow faster than the number of workers whose efforts support them.

Italy's problems are bad but not unique. Statutory charges on labor—that is, the sum of taxes and obligatory social-security contributions—now account for around two-fifths of the EU's GDP. In 1970, they took just over a third. By comparison, the proportion in America has remained stable at just below 30%, and in Japan it has risen from just under 20% to just over 30%. One reason for the proportional increase in Europe is that economic growth has slowed. But—welcome to another vicious circle—

FIGURE 10-3
Rich Man's Burden

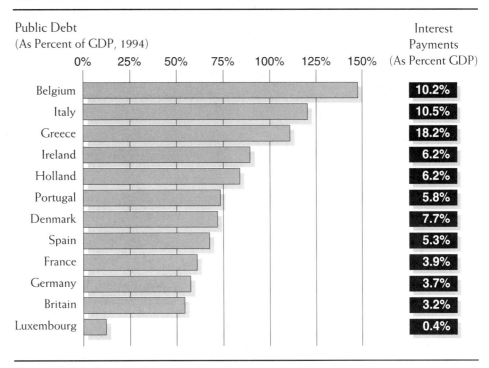

Public Debt (As Percent of GDP, 1994) — Interest Payments (As Percent GDP)

Country	Interest Payments (As Percent GDP)
Belgium	10.2%
Italy	10.5%
Greece	18.2%
Ireland	6.2%
Holland	6.2%
Portugal	5.8%
Denmark	7.7%
Spain	5.3%
France	3.9%
Germany	3.7%
Britain	3.2%
Luxembourg	0.4%

Source: OECD; European Commission.

a cause of that slowdown has in turn been the burden on employment and wealth creation of the statutory charges. Businessmen are deterred from investing and hiring by the extra cost.

Changes in the demographic profile will make the burden still heavier. At the moment every 100 European workers are supporting almost 40 retired people; in ten years' time, unless unemployment falls dramatically, this grey pressure on the workforce will rise, to almost 50 pensioners per 100 workers. No wonder EU governments are trying to stabilize or cut back on statutory charges as a proportion of GDP, for example by raising retirement ages (as in Italy) or by changing the rules (as in Britain) for inflation-linked pensions or by encouraging greater reliance on private pensions.

ENTER DELORS

All of which is expressed in admirable detail in that special report on growth, competitiveness and employment—commonly known as "the Delors white paper"—which was laid before last December's Brussels summit of Europe's heads of government, and portentously subtitled "the challenges and ways forward into the 21st century."

The stark conclusion of the white paper and other reports is that Europe's taxes, social obligations and rising real wages—plus the high interest rates that resulted from the cost of German unification—have combined to stretch public finances, reduce corporate profits,

FIGURE 10-4

Making Work

European Union
— Employment   ▬ Unemployment

United States
— Employment   ▬ Unemployment

1970=100

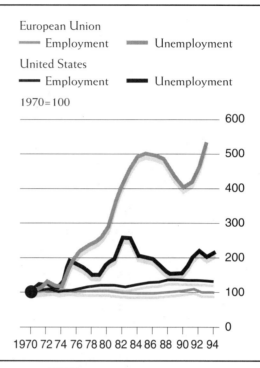

Source: European Commission; OECD.

constrain investment and inhibit the creation of jobs. Comparisons with America and Japan reveal a Europe that is singularly bad at creating employment even when its economies are booming. Over the past three decades, as America was adding to its store of jobs at a rate of 1.8% a year, the countries of the EU were managing an annual average growth of just 0.24%. In the past two decades America has created 30m private sector jobs, Europe just over 10m (see Figure 10-4).

Even in the second half of the 1980's, a boom period when Europe had recovered from the oil shocks of the 1970s and was investing for the impending "single market," the number of jobs rose by only 1.3% a year. That meant that even though Europe created 9m new jobs (mostly in the public sector), its unemployment rate fell from its 1985 peak of 10.8% to a still dismal 8.3% in 1990. Today the EU is back on that nasty peak with around 18m people, more than a tenth of the workforce, looking (at least in theory) for jobs. By contrast, America's jobless rate is about 6% and Japan's 3%.

You might conclude that Europe has a lot to learn from both America and Japan. Yet it is understandably reluctant to imitate what it sees. Japan has a culture of life-time employment (now eroding) and a willingness to accept wafer-thin profit margins and tiny share dividends. For its part, America's capitalism is too raw for most European stomachs. Whereas article 2 of the Maastricht Treaty specifically calls for "a high level of employment and of social protection," the American model combines a high level of employment with a low level of social protection. The result is that an American in the bottom tenth of the workforce earns less than two-fifths of median pay; his European counterpart earns more than two-thirds.

Britain's Conservative government may find inspiration in the American way—on the grounds that a low-paid job is better than no job at all—but the EU's other governments tend to shudder. Continental Europeans cherish the concept of "solidarity," the notion, held by Socialists and Christian Democrats alike, that people have a moral duty to help each other. To them, the American way smacks of an unnecessary drive to "align our costs on those of our competitors in the developing countries: socially unacceptable and politically untenable," in the words of the white paper.

What, then, is the remedy? The white paper's prescription mixes a dose of Adam Smith, a touch of Colbert and a hint of central planning. Let there be deregulated labor markets, lower taxes on labor and less profligate social spending—but also government-encouraged research into areas of high technology and a government-commanded infrastructure policy to create "trans-European networks" (TENs) of motorways, railways, energy pipelines and telecommunications links. Let there also, in order simultaneously to make up for the lost taxes on labor and to protect the environment, be new taxes on energy use.

MIX AND MATCH

Whether such a cocktail can be swallowed in one go is perhaps irrelevant. The point is that it contains at least one ingredient for every taste. The British will savor the stress on deregulation, the French the emphasis on high-speed railways, businessmen the stress on telecommunicating "superhighways," and so on. Politically, Mr. Delors's white paper is superbly adroit, not least in the way that it preserves a strong role—in coordinating the TENS, for example—for the European Commission.

That may sound somewhat snide. But the sneers will increase if the financial arithmetic goes astray. The white paper talks of financing needs that amount to 400 billion ecus ($492 billion) over the next 15 years, including by the end of this century 200 billion ecus for transport projects and 30 billion ecus for energy networks. Mr. Delors argues that such amounts can be raised easily, since much of the money is already there in the spending plans of member countries, and the private sector will happily provide the lion's share of what is not. But the figures are large enough to alarm the EU's finance ministers—who have vetoed Mr. Delors's plan for the commission to issue "Union bonds" (a clever ploy to increase the Commission's power) to help pay for the TENS. As for the private sector, the example of building a tunnel between England and France is one that will persuade most companies to proceed with caution.

It is possible to cavil at many bits of the white paper. Europe's industrialists, for example, reckoning that their energy bills are already on average 33% higher than in America, are particularly upset by the proposed energy taxes. But if the union is to, fulfill the potential of its single market, it needs to make a bigger collective investment in infrastructure. The finance ministers may worry, but Mr. Delors is adept at outflanking them. In June, at their summit in Corfu, the union's heads of government turned visionary and approved an early start for the first 11 transport projects, and an urgent examination of nine "priority" energy schemes. The challenge now is for Europe's industrialists and businessmen to seize the opportunity.

A QUESTION OF CULTURE

Carving gracefully through the dazzling sky of south-west France, an Airbus A340 is put through its paces. On the tarmac, other aircraft, slim A320S and bulky A310S, glisten in their fresh airline liveries, newly rolled out from the hangars that contain yet more airframes in various states of completion. The spirit of corporate pride at Airbus's Toulouse head-quarters is almost tangible: Airbus aircraft are glamorous symbols of effective European co-operation in high technology.

The feeling is much the same thousands of miles away on America's Pacific coast: a new Boeing 777 climbs on its test flight high above Seattle; the 747s—the original jumbo-jets—roll profitably off the Everett assembly line; and the workforce applauds yet more examples of America's high-tech superiority. And the passengers for these aircraft? Whether they fly in a Boeing or an Airbus, few will notice any difference.

If they are European taxpayers, perhaps they should. Airbus is constituted under French law as a *Groupement d'Intéret Economique*, which means that its accounts are available only to its four shareholders: France's state-owned Aérospatiale and Germany's Deutsche Aerospace Airbus (each with a 37.9% holding); privatized British Aerospace (20%); and Spain's state-owned CASA (4.2%). Whereas Boeing's profitability is a matter of public record ($1.2 billion net profit last year on revenues of $25.4 billion), Airbus's is invisible, hidden in the books of its shareholders. How, then, does one judge the success of Europe's best-known high-technology consortium?

By the amount of its subsidies, say Boeing folk, whose guesstimates start at $26 billion. By the excellence of the products and their share of the market, counters the team in Toulouse, adding that Boeing has enjoyed subsidies of its own from defense-contracting and federal research projects.

Both sides have a point. Since its first airliner entered service 20 years ago, Airbus has gained 30% of the market, compared with Boeing's 60%; in the next decade Airbus hopes to win a 50% share. Given that Boeing is America's single biggest exporter and that 80% of Airbus sales are beyond the national boundaries of its shareholders, the argument is a constant irritant in transatlantic relations—the Americans and Europeans are, indeed, still quarreling over a subsidies agreement concluded two years ago.

Over time, the subsidies issue may fade. Airbus is making profits on its A320 and may well do so on other models, too. Moreover, aerospace is a murky and incestuous world:probably half of any Airbus by value will go to contractors and engine makers in America, and they can lobby Washington as much as Boeing can. The real issue is whether Airbus's progress has been worth the taxpayers' investment. Lady Thatcher always had her doubts— but in the end her government, like its predecessor, stumped up the necessary "launch aid." By contrast,the Germans had rather fewer misgivings, and the French and Spanish none at all.

Some will say the difference is yet another example of Anglo-Saxon perversity, forgetting that Lady Thatcher's predecessors, both Labor and Conservative, were often very willing to pour the state's money into industrial ventures. In fact, the difference was doctrinal: Thatcherism decreed that governments had no business picking industrial winners—not least because, the Airbus example notwithstanding, they usually picked losers.

That Thatcherite dogma was surely right. The sectors in which Europe leads or matches the rest of the world—pharmaceuticals, retailing, fashion, recorded music—are precisely those in which governments have interfered least. Where they have interfered most, they have usually failed. Look at Europe's history of loss-making state-owned airlines and steel companies, or at Groupe Bull, France's struggling, state-controlled computer maker. Some inefficient state companies, such as Belgium's telephone utility, have made profits—but only by being monopolies. And some state companies, such as France Télécom, have given good service—but at prices which would have been too high in a free market.

Perhaps the dogma is a mite simplistic: some transport economists argue that the heavily subsidized French rail system is a much better deal for French taxpayers than the lightly subsidized British system is for British ones. Meanwhile, Airbus apologists will argue that it is a special case: aerospace is a business with lots of high-tech spin-offs, plenty of "value-added," and significant for defense.

Maybe. But it is worth remembering that aerospace sales are smaller than those of, say, cigarettes. In order to prosper, Europe needs to compete across the board, and grow new firms and industries. Ron Woodard, president of Boeing's Commercial Airplane Group, notes that the net worth of Bill Gates's Microsoft, a software company that did not even exist 20 years ago, is bigger than Boeing's, and yet "you could put all their assets in one of our parking lots."

It is a good point. Europe's real problem is that it has no Microsoft's, even though European brains are presumably as good as American ones, and its schools are arguably better. Why is Palo Alto in California crammed with the "start-up" companies that may provide tomorrow's Microsoft or Intel, while France's Sophia Antipolis science park, nestling in pine-clad hills just above the Cote d'Azur, is still struggling after 25 years to produce a home-grown Apple alongside such foreign residents as AT&T and Digital Equipment Corporation?

The answer is not an absence of raw material. Europe is full of small and medium-sized enterprises, ie, those with fewer than 500 employees. The European Commission reckons they provide 70% of EU jobs, including 29% provided by firms with fewer than ten employees. In the computer business there are almost 6,000 small companies. Yet somehow it is hard to see them sprouting rapidly to become the size of Microsoft, Apple or Compaq.

As for Europe's bigger computer companies, such as Italy's Olivetti and Germany's Siemens Nixdorf, they are having a hard time adjusting to a slowing market. As one EU official publication delicately puts it: "The key weakness in Europe seems to lie in its inability to integrate research, development and innovation in an overall strategy which both exploits and orients them." That sentence could have been written for Philips of Holland—a brilliant innovator of electronic gadgets which others, notably the Japanese, have then gone on to exploit more successfully.

THE WRONG MOOD

The explanation for this mismatch of talent and commercial success lies in a mix of history, geography and culture. For all its size, America has a common language and a well-defined view of the way the world should work. The "American dream" inspires New Yorkers in the same way as Los Angelenos. If you fail with one American start-up, then you move on to another. By contrast, the EU is a patchwork of individual nations, with different cultural values from one another—if your European start-up fails, don't bother to try again—and mutually incomprehensible languages (nine official ones at the moment, with more to come).

One result is that while a Californian whizz-kid, of whom there are many, will face few obstacles in selling to Floridians, his Danish equivalent, a rare species, will have real problems in selling to Italians. And despite a wave of privatizations, the age of national champions in Europe is not quite over: France seems obsessed with keeping Groupe Bull alive; Italy protects private-sector Fiat by limiting Japanese car imports; almost every government, except the holier-than-thou British (who privatized British Airways a decade ago), protects and subsidizes its flag-carrying airline.

If the European Union lived up to its political rhetoric, none of this would be happening. State aids would be disappearing; national borders would no longer equal market borders; and Europe's inherent creativity would be inspiring entrepreneurs by the thousand. Unfortunately, rhetoric and reality have yet to coincide.

A SINGULAR MARKET

Free movement for Europe's workers, goods, services and money—if there is one thing that squabbling Europeans can always agree on it is the importance of the "single market." And rightly so. A union that has internal frontiers is both a contradiction in terms and, since more trade creates more wealth, an economic opportunity forgone.

Hence a lingering mood of celebration. From January 1 last year, Europe's internal barriers (but for a few "temporary" exceptions) have disappeared: Spanish truck drivers who once needed 70 forms to cross a frontier can now truck oranges to Holland unhindered by customs officers and border police; German banks can open branches in Italy; Greek students can attend Danish universities as of right. From January 1 this year these same freedoms of the EU's single market have been extended to Austria, Finland, Iceland, Norway and Sweden to form the European Economic Area (add EEA to the list of acronyms). The result is a market more populous than America's, more valuable than China's.

Fine, except that it has all taken so long; that the freedoms are not fully exploited; and that so many in the union still try to limit the market's potential.

The four freedoms of the single market are part of the 1957 Treaty of Rome, establishing what was then called the European Economic Community, with its "common market." Unhappily there remained an uncommon number of differing technical standards, incompatible taxes and laws, close relationships between governments and their national companies: even without tariffs and quotas, protectionism still flourished at the ultimate expense of consumers.

The desire to end that protectionism is enshrined in the Single European Act, agreed in 1985 "with the aim of progressively establishing the internal market" over a period expiring at the end of 1992. The momentum owed much to the determination and vision of Jacques Delors, newly arrived as commission president; but also to the nit picking efficiency of Lord Cockfield, a British commissioner who listed and relentlessly pursued 300 actions (later consolidated into 282 pieces of legislation) that had to be accomplished by member governments to establish a single market.

Has it all paid off? Up to a point, certainly. Intra-EU trade as a proportion of all EU countries' trade has risen from just over half in 1985 to around three-fifths today: take in the whole of the EEA and the proportion rises to more than two-thirds. German students now escape overcrowded lecture halls at home by attending universities in Britain; north European pensioners retire in the sunny south. Only Britain, Ireland and—at least for the moment—Denmark still insist on frontier checks on EU visitors. Cross-frontier mergers and acquisitions (a simple way of exploiting the single market) rose from 2,190 in 1987 to 4,553 in 1992.

Yet the single market has fallen disappointingly short of its original expectations. In 1988 one lot of experts convened by the European Commission was predicting that the single market in its first five or six years would lower the EU's prices by 6%, create 2m new jobs, increase output by 4.5% and "put Europe on an upward trajectory of economic growth into the next century." There is still time for this body, the Cecchini committee, to be proved right; but in the single market's first year the EU's GDP shrank by 0.3% and its unemployment rose to 10.5% of the workforce. Meanwhile, some of the best business users of Europe's single market have been non-Europeans—Japan's car makers and electronics companies, for example, or a whole swathe of Americans, selling everything from IBM computers to McDonalds hamburgers.

The disappointment should not really be a surprise. For Europe's smaller companies the barriers of different languages and legal systems remain daunting. So, too, does the amount of paperwork. Customs formalities may have disappeared for truck drivers. But until 1997, when value-added tax on goods is supposed to be charged in their country of origin rather than, as now, in the country of final sale, the paperwork of VAT charges and VAT refunds remains a nightmare. And in the absence of a single currency there are still exchange-rate risks in venturing from home. Whatever the potential of an unfamiliar pan-European market, many a small company is bound to prefer to opt for the comfort of a familiar national one.

That choice is unavailable to non-Europeans, some of whom had started seeing Europe as a single market long before Mr. Delors arrived in Brussels. Ford of Europe, for example, was created by joining Ford's British and German subsidiaries as long ago as 1967 (when De Gaulle was still resolutely blocking Britain's membership of the European Community). But enthusiasm on a large scale came in the late 1980s when foreign firms could suddenly foresee a Europe free of national protectionism. Japan's direct investments in Europe amounted between 1970 and 1984 to $8.8 billion; from 1985 to 1993, they totaled $74.6 billion (see Figure 10-5).

FIGURE 10-5
Confidence Vote

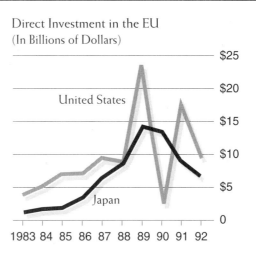

Direct Investment in the EU
(In Billions of Dollars)

Source: OECD.

About two-fifths of those Japanese investments went to Britain: a Nissan factory in the north of England, a Toyota one in Derbyshire, a Sony plant in Wales. Why Britain? In a survey this year by the Japan Institute for Overseas Investment, by far the main reason given by the investors themselves was the English language, better understood by Japanese managers than any other European language and familiar also from Japanese plants in America. Yet some Europeans cite another reason—Britain's willingness, with financial incentives for foreign investors, to be the "Trojan horse" by means of which Europe's rivals will invade its fortress.

UNFAIR COMPETITION

This accusation, with its implicit nationalism, illustrates the greatest problem for the single market: the readiness of member governments to conspire against their own creation.

At one level, this conspiracy consists of agreed delays in the single market: no free trade in insurance until July this year; none in investment services until January 1996; no compulsion to liberalize basic telephone services until 1998 (and up to five years later in poorer countries, so as to protect utilities such as Greece's from being crushed by the likes of Britain's BT or America's AT&T).

At another level, there are convenient parliamentary delays. Of the 282 measures needed to create the single market, some 222 have to be "transposed" into legislation in the member countries. The commission may boast that 87% of the necessary national laws have been passed, but only half of the 222 measures have been passed by all 12 member states. While the Danes and British have been the most active legislators, the Greeks, French, Spanish, and Irish have been rather slower. The delays could, of course, be innocent. But cynics note that the worst ones are in public procurement where by the end of 1993 only 59% of required national laws had been passed; company law (60%); intellectual and industrial property, such as designs, inventions and databases (61%); and insurance (73%).

Delays of this sort cost taxpayers dear: in public procurement, for example, which was worth some 595 billion ecus in 1990, the last year for which figures are available, the Cecchini report calculated that open competition could be saving member countries some 21 billion ecus a year. And yet the non-national share of contracts is stuck at 5% in public services and even less in public works. Worse still, few unsuccessful bidders complain, for fear that they would be ignored in future bids.

But the greatest insult to a free and single market remains the use of state aid. Provided it does not distort competition, this is allowed by the Treaty of Rome but it is perennially open to abuse—witness the loss-making survival of national airlines and state-owned makers of steel, ships and cars. What makes the abuse all the easier is that the treaty in effect condones the existence of state monopolies: telecommunications, postal services, energy and transport are all "reserved sectors."

Even in cases where monopolies have been legislated away, the market can be manipulated. From the beginning of last year Europe's airlines have been free to fly where, when and at what prices they want, save only for "cabotage" (the right to fly domestic routes in a foreign country)—and even that restriction will be gone by April 1997; theoretically, therefore, Europe's skies are now as free and competitive as America's. And yet governments protect their national carriers both by restricting foreign airlines' access to their airports and by pressing the European Commission to approve yet more state aid for airlines that in a free market would go out of business. It is a form of blackmail: if the subsidies are not approved, then thousands will be made redundant, governments will be under pressure and life will be made very uncomfortable for independent-minded commissioners.

With suitable promises to restructure the airline so that it will supposedly never need another subsidy, the blackmail usually works. In July the commission approved $7.1 billion in state aid to Air France, TAP of Portugal and Olympic of Greece. Herman De Croo, head of a committee that had advised the commission to be stricter with subsidies and link them explicitly to privatization, reckons that commission approval since August 1991 has added up to $10.35 billion in airline subsidies— "roughly $10m a day." Against this background, advocates of a single, free-trading European market may be tempted to despair.

They should not, for three reasons. The first is that state sectors, and therefore state subsidies, are getting smaller and will get smaller still—if only because privatization and budgetary discipline can hardly be avoided by governments attempting to meet the Maastricht treaty's criteria for economic and monetary union. The second is that rules for the single market are decided not by unanimity among Europe's governments, but by qualified-majority voting—so the illiberal will find it harder to defy the liberal, assuming the liberal are in a majority. The third is that market forces, once unleashed, are hard to resist. Assume success for commission plans to liberalize telecommunications and postal services and introduce competition into energy markets, and Europe as a giant zone of truly free trade will finally have arrived. The European Union's challenge, however, is to make itself into something rather bigger than that.

HISTORY MATTERS

Almost 50 years ago, the snow-covered hills of the Belgian Ardennes were stained with blood. In 34 days of siege and counter-siege, some 100,000 German soldiers, 80,000 Americans, and 1,500 Britons and Canadians were killed or wounded during the "Battle of the Bulge."

Today the Ardennes are tranquil. Villages once occupied by Germany's troops are now invaded by its weekend tourists. Europe's "low countries"— Holland, Belgium and Luxembourg—may traditionally have been a battleground of bigger powers, but today those powers are joined in solid peace. It seems inconceivable that Germany, France, Britain and Italy might ever again be at war. Preventing war was a main aim of the EU's founding fathers. Jean Monnet, a French civil servant, and Robert Schuman, France's foreign minister, did not want to foster a common market for its own sake but to bind Germany into a peaceful Europe.

Their first step was the creation of the European Coal and Steel Community. France had been worried that Germany would use the coal and steel industries of the Saarland to help regain economic strength and again dominate Europe. Monnet's solution was to put the development of the coal and steel industries of both West Germany and France under a single High Authority. When Schuman launched the plan in 1950 he declared: "The solidarity between the two countries established by joint production will show that a war between France and Germany becomes not only unthinkable but materially impossible." That sounded good not just to Germany's Konrad Adenauer but also to the governments of Belgium, Luxembourg, Holland and Italy: a year later, in April 1951, the six countries formally established the ECSC.

Six years later the same six signed the Treaty of Rome, establishing the European Economic Community (EEC), and a separate treaty setting up Euratom—the European Atomic Energy Community. In July 1967 the administration of the three bodies merged to form a single body, later to be known as the European Community, of six founder members. The British, Danes and Irish joined in 1973; the Greeks in 1981; and Spain and Portugal not until 1986.

Why these delays? Fascism in Spain and Portugal and military rule in Greece disqualified the southern Europeans from a club for democracies. For other peripheral Europeans there was the rival European Free Trade Association (EFTA), set up in 1960 at Britain's urging and embracing Austria, Denmark, Norway, Sweden, Switzerland and Portugal. And Britain, still with global ambitions, was bound to be ambivalent towards the ideas of Monnet and Schuman. Churchill had called in September 1946 for "a kind of United States of Europe," but immediately made it clear that Britain should not be a part of such an enterprise.

By 1961 Britain was realizing that the EEC was a bigger, and therefore better, bet for trade than one-year-old EFTA. Harold Macmillan sent in Britain's application, soon to be followed by those of Ireland, Denmark and Norway. All failed. De Gaulle, deciding that Britain was more interested in its special relationship with America than in any future relationship with continental Europe, vetoed Britain's bid—and so the other applicants withdrew too. Only when De Gaulle was gone did the French attitude change. The applications went in again, and an EC summit in 1969 agreed to consider new members. The bids succeeded, but the Norwegians, in a referendum in September 1972, decided they did not want to join the club after all.

Past Imperfect, Future Unknown

History may or may not repeat itself—the Norwegians, having this spring negotiated another treaty of accession, will hold a second referendum on November 28—but it always leaves its mark. Last month Germany's Christian Democratic Union the party of Chancellor Kohl, released an intriguing paper on the EU's future entitled "Reflections on European Policy." One of its propositions was that there exists a "hard core" in the union, consisting of the founder members minus Italy, and that "Germany and France form the core of the hard core."

Some member states, not least Italy, have reacted angrily. Britain's prime minister, John Major has talked in Orwellian tones of some countries wanting to be "more equal than others." Yet the CDU paper merely restates the insight of Monnet and reflects the original impulse behind the union namely that Germany needs to be integrated into a European economic and political structure both for its own sake and for that of its neighbors.

Another fact of history is the persistent nationalism of France. In June 1965, when France found itself alone in opposing some commission proposals on budgetary powers and the common agricultural policy, De Gaulle ordered a French boycott— the "empty chair" policy— of the community's ministerial meetings. Seven months later the five other members agreed to yield to France in what has become known as "the Luxembourg compromise": in decisions taken by majority voting, where "very important interests of one or more partners are at stake," the ministers will "within a reasonable time" try to reach unanimity. In other words, if it feels strongly enough, any nation has a veto.

This is a problem. Many Europeans are prepared to surrender big elements of sovereignty to embrace a federal Europe. But France and Britain continue to believe strongly in the primacy of the nation-state. France's tactics in l965 were echoed in the French attitude towards the GATT trade negotiations in 1993. The French insisted on a special place for their own narrowly defined national interests, and once again pushed their EU colleagues where the latter had not intended to go. Likewise John Major refused last June to accept Belgium's Jean-Luc Dehaene as the man to succeed Mr. Delors as commission president, later acquiescing to Luxembourg's Jacques Santer instead.

PERFIDIOUS ALBION

Britain's "problem" is that it has been a stable democracy for several centuries; has not been invaded for almost a thousand years; admits to losing no war in popular memory; and has never been subject to totalitarian rule. Since that makes Britain quite unlike fellow EU members, present or future, it is perhaps not surprising that Britain has so often been Europe's odd-man-out. Two decades after joining the EC, many British people still feel a relationship with America more special than the one they have with continental Europe.

Whether that is sensible is increasingly doubtful. It makes British attitudes within Europe, even when reasonable enough by British lights, seem either selfish or treacherous. By contrast, French pursuit of national interests, even when awkward for others, is tolerated because nobody questions France's European credentials. The natural consequence is that France is at the EU's "core" and Britain is not. Such self-willed exclusion, most marked over economic and monetary union and social policy, is bound to weaken Britain's influence.

Besides, America itself is adjusting its view of Europe. Asia's surging economies are continuing to shift America's geopolitical gaze from the Atlantic to the Pacific, and, with the cold war over, the need for American troops in Europe is less compelling. Their numbers have fallen from 300,000 to 150,000, and will soon reach 100,000. From America's perspective it is time for the Europeans to shoulder more of the burden of their own security.

On three visits to Europe this year President Clinton has stressed America's support for a bigger, and closer, European Union. In Paris he called for Americans and Europeans alike to set their sights "on a strategic star ... the integration and strengthening of a broader Europe." Monnet himself could not have wished for more florid phrasing.

Mr. Clinton's words are music to French ears. France has always wanted Europe to be as independent as possible of America. In De Gaulle's days that wish found expression in France's independent nuclear deterrent and a decision in 1966 (now being quietly reversed) not to be part of NATO'S command structure. Today France is enthusiastic about the "Eurocorps," the plan for an EU force of more than 40,000 troops announced three years ago by President Mitterrand and Chancellor Kohl (again, the core of the hard core). So far the Eurocorps has only 7,000 troops, drawn mainly from France and Germany but with Belgium, Luxembourg and Spain also involved.

One French politician, going against the grain, recently disparaged the corps as "but a symbol, if not an illusion." The British would agree with him, both because they distrust symbols and because they fear any development that might weaken the North Atlantic alliance. Just as France has resented America's leadership, Britain has cherished it.

THE BIGGER THE BETTER?

Yet in Mr. Clinton's message to Europe there is something for everyone. Consider his speech in Brussels: "The new security must be found in Europe's integration—an integration

FIGURE 10-6

Legend:
- ■ EU Countries
- ▨ Membership Agreed
- ▨ Already Applied
- ▨ Application Expected
- ✓ "Partners for Peace"
- ✗ NATO

of security forces, of market economies, of national democracies. The purpose of my trip to Europe is to help lead the movement to that integration and to assure you that America will be a strong partner in it."

Like the British and the Germans, the Americans see a need for Western Europe to embrace Eastern and Central Europe. Only thus, it is argued, can democracy and capitalism—and with them the European Union's eastern flank—be made secure in the ex-communist countries. But finding the right form for such an embrace is far from simple, as attempts to attach the new democracies to the NATO military alliance have recently shown.

Many Central and Eastern Europeans saw membership of NATO as their best security haven. But NATO foresaw logistical difficulties. More importantly, it was afraid of provoking the Russians. So a compromise has been put in place. This is the PFP, the "partnership for peace," a half-way house of military co-operation with NATO that is open to any supposedly well-intentioned, democratic country in Europe. There are now over 20 partners, from Albania to Uzbekistan, with Russia itself signing the PFP framework document on June 22.

This is at best an imperfect answer to the security problems of PFP signatories. The NATO alliance is based on the idea that an attack on one of its members is an attack on all. The PFP agreement, on the other hand, obliges NATO merely to "consult" with a partner under threat. If Russia were to send its army back into Latvia, or to decide to topple the government of Kazakhstan, NATO would not necessarily intervene.

As in defense, so in the economic sphere. For all the lip service it pays to the new democracies, Western Europe continues to put its own narrow interests first. The EU has celebrated the collapse of communism by concluding trade agreements with a crescent of former Soviet block countries, from the Baltic to the Black Sea. In Copenhagen in June 1993 the leaders of the EU went a step further: they recognized that "Europe Agreements" with Poland, Hungary, the Czech Republic, Slovakia, Romania and Bulgaria would be a stage towards their "ultimate goal" of full EU membership. A year later, in Corfu, the same leaders welcomed President Boris Yeltsin and signed a "Partnership and Co-operation Agreement" with Russia.

This is, says the EU, a genuine offer of help and friendship. The EU will offer the six countries with Europe Agreements free trade in industrial goods from next year, in steel from 1996 and in textiles from 1997. Russia will be treated not as a "state trading country" but as an "economy in transition" subject to no discrimination (most-favored-nation status); and in 1998 talks will start on the possible establishment of a free-trade area.

Is this realistic? The comparative advantages of the former communist countries are all-too-often in industries in which the EU is trying to preserve its own uncompetitive firms. Anti-dumping duties imposed on iron pipes from Hungary and Poland, and quotas on steel from Russia, are evidence of that. And the changing balance of trade between the EU and the six countries with Europe Agreements suggests that the EU maybe the bigger beneficiary. In 1989 the union had a deficit with its poor eastern neighbors of 600m ecus; by last year the deficit had turned into a surplus for the EU of 5.6 billion ecus, including, thanks to the subsidized exports of the common agricultural policy, 433m ecus in farm products.

All this suggests that the economies of these six countries may be too weak for any rapid accession to the European Union. Once in, moreover, they would become huge beneficiaries of a union budget that spends half its money on the common agricultural policy and much of the rest on the development aid known as "structural funds," were that structure to remain intact.

An American academic, Richard Baldwin, calculates that the 64m inhabitants of Poland, Hungary, the Czech Republic and Slovakia (the so called "Visegrad Four," which are far in advance of Romania and Bulgaria) are only 30% as rich as the EU average and far more reliant on agriculture. They would probably remain the poorest of the EU poor for at least two decades. Mr. Baldwin argues that to admit the Visegrad Four would mean either an increase in contributions to the budget of around 60%—or a severe cut in EU spending.

Some might think the price well worth paying; as a portion of collective GDP the EU's budget remains tiny. Others would welcome the chance to reform the budget.

But any enlargement of the union is bound to threaten the main beneficiaries of the present budget arrangements—notably farmers throughout the union and the four big recipients of development funds: Spain, Ireland, Portugal and Greece. They would object strongly to any newcomer grabbing a slice of the cake at their expense. Since the EU can take in new members only by unanimity, what will become of the grand vision of a bigger, better European Union?

1996 AND ALL THAT

Variable geometry, multi-track, multi-speed, two-tier, hard core, concentric circles, *à la carte*, deepening, widening . . . More than ever, Europe's politicians are mixing their metaphors.

The confusion stems from the part of the Maastricht Treaty that calls for a conference of member states in 1996 "to examine those provisions of this Treaty for which revision is provided, in accordance with the objectives set out in Articles A and B." Those objectives are economic and monetary union, "ultimately including a single currency"; a common foreign and security policy, "which might in time lead to a common defense"; and "close cooperation on justice and home affairs."

These are big ambitions. The job of the 1996 intergovernmental conference is to correct any mistakes the Maastricht drafters may have made in the "process of creating an ever closer union among the peoples of Europe." Since there are some profound disagreements over what this union should mean the 1996 debate could be extremely lively.

Why then has it started prematurely? The best explanation is that Germany, which now holds the six-month rotating presidency of the union, has a vision of an expanding, federalist Europe for which it feels that national electorates, and fellow governments, need to be prepared. After all, one lesson of the Maastricht process—shown by the wafer-thin referendum majority in France in 1992 and the need for Denmark to hold a second referendum in 1993—is that Europe's leaders can easily misread the public mood. Even those who do not share Germany's vision will concede that some kind of EU reform is inevitable.

AGE LIMITS

As presently constituted, the EU can barely cope with the present, let alone the future. Bear in mind that this is a club of unequals. Member states range from unified Germany, with 80m people, to tiny Luxembourg with a mere 395,000. They range in wealth from Denmark, with a GDP per head of over 21,000 ecus, to Greece, with about 7,500 ecus. Now look at three main institutions.

The commission is a body of permanent civil servants-and government appointees which administers EU business and proposes and drafts legislation. The Council of Ministers, attended by appropriate government ministers from the member countries, is the EU's legislature, the only one in the democratic world which normally deliberates in secret. The European Parliament, which holds its committee meetings in Brussels but its plenary sessions in Strasbourg, is the one EU body directly elected by the union's citizens and yet has few of the powers of any national parliament and counts for less than either the council or the commission.

This structure was designed for a club of six, and it has just about coped with the doubling to 12. But how can it deal, the rule-book unchanged, with a club that in the next two decades could expand to a membership of a score or more?

The bigger the club, the tougher it will be to maintain an acceptable balance between large countries and small. Of the six founding members, France, West Germany and Italy had big populations; Holland, Belgium and Luxembourg small ones. Today the big members have been joined by Britain, with Spain close behind, and the small countries have been bolstered by Ireland, Denmark, Greece and Portugal. Harmony of sorts is maintained by a system of checks and balances: big countries have more votes in the Council of Ministers so that they cannot be out-voted by a gaggle of small ones. In turn, small countries are protected by a system of weighted voting. Of the council's 76 votes, 54 are currently needed to form a "qualified," or decisive, majority—and only 23 are therefore needed to form a blocking minority.

So far, so good. The present arithmetic means that the big five, with 48 votes between them and representing four-fifths of the union's population, can muster qualified majority only if they gain the support of at least two small states. Similarly, to get their way the small states need the backing of three big states. Conversely, two big countries can form a blocking minority if they can get the support of any small country other than Luxembourg. Roughly speaking, a qualified majority normally represents 70% of the EU's people, a blocking minority 30%.

The problem is the future. From January 1 the EU is supposed to grow, by four more countries, to 6 members. Extend the arithmetic and the qualified majority will go up to 64 votes out of 90 (see Figure 10-7); and the blocking minority to 27. By John Major's pocket calculator that means that Britain, Germany and Holland, a liberal economic group, would be unable to form a blocking minority against illiberal nonsense even though they would represent over 40% of the union's population. By contrast, eight small countries could gang together and get 27 votes even though they represent only 2% of the European Union's people.

Viewing this as an unacceptable shift in the union's balance, Britain threatened until last March to hold up the accession treaties with the applicant countries. Then a compromise was reached: if two big countries wanting to block a decision could not gather the 27 votes needed, fellow members would try for a "reasonable" period to reach a compromise acceptable to them.

The British have a point—it is already bizarre that Germany should have only one council vote for every 8m people while Luxembourg has one for every 198,000—and the point will grow more obvious if tiddlers such as Malta and Cyprus join the union. But, in practice, council meetings tend to be bazaar-like bargaining sessions in which calculators are seldom needed. Of some 233 single-market decisions taken in the five years to last December only 91 actually went to a vote. The implicit message of Britain's obduracy was that it is more important to be able to block legislation than to pass it.

Is such an attitude sustainable in an expanding union? True followers of Monnet would say that no minority should be allowed to paralyze the European process. The concept of majority voting was in the original Treaty of Rome and was put into effect for all legislation affecting the single market. The aim must surely be to increase the scope for majority voting, not to go backwards towards more of the unanimity still needed for such areas as taxation and foreign policy—and for the revision of the treaties and the acceptance of new members.

FIGURE 10-7
Little and Large

1994	POPULATION EST. M	VOTES IN COUNCIL
Germany	81.6	10
Britain	58.2	10
Italy	58.1	10
France	58.0	10
Spain	39.2	8
Holland	15.4	5
Greece	10.5	5
Belgium	10.1	5
Portugal	9.4	5
Sweden	8.8	4
Austria	8.0	4
Denmark	5.2	3
Finland	5.1	3
Norway	4.3	3
Ireland	3.6	3
Luxembourg	0.4	2

Source: European Commission; OECD.

On the other hand, no club can be happy if some members are constantly overruled, especially if it is a club of conflicting interests and rival cultures. And that it surely is. Some members, such as Germany, Holland, Denmark and Britain, instinctively believe in free trade and open markets; others, such as France and Spain, mistrust market forces that they cannot influence. Some, notably Germany and Britain, put into the communal budget far more than they get out, while others, especially Greece, Ireland, Spain and Portugal, do the reverse (see Figure 10-8). There are plenty of what John Major once called "fault lines" to threaten the union's solidity.

SPEED LIMITS

Up to now the union has tried to finesse such differences. That is why the Maastricht Treaty deals with the single market, economic affairs and trade relations as communal matters to be supervised by the commission, but decrees that a common foreign and security policy, along with justice and home affairs, are matters to be settled between governments. This enables France and Britain, the two countries with lingering imperial responsibilities and also the will, tradition and—just about—the means to project military

FIGURE 10-8
Winners and Losers

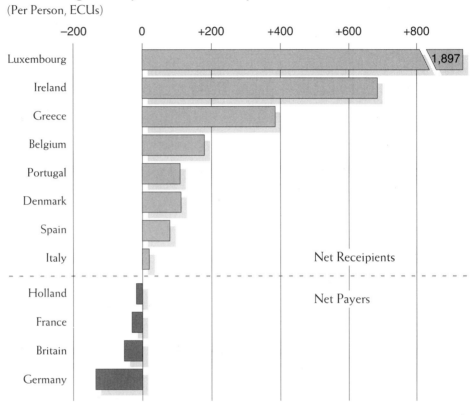

1992 EU Budget Net Payments and Net Receipts
(Per Person, ECUs)

Source: Royal Institute of International Affairs.

force around the world, to keep control of their foreign interests. Similarly Germany, which is particularly sensitive about immigration, can more easily ignore the liberal attitudes of the commission and the parliament.

Yet it is unlikely that intergovernmentalism, the practice of leaving tricky decisions-for agreement among individual member governments, can provide a perfect solution. René Foch, secretary-general of a lobbying group, the *Comité d'Action pour l'Europe,* argues that there are at least three weaknesses. One is inefficiency: since 1985 nine EU states—all except Britain, Ireland and Denmark— have signed the Schengen agreement to abolish all passport checks and other obstacles to the free movement within the EU of its citizens. And yet they have still not fully implemented the agreement. By contrast, the single market, achieved on a community basis and by qualified-majority voting, is up and (mainly) running.

The second failing is that intergovernmentalism can increase the "democratic deficit"—the extent to which EU affairs are decided outside the direct control of elected representatives. Mr. Foch cites the example of Europol, the body set up this year to foster co-operation among the union's police forces: it is specifically excluded by the Maastricht Treaty from supervision by the parliament and the European Court, but in reality is also beyond the supervision of national parliaments.

Lastly, intergovernmentalism does not fill in any fault lines, it merely papers them over. The theory is that all participants in intergovernmental organizations are equal—but the practice, from the United Nations down, is that some are more equal than others and a few may be dominant. As the EU expands, so the inequities will tend to worsen. "However democratic the new Germany may be," says Mr. Foch, "its sheer size and position in the heart of Europe would inexorably lead it—without seeking any such role and even against its will—to dominate a merely intergovernmental Europe."

Mrs. Thatcher's answer to that problem was to declare that only the military and political engagement of the United States in Europe, and close relations between the other two strongest sovereign states in the region—Britain and France—could balance German power. She went on to argue that no such balancing arrangements could be achieved within a European super-state. That, however, depends on how you design your super-state.

PICK THE METAPHOR

There are two kinds of design problem here. The first concerns the structure of the institutions. There are now 17 commissioners (two each for the five big countries, one each for the small ones), whose pronouncements have to be translated into nine official languages. If the union grows to 16 members on January 1 there will be 21 commissioners and 12 official languages (the Austrians speak German, which is already an official EU tongue); parliament will increase from 567 to 641 members; the European Court of Justice from 13 judges to 17.

And so it goes on … but not indefinitely. Before the union gets bigger still there will have to be a decision at the 1996 conference to have either a smaller commission, or one in which some commissioners are junior to others. Big countries, for example, could have one commissioner each; small countries could take turns to have a commissioner.

That will cause quarrels enough. So will the question of voting arrangements within an expanding Council of Ministers. In August 1993 Karl Lamers, the CDU's parliamentary spokesman on foreign affairs, suggested that successful votes should require a "double majority": a majority of member states representing also a majority of the EU's population. Votes that now need to be unanimous could in future be made by a "super-qualified" majority: say four-fifths, or three-quarters, of the member states representing four-fifths or three-quarters of the union's people.

But the worst quarrels could concern the parliament, not least because—at the urging of Chancellor Kohl—parliament's representatives are to help prepare the 1996 conference. Having won extra powers from the Maastricht Treaty (it can, for example veto much legislation and its approval is needed for the appointment of the commission and its president), the parliament will want still more. But only Germany and the Benelux countries are keen to transfer any more power to the parliament; France and Britain are firmly against.

Europe's institutions, however, are simply the means to an end. The real problem is the end itself, that "ever closer union among the peoples of Europe." Can the union become "ever closer" while it is also getting bigger—can "deepening coincide with "broadening"? Germany and the Benelux countries, true followers of Monnet, believe so almost as an act of principle. Pragmatic Britain, as ever, is skeptical.

Since Chancellor Kohl says that the EU convoy must not be forced to travel at the pace of the slowest ship, the solution will inevitably be some kind of agreement to disagree. There are good precedents: the Maastricht Treaty allows Britain to "opt out" both from the goal of a single currency and from the EU's commitment to enhance its "social policy"; Denmark has excused itself likewise from the single currency and, in an agreement after the treaty, from provisions on defense, foreign and judicial policies and European citizenship.

The question is how far there precedents can be taken before the club loses its sense of identity. That is what others object to in the British desire for an *"à la carte* approach": member states would sign up only to the policies they like—in other words, there could be lots of broadening but no need to deepen. Better, say France and Germany, to take the same path but let some proceed faster than others.

In May, in an article coinciding with a Franco-German summit in Mulhouse, Alain Lamassoure, the French minister for European affairs, called for a "new founding contract" by which a core group of EU members—including France and Germany— would commit themselves to some basics: economic and monetary union, a common defense policy (including Eurocorps), immigration control and co-operation on police matters. Any country not wishing to sign up to these areas would lose the right to vote on them.

Now add Mr. Lamassoure's article to the CDU's "reflections" and to remarks by his prime minister, Edouard Balladur, made just before the CDU paper. Mr. Balladur talked of an inner circle building a monetary and military union for themselves; other EU members, including new ones, could co-operate on foreign policy, security and trade; a third circle, embracing all of Europe, would co-operate still more loosely on diplomacy and trade. You do not have to be a conspiracy theorist—nor even John Major—to see a Europe which Antonio Martino, Italy's foreign minister, fears will be a Europe of "two speeds" and divisively "variable geometry."

But is there a better alternative? It is true that the: inner core might grow increasingly distant from the outer—and poorer—circles. Over time, the inner core might also be less prepared to foot the bill for the development funds that help the others. But the French and the Germans make one thing clear: any country—even Britain—is very welcome to join the inner core. Provided, that is, it believes in an "ever closer" Europe.

MIXED EXPECTATIONS

"First we must modernize France," said Jean Monnet to Walt Rostow, an American economist, in 1947. "Without a vital France there can be no Europe. Then we must unite Western Europe. When Western Europe unites and gathers its strength, it will draw in Eastern Europe. And this great East-West Europe rope will be of consequence and a force for peace in the world."

Monnet's dream has had its troubles—De Gaulle's chauvinism in the 1960s, the oil shocks of the 1970s, the anguish over the Maastricht Treaty, and then more recently economic recession and the humiliation (Jacques Delors's word) of Bosnia. Yet the dream is still intact: France is rich, the cold war is over, Germany is united. Whatever the latent truth of the caricature at the start of this survey, no country wants to leave the European Union; and plenty are waiting to join, attracted by its economic mass and its implicit promise of security in what, for Central and Eastern Europe, is a worryingly uncertain world.

Indeed, the attraction grows stronger with every report of the EU's resurgent economies. Even the timetable for economic and monetary union, dismissed as a pipe-dream during last year's exchange rate crisis, is beginning to look more feasible. True, a majority of EU members will not have fulfilled the necessary criteria of economic convergence to allow the creation of a single currency by 1997. But it looks as if France, Germany, the Benelux countries (with a little rule-tweaking for Belgium's public debt), and perhaps Ireland could yet form a single currency block by the second date envisaged in the treaty timetable of January 1, 1999. The EU would then have its inner core in place—and at least part of its single market would have the efficiency of a single currency.

Even so, it would be foolish to pretend that all is well. On January 5 Jacques Delors is due to step down, having proved himself the most dynamic president the commission has ever had. In his ten years in office, he has brought about—against all the odds—the single market, the Maastricht Treaty, and massive development aid (the structural and "cohesion" funds) for the EU's poorer regions and countries. All that leaves the new president, the unassuming, Luxembourgeois Mr. Santer, with a hard act to follow, not least because the parliament— which only grudgingly endorsed him—is determined to weaken the commission's powers. Assume some bitter wrangling for the 1996 conference (which will probably endure well into 1997 in order to leapfrog a British general election), and it is easy to see how Europe's self-confidence, slowly returning, could quickly fade.

THINK POSITIVE

Yet it need not. For all the liabilities of its social costs and lack of entrepreneurs, the EU has plenty of assets: for example, a well-educated workforce (although more investment is needed in education, especially in vocational training), good engineering skills, and a tradition of expertise in advanced technologies. But it can no longer take these advantages for granted, unless it modernizes economically. Even the biggest advocates of social "solidarity" and "cohesion" (the principle of using subsidies to promote development and so narrow economic divisions) talk now of deregulation and open markets; of the need to promote overall economic efficiency rather than pick winners; of the need to introduce cross-border competition into energy and telecoms.

True, some might be tempted to slip into old habits, but such backsliding has become more difficult: the Edinburgh summit of 1992, while approving more money for development, also checked agriculture as a proportion of the EU's budget. The GATT agreement, coming into force next year, will lower the EU's external tariffs and require cuts of 21% by volume and 36% by value of the EU's subsidized farm exports. Add GATT to the Europe Agreements with the union's eastern neighbors, and it will become increasingly hard for the EU to indulge its latent protectionism (although, amazingly, it recently penalized the garlic growers of Vietnam).

Unhappily, as the exemptions and delays to the single market show, deregulation is more easily preached than practiced—especially when so many Europeans associate America's job-creating deregulation with excessive inequality, and even crime. They have a point, but without a big jump in European productivity not much of an answer. If Europe makes that jump, it will be able to afford its life-style. If not, there can be only a gradual decline.

Whether it can be graceful is another matter. Too many in Europe, from factory workers to politicians, act as though the good times will inevitably return for those who wait. They should remember the economists' cliché that no lunch is free. The greatest problem for Europe today may not be unemployment but complacency.

PART III

Enlargement of the European Union

Germany: A Survey of the Economist

JOHN PARKER

HALF-HIDDEN AGENDA

Germany is the Mercedes s-class of countries, the largest and most luxurious model from the most dependable of producers. Three years after its introduction in 1991, the s-class had to be redesigned. Four years after unification, the German model itself is in need of change.

Like the s-class, it is too heavy and expensive. It is over-engineered. Nimbleness is not one of its virtues. But it is not just the design that is at fault: unification has altered its surroundings out of all recognition. Suddenly, the smooth autobahn has ended: the roads are crooked: the signposts are faded. Germany is an s-class hit side-on by a Trabant, dented piece of engineering perfectionism stuck on a dirt track going the wrong way.

Yet it is a Mercedes still—still the apotheosis of the well-ordered. And before considering its design problems, it is right to recall its successes, partly because they are so striking; partly because people want to copy them (Robert Reich, America's labor secretary, is a warm admirer); and partly because they are a source of strength that should make change easier.

Since the end of the second world war, Germany's success has been hardly less extraordinary than that of Japan, its ally in defeat. At *Stunde Null* (Zero Hour) in 1945, the daily ration for German civilians in the Allied zones of occupation was 700 calories—well below the minimum needed for proper health. Industry was in ruins. So was the political system: the country was sliced in two.

Now, Germany is richer than Japan (see Figure 11-1). It is not the richest of countries. But its "misery index"—inflation and unemployment combined—was for most years preceding unification the second lowest of any big, rich country, after Japan. Investment remains high as a share of GDP. Money has poured into public infrastructure.

Thanks to this, Germany is hard to beat for the unquantifiable benefits that make a country pleasant to live in. Its cities boast pedestrian precincts. Sleek autobahns and clean railways make it easy to get around; inter-city trains have on-board computers telling you how many minutes to go until the next stop. If you are ill, the treatment, courtesy of the social-insurance system, is among the best in the world; if you are unemployed, the benefits

The Economist (May 21, 1994).

FIGURE 11-1
Richer than Most

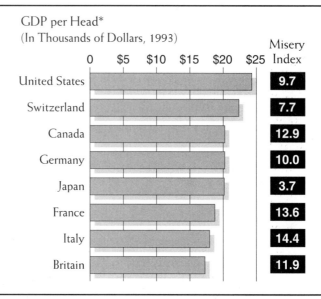

GDP per Head*
(In Thousands of Dollars, 1993)   Misery Index

Country	Misery Index
United States	9.7
Switzerland	7.7
Canada	12.9
Germany	10.0
Japan	3.7
France	13.6
Italy	14.4
Britain	11.9

*At purchasing power parities.
†Inflation plus unemployment.
Source: OECD.

among the most generous. If you are employed, the benefits are even better: high wages, long holidays and often lifetime employment. And beyond the utilitarian, German cities vie to support the best opera-houses and museums, producing a musical and artistic infrastructure unsurpassed anywhere.

The traditional explanation for Germany's economic success—"a more regimented national character," as Lady Thatcher put it in her memoirs—cannot be all there is to it. Germans do not fit their plodding, persevering stereotype. A public-opinion survey of Western Europe and North America, the International Values Study, found that Germans were more extreme in their feelings than anyone else (see Figure 11-2). De Gaulle's comment is nearer the mark: "a sublime green ocean where the net hoists a tangle of monsters and treasures."

That the stereotype lingers has a lot to do with ignorance. The same public-opinion survey found that half of French and two-thirds of British respondents had learnt nothing about Germany at school or university. In English-speaking countries, informed people with views on the Italian right or Edouard Balladur's popularity know next to nothing about Germany.

STABILITÄT ÜBER ALLES

A main explanation for the economic miracle lies in Germany's distinctive institutional arrangements. The most striking is *Ordnungspolitik*, defined by Wilhelm Ropke, an economist, as a system

FIGURE 11-2

'How Have You Been Feeling in Recent Times?'

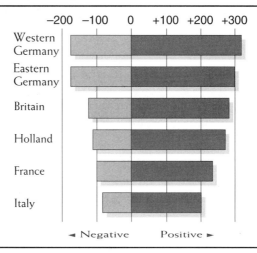

Source: International Values Study, 1990.

of measures and institutions which impart to competition the framework, rules and machinery of impartial supervision which a competitive system needs as much as any game or match if it is not to degenerate into a vulgar brawl ... This presupposes mature economic discernment on the part of all responsible bodies and individuals and a strong impartial state.*

In the 1950s and 1960s, the years of the economic miracle, market forces were allowed wide scope within this framework. But in the 1970s the "strong impartial state" evolved into a style of government that became gradually more interventionist. Growth slowed, even though the economy remained the strongest in Europe. By this time Germany was seen as a model of economic management distinct from, and more successful than, America. As another author, David Goodhart, says:

> Social-market institutions constitute a far more radical affront to the common sense of the Anglo-American market model than is often realized ... German labor markets are chock-a-block with rigidities, the freedom of capital is severely curtailed, company ownership is often lost in a blur of cross-holdings, taxes are high and unions remain strong.**

At the heart of Germany's social market economy is a system called *Mitbestimmung*, or co-determination, which gives workers extensive consultative powers. In a company, the boss may have the casting vote, but, by law, unions have half the seats on the supervisory board

---

*Quoted in "Germany in Transition." *Daedalus.* American Academy of Sciences, Winter 1994.
**"The Reshaping of the German Social Market." By David Goodhart. Institute for Public Policy Research.

and all of them on the workers' council, which must be consulted on most decisions. French firms have workers' councils too. But "in Germany," says René Lassére of the Paris Institute for the Study of Contemporary Germany, "*Mitbestimmung* . . . really means that, while in France the role of the *comité d'entreprise* is purely consultative." French firms are monarchies, run by the boss. German firms are closer to parliamentary democracies, run by company boards, specialists on those boards and trade unions.

This produces a distinctive form of corporate governance. Shareholders and stockmarkets, which disperse ownership widely, play a minor role. Many firms own shares in each other. Contested takeovers are rare (there have been four since 1945). Banks, which specialize in long-term "relationship banking" with firms, play a larger role in management decisions than they do in America or Britain.

The counterpart to these economic arrangements is a set of political and social institutions which have primacy over the operations of the market. But—and this is an essential feature of the German model—this primacy is not vested in the state, as in dirigiste France. First and foremost it is vested in the law itself, respect for which is stronger in Germany than in any other European country. As in America, there is a written constitution and a supreme court to interpret it. But Germany out-legislates America: it has regulations for everything. Shops close at 6:30 pm on weekdays; personal-insurance contracts must be approved by a federal office; construction projects must abide by thousands of building regulations.

Next, Germany has an elaborate system of checks and balances that restrict the power of the government. It is highly decentralized, with a strong role for provincial state (Land) governments. The country's financial capital is Frankfurt, its media capital Hamburg, its largest metropolis Berlin, its present seat of government a small town on the Rhine, and its Constitutional Court sits in Karlsruhe.

Third, the whole system is based on consensus politics. One prominent Social Democrat observes that the platforms of the two main parties, his own SPD and the Christian Democrats (CDU), could almost be exchanged for each other. Both stand for modest tax rises and cuts in the budget deficit and for a foreign policy based on closer ties with the European Union and NATO. Consensus is all.

This model has huge strengths. Because the framework within which markets operate is determined by consensus, it is less at the whim of passing politicians than it might seem. This restricts government tinkering. Monetary policy has been handed over to an independent central bank, the Bundesbank, which receives little parliamentary scrutiny. State governments have room to conduct experiments, making it easier to see which policies do and which do not work. Although labor and capital markets are rigid, companies compete with each other as fiercely as anywhere else in product markets. And the rigidities of the capital and labor markets are connected to one of Germany's principal economic strengths: the stability of relations among its economic actors—banks and borrowers, purchasers and suppliers, unions and managers. This confers huge advantages: for example, stability of employment and the commitment of workers and firms to each other encourages firms to invest in skills and training which they might not do if workers moved jobs frequently.

This has led some writers (especially management theorists) to claim that the German model is exhibit A of an alternative way of organizing societies. Completely free markets, they argue, produce internal friction that can be damaging to firms, and therefore to the economy as a whole (examples they give include the corporate massacres that accompanied restructuring in many American companies after takeover binges in the 1980s). The right kind of economic institutions, say these so-called "institutionalists," can resolve damaging conflicts without preventing healthier forms of competition.

The institutional arrangements favored by liberal market economies such as America's and Britain's—contested takeovers, arms-length banking, free wage bargaining—encourage, in Mr. Goodhart's words, "low trust relationships and individual opportunistic calculation." In contrast, German institutions—collective wage bargaining, consensus politics—produce continuity and stability. This is what happens within firms in liberal market economies. The German model extends the hierarchical and consultative arrangements that prevail within companies to the whole economy.

Whatever one thinks of these principles, it is important to recognize that, over the past decade or so, the German model has begun to change. In the 1970s and 1980s, governments at state and central level began to stress the regulatory parts of the model at the expense of the competitive ones. The welfare state has expanded relentlessly. Recession in 1991–93 raised worries about the end of the social market. Observers, especially outside Germany, began to see the country not as a new model but as the best example of a crumbling corporatism whose high-cost perfectionism was unsuited to a new world of low-cost international competition.

Then, in 1990, came the watershed of unification. This, many Germans hoped, would herald a break with the past. Left-wingers saw it as an opportunity to create a new citizen democracy combining the virtues of capitalism and socialism. Right-wingers hoped it would usher in a more assertive foreign policy. Some managers thought it would enable them to reduce the influence of the unions. idealists even hoped the dominance of the two big parties would be broken and a new political mold created.

Such hopes have been dashed. There has been incremental change but no paradigm shift. To its defenders, that was because of the underlying strengths of the system. Where change occurred, it merely proved the system's flexibility. In politics and foreign affairs, that seems a fair judgment. But, as this survey will suggest, in the economic and federal spheres, resistance to change has less to do with the underlying strength of the system than with the veto power of vested interests. Here, failure to reform is storing up trouble for the future.

No Escape

On the face of it, there is no reason why a consensus-based system should not cope with recession just as well as a more adversarial one. True, a country more accustomed to conflict might not be so affected by the strains of recession: it is used to such problems. But so long as it is capable of adapting reasonably flexible, a consensus-based country can, by sharing the pain of recession, overcome it.

There are plenty of signs that this is just how Germany is reacting:

- The economy is reviving (see Figure 11-3). After contracting by over 1% in 1993, GDP is likely to grow by a little under 1% this year, and by 2–3% in 1995. Unemployment in western Germany, at 8.3% of the labor force, is lower than the European Union average; even including the depressed new German states, joblessness is only a little over 9%.
- Restructuring has begun. Unit-labor costs could fall by 5% this year. Some big firms reckon they can do much better. Daimler Benz cut costs by DM4 billion ($2.4 billion) in 1993 alone, and says that by 1995 it will have reduced its workforce by almost 20% from its 1992 level. Its great rival, BMW, aims to boost productivity 20-30% in the next five years. All this, points out Norbert Wieczorek, an SPD member of parliament, has

FIGURE 11-3
Reviving

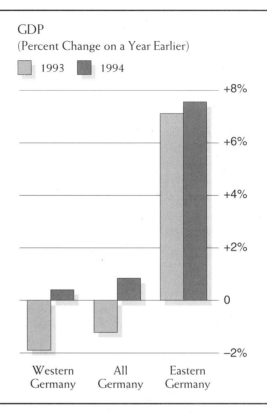

GDP
(Percent Change on a Year Earlier)

been achieved without the disruptive effects of speculative bubbles such as America's merger mania or Japan's property bust.

- Because of this, and thanks to exchange-rate changes, Germany's international competitiveness is improving fast. In 1992, Germany's wage costs were DM48 an hour and Japan's were DM33; now Japan's have risen to DM42–43, driven up by the yen, while Germany's have fallen to DM45. Allowing for greater German productivity, most estimates put German unit-labor costs in the middle of the range of industrialized countries, at about the same level as "low-wage" Britain.

- Despite the huge costs of unification—around DM180 billion a year, equal to half of total tax revenues—Germany has prevented double-digit inflation. At the peak, in mid-1991, prices were rising at 4.4% a year. "There were costs to this in the real economy," says Hans Issing, a member of the Bundesbank's board. "But these were much less than they would have been had we been trying to restrain 15% inflation."

- The government should be able to cut public spending's share of GDP from a worryingly-high 52% to roughly the level it was at on the eve of unification (45% in 1989). That sounds tough, but it has been done before: between 1982 and 1989, the government cut the share from 54% to 45%.

The conclusions to draw from all this must be that Germany is well on its way to overcoming the much-discussed problems of competitiveness and high labor costs and that it is not too seriously affected by the burden of government spending and debt. If this were all there was to it, then worries about the model's ability to survive recession might be overdone. It seems quite flexible enough to cope with the ordinary fluctuations of the business cycle.

FEWER PEOPLE, MORE TRADE

But that is not all there is to it. The country also has to cope with shocks and changes in its external environment. These the German model is less well equipped to deal with—mainly because the long-term relationships which it encourages take years to build up and work properly only under stable conditions. The most dramatic of these "external" shocks is, of course, unification, the subject of a later article. But the German model also has to adjust to two other pressures that have nothing to do with unification, which began to grow before it and will not go away as eastern Germany recovers.

The first of these is demographic change. Germany's baby boom ended early, about 1970, at a time when most other industrialized countries' populations were still growing. By 2030, according to Meinhard Meigel and Stephanie Wahl of Bonn's Institute for the Economy and Society,* the population will have fallen by no less than 15M (nearly the size of eastern Germany)—unless there is a now-unimaginably large influx of immigrants.

Of the population in 2030, 38% are likely to be over 60. That is almost twice the proportion today (20%). The extra welfare costs of these oldies will be borne by a declining group of economically active people (20–60-year-olds) who will by then have fallen to 46% of the population from 60% now. Throw in the fact that the average age at which men leave university today is 30 (28 for women, with the difference accounted for by a two-year national service for males), and it is clear that there will be many more dependents than wage-earners.

These demographic changes will force big changes in many aspects of German life. Some of them may help it to adjust. More women, for example, are likely to go out to work. At the moment, the female participation rate is only 58%. Germany might also let in more immigrants. That would boost the labor force. But it will not be unproblematic. Already the foreign population of the country is comparatively high, at 7.8%. In the past five years, Germany has taken in an average of 830,000 immigrants, as many proportionately as America did during its peak years of immigration in the early part of the century. This makes Germany the nearest thing Europe has to a melting pot—and a place where neo-Nazi groups and violent young people make foreigners the targets of their rage.

But however far such adjustments go, they seem unlikely to solve the basic problem. The welfare state, which is essential to the smooth functioning of Germany's consensus model, is already in crisis. It will not be able to cope without a thorough overhaul.

Germany's welfare-state benefits are generous, sometimes ridiculously so: health cures at spa resorts, for example, were until recently available at public expense. Total benefits for an unemployed man with two children come to 71% of previous, income; in America, the comparable figure is 55%.

As a result of such largesse, social spending's share of total public spending has risen from 27% in 1950 to 47% now. Merely to prevent it taking an ever larger share of output, real

*In "Das Ende des Individualismus." Aktuell.

GDP per head will have to rise by 3.1% for the rest of this decade. As Kurt Lauk, a member of the board of VEBA, a chemicals firm, laconically remarks, "when one considers that the average growth rate of real GNP per capita between 1950 and 1990—including the years of the German economic miracle—was approximately 3.8%, the prospect of a similar growth in the next few years is exceedingly unlikely." Unless there is either faster growth or more drastic reform, the share of GDP devoted to social spending could rise from 33% now to 50% by 2030.

No country could afford that for long. Benefits must be cut. Yet attempts to do this have so far been, at best, mixed. The basic dole is being trimmed from covering 63% of previous income to 61%. There has been a small rise in the pensionable age of civil servants. Health-service reforms in 1993 (mainly restrictions on doctors' limitless ability to prescribe) were unexpectedly successful, cutting spending by 2.7% in the first six months of the year. Yet, on the other side, the government is planning to introduce a new nursing-care scheme for the elderly. This is the biggest welfare reform of recent years and it will widen, not narrow, welfare's scope. So far, there is little sign of either big party contemplating a radical overhaul of the welfare state.

The second long-term trend affecting the German model is a change in international trade and competitiveness, which will affect Germany more than almost any other country because it has the largest share of the world's manufactured exports (its share OECD manufactured exports rose from 16.6% in 1970 to 17.5% in 1990). Services are becoming more important—and Germany's excellence in manufacturing has its counterpart in an ill-developed service sector. International capital markets, dominated by Anglo-American financial standards, are becoming more influential—which will make German firms less secretive with their books and force changes in the close relationship between firms and their bankers. "Lean production" stresses simple, modular assembly methods, quick start-up times, contracting out of supplies and sharing information between firms. German firms favor engineering perfectionism, long start-up times, in-house production and being proprietorial with information. East Asian markets are becoming larger— and Germany sends only 7% of its exports to them.

To see how all this is hurting Germany, consider the machine-tool business, a traditional pillar of the German economy (see Figure 11-4). Production fell by 16% in both 1992 and 1993. Export orders for German machine tools halved between the spring of 1989 and the autumn of 1991. As machine-tool output fell worldwide, America bore the brunt: its machine-tool output fell by nearly two-thirds during the 1980s. But it was Japan, not Germany, that benefited. The German share of the American market halved between 1974 and 1985.

This has worrying consequences for the pride and joy of the German economy, the *Mittelstand* of small and medium-sized firms. *Mittelstand* firms dominate the machine-tool business. But as a recent report by the Department of City and Regional Planning of the University of Wales points out "many fear that the industry is too fragmented to meet the two key challenges of the 1990s, namely to stay abreast of the new technologies, materials and organizational practices and to resist the growing threat of larger Japanese rivals . . . Turnover per employee in Japanese machine tools is more than double the equivalent figure for Germany." In response, two of the largest have merged; others have sacrificed once-fiercely guarded trade secrets to joint ventures with rivals.

The next section will look at how this new environment for business is beginning to affect the relations between workers and managers. But before that, it is worth examining how external constraints are affecting one other institution of the German model: the central bank.

FIGURE 11-4

Dipping

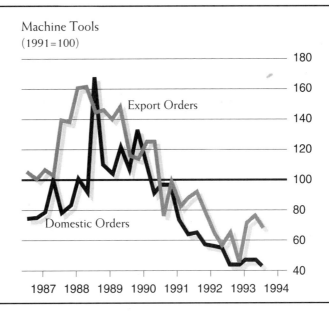

Machine Tools
(1991=100)

Export Orders

Domestic Orders

1987 1988 1989 1990 1991 1992 1993 1994

180
160
140
120
100
80
60
40

Source: VDMA.

The government's debt is now DM15 trillion (see Figure 11-5) and the cost of servicing it roughly DM100 billion a year. This makes debt-servicing the second largest item of public spending, after welfare benefits and ahead of defense. And that excludes the cost of servicing the debt of various municipal housing authorities, the road and rail networks, the post office and the Treuhand, the agency for privatizing eastern firms. Their total debts are around DM500 billion, costing an extra DM40 billion–45 billion of debt service every year. This makes debt interest the largest single item of public spending.

How to finance it? German taxes are now amongst the highest in the world and will rise further next year when an emergency income-tax surcharge comes into effect to pay for unification. This is at, or near, the upper tolerable limit of taxation. So spending must be cut. Germany's wasteful subsidies to inefficient industries should be a prime target. But such budget cuts have been fought off before; in a recession (and in an election year) they look politically impossible.

If spending is not cut, and taxes cannot be raised, the pressure to increase the country's debt will be relentless. This puts tremendous strain on monetary policy and the Bundesbank. The role of the central bank is rarely questioned in Germany. It is the keystone of the system, its power buttressed by old memories of hyper-inflation and a new triumphalism engendered by the collapse of the European exchange-rate mechanism.

Now the Bundesbank's monetary policy has to cope at the same time with the inflationary shock of unification, past cost-push pressures from wages and benefits, and growing government debt. In response, it has forced short-term interest rates above long-term ones to squeeze inflation, and in effect to attract foreign capital, a strategy which admits that the defense of the D-mark has become ever more dependent on the confidence of foreign

FIGURE 11-5

In the Red

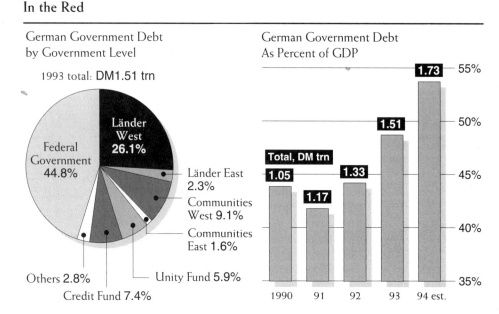

German Government Debt by Government Level

1993 total: **DM1.51 trn**

Länder West 26.1%
Federal Government 44.8%
Länder East 2.3%
Communities West 9.1%
Communities East 1.6%
Others 2.8%
Credit Fund 7.4%
Unity Fund 5.9%

German Government Debt As Percent of GDP

Total, DM trn
1.05   1.17   1.33   1.51   1.73
1990   91   92   93   94 est.

Source: OECD.

investors. At the same time, the bank's insistence that the convergence criteria for European monetary union be so strict that even Germany cannot meet them is described by Helmut Schmidt as "a diligent power play based on pure turf motivation, an interference in foreign policy." His party, the SPD, wants greater parliamentary scrutiny over the Bundesbank.

No one thinks that the Bundesbank will ever become an obedient handmaiden of government, or slacken its monetary vigilance. But the fact that it is now attracting significant criticism shows that even the most rock-solid and successful parts of the German model cannot escape the pressure of change. That applies with yet greater force to the central-ized wage-bargaining system, to which we turn next.

THE PERILS OF COZY CORPORATISM

Germany's labor market is based on a set of assumptions fundamentally different from those of post-Thatcher Britain and post-Reagan America. The Anglo-Saxon model is one of "atomised competition." Workers compete for jobs in the labor market rather as goods com-pete for customers in the shops. And, just as price-fixing cartels are frowned upon, so is excessive intervention (eg, by trade unions). Germany's labor market, in contrast, is more like a medieval guild system in which craftsmen run closed shops that set wages, defend quality standards and discourage outside competition.

Employers belong to industry associations, employees to trade unions; and they nego-tiate wages between them. These wages are determined not at company level but across whole industries. The recent deal struck by Gesamtmetall, the industry association, and IG Metall, which with 3.4m members is the largest trade union in Western Europe, will apply to all the businesses they represent: cars, engineering, shipbuilding and electronics. Similarly, the deal struck by IG Chemie, which has 820,000 members, will set the same wage scale in the chemical, rubber, glass, paper and recycling industries. Except that the government does not intervene, Germany's wage-bargaining system is a bit like that in centrally-planned economies in the 1960s and 1970s. Firms which belong to the industry association may pay more than the negotiated wage but are not free to pay less; over time, the negotiated minimum has become the standard, so even this flexibility has narrowed.

"Filthy competition" is what Germans call the notion that firms should instead compete on the basis of lower wage costs. The German model, says Rüdiger Soltwedel of the Institute for the World Economy at Kiel, provides for competition on the basis of the same cost. This is not as ridiculous as it sounds. By blocking lower wages, it tends to force wages up in an economy in which the government, by and large, does not intervene to stop firms going bankrupt. This means that, if firms are to survive, they must shift to higher-value goods like luxury cars and top-of-the-line refrigerators or machine tools—products for which Germany has for years led the market.

The system benefits workers, of course, by giving them high wages. It benefits unions because, even though there is no closed shop forcing workers to join them, they have power to co-determine wages. Surprisingly, it benefits employers too, even though individual firms lose the ability to set their own wages. The reason is that strong unions are predictable. They have as much interest as managers in preventing wildcat strikes, which undermine their authority. The system prevents multiple union firms, so a factory cannot be halted if a union representing a small part of its workforce calls a strike. Germany loses fewer man-days to strikes than almost any other industrial country.

So it is the managers, not the unions, who are the bigger supporters of centralized wage bargaining. Little more than one-third of those currently in work are members of unions (precise figures are hard to come by, because in Germany unemployed people and pensioners may keep their union membership). In contrast, nearly three-quarters of all firms making capital goods are members of employers' associations. Above all, the *Mitbestimmung* system gives unions a stake in ensuring that the demands of their members do not put firms and industries in jeopardy. It turns workers and managers from opponents into partners and, says W.R. Smyser, a professor at America's Georgetown University "accounts to a considerable degree for [German economic] success."*

Yet this system is now under threat. Germany's largest car company, Volkswagen, has always operated outside centralized wage bargaining system, but until last November it had deviated from its terms only marginally. The in-house deal it struck then, including a four-day week, went much further. It had the agreement of IG Metall, so the challenge was to co-determination, not to labor-management co-operation as a whole. IG Chemie has since come to a deal with firms in its industries that allows the firms to take on, at less than the usual minimum wage, people who have been unemployed for over a year. This was an even bigger challenge to the notion of "clean" competition. By German standards, it was revolutionary.

To most managers and trade-union leaders, however, such deals show that the system is proving its worth by adjusting smoothly to recession (both were achieved without strikes). On average, western German wages have fallen 1% in real terms since the start of

---

* "Germany at the Crossroads." Hurst and Co.

1993, after rising by 4% in 1991–92: and unit-labor costs have fallen an unprecedented 6%, after rising by 7.5% in 1990–92. The long-run performance of the German labor market is no less impressive. Since 1979, unemployment has averaged 5% in Germany, and 9% in Britain, which has a free labor market. German unit-labor costs have fallen 5%; Britain's have remained the same.

Nowhere else, say supporters of the system, have labor costs fallen so far, so fast—not even in America, where spectacular wage concessions in some industries (such as airlines) have been counter-balanced by rises elsewhere. The reason for this, argues Enno Langfeldt of the Kiel Institute, was that centralization has made for across-the-board wage restraint. At the same time, it has allowed more and more deals on working hours to be negotiated by the factory council, not the big unions. In sum, the recent round has shown that the system is tough enough to push wages down and flexible enough to permit special cases.

The worry is, however, that even that is inadequate. For other problems are building up in Germany's labor market that look too formidable to be solved by a year of wage restraint and a special case or two.

THE EASTERN FRONT

The system is being attacked on several fronts, many to do with recession. Recession increases the system's inefficiency costs. These arise because wages are set across industries and regions. A troubled firm in one business cannot respond by reducing wages below those of more profitable competitors. Different industries must pay the same wage scales. Thus wages and conditions in the shipbuilding and computer industries are the same (IG Metall represents both), even though the two have quite different requirements. IBM Germany left the employers' association, Gesamtmetall, over this. Wage inflexibility is also a big reason for huge government subsidies to bankrupt industries such as coal and steel.

A change in the balance of power between unions and managers now looms. As in other countries. German unions are losing membership. Deals that allow local workers more say over working patterns are bound to erode the unions' power further. Since the system is a partnership of equals, a decline in union membership will affect it radically.

Changes are coming on the employers' side too. *Mittelstand* firms are reacting against the traditional wage-bargaining system because, they say, it discriminates against them. A small firm can pay engineers different wage rates relatively easily: the boss knows who is worth what. A firm with 10,000 employees tends to have more inflexible wages. The centralized wage bargaining system is a way of forcing small firms to be as inflexible as big ones. This year they began to rebel, ousting the representatives of big firms who usually take the lead in wage negotiations. That is likely to make wage bargaining more conflict-ridden. Big firms have a cosier relationship with unions than small ones, which have a lower level of unionization.

The third threat to the centralized wage-bargaining system comes from long-term unemployment. Total joblessness in Germany is 4m: 35% have been without work for more than a year. They tend, inevitably, to be the people with the fewest skills. There are two ways to get them back to work. One is to price them back into a job. The centralized wage bargaining system hinders this, although the chemical industry's deal on low wages, if copied, might provide the necessary flexibility (but other unions are opposed to the idea).

The other is to find the unemployed jobs in services. That would require Germany's restrictive laws on such things as shop-opening hours and personal-insurance contracts to be relaxed or abolished. It would also mean changes to conditions negotiated between unions and workers, since a service sector cannot function properly with a working week limited to 35 hours.

But the biggest pressure for change is coming from eastern Germany. In 1990 managers, unions and politicians all colluded to reject any sort of "Mexican solution" (i.e., increasing eastern living standards by fast growth based, initially, on low labor costs). Instead, unions and workers demanded that wages in the two parts of Germany should be equalized by 1994. This failed utterly. Last year, the two sides agreed that the aim could not be achieved, and allowed struggling firms (i.e., most of them) to opt out of their contracts and reduce wages in circumstances agreed in advance with the unions. In theory, another sign of flexibility. In practice, another sign of insufficient flexibility: the opt-out clauses were so narrow that few firms have taken advantage of them.

Many eastern German firms are therefore ignoring the wage bargaining system altogether. In western Germany, around 70% of engineering and electronics firms belong to their industry association. In the east, fewer than half do. And even those who have joined are ignoring the system's demands by paying less than the negotiated wage—and are getting away with it because the unions know that, if they take a firm to court, they risk driving it bankrupt and so losing their jobs. This rebellion against centralized wage-bargaining is concentrated in the east; but not confined to it. As the decline of the unions, the shift into services, and the economic distortions all continue, the pressure will grow to decentralize wage bargaining further.

That poses its own danger. Free and centralized labor markets both work better than something that mixes the two (as Britain found in the 1970s). If Germany decentralizes too much, the cure could be worse than the disease.

Germany's Mezzogiorno

In 1990, the West German system of government, with its complex legal code developed over 40 years, was transferred to the East in one blow. The outcome, says Jürgen Kocka, a professor of history at the Free University of Berlin, has been this:

> The transfer of the West German order to the eastern *Länder* has worked relatively well on the constitutional, legal, and institutional level. However, it has met with stiff resistance and has not progressed far on the level of social relations, political culture and everyday life. On another level (i.e., the economy), the transfer of the West German order has led to destruction and crisis.

The severity of this crisis is still underestimated in western Germany, where it is seen as a problem of financial aid. Considering how big the aid is, that view may be pardonable. This year, and for the next five years, assistance to the east—including everything from unemployment benefits to debt write-offs to road investment—will amount to DM180 billion (see Figure 11-6). That is nearly half of all western tax revenues; and it goes to six states whose combined population is no more than that of North Rhine-Westphalia. If assistance on the same scale were given to Russia, it would cost DM2 trillion a year, 50 times what was sent by the West in 1993.

Yet the crisis is not in the west; it is in the east. Abrupt restructuring that followed unification led to unparalleled industrial collapse (industrial output fell by 65% in 1990–91) and the loss of nearly 3m jobs (manufacturing employment fell from 3.2m in 1989 to 1.2m in 1993; jobs in farming fell from 1m to 250,000). The result has been open unemployment of 17.6%; and hidden unemployment of 30–35%.

FIGURE 11-6
Western Public Transfers to the East

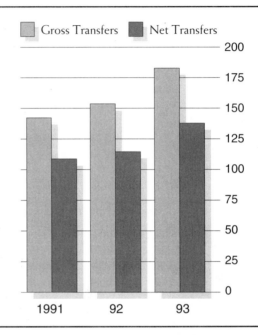

Source: OECD.

Thanks to financial transfers, the sudden imposition of the western model has not led to mass poverty in the east. But, although that was avoided, some of the demographic consequences associated with it were not. According to Mr. Kocka, "the east German birth rate has fallen by 60% and the marriage rate by 65% between 1989 and 1992. Declines of this magnitude are extremely rare in history. Only the Great Wars offer similar examples." It is as if unification had sent family life into a state of shock for three years.

This sort of trauma can be excused only if it could not have been avoided. And even then, it might at least have been mitigated. But most people think it could not have been. They make three arguments: that the differences between east and west were much greater than anyone had expected, suggesting that traumatic change was inevitable; that the policies chosen by the west were unavoidable given the circumstances; and that the policies are now beginning to work anyway. This adds up to less than complete justification.

East Germany is the land of inflated expectations. In 1989, Hans Modrow, the last communist leader of the German Democratic Republic, gave his estimate of the country's net worth: DM1.5 trillion. In 1990, his Christian Democrat successor, Lothar de Maiziére, halved that: DM800 billion. After unification, Detlev Rohwedder, the head of the Treuhand, gave a comparable estimate for the value of the assets on his agency's books: DM600 billion. A year later, he admitted that assets and liabilities would only balance each other: zero. Even that was too much. This year, his successor, Birgit Breuel, presented the agency's balance, with most firms privatized and the Treuhand winding down. Liabilities exceeded assets: minus DM300 billion.

Western views about their eastern cousins followed a similar path. Divided, both Germanies regarded each other as fundamentally similar. Yet Stefan Heitmann, Saxony's justice minister—and at one time Helmut Kohl's candidate for the German presidency— points out that easterners lived under communism for 45 years, much longer than under the Nazis (13 years). They started with different attitudes, more influenced than westerners by the paternalist traditions of Prussia. And they ended the communist era with no experi- ence of how markets work, but with a dispossessed and discontented group of intellectuals who, having been pampered by the communists, were quick to articulate new grievances.

So the persistence of a distinct set of mental attitudes in eastern Germany is not sur- prising. But it is significant. In 1992, according to the Allensbach Institute, 57% of east- erners thought "socialism was a good idea that was badly implemented"; 47% said they wanted a "third way" that combined a market economy, humaneness and socialism (against 11% of west Germans). When asked to choose between freedom and equality, westerners chose freedom before equality by 2 to 1 but easterners were evenly split (see Figure 11-7 and 11-8).

All this—argument number one of those who defend the way in which unification was handled—explains why, though western German social and political institutions have spread to the east, they have not taken root there. Church membership is far below western levels. So is membership of political parties. In the west, nearly three quarters of voters sup- port one of the two big parties, the CDU/CSU or the SPD; in the east, the share is little more than half.

These differences, say many Germans, would have caused problems under virtually any unification politics. As to the particular policies chosen—argument number two—they were inevitable. The collapse of the East German economy, instability in the Soviet Union (whose permission was needed for unification) and the widespread acceptance of the west's Constitution required a one-step transfer of the western system and the cold-turkey indus- trial restructuring that went with it. Extending the model eastwards gradually was not an option. Anyway, the constitutional transfer worked reasonably well. Certainly, the new state parliaments have taken to it with enthusiasm. Mr. Heitmann proudly brandishes a cubic volume of laws passed by the Saxon parliament since 1990 alone.

As for argument number three, the economy hit rock bottom in the fourth quarter of 1991. It is now bounding back. Thanks to investment running at a tigerish 40% of the east's

FIGURE 11-7

'Socialism Was a Good Idea that Was Badly Implemented'

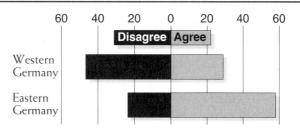

Undecided not included.

Source: International Values Study, 1992.

FIGURE 11-8 ─────────────────────────────

Looking for a Third Way

Compare two different states. One takes a lot of care of its citizens, insuring them completely and intervening in the economy as soon as difficulties arise. The other does not intervene in the economy and provides only the basic necessities of insurance for its citizens.

	WESTERN GERMANY		EASTERN GERMANY	
	HIGH INSURANCE	LOW INSURANCE	HIGH INSURANCE	LOW INSURANCE
Which is more humane?	57	21	79	7
In which is there more justice?	54	28	74	12
In which is there more welfare?	44	32	54	22
In which is there more freedom	22	59	32	40

Source: International Values Study, 1994.

GDP, long-term growth of up to 7% a year is possible, a rate that will double the size of the economy in a decade. Much of this is coming courtesy of West German taxpayers, of course. But, says Birgit Breuel, the head of the Treuhand, privatized east German firms are now investing 140% more per employee than the average western firm. Where big investments have taken place, firms can outperform western competitors. Productivity at Volkswagen's plant in Zwickau, Saxony, is higher than at its headquarters in Wolfsburg, near Hanover.

An equivalent of the *Mittelstand* is coming into being: the state of Saxony (population: 4m) is third in new-firm creation after North Rhine-Westphalia and Bavaria (populations: 17m and 11m respectively). In places where restructuring has gone furthest, like Dresden and Leipzig, unemployment, though high, is no worse than in the big depressed cities of the West, such as Bremen and Kiel.

One indication of the improving health of eastern Germany's economy is its ability to pay taxes. Already, the amount of tax paid per head has risen from 20% of western levels in 1990 to 30% in 1993. In the new states, tax rises disproportionately fast because many people are moving from paying no tax to paying some. At the moment, estimates the German institute for Economic Research in Berlin, a 10% rise in GDP produces a 25% rise in tax revenues. Such high elasticities could lead to a tax boom in the new states. This will help to ease fiscal federal problems.

HOW NOT TO TAKE OVER YOUR NEIGHBOR

Yet even if you think that these rosy prospects outweigh the trauma experienced in 1990–92, that still invites the question: might those problems have been less traumatic under different policies? The question is a reasonable one given that eastern Germany's economic growth has not been all that much faster than that of Poland, whose shock therapy was comparatively low-voltage.

And doubts about the east German model do not rely solely on comparison with their neighbors. In several areas, policies were carried out that were mistakes by any standard. First and most important, westerners were too inflexible in applying economic policies that were bound to cause a huge slump. In 1989, Chancellor Kohl promised that no tax increases were needed to pay for unification. German voters and businessmen fell for this propaganda, blinded to the gathering problems by a vision of cost-free unification. Employers and unions in the west agreed in 1990 to push east German wages up to western levels by 1994 (a date now postponed to 1996). There was no economic justification for this; wage differences can and should persist quite easily between rich and poor parts of a single country. Worst of all was the government's decision to exchange worthless East German marks for hard D-marks at one-to-one. This accelerated the collapse of eastern companies and necessitated high subsidized investment which, when combined with high wages, produced an instantly expensive production base (east German unit-labor costs are now 160% of west German ones). The east has gone from a labor-intensive economy with funny money to one with masses of capital and a small workforce on high wages. No wonder employment has fallen so fast.

Second, there was a dismal failure by the political leadership to include easterners in positions of authority in united Germany. Only one easterner who was elected is still in post as prime minister of any of the new states (in Brandenburg); the rest are either westerners or easterners appointed after the resignation of the previous government. This does not signal to voters that they are getting their own people in positions of power.

Hundreds of miles away, in Bonn, there are no permanent secretaries of state and precious few top civil servants of any kind from the east. The performance of the foreign ministry has been particularly shameful. Russian-speaking Soviet experts from the former East German foreign office were queueing up for jobs. Yet it has appointed fewer top officials from the east than the army, which has greater security worries. As Brandenburg's justice minister, Hans-Otto Bräutigam, puts it: "Easterners feel as if they are for the skivvy work. To some extent this is true. To some extent it is even justified. But the result is that they feel discriminated against." Many western businessmen and civil servants in east Germany act like posturing conquistadors. The business of moving the capital to Berlin has been conducted with painful reluctance. The attempt to run Mr. Heitmann for president (the election is on May 23) collapsed in embarrassment when he made various gaffes over women and foreigners.

A third mistake concerned the property rights of those whose assets had been expropriated by the communist government. The principle seemed generous: former owners could claim their property back if it had been requisitioned between 1949 and 1989. But that meant that those whose property had been stolen at the start of the communist period or privatized at the end got compensation to the value of 20% of the property if they were lucky. Those living in the property, even if they had spent half a lifetime's savings on improving it, were evicted. Brandenburg's justice minister calls this "grossly unjust." To add insult to injury, 80% of those who have got their property back promptly sold it again, usually to westerners (easterners do not have the money). And arguments over who owned what have discouraged investment and harmed the economy. This debacle has affected millions of people on both sides. It is, thinks Mr. Brautigam, "the biggest failure of unification."

Last, the hounding of those involved with the old secret police or *Stasi* is in danger of turning into a witch-hunt. There is no question of excusing those who committed crimes in the service of the old regime or even those who worked part-time for the secret service. But almost all of these have already been dealt with. The hard question is how much responsibility people should take for their behavior under the old regime. It has been brought home in an acute form by the case of Manfred Stolpe, prime minister of Brandenburg.

Mr. Stolpe was the chief lawyer of the Protestant Church, the only large public institution not directly controlled by the government of the former East Germany. As such, he dealt with virtually everyone of any influence in the Communist party, using his influence to further the interests of the church. Though he has never been accused of betraying the church, there is not much doubt that to keep these channels open, he collaborated in some way with the secret service (how much is not known). Mr. Heitmann sneers that Mr. Stolpe would not have got a job as a janitor in a public building in Saxony. Yet, as the extent of Mr. Stolpe's collaboration became clearer, his popularity among his own voters rose. Whatever the rights and wrongs of his particular case, it has made clear that easterners and westerners have different views about the responsibility that such people bear for the old system—and that, in eastern eyes, many westerners take a holier-than-thou attitude to a regime of which they had no experience.

All this is more than just water under the bridge. It explains why, in the economic sphere, the west German model has fared badly in the east. It has been associated with traumatic changes, some of which were inevitable but some of which it exacerbated. As Italy's Mezzogiorno suggests, a hugely subsidized poor region with high unemployment can stay depressed and troublesome for decades.

WHERE FEDERALISM NEARLY WORKS

Germany is a single country with 17 governments: one in Bonn and one in each of 16 states. Switzerland and Belgium apart, it has the most decentralized system of government in Europe. The states are solely responsible for the police and "culture," which includes everything from education to broadcasting. Jointly with the central government, they control civil and criminal law, labor law, and some aspects of economic policy, such as foreign trade. These areas are "joint" in that the central government has a prior right of legislation but the states can write laws if the central government chooses not to. And unlike America, Germany does not have an extensive system of federal bureaux for federal laws. This gives the states even more influence over policy because central-government intervention often takes the form of guidelines which the states have discretion in applying.

Most importantly, German states have a more direct influence over the federal parliament than do states in America. American senators, for example, are directly elected by voters and do not represent their state governments. Not so in Germany. Members of the upper house, the Bundesrat (which, while not an equal chamber to the Bundestag, still has to approve most legislation) are appointed by state governments as their representatives in Bonn. They hold local office as well as office in the Bundesrat (serving as mayor of a town, for example). And even more than American senators, they act for local interests. Where these conflict with central government or national-party considerations, it is local interests that tend to prevail. Last year, when central and local governments were arguing about a revision to the way taxes are shared out, the prime minister of Brandenburg, Manfred Stolpe, defied the opposition of his own party to the proposal and voted for it, ensuring its approval.

FIGURE 11-9
Federalist Dream

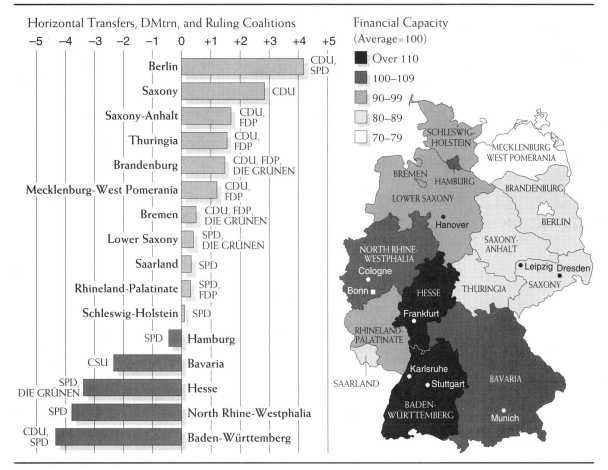

Horizontal Transfers, DMtrn, and Ruling Coalitions

Financial Capacity (Average=100)
- Over 110
- 100–109
- 90–99
- 80–89
- 70–79

State	Value	Coalition
Berlin	+4	CDU, SPD
Saxony	+3	CDU
Saxony-Anhalt	+2	CDU, FDP
Thuringia	+2	CDU, FDP
Brandenburg	+2	CDU, FDP, DIE GRÜNEN
Mecklenburg-West Pomerania	+1	CDU, FDP
Bremen	0	CDU, FDP, DIE GRÜNEN
Lower Saxony	0	SPD, DIE GRÜNEN
Saarland	0	SPD
Rhineland-Palatinate	0	SPD, FDP
Schleswig-Holstein	0	SPD
Hamburg	−1	SPD
Bavaria	−3	CSU
Hesse	−4	SPD, DIE GRÜNEN
North Rhine-Westphalia	−4	SPD
Baden-Württemberg	−5	CDU, SPD

*Estimated financial equalization in 1995.

†With Statt party.

‡As defined under the financial equalization scheme.

Source: OECD.

Some Germans argue that all this reflects something about their country that differs from other European states: that Germany is not a nation at all, just a collection of provinces. As John Ardagh points out in his useful "Germany and the Germans,"* the sentence "we have seen it" is *"Wir haben es angesehen"* in standard High German, *"Wir haben's angekiekt"* in Berlin, *"Mir hens a'guckt"* in Bavarian and *"Mir hannet gesäh"* in Swabian (around Stuttgart). Primogeniture was the rule in northern Germany, making possible the huge holdings of the

* "Germany and the Germans." Penguin.

Junker aristocracy. In the south, land was divided among male heirs, producing, argues Norbert Walter, Deutsche Bank's chief economist, a society in which, since people could not earn enough from subdivided farms alone, small businesses emerged that have become the basis for the economic success of the southern states.

Differences shout at the traveler as you move from state to state. The Free State of Bavaria is all gold-leaf and marzipan, showy, vulgar yet cultured; its capital, Munich, is a city of the theatrical baroque, the heart of a central, not a northern European region, the city of Wagner. By contrast, the Free and Hanseatic state of Hamburg is austere, gentlemanly, and sedate, more English than Austrian, the city of Brahms. Stuttgart is cosy, pious, tidy. Free-wheeling Cologne exemplifies the boisterousness and quirkiness of the Rhineland.

All this is enhanced, even entrenched, by decentralized government. Yet it is doubtful whether underneath it all the citizens of Munich and Hamburg really differ from each other more than those of Glasgow and London, Paris and Marseilles, Milan and Naples. Rather, Germany's decentralization is a product of history and self-interest. The history was Bismarck's blood-and-iron forging of a united Reich out of more than a dozen reluctant fiefs; and the self-interest that of checking the dominance of Prussia. This the federal system has achieved for decades, even though Prussia's economic heartland survived in one block as Germany's largest state, North Rhine-Westphalia, which alone is larger than all but five European nations. But products of history can be changed by history—and unification was a seven-point upheaval on history's Richter scale. How will federalism be affected by unification?

At first sight, not much. Unification was undoubtedly easier under a federal system than it would have been had Germany been highly centralized. The so-called "new states" of eastern Germany are not new: they were old units that had been abolished only in the 1950s. This link with the past made unification easier because it offered easterners a way of identifying themselves with their new state. So federalism underwent an expansion, not a renewal.

Yet the arguments of those who say that Germany's federal arrangements need reform still deserve attention. Considered simply in terms of the balance of power between the center and the states, unification is likely to weaken the states' coherence because they are now 16, not 11. As the European Union found when it fell out recently over changes to its voting rules, increasing a group to 16 can cause big ructions. At the same time, the federal government has assumed responsibility for most of the debts incurred by unification which, other things being equal, will increase its influence over how the money is spent.

But unification is only part of the problem, and not the larger one at that. The larger one is connected with the basic feature of the German model—consensus. Because there is supposed to be consensus between different levels of government, Germany often has more overlap between tiers than America. And because there is supposed to be consensus among the states, those areas in which they have to act together require unanimity.

To see how all this causes problems, consider the interaction between the social-security and unemployment-benefit systems. The central government is responsible for unemployment benefit while local government assumes the burden of social-security pay, the basic safety net. If the center reduces the value of the dole or cuts the length of time for which it can be drawn, then the income of some recipients will fall to the point at which they can claim social security. This shifts the burden of supporting them from the center to local governments. Local governments can then retaliate by handing out jobs to their new dependents in public-works projects, re-introducing them into the job market, and making them eligible for unemployment benefit. This shifts the burden back to the center. Thus recession turns central and local governments from partners in consensus into tennis players, batting welfare claimants back and forth between them.

Recession, combined this time with demographic change, is also affecting consensus among the states. As the tax base shrinks and the student population rises, reform of education, a state responsibility, is becoming urgent. But any serious change in, say, the university system requires the agreement of all states. So unlikely is this that the universities—which urgently need reform—are off the agenda. One of the more absurd features of German federalism is its inability to resolve a debate over cutting the number of years spent at secondary school from 13 to 12. The obvious solution would be to allow those states which wish to do this to try it out (as several would like to do). But because some states are opposed to the idea, nothing gets done.

And as if the strains of recession were not enough, the needs of the European Union are requiring German states to perform a role they are not equipped to play. Because Germany has taken the EU more seriously than most other countries, its states are being required to play a big role in European decision-making. So there is a standing committee for Europe in the upper house, a standing conference of state prime ministers, a standing conference of ministers for Europe and state representatives in the European Union's Assembly of the Regions. For small states especially, this is a bureaucratic nightmare. Thomas Mirow, who helps Hamburg's state government fulfill its responsibilities under this says that "it is a fiction that Hamburg can influence European affairs."

In short, the growing rigidities of consensus, exaggerated by unification and recession, are raising doubts about whether Germany is any longer a decentralized country. "The extent of German federalism," concludes Klaus von Dohnanyi, a former mayor of Hamburg, "is exaggerated."

ALL THE GERMANIES

One of the big open questions of the next few years is how much unification will affect this already strained consensual federalism. It has already forced substantial change to the tax revenue-sharing arrangements that underwrite the consensus. That was inevitable: to boost consensus, this system redistributes income from rich to poor states. To have applied it to the much poorer eastern states would have bankrupted it. So, in 1990, the law, with the convoluted title of *Finanzausgleichgesetz*, was temporarily suspended while the federal government took over responsibility for the east.

Next year, the system will start again. The state governments' share of value-added tax will rise from 45% to 52%; the central government will receive, by compensation, a 7% income-tax surcharge also to be levied next year. That surcharge, says the economics minister, will be temporary. When it lapses, the states will be left with a higher share of overall revenue than they had before unification, while the central government will be left with a higher debt to service. That raises worrying possibilities: will the states seek to spend their extra revenues at home and balk at helping the center finance its debt? If they do, will the federal government be forced to reduce its spending further, throwing greater spending responsibilities onto the states? Both developments could shift more power to the states.

That possibility will arise at a time when the reappearance of the system that redistributes income among states will be causing worries. In the late 1980s, before unification, around DM3 billion–4 billion was flowing from rich states to slightly less rich ones. From next year, DM12 billion–15 billion will be flowing through the system, all of it from west to east, turning several former recipients into donors. It seems unlikely that a change of this order can be managed smoothly, even in Germany.

Few Germans are willing to contemplate the possibility that these strains require a redesign of the system that has served them so well in the past. Yet it does not seem plausible to think the system can continue unchanged. But how to change it? The simplest way would be to keep the consensual system more or less as it is but to alter the boundaries of the states, creating, say eight states of roughly equal size and income. There is a precedent: Baden-Württemberg is the product of a three-state merger negotiated in 1952 between Baden, Württemberg and a region called Hohenzollern. Another round of boundary changes would be in redesigned states' interests because they would find it easier to defend their joint interests against the center. It would also radically reduce the redistributive part of the system (if, say, Saarland were part of Rhineland-Palatinate, it could no longer qualify for special help).

Yet only Berlin and Brandenburg are negotiating a merger; others are either unwilling to give up power or reluctant to face the referendums that any change would require. So Germany may have to take a more radical alternative: to redesign its federal system to make it more flexible. That would mean:

- Increasing states' independence in those areas where, nominally, they are already solely responsible, such as education. That would mean more variation in states' education policies, which would speed reform of the system.
- Making the division of responsibility between states and the federal government clearer. That would require giving states more discretion over social spending.
- Most controversially, giving states some independent tax-raising powers, so that those that think they could afford to raise taxes to improve public services could do so without requiring others who are less well off to spend more than they need.

The cost would be a wider range of income differences among states than now exists, something which unification will make inevitable anyway. The benefit (though few Germans see it this way) is that this will mean shifting away from consensual federalism towards a more competitive version.

SYSTEM FAILURE

Consensus politics has shaped the German model for 50 years—and been shaped by it. With the labor market defusing conflicts between managers and workers and the federal system reducing many, though not all, conflicts involving states, national political parties have mostly operated within a narrow range of opinion (the more so since the SPD moved to the right after the Bad Godesberg conference in 1959). This has helped to give Germany its social peace and prosperity. But if the underlying model is changing, will the national political consensus change too? In the end, it must. Indeed, it has already begun to. Yet, as with so much else in Germany, change will be incremental.

The old political system in western Germany was stable partly because it revolved around a central feature that exercised an irresistible pull on all parties. This was the Free Democrats, whose support was necessary for either of the large parties to form a government. Between 1945 and 1994, Western Germany had 29 years of Christian Democratic rule and 13 years of rule by the Social Democrats; but for all but 4 of those years the Free Democrats were part of the governing coalition.

This helped keep German governments committed to free markets. The Free Democrats are a liberal party, keen on free trade and small government. In contrast, the Social Democrats are left-leaning believers in interventionist government; while the Christian Democrats, though a conservative party, are no less committed to the social-market economy than the SPD.

The pull of the center worked in other ways, too. The SPD's ability to move to the left was restricted by its wish to distinguish itself as sharply as possible from East Germany's communists and by its need for FDP support in government. The CDU's ability to move to the right was similarly constrained by a need for FDP support; and by a desire to distinguish itself sharply from any links with neo-Nazis.

Unification has not destroyed the center of politics; but it has changed the old pattern, widening the spectrum of opinion by including in it the Party of Democratic Socialism (PDS), the reformed rump of the East German communist party. In elections in Brandenburg at the end of 1993 the PDS won 21% of the vote, which was not a freak: according to national opinion polls, the "Red Socks" have the support of 15–20% of all voters in the east. That still means that, nationally, the PDS has less than 5% of the vote, the normal threshold for seats in the Bundestag. However, any party whose representatives win three constituency seats outright gets a share-out of the proportional-representation seats in parliament (in a general election, Germans have two votes: for constituencies, and for party lists). This year, the PDS may get into parliament even if its voting share is below 5%.

Some Germans worry about ex-communists in the Bundestag. Yet the PDS's ideology (in so far as it has one) is now that of an ordinary socialist party, like the reformed communists of Hungary or Poland. There is no evidence that it is spearheading a drive to return east Germany to communism. Instead, it is playing a valuable role in incorporating the old communist party into the new democracy.

In any case, the consensus model has operated perfectly well for 50 years with a regional party inside it. This is the Christian Social Union (CSU), the conservative party that rules Bavaria and has been in permanent coalition with the main Christian Democratic Union (CDU). It is rather as if the Democrats of the American South were a separate party, in permanent alliance with the rest of the Democratic party. Except when the CSU's once-dominant figure, Franz Josef Strauss, was running for the chancellorship in 1980, the separateness of the Bavarian conservatives has not hindered consensus politics-indeed, it may have encouraged it because the CSU provided a safety-valve for Bavarian right-wingers.

Nevertheless, a second regional party may prove harder to absorb, both because it is too left-wing to be in permanent alliance with the SPD and because of other changes to the political landscape that followed unification. The post-unification period has seen the revival of the Green Party, which had lost all its seats in the 1990 general election. The slaughter of that election has, oddly, made the Greens a more plausible party of government, because it helped end a damaging conflict between fundamentalists who opposed any concessions to the messy business of traditional politics and realists who were willing to make compromises to advance the cause. Thanks partly to self-destruction by the fundamentalists, partly to the post-cold-war collapse of the peace movement (once part of the fundamentalist wing) and partly to the experience of working in coalition with the SPD in state government, the "Realos" have won the fight. The Greens now, according to the opinion polls, command over 10% of voters' support. Most of their supporters are under 35; one study found a new three-way split among 18–24 year olds, with the CDU/CSU, SPD and Greens each sharing 20% of the vote (and the remaining 40% undecided). Thus, uniquely among western European countries, Germany has a youth party.

With smaller fringe groups also growing—such as the far-right Republicans, who might win 7–8% of the vote in Bavaria, and the Statt party, an anti-corruption group that is the junior coalition partner in Hamburg—support for the three traditional coalition members is clearly dwindling. Combined support for the big two parties, which stood at around 70% before unification, has fallen to around 60%. For the FDP, the change has been exacerbated by the pains of generational change. Long regarded as the home of all the best politicians in the country, it has been losing credibility since the retirement of Hans-Dietrich Genscher, its old leader, perennial foreign minister and for years Germany's most popular politician. And, unluckily for the party's new boss, Klaus Kinkel (also foreign minister), the FDP's main concerns–free markets and civil liberties–have been overtaken in voters' minds by worries over unemployment and crime.

FOUR COALITIONS IN SEARCH OF GOVERNMENT

How might all this affect the political landscape after the general election in October? One possibility is that a new, more fractured multi-party system might emerge, with both the SDP and the CDU splitting (the SDP has an isolationist wing, while the divisions within the CDU might be opened if they suffer a heavy electoral defeat in the eastern states, where they won handsomely in 1990). With the Greens, Liberals, and PDS all jostling with splintered large parties, the result could be the kind of fluid party line-up characteristic of other European countries with proportional representation, such as Belgium or Holland.

Yet this seems far-fetched. Opinion polls continue to show a drop in support for the two big parties. But in March's election for the state parliament of Lower Saxony (Germany's second biggest state), the big two took 70% of the vote in an 84% turnout: hardly evidence of rejection of the traditionally dominant parties. The Greens might yet add themselves as a fourth big party. But none of the fringe groups seems capable of following suit. Germany is unlikely to see the multiple parties that prevail in Holland, still less anything like Italy's wholesale breaking of the political mold (there is no public pressure to change the system of proportional representation, for instance).

A second possibility is that the two main parties begin to compete with each other more by moving away from the center and towards their left and right wings. This is conceivable in the long term. But right now the two parties are closer than they have been for many years. The differences between their manifestos are not that significant: the CDU is slightly more committed to NATO, the SPD slightly more willing to impose redistributive taxation. Any real move away from the center would have to await new, less consensual leaders. Helmut Kohl and Rudolf Scharping share the same home town (Mainz), have similar political experience (Mr. Scharping is now doing the job that Mr. Kohl had in the 1970s, prime minister of Rhineland-Palatinate) and have the same commitment to binding a united Germany into the European Union.

That leaves a third, and by far most likely, possibility: that the two large parties will in future continue to alternate in forming coalition governments, but with untraditional parties, such as the Greens. It is risky to speculate about the outcome of an election that is still five months away (psychological evidence shows that five of the past eight elections have been decided in the last 10 weeks of the campaign). But it is worth noting that, if an election were held today, the result might well be a red/green coalition.

Such a prospect might alarm the neighbors. The Green manifesto includes commitments to leave NATO and abolish the army. Green leaders play down the significance of this, saying that none of them take it seriously (the full text calls for them to "dismantle NATO within the context of a new system of collective security for Europe," suggesting that the Greens would be willing to stay in NATO so long as it still exists). Yet the Greens could still prove awkward, if only because of their influence on the isolationist wing of the SPD, which supports a new post-cold-war collective security system and has prevented Mr. Scharping from giving unequivocal support to the stationing of German troops out of the NATO area. Not surprisingly, Mr. Scharping would prefer to revive the old SFD-FDP coalition of the 1970s after the election. As prime minister of Rhineland-Palatinate, he already leads such a red-yellow coalition.

For this election, however, there may be a fourth option, which nobody really wants: a grand coalition. This could be produced in various ways: if, say, the far right (with whom no one will make an alliance) wins enough seats to prevent other parties forming a viable coalition, or if the FDP falls below the 5% threshold, or if the PDS gets above it.

Grand coalitions tend to drive opposition out of parliament altogether and to deepen divisions within party ranks. Germany's previous one—in 1966–69—was just such an unhappy time of extra-parliamentary turmoil. (Although against this experience should be set the more constructive one now running Baden-Württemberg, which is starting to take an axe to the overblown public sector and is popular with local businesses.) At the moment, however, any outcome that might precipitate a grand coalition of losers seems far-fetched. The FDP seems likely to clear the threshold. The PDS is unlikely to. The Republicans have about 10% of the vote in Bavaria, where they seem likely to get into the state parliament. But polls suggest they will not win any seats nationally.

THE NEXT 50 YEARS

Yet the big question is not really what government is likely to emerge from the changing pattern of politics after unification. It is whether any new coalition can adapt itself to the changing German model. As this survey has argued, the record since unification has been mixed. Of the various elements of the model, the labor market has responded well to recession but not to the economic problems of the new states, in which it pushed wages up too far, too fast. Political stability is assured, yet politicians are barely starting to get to grips with the problems of the welfare state and public debt. The federal system needs to be made looser, but has instead become more inflexible. Yet at a time of 4m unemployed, recession, huge and unsustainable financial transfers to the east, and a revulsion against traditional politics, it is a tribute to the strength of the German model that the best way of reforming it seems to be incremental change, not a return to the drawing board. The paralysis that followed unification is now giving way to such change.

Editor's note: In addition to "Germany in Transition" and other sources mentioned in the footnotes, this survey is indebted to the Kiel Institute's discussion papers (especially "Challenges Ahead," by Karl-Heinz Paqué and Rüdiger Soltwedel), to the Economic Bulletins of the DIW, Berlin, and to the archives of the Allensbach Institute.

Austria and the European Union

WIGBERT WINKLER

Austria will become a member country of the European Union (EU) on January 1, 1995. The Austrian population voted by a two-thirds majority in June 1994, to join the EU. This decision established a precedent for Sweden, Finland and Norway to join in the following months. Their decision to join the EU, however, was preceded by a long period of tricky discussions during which it was not always easy to distinguish between truth or polemic.

AUSTRIA—A COUNTRY INTRODUCES ITSELF

REPUBLIC OF AUSTRIA

Form of Government	Parliamentarian/Democratic; Federal Republic
Regions	9 Federal Regions
Head of State	Federal President Thomas Klestil (since 1992)
Head of Government	Federal Chancellor Franz Vranitzky, Social-Democratic Party, (since 1986)
Capital	Vienna (1.6 million inhabitants)
Area	83,856 km²
Inhabitants	7.8 Mill. (94 / km²)
Language	German
Currency	1 Austrian Schilling = 100 Groschen
Religions	80.6% Catholics, 4.9% Protestants, and 1.5% Moslems
Foreigners	6.6% (550,000); 49% from the former Yugoslavia and 21% from Turkey
GNP per Inhabitant	AS 201,830.00 (1991 ⇒ approx. U.S.: $18,100
Agriculture	GNP: 2.9%
Employment	5.9%
Industry	GNP: 36%
Employment	36.9%
Unemployment	5.8% (1992)
Inflation	4.1% (1992)

ECONOMIC POLICY

Austria's strongest motivation to join the EU was its economic policy. Austria is a relatively small country with high rate of exports; industry consists mostly of small-and medium-sized companies, except for state-owned companies.

Almost three-quarters of Austria's trade exchange is with the European Economic Area. Austria is the third most important trading partner of the EU.

The following list represents most important trading partners of the EU*:

USA	88.7
Switzerland	49.2
Austria	35.9
Japan	27.5
Sweden	27.2
Norway	12.0

*($ billions); source: OECD.

WHAT WILL THE TRADE INTERLOCKING WITH THE EU PRODUCE?

1. There will be a lifting of technological, tax, and bureaucratic trade barriers.
2. As frontier-crossing traffic becomes less restricted, trade and distribution structures will change.
3. The removal of trade barriers will benefit the Austrian economy. However, competition will increase in many sectors—with benefits for companies that accept the challenge and drawbacks for the companies that are not flexible, or that suffer from competitive disadvantages due to their small size. One can predict that changing the structure of the Austrian economy will be a difficult task. But if this task is achieved, it is certain that Austria will emerge strengthened from this transition period.

The following is a forecast of Austria's economic balance/statement over the next 6 years*:

	WITHOUT EEA** (IN %)	WITH EEA (IN %)	AS AN EU-MEMBER (IN %)
Economic Growth(GNP)	+ 1.5	+ 2.3	+ 3.6
Balance of Performance	+ 0.7	+ 0.3	− 1.4
Price Standard	− 1.8	− 3.4	− 5.2
Real Income	+ 1.8	+ 2.2	+ 4.1
Employees	+ 0.7	+ 1.1	+ 1.9

**Under the assumption of an otherwise steady economic development.

WHAT CAN AUSTRIA'S INDUSTRIES EXPECT?

Wood Processing	Increased orders from the EU, export releases through removal of customs formalities. Impairment of competition is not expected.
Machine and Steel Building	They profit from harmonized norms and removal of customs formalities and origin regulations. Because of the existing strong links with the EU, no dramatic change of competitive capabilities will occur.
Metal-working	Due to high transportation costs, almost no intensification of competition in the home country. Simplification due to removal of origin regulations and technical trade barriers.
Food Industry	In important branches, there is a strong threat of competition caused by large EU retail chains, but sales possibilities will increase for quality products produced by Austrian companies. Clear advantages exist for fruit-juice producers. Disadvantages exist especially for dairy products, spirits, tobacco, meat, spices, cooking oil, and yeast products.
Paper	Manufacturers want to keep their good position in the EU. Further export possibilities exist because of Austria's agreement with in the EU customs and trade policy against third-party countries.
Clothing	Without EU membership domestic manufacturers are disadvantaged through existing origin regulations. Adoption of low EU external tariffs and exemption from duty for developing countries could increase import pressure.
Mining	Because of previous strong links with EU markets already prepared for joining the EU. Advantages through removal of administrative obstacles as well as technical trade barriers and through easier access to a EU call for bids. The Austrian salt monopoly is already becoming adjusted to EEA norms (until 1995).
Construction	Expects more public orders from the EU region and advantages from the increased mobility of workers. It will profit from cheaper purchases of building materials and machines. But it will suffer from increased competition in the domestic market through a EU-wide call for bids on large building projects.
Chemical	Prematerials will become more expensive due to a common EU external tariff, but the removal of customs formalities will bring process simplification as well as standardized norms and acceptance of test attestations. Advantages also through the possibility of participating in EU research programs.

| Iron and Steel | Depends on the common European market, because the EU is the most important sales market. Increased export possibilities without administrative barriers (like test pressures) through removal of trade obstacles. |
| Electrical and Electronics | Improvement of the competitive position through removal of existing trade and administrative barriers as well as the acceptance of technical test attestations. Acceleration of innovation through participation in EU research programs. Increased competition through liberalization of public orders. |

How Will Consumers Be Affected?

Due to the intensified participation of foreign retailers and the removal of trade, consumer prices for food, clothes, and other goods will decrease by 3 to 30%. But there is a remaining threat that legal regulations on the environment and food laws will diminish the quality of the goods. The higher customs free quota also favors consumers.

Traffic Policy or the Eye of a Needle in the North-South Transit Traffic

Traffic policy was one of the most difficult topics discussed during the negotiations in Brussels. Maintaining efficient transit between Germany and Italy is of primary concern to the EU. The negotiations were difficult because:

1. The Alps reduce the number of possible traffic routes to only a few, with many tunnels and bridges.
2. Switzerland has an independent traffic policy. It favors the railway and discriminates against truck transport through a low maximum weight limit (CH: 35 tons, A: 38 tons + 5%, EU: 40 tons).
3. There are no reasonable alternatives in the connection between Germany and Italy. The former Eastern European countries lack good roads, and bypassing through France is impossible because of the Alps.
4. In Austria an attempt is underway to reduce the pollutant and noise burden —or at least not allow it to rise.
5. A transit contract passed in 1991 was implemented on January 1, 1993, with a duration of 12 years (until 2005). The purpose of the contract was to shift from truck transport to rail.

Membership in the EU resulted in the following changes:

1. The duration of the transit contract will be reduced by one year. It will be checked twice during its duration. At the moment its effects cannot be predicted.
2. The weight limit of 38 tons will change to the EU standard of 40 tons.
3. The EU will participate in large capital expenditures related to the expansions of traffic routes.
4. The largest planned capital expenditure is the "Brennerbasistunnel" (55 km long) from Innsbruck to Italy; it will be 15 km longer than the just-completed Eurotunnel.

AGRICULTURE AND THE FUTURE OF AUSTRIA'S FARMERS

The adaptation to EU agricultural policy remains a difficult issue. Austrian agriculture is based on relatively small farms. The mountains and related climate impede agricultural efficiency, especially in production costs, which are higher than in Germany, France, or Italy. The goals of the EU are to allow free trade and to limit subsidies for exports.

Accelerated changes in agricultural structures will include:

1. Operational and regional specialization will increase markedly.
2. Larger land units will develop.
3. Fewer fertile/productive areas will be cultivated, thus threatening the care and maintenance of the landscape in economic borderlands.
4. Financial support will be given for concrete achievements, such as landscape conservation, in contrast to the previous practice of supporting agricultural exports. These changes, although difficult for Austria's farmers, are part of a general trend. Also, the 1993 GATT contract signed by Austria may result in a reduction of high agricultural prices and export supports for agricultural products.

PRICE DIFFERENCES OF AGRICULTURAL PRODUCERS

According to the 1991 statistics, a take over of the EU agricultural policy would cause the following price shifts:

Wine	+ 3%
Wood	+ 5-10 %
Sugar-beets and slaughter cattle	– 8%
Fruits	– 10-20 %
Eggs	– 15%
Pigs	– 15%
Vegetables	– 15-25 %
Brewing crop and corn	– 20%
Potatoes	– 20%
Milk	– 23%
Poultry	– 25%
Oil-bearing seeds	– 30%
Bread grain	– 35-45 %

Source: WIFO (Wirtschaftsforschungsinstitut);
(Austrian Economic Research Institute).

FOREIGN AND SECURITY POLICY

Although the integration of Europe dealt only with economic questions at the beginning, political Union has been a long-term vision since its foundation. This goal is not easy to accept for neutral countries such as Austria or Sweden.

For the foreign policy and security needs of the EU, institutions such as NATO and the Western European Union (WEU) exist. The WEU has been an entity in name only, but it might be useful to strengthened it now. The dream of a pan-European army is still far from a reality, though there are some integrated units of French and German troops.

The Austrian government insists on the statement: "We walk neutral in the EU," because there is no obligation to join the WEU. But it could easily be that this viewpoint may have to change, though it is a highly charged topic in Austria at the moment. The reason for this attitude lies, first, in the fact that neutrality was a policy established under special circumstances after the Second World War, and, second, that the small budget allocated to the Austrian Army is not sufficient for external security purposes.

ENVIRONMENTAL POLICY—IS EUROPE'S FUTURE GREEN?

Austria is a global leader in environmental policy. Almost 2% of the GNP is used for environmental expenses. A comparison of expenditures for pollution control (1991) follows:

COUNTRY	% OF GNP	EXPENDITURES OF COMPANIES
Sweden	0.87	0.30
France	0.91	0.34
United Kingdom	0.93	0.48
Holland	1.46	0.33
Germany (West)	1.74	1.10
Austria	1.94	1.27

Source: BWK (Bundeswirtschaft skammer); (Federal Chamber of Commerce).

Austrian environmental policy is in some aspects stricter than the EU's. In other areas, Austria has already lifted existing standards to match those of the EU. Stricter regulations can be retained and new ones can be enacted, as long as they do not represent an arbitrary limitation of free trade. In some branches of industry, the stringent environmental regulations considerably affect competitive strength. Membership in the EU will increase pressure on the Austrian economy to adjust the valid norms to the lower ones of the EU. Enactment of a stronger environmental policy, with basic changes such as the introduction of an ecological tax, can only be achieved if there is international consensus.

INTERNAL SECURITY—WILL ORGANIZED CRIME CONTROL AUSTRIA?

Austria is one of the safest countries in the world. All countries that border Austria have a higher crime rate, and the opening of Eastern Europe has increased the percentage of capital crime. Removal of border controls could result in an increased percentage of drug-related crimes.

At present, crime is rising on a global level. Entry into the EU could have negative effects for Austria unless there is better international coordination among national police organizations.

FINANCE AND CURRENCY—WHAT REMAINS OF THE AUSTRIAN SCHILLING?

The creation of one single currency, the ecu (European Currency Unit) is a main objective of the EU, although currently only Luxembourg fulfills all the necessary criteria.

EU COUNTRIES	RATE OF INFLATION	BUDGET SALDO (IN %)	NATIONAL DEBT (IN %)	LONG-TERM INTEREST RATES
Belgium	2.4	− 6.1	134.4	8.7
Denmark	2.1	− 2.6	62.2	9.0
Germany	4.0	− 3.2	44.0	7.9
France	2.8	− 3.2	50.1	9.0
Greece	15.9	− 13.2	84.3	26.0
United Kingdom	3.7	− 6.6	41.9	9.1
Ireland	3.2	− 2.5	98.1	9.1
Italy	5.3	− 11.1	108.4	11.9
Luxembourg	3.1	− 1.9	7.2	7.9
Holland	3.6	− 3.8	78.3	8.1
Portugal	8.9	− 5.4	66.2	15.5
Spain	5.9	− 4.7	48.4	12.2
Finland	2.6	− 8.2	29.0	13.8
Iceland	4.2	− 2.7	31.6	10.0
Norway	2.4	− 3.4	43.9	9.6
Austria	4.1	− 1.9	56.2	8.3
Sweden	2.3	− 7.9	54.4	10.0
Switzerland	4.1	—	—	6.4

Source: Austrian Federal Statistical Bureau (1992).

If the current rate of inflation were used, Austria would also qualify. However, the national currency is part of the identity of a country. It is not easy to change. (Just think of what it would mean to combine the U.S. dollar and the Japanese yen into a single new currency).

At the moment it is very difficult to imagine controlling all the different countries of Europe with prices and wages alone. If inflation increased in one country, real incomes would decrease, instead of having devaluation of the currencies of other countries. Still, Austria is in a fortunate position, as it has one of the hardest currencies in the world.

In the financial arena, Austria will be a net payer, which means that it will pay more to the EU than what it will receive. Raising the required capital to join the EU will be very difficult for Austria, with its deficit budget. It is more than questionable whether it will be possible without raising taxes. The current forecast for economic development is 3%, but it is impossible to predict how much entry will really cost.

ACQUISITION OF LAND WITHOUT SELLOUT

According to EU law, a member country is not permitted to discriminate against foreign nationals who want to buy land. Austria expects to have to sell much of its land under these new conditions.

The unique Austrian countryside and the liberal Area-dedication-law means that many beautiful building sites are available and that with development a deterioration of the countryside may occur. In other countries, there is a clear separation between urban areas and countryside; one cannot buy a house at the edge of a forest or at a lake. But in Austria, these types of building sites are available, and their high prices are more affordable to foreigners than to many Austrians.

From the perspective of regional planning, the main problem is not the origin of the buyers but how they intend to use the property—either as a permanent residence or a vacation home. This determines factors such as increased ground prices or the appearance of ghost towns (that is, empty towns, no citizens) during out-of-peak seasons.

In other EU countries, laws have set forth limitations for foreigners concerning the purchase of land. The decision-making process in Austria on this issue has not been completed.

LIBERAL PROFESSIONS—INTERNATIONALITY DESIRED

Members of liberal professions (medical doctors, lawyers, etc.) are allowed to practice in all EU member countries. This means that diplomas or certificates are accepted throughout the EU. For some professions (for example, medical doctors, dentists, architects, druggists, and midwives), special EU guidelines will result in an alteration/adaptation of existing programs of studies.

In other areas Austria must expect increased foreign competition. In turn, however, Austria will try to profit from these new market opportunities. It is probable that the number and variety of languages in the EU (there will be 14 different official languages), as well as different traditions and customs, will result in natural barriers.

HARMONIZING IS A LONG-TERM PROCESS

In many areas laws and prescriptions will need to be adapted. Harmonization will take time, because only some of the likely effects are known. The speed of change and its real time frame, among other factors, are not known. The experiences of other countries reveal that joining the EU can sometimes be a painful process.

In all areas, integration and adaptation will cause different advantages and disadvantages. But, as Julius Caesar once said, "The die is cast!" Austria has made a decision and the EU has accepted Austria. Nobody can forecast the real consequences, the advantages, or the disadvantages that entry in the EU will bring.

BIBLIOGRAPHY

Bundeskanzleramt. *Bericht über das Ergebnis der Verhandlungen über den Beitritt Österreichs zur Europäischen Union.* (*Report of the Results of the Negotiations Concerning Austria's Entry in the EU*). Wien: April 1994.

Bundeskanzleramt. *Europa—das Buch 11.* Wien: 1994.

Global 2000. *Das EU-Umweltbuch* (*The EU Environmental Book*). Wien: 1994.

Schwab, Klaus. *Der Vergleich—Freihandelsabkommen, Europäischer Wirtschaftsraum, EU-Mitgliedschaft.* (*The Comparison—Free Trade Agreement, European Economic Area, EU-Membership*). Wien: 1993.

Schwab, Klaus. *Risiken und Chancen: Österreich und die EU* (*Risks and Opportunities: Austria and the EU*). Wien: 1994.

WIRTSCHAFTSKAMMER (CHAMBER OF COMMERCE) SERIES:

Benedikt, Oskar. *Kleinere und mittlere Unternehmen in der EU.* 4th ed. (*Small and mediun-sized companies in the EU*). Wien: 1994.

Maltz-Strassnig, Huberta. *Europäische Normung.* 3rd ed. Wien: 1994.

Mille, Annemarie. *Produkthaftung in der EG.* 3rd ed. (*Product Liability in the EU*). Wien: 1993.

Schweng, Christa. *Niederlassungs- und Dienstleitungsfreiheit.* 5th ed. Wien: 1994.

Sollgruber, Johannes, and Huemer, Gerhard. *Öffentliches Auftragswesen in der EU.* 4th ed. Wien: 1994.

Heading South:
A Survey of the Nordic Countries

Frances Cairncross

By the end of this month, if all goes to plan, the four main Nordic countries will at last all face in the same direction: south, towards the European Union. For two decades only Denmark has belonged to the club. Now Finland has voted to join it. Next week it will be Sweden's turn to choose, and a fortnight later that of Norway, the most reluctant European of the group. If all say yes, only Iceland will remain outside, adrift in mid-Atlantic.

As the doubts about the three referendums have confirmed, the newcomers are unenthusiastic Europeans. If they join—and remember that Norway's voters backed off in 1972—it will not be thanks to any high-falutin' belief in a common European destiny. Rather, it will be because they see nowhere else to go. For Sweden in particular, crippled by economic problems, the EU appears to offer a crutch to lean on. The lurch towards western Europe has also been encouraged by the revolution in Eastern Europe. Suddenly, Sweden's 150 years of neutrality and Finland's obligation to keep cozy with Russia are no longer obstacles to EU membership. The Norwegians, long NATO stalwarts, see the United States starting to disengage from Europe. All are conscious of the drawbacks of political isolation on Europe's rim.

The three countries' economic arguments for joining the EU are essentially defensive too. Just as Denmark joined in 1973 mainly because Britain the biggest market for its agricultural exports, was going in, so the other Nordics want above all to have a say in devising common policies that might otherwise be used to hamper their exports. All three applicants already belong to the European Economic Area, a free-trade arrangement with the EU. But standards, not tariffs, are the barriers that they will wish to influence.

Unenthusiastic they may be. But the new members will still have a considerable impact on Europe. For the first time, the EU will acquire a group of members that have more in common than most existing EU countries do. The Nordics insist that they have no intention of forming a "Nordic block." Yet they already co-operate with each other on everything from foreign policy to folk dancing. And their common culture binds them in profound and subtle ways. Even though, close up the differences among them are as striking as the similarities, it is the similarities that are likely to impress the rest of Europe.

The Economist (November 5, 1994).

To take one example: the Nordics can talk to each other. It is not just that, throughout the region, English is spoken with a fluency that shames the monoglot British visitor. The Swedes, Danes and Norwegians can more or less understand each other's tongues: indeed, until the turn of the century, Danish actors appeared in Swedish plays. In Finland, Swedish is the second official language, compulsory at school. Many Icelanders speak Danish.

These linguistic links are no accident. For three and a half centuries Norway was part of Denmark (and then, for another century, run by Sweden). Iceland was ruled by Denmark for centuries. Finland was part of Sweden. Sweden's southern strip, the hinterland of Malmo, was long part of Denmark: Danes still take the 45-minute ferry ride to Malmo's lively theaters, or commute from there to work in Copenhagen and escape Denmark's high taxes. (If the idea of Sweden as a tax haven sounds odd, Denmark's tax rates are odder.)

Such an intertwined history has left its mark. There is a common religious heritage: Lutheran for the most part, nationalist, deeply anti-Catholic. Hostility to the Vatican has tinged the campaigns against EU membership. From Luther has come a strong sense of individual responsibility. A line of Swedish pedestrians waiting beside an empty road for the traffic lights to change is an awesome lesson in civic self-discipline. A Lutheran dislike of flamboyance and swank is apparent both in the sparse lines of Ikea's furniture and in the understated style of Nordic monarchs, driving themselves to work at their modest palaces.

Above all, Luther has endowed the Nordic people with a feeling of responsibility for the welfare of others, and a belief in the virtues of equality. Caring for others has made Nordic countries generous donors of overseas aid and supporters of multilateral organizations such as the UN. Denmark, Norway and Sweden all meet the UN's aid target of 0.7% of GDP, and give much of their aid to the poorest countries and to the multilateral institutions—ie, in ways least likely to bring commercial return.

But it is at home that this desire to use taxpayers' money to build a better world has been most striking. Social democracy, whose adherents have run the Nordic countries for most of the post-war years, has not gone out of fashion, as in other parts of Europe. Social Democrats are currently in government in every country in the region except Finland—and even there, they are expected to win next year's election. The basic concept of social democracy—that the machinery of the state should be used to plan and redistribute the fruits of the market economy—remains deeply entrenched. It is a concept that is perhaps more workable in these small, homogeneous countries (the five Nordic countries have among them a population of only 23.4m, roughly that of Peru). But it is also a concept that works best when there is wealth to spare. The Nordic countries—especially Sweden—have got all too used to thinking of themselves as wealthy.

CHIPS OFF THE BLOCK

Once inside the EU, the influence of the four Nordic countries will be greater than their populations alone would suggest. The new voting structure agreed in the Maastricht Treaty, gives small countries extra muscle. In total, the four will have 13 votes out of 90: fewer than half the number needed to form a blocking minority, but more than Germany's ten. More important maybe the fact that a Nordic country will now preside over the Council of Ministers one time in five.

FIGURE 13-1

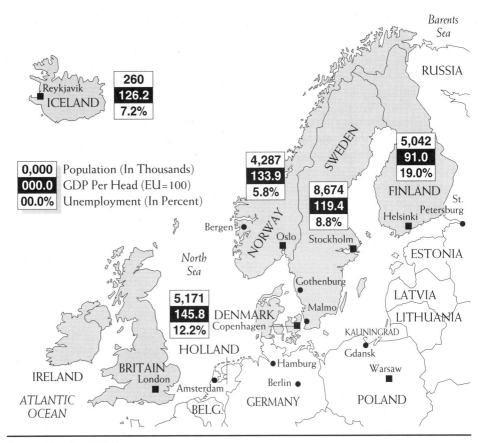

| 260 |
| 126.2 |
| 7.2% |

Reykjavik
ICELAND

0,000	Population (In Thousands)
000.0	GDP Per Head (EU=100)
00.0%	Unemployment (In Percent)

Barents Sea

RUSSIA

| 5,042 |
| 91.0 |
| 19.0% |

FINLAND

St. Petersburg

Helsinki

| 4,287 |
| 133.9 |
| 5.8% |

SWEDEN

| 8,674 |
| 119.4 |
| 8.8% |

NORWAY

Bergen

Oslo Stockholm

ESTONIA

Gothenburg

LATVIA

LITHUANIA

North Sea

Malmo

| 5,171 |
| 145.8 |
| 12.2% |

DENMARK
Copenhagen

KALININGRAD

Gdansk

HOLLAND

Warsaw

Hamburg

IRELAND BRITAIN
London Amsterdam

Berlin

ATLANTIC OCEAN

BELG. GERMANY POLAND

Source: EuroStat; OECD.

The four will be reluctant to be seen as a block. Old rivalries divide them: Denmark is uncomfortable at the prospect of ceding to Sweden its place as Nordic spokesman in the EU, while Norway and Finland both view Sweden with the ambivalence that ex-colonies always feel towards a former master. The widely differing structures of their economies gives each country interests that it may not share with its neighbors: a world class food industry in Denmark's case, for instance, but staggeringly uneconomic agriculture in Norway's and Finland's. Even in the realm of environmental policy, to which all Nordics claim to be devoted, there are differences: Denmark is keen on recycling packaging, a neat way to keep out foreign food-and-drink suppliers, while Finland fears that recycling rules would reduce demand for pulp from its vast forests.

So the changes to the EU are more likely to be ones of tone and style. The newcomers will be anti-federalist, careful about elaborate commitments to economic and monetary union, cautious on common security (Sweden and Finland are still, formally, neutral). There will be more emphasis on openness and transparency—more insistence that countries that sign up to directives should enforce them, for instance, and more scrutiny of the EU's institutions. And there will be even greater enthusiasm for interventionist social policies.

The EU's center of gravity will also shift north and east. For the first time, it will acquire a frontier with Russia—and one that runs past some of the most disputed (and polluted) border territory in Europe. One of Norway's arguments for joining the EU is to help it resolve differences with Russia over the Barents Sea, with its potential energy resources. Finland's dowry will be a better understanding of Russia: "To be a Finn," grumbles Pertti Salolainen, the foreign-trade minister, "is to be asked everywhere about Russia." The EU will also come closer to the Baltic countries, which the Nordics have been supporting and advising, giving it a possible stake in any future quarrel between those countries and Russia. In general, the newcomers will be keener to see the EU "widened" to admit countries from Eastern Europe than to see it "deepened."

Membership of the EU will of course also shape the Nordic applicants. But a different worry is, for them, more immediate. In all three, searching questions are, not before time, being asked about the future role of the state. Led by Sweden, the Nordic countries once thought they had found a "third way" between Russia's stultifying communism and America's brutal market liberalism. Now, one of those three ways has gone for good. And the market, brutal as ever, is forcing Nordic Social Democrats to contemplate the policies of Thatcherite Britain rather than Olof Palme's Sweden.

This survey takes a broadly optimistic view of the ability of the Nordic countries to adapt: their cohesion, small size and sheer common sense will see them through. But the pressures on each are different—as will be their responses. The place to start is Sweden, the biggest and in some ways the most troubled of them all.

A Case Study in Collapse

The Nordic economies play several variations on a single theme: how to finance a large public sector out of relatively modest economic growth. Denmark has managed it mainly by putting its citizens on a "potato diet": stabilizing public spending in the mid-1980s, when other countries were still expanding it. As a result, Denmark's economy is now impressively well-balanced. Norway's answer has been mainly to use its oil money. Iceland has trimmed welfare benefits. But Sweden and Finland, which both enjoyed heady economic expansion in the late 1980s, have since undergone a parallel plunge into recession and debt, from which they are finding it hard to resurface.

Such problems have been aggravated by a heady bout of monetary expansion that brought soaring asset prices—and inflation. One after the other, the governments of Norway, Sweden and Finland pegged their exchange rates to the ecu in a search for stability. The upshot in each case was a leap in interest rates, a collapse of property prices and a banking crisis. Hit by the crisis in the European exchange-rate mechanism in 1992–93, the currencies of the applicant countries have since been floating, mainly downwards.

For Richer, for Poorer

Sweden's economy is by far the biggest in the region. Just as its GDP outstrips those of any of its neighbors, so its economic woes are also more serious. True, Finland has seen an even larger collapse in domestic demand and Iceland, a one product economy, has endured a longer period of stagnation. Denmark shares some of Sweden's long-term problems: a bloated public sector and two decades of relatively slow economic growth. All five have uncomfortably large numbers of their citizens out of work or on make-work schemes. But none has such a glaring combination of stagnation with public-sector extravagance as Sweden.

It is hard for the outsider not to feel a touch of Schadenfreude when contemplating Sweden. Its past century has been glorious; its immediate past, catastrophic. For 100 years from 1870 Sweden grew faster than any country but Japan. The companies it has inherited from that era—giants such as Volvo, Ericsson, ABB, and Electrolux—are true multinationals, selling (and increasingly, manufacturing) in every corner of the world. Coming late to industrialization, Sweden benefited from strong central government, plenty of the right sort of raw materials and well-educated engineers. By 1970 it was one of the richest countries in the world.

Now, the economy looks a pale shadow of its old self. The immediate preoccupation of its politicians and bankers is an alarming budget deficit (at 12.9% of GDP in 1993, one of the highest in the OECD) coupled with a huge public debt (83% of GDP, much of it in foreign hands). And behind this debt crisis, which has been precipitated chiefly by a 6% decline in GDP between 1990 and 1993, lies a still more disturbing trend: the sharp slowdown in economic growth since the early 1970s.

In 1970 Sweden's GDP per head, measured in purchasing-power parity terms, was fourth in the OECD (after Switzerland, the United States and Finland); by 1992 it was 13th (see Figure 13-2). When a group of economists, led by Assar Lindbeck, reported at the government's request last year on the state of the economy, they made this chilling point: "It may take a long time before changes in the official GDP statistics are experienced as a real problem in everyday life. This is because the standard of living, both for a single household and for a country, depends not only on the flow of income during a single year . . . visitors to Stockholm of the 1990s therefore find it difficult to detect the ongoing relative decline. In the same way, however, visitors to Buenos Aires of the 1950s and London of the 1970s found it difficult to detect the ongoing decline that is so apparent today."* Swedes find it hard to imagine a fall in living standards, and yet that is the prospect that faces them over the next decade.

The economic slowdown, which seems to have started around the time of the 1973 oil shock, was initially masked by the government's response. Sweden was an early and enthusiastic convert to Keynesianism. The country has produced more than its fair share of economists, some of whom, such as Gunnar Myrdal and Bertil Ohlin, were preaching the need for active countercyclical policies even before the publication in 1936 of Keynes's "General Theory." Over time, such policies were increasingly directed towards keeping down unemployment, whatever the cost. Until the end of the 1980s, Sweden's vaunted labor-market policies helped to keep unemployment within a range of 13%, far below levels in most OECD countries.

The policy seemed at the time to be a triumph for the philosophy of the Social Democratic Party, which ran the country either alone or in coalitions for all but six of the

*"Turning Sweden Round," Assar Lindbeck and others. MIT, 1994.

FIGURE 13-2
Falling Back

Real GDP Per Head at Purchasing-Power Parities
(1992 Prices)

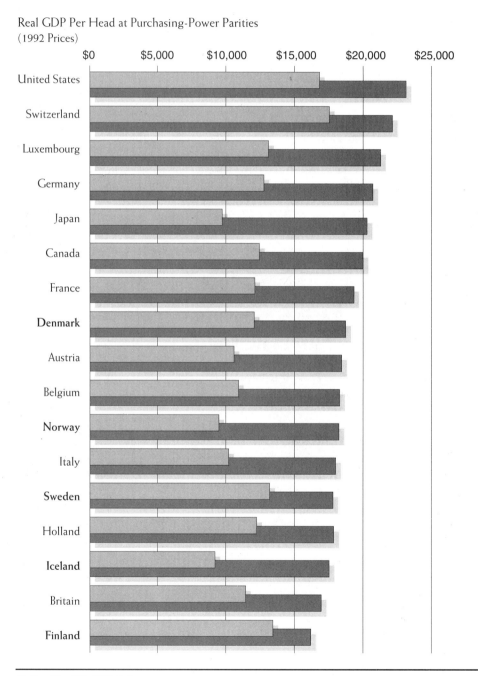

*Inflated by US GDP deflator.
Source: OECD; World Bank.

years between 1932 and 1991— the longest stretch of power for any party in a European OECD country—and was returned to power under Ingvar Carlsson in September's elections. But the costs of success have been considerable. In the 1970s, when the oil shock forced most governments to deflate sharply, Sweden ploughed on with fiscal expansion. Government debt began to rise and the balance of payments to deteriorate.

A series of devaluation's intermittently rescued the foreign balance, at the cost of recurrent inflation (which had the convenient side-effect of reducing the real value of the public debt). Devaluation's also bought off some of the damage done by a highly centralized (and politicized) wage-bargaining system, which continued to push pay levels up. And whenever domestic demand flagged, the buoyant public sector would take over, pouring subsidies into shaky industries and private housing, and inventing new services to mop up the jobless. Not surprisingly, the state's share of GDP ballooned. In 1950 Sweden had one of the lowest ratios of public spending to GDP in the industrial world. By 1960 it was just above the OECD average. By 1983 it was almost 25 percentage points above that of other industrial countries; and the share of government consumption was two-thirds larger than the OECD average. After the recession of the early 1990s, government spending reached 73% of GDP in 1993.

The recession was aggravated by a financial collapse. Financial deregulation in the mid-1980s, coupled with a heavily subsidized boom in house building, led to a spurt in borrowing and a surge in property and other asset prices. In an effort to curb inflation, the krona was tied to the ecu in the spring of 1991. In the backwash of the European currency crisis of autumn 1992, interest rates soared before the currency was cut loose.

By then, a clash between a slow-growing economy and an expanding public sector had become inevitable. The recession that began in 1990 has been particularly ferocious: industrial production fell by 17–18% in the three years to 1993, as steeply as during the depression of the 1930s. The effect has been a savage rise in unemployment, to 9%—or 14%, if one counts workers on various make-work schemes. The rise in unemployment has been matched by an increase in spending on benefits and a fall in tax revenues, pushing the public sector, which was in surplus in the late 1980s, into a spectacular deficit.

SCYLLA OR THE OTHER PLACE

In the eyes of the Social Democrat government, the main danger ahead is that high unemployment will become entrenched. Swedes look fearfully at the underclass emerging in other parts of Europe. To the financial markets, the main danger is a different one: that, as world interest rates turn upwards, the costs of servicing Sweden's debt will out pace nominal GDP. Official forecasts, which show an eventual decline in the ratio of debt to GDP, tend to assume faster rates of growth than the economy has achieved in the past two decades.

From such a debt trap, there could be only three possible exits: default, inflation, or savage tax increases and public-spending cuts. The first is unimaginable; the second is barred by the readiness of the markets to drive up interest rates, and so the krona value of foreign-currency debt (one-third of the total). Sweden's Social Democrats will therefore have to find ways to reduce the budget deficit without destroying private-sector growth—which means cutting spending more than raising taxes.

As Klas Eklund, chief economist of SE Bank, points out, the country has plenty of advantages. Exports are booming. Inflation is negligible. Productivity is soaring. Output has recovered almost to pre-recession levels. The rest of Europe is turning up. But a lot of things still need to go right over the next two years. Export industries must avoid capacity constraints. Pay rises have to stay low, especially in the public sector. The markets need to feel sufficient confidence in the policies of the new government to allow interest rates to fall. Failure on any of these fronts could provoke a new and even more dramatic economic crisis.

It is not at all clear that Swedes realize how big a problem their country has. The election of a Social Democrat government suggests that voters still imagine that the old answers can be made to work again. The new government plans to rescind most of the measures to reduce taxes and reform labor laws that had been started by the outgoing Bildt administration, which hardly suggests that it appreciates what needs to be done. It still seems to prefer tax increases to spending cuts. But measures taken to deal with the deficit will succeed in changing the economy for the better only if they also tackle the underlying problem of the Swedish model: the decline in long-term productivity growth.

Reducing the size of the public sector, where productivity (except in the Bildt years) has tended to decline, will put a severe strain on Sweden's cherished traditions of consensus and caring. The goal of full employment will have to be set aside for the next decade. It is hard to see how such a revolution can be achieved by a minority Social Democrat government. Some sort of cross-party coalition may be the only way to turn Sweden into a flexible and prosperous economy once more.

IN SWEDEN'S WAKE

Flights from Stockholm to Helsinki these days carry a procession of Swedish economists, off to compare and contrast their country's woes with those of their erstwhile dependency. The experiences have been surprisingly similar.

The two economies have long shared a number of undesirable characteristics. **Finland,** like Sweden, has had tough trade unions and a centralized pay-bargaining system. Both countries have become used to a regime of high employment, bought partly at the expense of the exchange rate. The markka has lost even more of its value over the past 20 years than the krona. Both countries have suffered from repeated doses of inflation.

Finland's economy bubbled even more than Sweden's in 1985–90: it expanded at an annual average of 3.4% a year, compared with Sweden's 2.2%. Its GDP contracted even more sharply than Sweden's in 1991–93; by an average of 4.5% a year, compared with Sweden's 1.7% a year. Sweden's recession was as bad as its experience in the Great Depression: Finland's has been even worse. It was aggravated by the sudden collapse of its largest trading partner, the Soviet Union, which had been taking 15% of its exports in the late 1980s and providing jobs for some 100,000 people, mainly in labor-intensive industries such as shoes, textiles and furniture.

As in Sweden and Norway, Finland's boom was fomented by financial deregulation and an explosion of lending, and its recession accompanied by a banking crisis. Like Sweden and Norway, Finland sought to steady itself by pegging its currency to the ecu in 1991; high interest rates aggravated the downturn; and the markka had to be cut free. Sirkka Hamalainen, governor of the central bank, now regrets that the currency did not float sooner.

As in Sweden, the recession has driven unemployment to new heights. But because Finland has fewer make-work schemes than Sweden, unemployment has risen by 15 percentage points in four years, to 19%. Not only is that far above the 7% peak in Finland's unemployment in 1931; it is the sharpest increase seen in any OECD country since the second world war, and a level unprecedented in the Nordic world. And as in Sweden, unemployment has wreaked havoc with the public finances. The public-sector deficit is likely to be over 8% of GDP this year, mainly because of a sharp rise in the central-government deficit, which has more than doubled since 1991 to 15% of GDP this year. Public debt is 73% of GDP—almost on a par with Sweden.

The Finnish government has reacted differently from its Swedish neighbor. Fiscal policy has been tightened more, and interest rates cut more rapidly. An export-led recovery is now clearly taking place, benefiting from Russia's new market economy: the grander shops in Helsinki are keen to advertise the fact that sales assistants speak Russian.

"Finland has never produced more, never exported more," says Mr. Salolainen. But it is doing so with 500,000 fewer employees than before the recession. The government's apparent willingness to put the budget deficit before unemployment horrifies some of its Nordic neighbors. Last year the Bank of Finland bravely asked three foreign economists to assess Finland's economic crisis. Hans Soderstrom of the Stockholm School of Economics urged a more expansionary fiscal policy to prevent the loss of public-sector jobs in a market with no job opportunities, to stabilize private consumption and to encourage public investment. "Swedish bond economists are stupid," growls one Finnish official. "They downplay the role of budget deficits."

Finland's economy is now healthier than that of its bigger neighbor. In the 1970s and 1980s it grew faster than almost any other in Europe. Now, partly because its recession was so deep, its recovery looks vigorous. ETLA, a Finnish research institute, reckons Finland's economy will grow twice as fast as Sweden's this year and next, and faster than any other Nordic country's. That means the tax base will grow faster too.

But the test will be how well Finland (like Sweden) copes with the mammoth task of rebalancing its economy: shifting resources from the domestic to the foreign sector, and from public to private. Again, Finland has a head start. Its public finances entered the recession in better shape than Sweden's. Until 1990 the country's public spending, as a proportion of GDP, was below the average for European OECD countries. As in Norway, the public sector had been a net lender for many years. Since 1990, its net borrowing as a proportion of GDP has risen—but only to the average for OECD Europe.

Ministers in the present government expect their successors to announce big cuts in a post-election budget next spring. They have little choice. "We have to stop the growing debt ratio before the next downturn," says Ms. Hamalainen. Otherwise, Finland, like Sweden, risks falling into a debt trap. Even on favorable assumptions, Juha Ahtola, chief economist at Union Bank, reckons public debt will peak at 87% of GDP in 1997 and still be higher than today at the end of the century. Like Sweden, Finland has caught the international economic cycle at just the wrong moment: its boom was aggravated by the world boom, its slump by the world slump, its interest-rate bill by the indigestion in the world markets. No wonder both countries look wistfully across the Oresund to Denmark, whose timing has been so much better.

Denmark, ever Sweden's rival, feels a little smug about the mess to the north. Ten years ago Denmark had a budget deficit of about 11% of GDP and was heading into an inflationary boom. A non-socialist government raised taxes, curbed spending and abolished 30 years' practice of indexing wages to prices. Membership of Europe's exchange-rate mechanism enforced monetary restraint. Six years of stagnation from 1987 ended last year, when the new Social Democrat government boosted demand. Now Poul Nyrup Ramussen, the Danish prime minister, is delighted with his country's economy. "Our wage and salary costs are 30% lower than Germany's," he boasts. "We have achieved high growth and the lowest inflation in Europe." The foreign debt is falling rapidly, and interest-rate payments are shrinking.

Can it last? Knud Sorensen, chief executive of Den Danske Bank, worries about overheating: he notes that brick prices have jumped 50% in the past few months. Next year, fiscal policy will be tighter. In fact, there are signs that higher interest rates are already cooling the economic boom. The main problem now is that unemployment has barely budged from the post-war high of 12.2% that it hit last year. Mr. Ramussen hopes that the economy will create 200,000 net new private-sector jobs over the next five years. But creating new jobs has so far proved easier than reducing unemployment. Denmark's recovery from 1983 to 1987 brought unemployment down from around 11% to 8%. At that high level, however, capacity shortages began to appear in the economy, and wages to rise. This time, the government has introduced a temporary-leave scheme, which pays people to take time off work to study or care for children. This has proved popular: 100,000 people will use it this year. But the scheme looks a better way to cut employment (and national income) than to reduce unemployment.

WELL OILED

When people in **Norway** look at the plight of the Swedes, they usually blame the country's difficulties on three failures: to unpeg the currency quickly enough, to push through a tough budget once they did so, and to persuade trade unions to co-operate. For Norway also had a boom in the second half of the 1980s, pegged its krone to the ecu, and experienced a sharp rise in interest rates and a collapse of demand. But it swiftly unpegged, and it has cut public spending. However, it had an even nastier banking crisis than Sweden, brought on partly by a combination of lax monetary policies and financial deregulation in the early 1980s. Most of the banks ended up in government hands; and although depositors did not lose their money, lots of middle-class shareholders lost all their savings.

A prompt cut in interest rates has now helped to generate a swift recovery: the non-oil economy is officially forecast to grow by 3.3% between 1993 and 1994. Unemployment is falling. The government congratulates itself on having used incomes policy to hold down inflation, which hovers around 1%. It is now tightening fiscal policy. The budget has traditionally been balanced, but the recession pushed it into deficit. Now the deficit is dwindling, although the public sector is likely to be a net borrower until at least 1998.

Too good to last? Norway has some reasons to be optimistic. One is that, as a producer of raw materials and energy, the country should do well from the global recovery. Another, says Finn Hvistendahl, chief executive of Den Norske Bank, is that industry has undergone substantial restructuring in the past five years. The present recovery is taking place without much increase in loan demand—a sign that industry is using its existing capacity better. More restructuring is needed, partly to wean business off subsidies which cost about 7% of GDP in 1992, compared with an OECD average of 2.1%.

In the longer run, Norway faces two more enduring structural problems. One is how to develop a non-oil economy while a third of its exports are oil and gas. The dominance of the oil industry tends to reduce the competitiveness of the rest of the economy. Norwegian workers are expensive: in manufacturing they cost 5% more to employ than Danes, and 11% more than Swedes. In one sense Norway may not need to develop its non-oil sector: although oil output is expected to peak at the end of the century, it will remain high for the first decades of the next century. But Norwegians have rightly spotted that Russia has much the same range of exports—oil, gas, minerals, timber—and may become a formidable competitor. Too much dependence on one commodity is risky.

The other problem, which other Nordic countries share to some extent, is a failure to save. Asked what has happened to the country's vast oil revenues, Torstein Moland, governor of the central bank, says simply: "We spent them." He remembers the papers written 20 years ago by the economists in the Ministry of Finance, urging that the equivalent of the oil money be saved. But "in a sense, we have invested in not having a large public debt." Norway's public sector (like Finland's) has net assets. But then so it should, given the oil revenues. More ominously, the budget deficit implies that the country is spending substantially more than the oil brings in. And private saving has not been high enough to compensate.

FLAT FISH

Even more than Finland and Norway, **Iceland** lives off a natural resource whose price is set in the world market. Fish make up 70% of its exports; cod alone is 40% of the total. Overfishing now appears to have destroyed stocks to the point where the government has halved the amount of cod fishermen may catch, in order to allow the fish population to recover. That may take until the end of the century. To compound the misery, fish prices have declined over the past two years to historically low levels.

The result is that the country has had seven years without economic growth. Real household incomes have fallen, and are now 20% lower than in 1987. The country has a hefty foreign debt. Unemployment is high for the first time since the war ("high" in Iceland, as in Norway, means 5%) and inflation, frequently at South American levels in the past, is now a sedate 22%. When the economy passed through an earlier bout of high unemployment in the early 1970s, says Halldor Gronvold of the Icelandic federation of labor, "everyone knew it was temporary and that the economy would recover. Now, many people wonder whether things will ever get better. We never used to have unemployment: now, people have been out of work for two or three years."

Clearly, the country needs to diversify its miniature economy. But into what? Its most obvious asset is electricity, in which it has grossly overinvested. But that is hard to export. Hopes of building an aluminum smelter were crushed when Russia began to dump the metal on the world market. Hopes of selling power direct to mainland Europe have so far got nowhere. Tourism is growing, but with beer at $7.50 a bottle and a long Arctic night, the potential is limited. Even so, seven lean years have begun to bring changes. The fishing fleet has found another species, the capelin, to overfish. The balance of payments is in surplus, and the foreign debt being paid off. Productivity is rising sharply. "Companies are beginning to compete on price," says Thorarinn Thorarinsson, the head of the employers' confederation, "and the unions have stopped pressing for wages to match inflation."

All the Nordic countries need economic reform, not only in order to deliver higher living standards. They have a more pressing concern, to which this survey turns next and which is easiest to deal with against a background of economic growth: the partial dismantling of their welfare states.

WOMB TO TOMB

Nowhere in the world has the concept of the welfare state been developed as fully as in the Nordic countries, and especially in Sweden. But throughout the region, this humane and well-meaning invention is now in dire trouble. People are no longer willing to pay ever higher taxes to finance it. With incomes from employment under pressure, the gap between what people can get in and out of work has become dangerously narrow— or even disappeared—lessening the incentive for the unemployed to go back to work. And high taxes and lavish welfare have other distorting effects, for instance on patterns of saving and education.

As a proportion of GDP, public spending on social protection is high in all the Nordic countries by comparison with the rest of Europe, let alone the rest of the world. In Sweden the figure hovered around 33% in the 1980s, more than double America's 15%. Even in Finland, where the proportion (at 27%) is the lowest in the Nordic group, it is still above that of any EU country except Belgium, Luxembourg and—of course—Denmark.

As Anders Isaksson, whose recent book "Always More, Never Enough" criticizes Sweden's welfare culture, puts it: "Everything was well intended." But now public services and transfer payments underpin the living standards of a majority of people in the region. In both Sweden and Denmark there were fewer private-sector jobs in 1992 than there were in 1950; jobs in the public services have been, the main source of new employment. In Sweden, even at the height of the boom of the late 1980s private-sector employment was lower than it had been at the start of the 1960s (see Figure 13-3). In 1960 about one Swedish worker in eight worked in the public sector; by 1990 the proportion was one in three. This switch was aggravated by Sweden's much hyped worker-retraining schemes, through which the public sector became, in effect, the employer of last resort.

To public-sector employment, add an elabourate array of transfer payments—at its most imaginatively extravagant in Sweden, where transfers provide 45% of personal disposable income. Overall, says Bo Ekman, head of SIFO, Sweden's biggest market-research institute, perhaps 65–70% of Swedes depend on the public sector for their livelihood—almost twice as many people as did in 1970. Much the same applies in Denmark, where about two-thirds of the population either works in the public sector or receives state benefits. In Norway, too, the number of industrial jobs has fallen by 100,000 since 1972 while public-sector employment has doubled.

Such figures help to explain the anachronistic power of Social Democratic parties in the region. There is a large constituency in favor of maintaining and expanding the welfare state. Its grip is strengthened by two other characteristics. First, in all the Nordic countries except Denmark, employers pay unusually heavy social-security contributions, while employees pay little—encouraging the impression that benefits cost nothing. Second, benefits have been linked to employment and sometimes to trade-union membership. That has encouraged people to get into the labor force, though not necessarily to work hard once they are there. In Finland, where the unemployed retain their trade-union membership, representation has actually risen in the recession, making trade unions enthusiastic supporters of welfare.

FIGURE 13-3
Too Few Producers

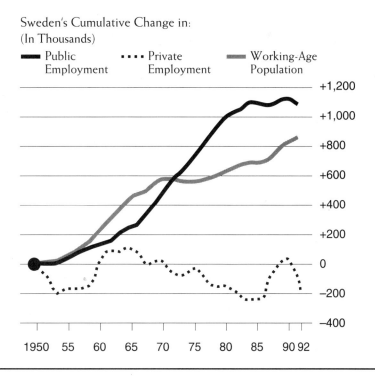

Sweden's Cumulative Change in:
(In Thousands)

■ Public   •••• Private   ▬ Working-Age
   Employment   Employment   Population

Source: SNS Economic Policy Group.

DOWN THE PRIMROSE PATH

How did the Nordic countries end up cosseting their citizens at such expense? Part of the blame is ascribed by Mogens Lykketoft, Denmark's finance minister, to the entry of women into the job market. "Functions that used to be carried out at home are now done by the public sector," he points out. "Often, especially when the children are small, the women don't earn much. But it's politically unthinkable to turn back this development." The proportion of women employed in the Nordic countries is indeed striking. In Sweden in 1992 80% of women were in the job market (and 85% of men): the highest rate by far in the OECD. In Norway, Finland and Denmark around 70% of women of working age are in the labor market. Such figures are also a consequence of highly progressive income tax schedules, which ensure that two modest wages are worth more after tax than one large one.

Most of the services intended to improve women's lives, however, are provided directly by the state, not by the private sector. Scandinavian homes are, by British or American standards, extraordinarily short of domestic help. British working mothers may swear by their Scandinavian au pairs; Scandinavian families are squeamish about employing "maids." Life for young professional parents is not easy; and a good slice of public spending has been devoted to helping them. Norway, which had hardly any kindergartens in 1970, now has lots. In Finland, mothers get state-subsidized care for every child under three. Sweden's child care is even ritzier: a place at one of its state nurseries costs the government about as much as a place would at Eton, and child care overall absorbs about 6% of GDP. Nordic countries also have generous maternity-leave provisions: Sweden gives mothers 11 months, and up to 120 days' paid leave—per child—to care for sick children.

Many of the women whose employment is subsidized by fellow taxpayers work in the public services: in health, child care, education and public administration. They form the core of resistance to cuts in public spending. Perhaps not surprisingly, women are well represented among the ranks of Social Democratic politicians. In Sweden, they account for half the party's members of Parliament, in Norway for half the government ministers. Even so, Nordic governments are at last starting to ask whether they can afford to be so kind to women. Persistent unemployment, especially among men, may change attitudes. So will budget deficits that are going to force painful spending cuts.

Such cuts will be politically more difficult than raising taxes yet again. But the reasons for curbing the growth of the public sector are not mainly budgetary. More important are the effects of high taxes and high benefits on the labor market and on savings (discussed in the next section) and the fact that the declining productivity of the large public sector drags down the region's economic performance.

Part of the answer is to improve the efficiency of Nordic public sectors. In Sweden, local government has been allowed to decide whether to pay for an old person to be cared for at home or in an institution. Finland is introducing a voucher scheme for higher education. Denmark is experimenting with private providers of state services. Falck, a company that has long provided ambulances and fire-fighting, is teaming up with ISS, a Danish office-cleaning firm, to persuade the government to pay them to offer a complete service of care for the elderly. ISS already provides all the non-medical services for a state hospital in southern Jutland.

Many more such experiments are needed. But it will not be enough for governments to run public services as though they were in the private sector. They will also have to hand back to the private sector many of the tasks that the state has taken over in the past. Child care, saving for old age and insuring against unemployment and ill health should all be candidates for at least partial privatization too.

THE CONSEQUENCES OF KINDNESS

All the Nordic countries need more flexible labor markets. Nowhere is that more true than in Sweden and Finland, where there is a danger that the booming export sector, stimulated by currency depreciation, will drag up costs. All but Norway also have high unemployment, which is proving hard to reduce even when economies recover. Industrialists throughout the region complain of inflexibility in the labor market: "a stiffness, a certain lack of dynamism," in the words of Johann Schroder, chief executive of Radiometer, a Danish manufacturer of medical instruments. Among the reasons most commonly cited are high taxes, generous benefits, centralized pay bargaining and narrow wage differentials.

A high tax burden is the inevitable price of generous welfare benefits. In all the Nordic countries, tax revenues as a proportion of GDP are well above the European average— Finland is at first sight an exception, but not if social-security contributions are included

FIGURE 13-4

Taxing

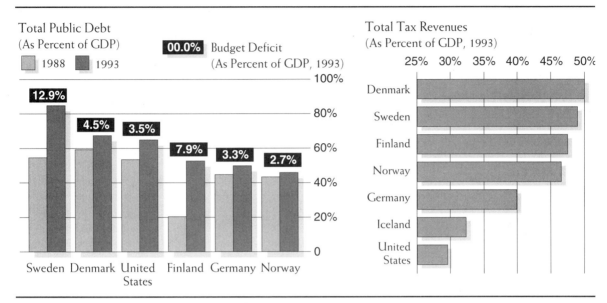

Total Public Debt
(As Percent of GDP)

☐ 1988 ☐ 1993

00.0% Budget Deficit
(As Percent of GDP, 1993)

Total Tax Revenues
(As Percent of GDP, 1993)

Source: OECD.

(see Figure 13-4). Moreover, except in oil rich Norway, personal income tax accounts for an unusually high proportion of taxes: around 40%, compared with a European average of about 25%.

The effect of high taxes on the job market is compounded by a strong belief in the virtues of small pay differentials. Relative wages have to a large extent become tools for redistributive ambitions," says the Lindbeck report. There is deep public resentment of large pre-tax salaries, even for the most successful senior executives. In Finland Jorma Ollila. boss of Nokia, got a total package of only $350,000 last year, before tax, for running a company with one-fifth of the world market for mobile phones. His fellow Nordics think that even this is extravagant. In Sweden earlier this year a 100% pay rise for the highly capable head of the country's profitable (and competitive) post office was greeted with so much public fury that the prime minister was forced to step in and quash it. "Swedes should beware of conspicuous consumption," murmurs SIFO's Bo Ekman.

Senior Scandinavian executives complain about high marginal tax rates, typically running to 65–70% (see Figure 13-5). Managers have in the past put up with low pay and high tax rates partly because life in a country such as Sweden has lots of pleasures: a country cottage, a boat and a large house are readily available compensations. Foreigners are different. Pharmacia, a recently privatized Swedish company, reckons that pre-tax pay for its senior managers is roughly half the level paid for equivalent staff in France or Italy, and complains that it is far easier to move Swedish managers to Italy than Italian managers to Sweden.

A consequence of the removal of exchange controls in the late 1980s has been to make it easier for good managers to take their money and walk. That will become easier still in countries that join the European Union. But there are other reasons to reduce high

FIGURE 13-5

Disincentive Effect

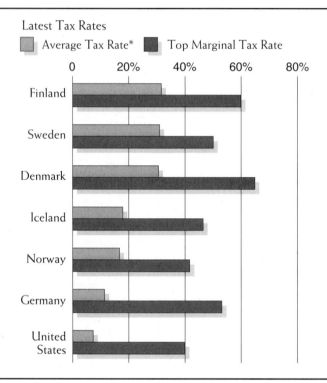

*Average married man with two small children earning $30,000.

Source: Price Waterhouse.

tax rates and to allow pay differentials to widen. One is to cut the tax wedge": the difference between what an employer pays and what a worker takes home. In 1989 the percentage increase in an employer's wage bill required to give a typical household a 1% rise in its net wage ranged from 2.6% in Finland to 5.6% in Sweden.

Another concerns education. One striking conclusion of the Lindbeck report was that the rate of return on education in Sweden had become dangerously low. In most industrialized countries, people expect to boost their incomes by at least 12% as a result of taking a university education. In Sweden, some estimates suggest the premium is only 3.5%. The fall in the premium may help to explain the fact that, by international standards, a relatively small proportion of young Swedes go on to universities. Companies complain: Pharmacia, for example, says that Sweden does not, produce enough good scientific researchers.

Not only have Swedes gained less than people in other countries from investing in education as youngsters; they have also gained little from investing in training over the course of a working life. Wages barely change as people become more experienced: they start high and stay flat. The Lindbeck report draws attention to a perhaps unique curiosity in the Swedish labor market in the past two decades. In 1968 18- and 19-year-olds earned 55% of the pay of 35–44-year-olds. By 1986 their earnings had risen to 80%. The problem is worst in the public sector, which finds it "easy to attract the newly educated, but difficult to keep those with more experience and qualifications."

A consequence of flat differentials is described by Jorgen Sondergaard, head of the secretariat of Denmark's Economic Council, which advises the government on pay trends. "Some skilled unions have almost no unemployment, while about 20% of the unskilled are out of work," he says. Danish unions compound skill shortages by refusing to allow employers to take on staff who have not undergone lengthy training. The centralized pay-bargaining arrangements common in Nordic countries aggravate the compression of differentials. The unions representing the unskilled know well, says Mr. Sondergaard, that such centralization is in their interest, because it gives them more political clout. Mercifully, centralized bargaining is now breaking down in Sweden, and to a lesser extent in Finland, under the pressure of the recession.

LUCKY COMPANIES

Income-from capital has typically been taxed every bit as heavily as income from employment; capital gains have been taxed relatively lightly. One result of that, coupled with low property taxes, has been to discourage people from building up financial assets and to encourage them to put their money into bricks and mortar instead. Swedes in particular are lavishly housed, with an average of two rooms per person. Another effect has been to discourage the build-up of medium-sized businesses. In Sweden, about 56% of people employed in manufacturing work in firms employing more than 200 people, and a mere 6% in firms with fewer than 20 workers—proportions that are radically different in other rich countries.

While taxes on incomes have been high, taxes on retained profits have been low. In Sweden, in the words of Kjell-Olof Feldt, Social Democrat finance minister in the late 1980s: "the Social Democrats wanted rich companies but poor owners." Successive Social Democrat governments have enjoyed a comfortable relationship with the Wallenberg group, which controls an estimated 40% of companies quoted on the Swedish stock exchange. The group's rumpled boss, Peter Wallenberg, has been pretty successful at persuading the left that what is good for his group is good for Sweden.

Low taxes on retained earnings have helped to build Sweden's corporate giants. But they have also depressed the internal rate of return and encouraged cash-rich mammoths to look round for ways to waste money—such as, in Volvo's case, diversifying into the food industry. The wiser mammoths have invested more profitably—but abroad, not in Sweden. A similar trend has been apparent in Finland, a country with a similar tax structure. In 1985–88 Swedish direct investment in the EC rose almost sevenfold; Finnish direct investment more than quadrupled. By the end of the 1980s 52% of the employees of Sweden's 30 largest manufacturing companies (ranked by employment) were working in foreign subsidiaries; as were 30% of the employees in Finland's 30 largest manufacturers. If there are plenty of good reasons why large companies based in small economies might expand mainly overseas, there is no case for keeping a tax structure that seems to be hastening the trend.

Attempts have been made to reform Scandinavian tax structures, mainly by broadening the tax base and closing loopholes. Denmark, for example, plans to reduce income tax over the next two years filling half the gap with a large increase in social security contributions. The aim is to encourage workers to connect contributions with welfare spending. Denmark also plans to increase revenue by raising taxes on environmental pollution. Sweden introduced a reform in 1991 that broadened the base and lowered marginal rates to 50% for the best paid and 30% for the average worker. But the scale of the budget deficit will make further reform difficult. Indeed, the new Social Democrat government plans to raise income tax—which will swing attention back to the labor market.

WHY WORK?

It is the combination of tax disincentives with generous welfare systems in Nordic countries that does most damage to the working of the labor market. Benefits to the unemployed have become a bit less generous since the start of the 1990s, but they have generally held their value better than real after-tax wages, especially when combined with other benefits, which are increasingly means-tested. In Finland, for instance, Sixten Korkman, director-general of the finance ministry, fears that benefit levels are discouraging people from taking jobs at the rates employers are willing to pay (see Figure 13-6).

Moreover, while the value of benefits may have been trimmed, the length of time for which the unemployed can draw them has not. Denmark cut benefits in the 1980s with

FIGURE 13-6
Unwork Ethic

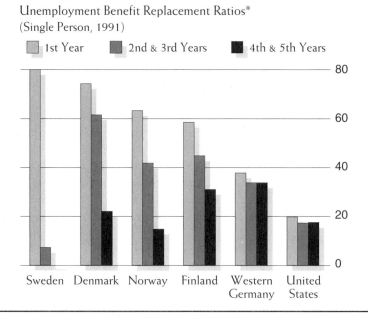

*Unemployment benefit as % of previous salary.
Source: OECD.

little impact on unemployment; now the debate has moved on to whether to cut their duration—up to seven years—by putting more pressure on the jobless to take up job offers. In Norway, older workers can easily get disability pensions. An unintended consequence has been that companies feel happier about putting their older staff out to grass. But the real fear is that these benefits may help to entrench high unemployment. Until recently, long-term unemployment has been a rarity in Sweden and Finland, and around the European average in Norway. Only in Denmark, which went into its recession earlier than its Nordic neighbors, has long-term unemployment been obstinately high.

In all the Nordic countries, one hears tales that suggest that many of the unemployed have now discovered an alternative to the famous Nordic work ethic. They are most widespread in Finland, where the recession has been deepest. A man in Helsinki hiring bus drivers, complains that eight of the ten who arrived for interview had come merely because they had to do so in order to keep their entitlement to benefit; a Finnish journalist reports that he was pleasantly surprised to find how little difference his first experience of unemployment made to his standard of living. "Everybody knows people who are cheating," he says, "and it's eating public morale. Everyone, both the employed and the unemployed, feels cheated."

The interaction of taxation and benefits also appears to have a negative impact on saving for retirement. The most numerous recipients of Nordic generosity are not the out of work but the old. All Nordic countries bar Iceland have relatively elderly populations: 17% of Swedes are already over 65, the highest proportion in the world. The costs of support for the old have risen dramatically. An earnings-related pension scheme, paid on top of the basic pension and introduced at the end of the 1950s, now costs more than 5% of GDP. Like the basic pension, it is financed by the taxpayer and by levies on employers and the self-employed: employees contribute nothing.

Sweden's state pension is, at least, partly funded. But the effect of the scheme is to breed the view that extra benefits cost nothing. Together with high taxes on income from capital and a history of rapid inflation, it also helps to discourage thrift. Although savings rates have recently risen sharply in the wake of the financial crises in Sweden, Finland, and Norway, all the Nordic countries have long had low rates of personal savings (see Figure 13-7), narrow capital markets and underdeveloped institutional investment. Thanks to a period of negative savings in the mid-1980s, net household savings in Sweden averaged 0.9% of GDP a year in 1980–92. With benefits to help pay for every contingency, from pregnancy to old age, Swedes have rarely seen the need for money in the bank.

Now an all-party committee has suggested a radical overhaul of state pension arrangements. The proposed new scheme would be financed by contributions split equally between employers and employees, with entitlement tied partly to the amounts that individuals pay in. One effect should be to encourage savings, albeit in a state-run fund. The Social Democrats have recently announced that they will no longer fully index pensions. In time, that may at last persuade Swedes to build up financial assets.

All the Nordic countries are now worrying about the generosity of their welfare systems. The non-socialist government in Sweden cut unemployment benefits from 90% to 80% of average pay. State sickness benefits, which once paid 90% of salary from the first day off work, now start only after a fortnight away from work, and at 80%. A consequence has been a dramatic decline in Sweden's notorious absenteeism, and a cheery suggestion that the finance ministry should be awarded the Nobel prize for medicine.

FIGURE 13-7 ——————————————————————————
Spendthrift

Household Savings
(As Percent of Disposable Income)

■ 1983   ■ 1993

Source: OECD.

Other countries are also considering changes. Denmark has recently conducted a review of social security. In Norway, a white paper is due shortly which will ask whether people should pay directly for some health care, whether state child support should be paid regardless of income and whether more social-security payments should depend on income. In Iceland, people now pay more towards the cost of healthcare, while payments to help with the costs of child-rearing and rent are no longer dished out to everyone.

Such changes are essential. The sight of a large minority of citizens living indefinitely on the state has begun to undermine the mutual trust that has been an important characteristic of the Nordic system. People have been willing to provide benefits to relieve the misfortunes of others, and have widely assumed that their generosity would not be abused. But now the cost of supporting public services is creating increasing frictions in those countries where the burden is greatest.

INTO EUROPE

To join or not to join? The debate over membership of the European Union has sharply divided voters in all four Nordic countries that are not already members. But it has taken different forms. In Sweden, where the decision to apply was announced to calm the markets in the thick of the 1990 economic crisis, the key issue has been industrial investment. In

Finland, with 1,000 km (620 miles) of shared border with Russia, much of the argument has been about security. Security has also been important, for different reasons, in Norway, worried about its position given the prospect of American disengagement from Europe.

In all the applicant countries, most political and business leaders and nearly all national newspapers have backed membership. Opposition has come mainly from farmers, other rural folk and from women, many of whom are employed in public services which they fear would be threatened by EU membership. Social Democrats are more nervous than members of center parties and conservatives. Bizarre though it sounds to those who are already members of the EU, the opponents of membership in all the applicant countries play on a deep fear that the EU stands for liberal markets and a loss of national control.

Opposition has been weakest in Finland (which is why the Finns held their referendum first); strongest in Norway, which votes last. In Finland, the vote in favor of membership has been won in spite of tension between Esko Aho, the pro-European prime minister, and the mainly anti-European Center Party that he leads, which has strong rural support. In Sweden, had the center-right Conservative government of Carl Bildt won the September election, the chances of a "yes" vote would have been diminished because the Social Democrats, who have been ambivalent Europeans, might have been half-hearted supporters. Victory has given Mr. Carlsson, the new prime minister, a better chance of persuading his supporters to vote yes.

In Norway, the outcome looks more finely balanced; but the sight of Finland and Sweden voting yes should tip the balance. However, the argument may not stop with the referendum. As in the other Nordic applicants, it is not binding, and enough members of Norway's parliament belong to parties opposed to membership to make it hard to reach the 75% parliamentary majority on which the constitution insists. Gro Harlem Brundtland, Norway's formidable Labor prime minister, has avoided threatening to resign if she fails to get a "yes" majority in the referendum: when her Labor predecessor, Trygve Bratelli, did that in 1972, the electorate called his bluff. But a "yes" vote in the referendum followed by a "no" vote in parliament would precipitate a constitutional crisis, a thought that may deter mutinous anti-Europeans from ignoring the referendum result.

The economic arguments for or against membership differ from one applicant country to another. Tariff barriers have played little part in the debate: as members of the European Economic Area, the three Nordic applicants have been part of a free-trade zone with the EU since the start of this year. In Iceland, which has not applied, much is made of the fact that the free-trade area brings most of the benefits of EU membership with few of the costs. The difficulty is that, once Austria and some Nordic countries join the EU, the economic area will seem less important. More crucially, the EEA offers its members no "seat at the table." Each applicant country has reasons for wanting a say in Europe's standard-setting, to avoid the trade-thwarting impact of non-tariff barriers.

In the case of Norway, Europe's biggest energy exporter, the main concern is how the EU organizes its energy market. Without Norway at the table, the EU's energy policy, still under construction, is likely to be built around the coal and nuclear power that the rest of Europe mainly produces. Norway produces much more oil than gas, but it has more reserves of gas than of oil. As Harald Norvik, chief executive of Statoil, the country's main state-owned energy company, points out, whereas oil is a global industry, gas is more of a local one, so its distribution is more subject to political interference. Norway already exports all its gas. Russia will be Norway's main competitor in

Europe's natural-gas market; a say in shaping EU energy policy offers a way to protect access to that market.

In Finland, timber and associated industries account for half the country's net exports, the great bulk of which go to Western Europe. The Finnish forestry industry has watched with dismay the growing pressure in EU countries to insist on minimum levels of recycling and of recycled content in paper products. "If we are not at the table where the decisions on standards are taken," says Jarl Kohler of the Finnish Forest Industries Association, "these can become protectionist." The foresters have good reason to worry. They are anxious to draw attention to the high environmental standards their industry now applies: trees are replanted faster than they are cut down, a variety of species makes the forests nicer to look at, and growing trees are good absorbers of carbon dioxide. But without a seat in Brussels to make this case, the industry fears that the recyclers may win the argument.

In Sweden, a group of big industries this summer publicly urged a "yes" vote in the referendum. Peter Wallenberg sums up the feeling: "The important thing is to be a full member, because that is the only way you can gain access to all quarters and influence people's way of looking at things. Besides, Sweden's market is too small to keep individual industries going." Swedish industry sees a vote for European membership as a way of helping to rebuild confidence. Swedish companies have not invested much at home for 20 years. Since the early 1960s, when industry invested some 24% of GDP, the ratio has dwindled to 13%. Companies have continued to invest, but abroad, not at home. This failure has lots of causes; but many people, including Anne Wibble, finance minister in the non-socialist government that lost power in September, ascribe it partly to uncertainty over EU membership. They may be right that uncertainty has encouraged the outflow and that a "no" vote would make it worse; the trouble is, without the other economic reforms, membership is not likely to bring industry back.

FARMS AND FISH

The strongest opposition to EU membership has come from those in Norway and Finland who worry about the effect on farmers. Farmers are the core of Norway's "no" movement, which its leader, Kristen Nygaard, describes as being "by far the largest political organization in Europe." The farmers' party is the second biggest in Norway's parliament, drawing support not only from the countryside but also from the many urban Norwegians whose families left the land only a generation ago. The passion behind the farmers' campaign is not surprising: they enjoy one of the highest levels of support in the world (see Figure 13-8). But on January 1 next year prices will have to fall to EU levels, although income support, paid for by the national government, will be increased to compensate farmers in the inhospitable north.

Norway has pursued a deliberate policy of cosseting its wildly uneconomic agriculture in order to preserve a rural society. It subsidizes other aspects of country life: "The standard of living is higher in rural districts than in cities," says Thorbjorn Jagland, leader of the Labor party, "because the public sector is more developed there. We are very aware of the problems of city life. It would be much more expensive if people moved to towns and we had to deal with all the accompanying social problems." One result is lots of small communities with expensive public administration.

But farmers are growing old. Rural employment has been falling by 2% a year for two decades. The real danger with EU membership may be not that it drives farmers off the land, but that it slows down the process, because the government is to be allowed to continue to pay large subsidies. That is mainly a risk in the north. Farmers in the east and south will receive less help than they do now, and will compete directly with the efficient Danes. So Norway's least inefficient farmers will be hurt most.

In Finland farmers have had an even better deal. Indeed, it has been so good that the country produces a surplus of milk, beef, pork and (incredibly) grain. One of the transitional costs to the public sector of joining the EU will be the need for the government to compensate farmers for the losses they will incur on their surpluses next year, because EU farm prices are 40% below Finnish levels. In Sweden, by contrast, where a brave attempt has been made to dismantle farm subsidies, EU membership will result in an increase in protection for some agricultural products.

Norwegian fishermen are another group that has always opposed membership. But they have won a much better deal than they ever expected: so good, indeed, that Iceland has had second thoughts about its decision not to apply. Norway's fishing industry is now split down the middle on EU membership. Those who fish at sea hate the thought that Spanish fishermen will be allowed to plunder Norway's coastal waters. But fish-farmers, who now produce as much as sea fishermen, are keen to sell processed fish to the EU. Tariffs on

FIGURE 13-8
Outcapping

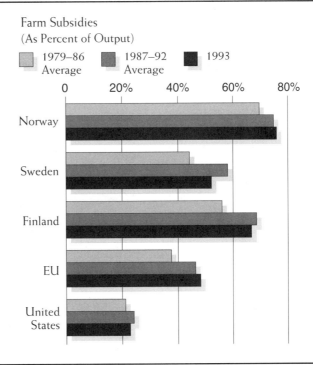

Source: OECD.

processed fish, which the EU refused to give up during the talks on the EEA, are thought to have driven the Norwegian fish-processing industry south to Denmark.

As for the Danes, their impressively efficient food industry expects to feed a lot more Finns and Norwegians. At the Agricultural Council, which represents Danish farmers, Henning Otte Hansen cheerfully points out that pork, eggs and poultry get little protection in the EU, but are the areas where Denmark is most competitive. In other words, Denmark is producing almost at world prices. Not surprisingly, Danish food companies have been buying into the industry in the three applicant countries to gain a foothold.

If all three applicants go in, the smallest Nordic country of all will be left alone (with Switzerland), in the outer circle of the EEA. Iceland has Europe's only unsubsidized fishing industry, though it has protected its fishermen by keeping almost all other fishing fleets out of its coastal waters. The fall in the fish catch means that nobody is keen to change that policy. But 80% of the catch is sold to Europe, if Norway joins, its fishing industry—Iceland's main rival—may gain at Iceland's expense.

The ruling Conservative party is backed by farmers who are even more fabulously protected than farmers in Finland and Norway, and just as fearful of Europe. The prime minister and most of his government are skeptical: most of the benefits of EU membership already come from belonging to the EEA. Besides, argues the opposition People's Alliance, Iceland's tiny civil service and sparse flights to Brussels would make membership an intolerable burden for the public administration.

But the alternative is political isolation. Already Icelanders wince when (as happens all too often) newspapers inadvertently leave their island off a map. Worse lies ahead. "After 1996 the EU will be preoccupied with applications from Eastern Europe," argues Jon Baldvin Hannibalsson, the foreign minister, chairman of the Social Democrats and the government's main Euro-enthusiast. The United States has withdrawn most of its troops from the naval base at Keflavik. Last May, a parliamentary delegation visited the United States and broached the possibility of Icelandic membership of the North American Free-Trade Agreement. Latin America, the Icelanders were told, was first in the queue. Iceland would have to wait.

CROSS YOUR FINGERS AND JUMP

The fear of isolation may be enough to persuade all three Nordic applicants to go in. All three have turned south because they feel less confident about their ability to continue alone. Sweden and Finland in particular are hunting for economic security under the Euroblanket. But the experience of plenty of EU members is that joining the club is no magic cure. Indeed, life in Europe will in some ways be tougher than life outside. It will be easier for the young and the skillful to emigrate. It will be more difficult to preserve the peculiarities of the tax system. It will be harder to prevent companies falling into foreign hands, something the Swedes have been particularly clever at in the past.

These pressures will be good for the Nordic countries. Others will not. The protection of Europe's farmers will legitimize the protection of farmers in Finland and Norway. The EU's interventionist instincts will bring out the worst in Nordic Social Democrats, discouraging them from liberalizing their job markets and from dismantling, at least partially, their bloated welfare systems.

The Nordic countries have plenty to teach the rest of Europe about openness and honesty in public life, social responsibility and pragmatism. Their arrival could change the outlook of the Union more radically than any event since the arrival of Britain over 20 years ago. But if the change is to be for the good, the Nordic countries will need to see membership as an opportunity to continue to make their economies more flexible and to reduce the role of the state, rather than as one more chance to postpone reform.

PART IV

Industrial Development and Marketing in the New Europe

An Industrial Policy for Europe: Concept and Applications

HARRY COSTIN

This paper will discuss and contrast interpretations of industrial policy rooted in political, economic, and strategic approaches. The concept of industrial policy will then be applied to a non-traditional unit of analysis—a regional economic group rather than only one country. The specific focus will be twofold: (1) to explore whether the European Union has developed an industrial policy and (2) to examine the institutions with the powers to design and implement it.

INDUSTRIAL POLICY: A FRAMEWORK OF ANALYSIS

In order to analyze industrial policy as a set of government choices and actions, the following questions need to be addressed:

1. What is an industrial policy?
2. Is an industrial policy necessary and useful or detrimental to economic growth?
3. Is it a necessary evil in a world where free trade remains an elusive goal?
4. How is an industrial policy implemented?
5. What is the best method of analysis of the results of implementation?

Industrial policy is inherently political in questions such as the role of government in society, the legitimacy of economic institutions, and how they interact with the private sector.

For example, southeastern Asian countries such as South Korea have for decades developed five-year economic development plans. These plans detail national priorities and support given to specific industries. Such a plan would be unthinkable in the United States, where any argument concerning the logic of systematic support to chosen industries by the federal government would counter a long-standing political tradition that limits the role of government in running the economy.

This example illustrates the complexity of the concept of industrial policy. For further discussion it is useful to distinguish three variables in the process of formulation and implementation of industrial policy: logic, ideology, and performance.

The first variable is the **logic** or rationale for use of an industrial policy. Analyses focus on results such as predicted employment rates and low inflation derived from such policies, based on economic theory. Nevertheless, although some of the basic premises may be common among analysts, different schools of economic thought prevail (for example, Keynesian, Monetarist, and Marxist). Following a Keynesian interpretation of economic growth, the implementation of an industrial policy might be seen as a useful policy tool. By contrast, following a Monetarist approach, an industrial policy would likely be seen as largely detrimental to growth and stability. A Marxist state would probably implement an industrial policy for reasons other than economic rationality.

A prevailing **ideology** may justify the use of an industrial policy for reasons other than economic rationality, such as national pride. Ideology and values determine policy making and implementation, based on different national and individual priorities. Ideology in this context can be compared to the set of axioms on which a logical system is based. Ideology and logic are different, since logic is a system of inferences based on a set of "given" premises. Ideology relates to the "given" premises, to a set of fundamental values and choices, on which all other inferences are made.

The third variable is **performance**. Performance is commonly measured using both macroeconomic (for example, growth, employment, and inflation) and socio-economic (for example, income distribution) indicators and relates to the fundamental question: Is industrial policy an effective means to achieve objectives such as national industrial competitiveness and sustained economic growth?

DEFINING INDUSTRIAL POLICY: AN OVERVIEW OF EXISTING APPROACHES

Industrial policy is commonly defined as a set of government initiatives designed to protect and promote the development of particular industrial sectors. These initiatives may include incentives to investment in capital goods, or R&D efforts. Direct governmental acts may include legislation such as import quotas and tariffs. The concept that underlies all interpretations of industrial policy is the idea that *government*, rather than the free play of economic market forces, decides which particular industries and firms are to be promoted. A commonly cited example is the decision of the Japanese government, through the Ministry of International Trade and Industry, to promote the shift of resources from the "sunset" high-energy industries (for example, steel) to the "sunrise" high technology industries, as a planned reaction to the oil shocks of the 1970s.

Industrial policy, as a set of government choices and actions, can be interpreted in different ways related to the three variables (logic, ideology, and performance) discussed earlier:

1. An industrial policy is a rational mechanism of policy formulation and implementation used by governments to promote economic growth based on fundamental economic logic (for example, need for economies of scale in certain industries). An industrial policy may also serve to advance other national priorities such as national defense and political independence (for example, the French military complex). Every government has some form of industrial policy, whether openly defined or not.
2. The basic values of a society are the ideological origin of an industrial policy. A particular country has been shaped by a historical legacy of the distribution of political powers and collective preferences, from individualism to collectivism (Lodge, 1990). For example, Japan's industrial policy clearly reflects collective values that emphasize the common good, while the prevalent American aversion to any industrial policy reflects

    a long tradition of individualism, with distrust in government to be an efficient allocator of economic resources.

3. An industrial policy is a necessary evil. When some governments intervene to boost artificially the competitiveness of their industries, it is only fair that others do the same. The efforts of international forums (primarily GATT) to settle such disputes have proven largely ineffective to curb such infringements on free, global competition. Therefore, "reciprocity" is only fair. The emergence of regional trading blocks (North America, the European Union, and Southeast Asia) and "bilateralism," as opposed to "multi-lateralism," is a new economic and political reality.

4. The concept of industrial policy has also been discussed in the context of economic development models. For example, Rostow (1961) has described how developing countries commonly go through a stage of "Import Substitution Industrialization" whereby local industry, protected under a national industrial policy, begins to produce goods that were previously imported. Also, during this stage, industries with "spillover effects," such as construction and automobile manufacturing, are promoted and protected from cheaper imports.

In the United States, the discussion regarding the need to implement an industrial policy has had strong political overtones. An industrial policy is seen by some (usually from the political right) as a flagrant symbol of the sort of government interference in the economy that should be avoided at any cost.

The European approach to industrial policy is altogether different. It is partly rooted in a welfare tradition, described in the following terms by Ralf Dahrendorf, who referred to Great Britain's strengths and weaknesses:

> The persistence of certain social and political values in this country is one of the main reasons for its weaknesses in political performance, but at the same time, the persistence of these social and political values is one of the main reasons for a degree of social and political welfare, which is not characteristic of many other developed countries. (HBS case 386–134, p. 11)

Industrial policies implemented in most Western European countries seem to have three main purposes: first, to stimulate industries that are crucial to global industrial competitiveness (for example, semiconductors) in order to avoid a dangerous dependency on foreign technologies; second, to promote employment; and third, to promote industries for other purposes, such as national security, in the name of national or pan-European interests (for example, the French defense industry and the Airbus consortium).

There is also a fourth goal, that of social welfare. The implementation of policies that will achieve this goal is more difficult to measure, except in cases where government decides to control the industries that are considered key to the general welfare of the population (for example, nationalized health care).

INDUSTRIAL AND TRADE POLICY

The mechanisms available to government to implement an industrial policy include national trade policy. A recent study of the International Monetary Fund illustrates this relationship:

> Industrial policy is broadly defined as the deliberate attempt by a government to influence the composition of a nation's output. The definition encompasses all government actions to foster

activity in specific sectors, either to shift resources to higher-productivity activities in support of adjustment objectives or to maintain resources in existing activities for security, political, and other reasons. A number of domestic and trade measures are used by governments to implement industrial policies. An indicative list of selected domestic measures would include subsidies (cash transfers, research and development funding, tax concessions, loan guarantees and insurance, subsidized credits, capital grants, regional aids); government procurement; national product standards; and commodity-specific indirect taxation. An indicative list of selected trade measures would include tariffs (peaks: high tariffs on selected products in a structure with otherwise low overall tariffs; escalation: progressively higher tariffs, within a product category, as the level of processing and value added increases), and nontariff measures (import quotas, voluntary export restraints, tariff quotas, discretionary and nondiscretionary import licensing, countervailing and antidumping investigations and duties, health standards, and export subsidies). (Kelly 1988, 15)

IDEOLOGY AND INDUSTRIAL POLICY

When it comes to the discussion of ideology and its relationship to industrial policy, we need to differentiate descriptive from normative methods of analysis. Purely descriptive approaches are rare, since it is difficult to analyze objectively ideology without taking sides. These descriptive analyses attempt to provide a historical and cultural perspective that emphasizes how a given state of things came to be. Most studies, such as country analyses done by multilateral development institutions, have a strong normative component, providing guidelines on how things ought to be.

The work of George C. Lodge provides useful insights to the relationship between the concepts of ideology and industrial policy. He defines industrial policy as

> ... a set of procedures through which government and business join together to determine community needs, organize and allocate resources to fulfill them, and adopt in particular a wide range of instruments to achieve global competitiveness. (1990, p. 66)

Lodge's definition and further discussion of industrial policy are closely related to the broader concept of business/government relationships. In his view, these relationships are strongly affected by national history and ideology. He departs from the one-dimensional analysis that places totalitarianism at one end of the spectrum and democracy at the other, and describes another continuum:

> There are two ideological paradigms concerning the role of government: **individualistic**, which stresses the individual over the community, and **communitarian**, in which the reverse is true. In actual practice, most nations display a mix of these two types.

> In an individualistic society, the role of government is limited. Its fundamental purposes are to protect property, enforce contracts, and keep the marketplace open so that competition among firms may be as vigorous and as free as possible. Government is essentially separate from business. It intervenes in the affairs of business only when the national health and safety are involved ...

> The role of government in a communitarian society is quite different. Here government is prestigious and authoritative, sometimes authoritarian. Its function is to define the needs of the community over the long as well as the short term, and to see that those needs are met (although not necessarily through its offices). It sets a vision for the community; it defines and ensures the rights and duties of community membership, and it plays a central role in

creating—sometimes imposing—consensus to support the direction in which it decides the community should move . . .

To oversimplify, among the so-called capitalistic countries, the United States has tended traditionally to be the most individualistic, Japan the most communitarian. Other nations can be placed somewhere along the continuum between these two extremes. Germany is more communitarian than the United Kingdom, but still less so than Japan. France is a complex mix that in the 1980s allowed a communitarian president and a more individualistic prime minister to share power effectively. (1990, 15–16)

Another duality relating to national perspectives is characterized as "inward looking," when countries focus on domestic considerations, vs. "outward-looking," as countries aim to achieve a global political or economic position.

According to Lodge, the traditional Western predominance of the "individualistic" paradigm has to be challenged in terms of economic effectiveness. ". . . Japan and other Asian countries . . . have benefited greatly by acting contrary to the tenets of individualism." (1990, 17). Free trade as advocated by the individualistic ideological model is at odds with reality. As Lodge notes, "nearly 75% of world commerce is conducted by economic systems operating with principles at odds with American individualism."(17)

Lodge is a strong advocate of a U.S. industrial policy, but cautious regarding the prerequisites for an effective formulation and implementation of such a policy, which would require coordination across different government agencies.

INDUSTRIAL POLICY: A MANAGEMENT POLICY PERSPECTIVE

The distinct approaches of the fields of Economics and Management Policy to the concept of industrial policy relate to the units of analysis selected, the concepts of decision making and choice (rational vs. organizational processes or political paradigms. See: Allison: 1971), and the importance of time adjustment to impersonal market forces (long vs. short term).

Economic analysis describes a set of impersonal forces of supply and demand that, in the long term, work independently of ideology. These forces are based on existing national endowments of resources that are unequally distributed. More recent economic approaches have begun to emphasize the role of "created comparative advantages," based primarily on the successful development of countries like Japan and the Four Dragons (Hong Kong, South Korea, Taiwan, and Singapore), which are not richly endowed with natural resources.

Management Policy emphasizes the concept of choice at all levels: individual, organizational, national, and international. Choices, such as whether or not to enter specific markets, by identifiable political actors, matter fundamentally, and although basic economic forces continue to prevail, the time effect of market adaptation to shifts in supply and demand curves may be significant.

From a Management Policy perspective, an industrial policy is not simply a given environment in which managers have to learn how to operate, but one in which managers should influence and help to reframe. (Pfeffer & Salanclk 1978, Thompson 1967). Too often managers react to a given environment, rather than acting to shape a new one.

These two different perspectives can be illustrated using the example of the Europe 1992 program for the completion of the internal market in the European Community. The industrial policy components of the program can be seen as a rational set of choices to a growing concern about the lack of competitiveness of European industries in the early 1980s. Several economic studies such as the celebrated Cecchini Report provided a rationale, based on long-term employment, inflation and growth effects for an integrated European market and the fostering of key industries (for example, high technology).

A very different analytical approach examines the political role of key players in the framing of the original legislative agenda, known as "The White Paper" on the Completion of the Internal Market. The CEO of Philips, Wise Dekker; the President of the Commission, Jacques Delors (a former French Finance Minister during a socialist administration); and Lord Cockfield, the main author of the White Paper of 1985, played key roles in the creation of the original program. From this Management Policy perspective, the 1992 program is essentially a political agenda strongly influenced by individuals and the national priorities of the strongest members of the Community, such as Germany, France, and the United Kingdom.

One of the key differences between these two approaches lies in the choice of unit of analysis. Macroeconomics focuses on regional blocks, countries, and industries (aggregated industries). Management Policy focuses on segmented industries, specific companies, and key decision makers. A Management Policy perspective to the analysis of industrial policy can provide useful insights into the complex question: how useful is an industrial policy, and how can performance variables be defined and measured? An example of such an approach can be found in Porter (1990), who addressed the issue of the competitive advantage of nations in a multi-industry, multi-country study. Porter's study focused on industries in different countries which have demonstrated consistent superiority in specific industrial sectors.

Some of Porter's conclusions were:

1. Firms in specific industry segments compete; countries do not.
2. Competitive advantage in industry clusters is created, not a consequence of natural resource endowments. The most important resources are highly specialized and created. No country can achieve sustainable competitive advantage in all industries.
3. A strongly competitive national environment leads to sustained competitive advantage, not a highly protected one.
4. The role of government is auxiliary, not fundamental in achieving sustainable competitive advantage. Government can influence in a limited way only the four key variables related to competitive advantage: firm strategy, structure, and rivalry; factor conditions; demand conditions; and related and supporting industries. Government can not immediately influence or create these conditions, which are related to the historical development of specific countries. Nevertheless, government can provide focus and market intelligence, for example, (Ministry of International Trade and Industry) role in directing industry attention to research in leading edge technologies.

According to Porter:

Government plays a prominent role in international competition, but it is a different one than is commonly supposed. At one extreme, some view government as at best a passive participant in the process of international competition because the determinants of national advantage are so deeply rooted in a nation's buyers, its history, and other unique circumstances, it could be argued that government is powerless ... the evidence from our research, does not support this view. Government policy does affect national advantage, both positively and negatively. While the role of government in creating and sustaining national advantage is significant, however, it is inevitably partial. Without the presence of underlying circumstances that support competitive advantage in a particular industry, the best policy intentions will fail, Governments do not control national competitive advantage: they can only influence it. The central role of government policy toward the economy is to *deploy a nation's resources (labor and capital) with high and rising levels of productivity.* (1990, 617).

The implications of Porter's conclusions, which he claims are empirically (rather than ideologically) based, are significant. For the effective implementation of an industrial policy, he advocates focused, non-politically motivated stimuli by government to specific sectors, where competitive advantage based on fundamental factors and history already exists, rather than broadly based protectionism of generic industries. Experience shows that protectionism only results in the opposite of the stated objectives of such efforts: long-term decline and lack of national competitiveness.

Though important, Porter's analysis falls to address a basic question: What are the political conditions necessary to select "strategic industries" and to implement policies that will inevitably result in "winners" and "losers"? For example, although MITI's efforts contributed to industrial restructuring from energy-intensive to technology-intensive industries after the oil shocks, the inefficient Japanese rice industry is politically untouchable.

INDUSTRIAL POLICY IN THE EUROPEAN UNION

Traditionally, industrial policy as a concept has been used in the analysis of government choices and actions of specific countries such as Japan, Germany, or the United Kingdom. There is no clearly established framework that uses industrial policy as a conceptual tool to analyze concerted economic action at the level of a regional economic group such as the European Union. Still, references to the Community's industrial policy are frequent. The following questions have been posed: Does the European Union have an industrial policy? Is such policy in the best interest of its members? To answer these questions, the basic conditions for the formulation and implementation of an industrial policy need to be defined.

Industrial policy, understood as a set of economic and political choices and actions to promote specific industries likely to have a positive economic growth effect, requires: first, government actors such as agencies in charge of planning and "designing" a set of coherent policies; second, implementation mechanisms like tariffs, or financial and information resources, funneled to the chosen industries to be promoted; and third, enforcing and control mechanisms for government policies.

Policies need to be planned or designed, implemented and enforced, and results evaluated. For the purposes of our analysis, we must determine whether the political agencies and mechanisms necessary to design and implement an industrial policy exist at the Community level. The answer to this question is complex, as it has evolved with the enactment of the Single European Act in 1987 and the Maastricht Treaty in 1993.

THE TREATY OF ROME AND THE SINGLE EUROPEAN ACT

The Treaty of Rome of 1957, the founding charter of the European Economic Community, called for concerted action in specific industries such as coal, steel, and agriculture. For example, significant support was given to agriculture under the framework of the Common Agricultural Policy, which has amounted until recently to two-thirds of the Community budget. Without such support, and left to market forces, the agricultural sector would have decreased even further throughout the Community than it has over the last three decades.

During the 1980s, while such sectorial policies continued to be implemented (inevitably creating "winners" and "losers"), every effort was made in Brussels not to refer to such initiatives as a European-wide "industrial policy." The Commission stressed repeatedly that sovereignty rested with the individual member countries, which was true until the passing of the Single European Act in 1986, as individual member countries could effectively exert a veto on most decisions.

The Single European Act modified the existing decision-making process by introducing qualified-majority voting in the European Council (34 out of 56 votes). With this modification, binding community legislation could be passed in many areas, bypassing the wishes of an individual member country. In effect, a country could be forced, under community legislation, to accept and also incorporate into national laws legislation with which it might not agree.

The Europe 1992 program, defined in the Single European Act, and detailed in the White Paper of 1985, significantly altered industrial and business practices in the Community and introduced a set of some 300 new Directives, that is, European laws that needed to be translated into country laws. Most of these Directives were passed using the new "qualified majority" process.

During the implementation of the legal framework (300 Directives) of the Europe 1992 program, Community officials remained reluctant to make reference to a potential "industrial policy." Rather, a new context for community-wide "free competition" was stressed. In 1989, Bangemann, vice-president of the Commission stated:

> There is widespread misunderstanding about the industrial policy concept advocated by the European Commission. We neither seek to copy the Japanese M.I.T.I. (Ministry of International Trade and Industry) with its quantified objectives for market shares and support for industry from massive public funding, nor can we accept a free-for-all based on market forces alone.
>
> The approach that we recommend for European Industry lies between those two extremes. We have to create a legal and tax environment which promotes investment and economic cooperation in Europe.

Mr. Bangemann went on to point out that this approach requires:

- a truly European competition policy,
- an open commercial policy (competitiveness is the only true effective weapon against protectionism), and
- intensification of R&D policy.

In short, he pointed out, we must drop the defensive attitude that too often typifies the debate on industrial policy in Europe.

This represented a rare occurrence of a specific reference by a high-level Community official to the elements of a European "industrial policy."

The London *Economist* commented on such reluctance and the potential for a European Industrial Policy:

> Ever since Project 1992 began, industrial policy has been Europe's issue that dare not speak its name. As more and more barriers between the EC's national markets have been dismantled, and as the European Commission has gained the power to oversee competition policy in the Community and to attack state subsidies, so the ability of national governments to protect, nurture, finance or otherwise encourage domestic businesses has been diminished. Allowing such national nurturing would make a nonsense of the idea of a single, open market. But not all governments accept this. *France, in particular, has regularly tested the commission's resolve over state aids and competition policy. And this process has left unanswered the question of whether something supranational might replace these paroquial industrial policies—an effort to produce European champions rather than national ones.*
>
> The question is unanswered because the Community is divided over the issue, as is the commission itself France and Italy lead the interventionist camp; Britain and Holland lead the opposition. (Jan. 25, 1992 editorial)

A further analysis of the potential for a European industrial policy under the Treaty of Rome and the Single European Act requires an understanding of the role and powers of the Commission, of European Competition Policy, and a brief overview of sectorial policies.

THE COMMISSION

Ludlow provided a clear synthesis of the role and powers of the Commission:

> The Commission is charged by the Treaties to act "in the general interest of the Communities." More specifically, it is given three functions:
>
> - to initiate the policy process and more generally serve as the driving force behind European integration within the terms of reference laid down by the Treaties,
> - to act as guardian of the Treaties themselves, both in its own right and by recourse to the Court, and
> - to implement Community policies in terms laid down by and with the Council.
>
> The Commission's mandate [as initiator of policy and legislation] ... is not simply optional, it is binding. The Commission is obliged by the Treaties to take the initiative in ensuring that their provisions are transformed into practical policy. Its actual fulfillment of these tasks is probably best considered under five headings: strategic goal setting, policy formulation, the drafting of legislation, preparation of the budget, and political management. (1991, 96ff).

The Commission with its XXIII Directorate Generals (DGs), headed by 17 commissioners, is the entity that can design and, to a large extent, enforce an industrial policy. The Commission develops the European legislative agenda, including the one affecting the different industrial sectors, but it is the Council of Ministers, which represents the current governments of the twelve EC members, that votes on legislation that will have a Community-wide impact.

Before 1987, European laws were difficult to pass because each EC member had a right to veto most legislation. This changed with the passing of the Single European Act in 1986, a modification to the founding charter of the EC, the Treaty of Rome of 1957. Today, the passing of European "laws" (Directives and Regulations), except for specific cases such as fiscal matters, does not require unanimous consent of the twelve Community members, but only a "qualified majority." With the Single European Act and the Maastricht Treaty, the European Parliament, comprising over 500 Members of Parliament (MPs) directly elected by the European citizens, also has veto power on legislation.

Several of the XXIII DGs of the Commission represent specific industrial sectors such as Agriculture (DG VI), Telecommunications (DG XIII), Financial Institutions (DG XV), and Small- and Medium-size Enterprises (DG XXIII). As could be expected, the specific interests of these sectors can be at odds, as evident in intra-Commission disagreements during the last few years.

EUROPEAN COMPETITION LAW

The framework for "free competition" in the European Union, a concept repeatedly highlighted by EU officials in contrast to "industrial policy," is provided in the Treaty of Rome. Peter Sutherland, former Commissioner for Competition, provided the following description (1985):

> EEC competition law is based on specific provisions in the Treaty of Rome which take precedence over national anti-trust laws, although it does not replace them. The treaties require the Commission to take action against anti-competitive practices that partition the Common Market or distort competition; at the same time, it enables the Commission to favor cooperation among companies that promote the overall policy interests of the Community, and particularly the unity of the Common Market.
>
> Action can be taken against the following varieties of anti-competitive behavior:
>
> (i) government subsidies or state aids to particular firms or industries under Articles 92-94 of the EEC Treaty; the policy seeks to ensure that competitive firms do not suffer through unfair subsidies to weaker competitors.
>
> (ii) control over public undertakings and monopolies under Articles 90 and 37 of the EEC Treaty to ensure that there is no discrimination between private and public sector enterprises.
>
> (iii) restrictive business practices such as price fixing, market sharing, anti-competitive discrimination, etc., under Article 85 of the EEC Treaty.
>
> (iv) abuses of dominant position by a firm or group of firms under Article 86 of the EEC Treaty.

This framework is translated into specific business and industrial practices to be avoided, described by Wistrich (1991, 47–48):

> The Treaty of Rome outlaws deals between companies to fix prices, share out markets, place limits on investment, development and production, or adopt other restrictive practices. It bans abuses of dominant position by firms or groups of enterprises and forbids government subsidies that distort or threaten to distort competition . . .

Price-fixing agreements, such as the dye-stuffs cartel which in 1969 controlled 80 per cent of the European market, were outlawed. Firms with head offices outside the Community were fined because they were operating within the Community in a way damaging to its interests.

There is a ban on agreements to buy only from specified manufacturers or importers, and to sell only to certain buyers, because they carve up the market and give unfair advantages which distort free trade. The products involved range from gramophone records to heating equipment. (1991, 47–48)

This framework existed since the founding of the EEC in 1957, but was frequently bypassed using exemption clauses of the Treaty of Rome. The practice persisted until the mid-80s when DG IV (Competition), under the able leadership of Sir Leon Brittan, began to use its powers more effectively to curb abusive practices. In one case, the French government was required to suspend subsidies to French automobile manufacturers.

The European Court of Justice also played an important role in enforcing free competition. The celebrated Cassis de Dijon case represented an important precedent for legislative supranationality. In this instance, Germany was not allowed to suspend imports of the French liquor as not conforming to German laws for classification of spirits. This decision spearheaded a powerful movement toward a new approach to competition throughout Europe.

SECTORIAL POLICIES: COAL, STEEL, AGRICULTURE, AND TECHNOLOGY

The sectorial policies of the EU bear the mark of what would normally be considered an industrial policy. Several of these policies also constitute good examples of the type of behaviors and performance criticized by those who fundamentally oppose the formulation and implementation of an industrial policy.

The coal and steel industries are basic to European Community concerns, and have been since its inception. These concerns were enshrined in one of the sister institutions of the EC, the Coal and Steel Community, founded in 1951. The Community has systematically protected the interests of these industries, through strong subsidies that have at least partially resulted in obsolete technologies and excess capacity. Those arguing in favor of economic rationality and the need to let market forces prevail have strongly criticized the heavy subsidies given to these industries. One such example is the London *Economist's* criticism of recent support to the steel industry:

History has a nasty habit of repeating itself in Western Europe's steel industry. After running into trouble in the early 1980s, steel makers were rescued by a special "crisis regime" enshrined in the 1951 treaty which created the European Coal and Steel Community (ECSC). Now, after a brief period of profit, big steel has more big problems. Yet again there are too many mills in Europe churning out too much steel. Yet again, prices are plunging, losses are piling up and steel companies are clamoring for subsidies and other kinds of support. And yet again the European Community's proposed solution to the industry's ills is not really a solution at all. Just the reverse: it is part of the problem. (March 6–12 1993, 17)

But apart from concerns of economic rationality, coal and steel remain politically delicate subjects. This became evident in the British government's failed attempt to close coal mines, which almost toppled the Tories in 1992. A quick reversal of intentions was necessary, despite the fact that coal production costs were running higher than market prices, with no possible trend reversal in sight.

A further example of EC sectorial policy is the "Common Agricultural Policy" (CAP), in place since the founding of the EC. The CAP is a system of tariffs, subsidies and other mechanisms of protectionism of Community agriculture, and currently constitutes two-thirds of the EC budget.

In the 1950s almost one-third of the Community members' population depended economically on agriculture. It was the primary economic activity of many regions, and of some countries. However, the income of this sector was a third lower than the general average. In this context, the CAP was implemented to increase agricultural productivity, raise the standard of living of those working on the land, stabilize markets and guarantee a regular flow of supplies, and ensure stable and reasonable prices to consumers.

In the early 1990s protectionism of agriculture led to a deadlock between the Community and the United States in the GATT Uruguay Round of Trade talks, and, according to the *Economist,* to price instability rather than the hoped-for stability to be promoted under the original objectives of the CAP.

EUROPEAN TECHNOLOGY POLICY

A more positive example of sectorial policy can be found in the Community's efforts to promote European technological interests. Marchipont et al. (1992) have offered several arguments that justify an industrial policy in technology. Recognizing the complex dynamics of international competition, they favor policies that will stimulate the creation and implementation of key technologies on Community soil rather than simple protection of what can only dubiously be referred to as Community vs. non-Community companies, given the complex patterns of ownership that exist.

The promotion of research and other technology-related efforts by the Community is justified since many technologies involve large sunk costs in their development and often constitute a quasi "public" good, that is, their benefits are often not proprietary but accrue to third parties at a marginal cost, once developed.

Specific cases, such as the development of a European standard for High Definition TV, justify even further the intervention of Community level entities. In this case, the Community's role is not only to foster the development of expensive core technologies, and thereby decrease the existing technological dependence from the United States and Japan, but also to help generate a market large enough to justify these technologies.

Currently, many European technology programs are actively supported by the Community. Some go beyond Community borders and include EFTA members.

Examples of these programs are:

- ESA (**European Space Agency**), set up in 1975, its objective is "to provide and promote, for exclusively peaceful purposes, cooperation among European states in space research and technology and their space applications, with a view to their being used for scientific purposes and for operational space application systems."
- SPRINT (**Strategic Program for Innovation and Technology Transfer**) launched in 1986 with the purpose of helping small- and medium-sized enterprises in their needs for skilled support for R&D of new products and transnational marketing.

- **RACE (Research and Development in Advanced Communications Technologies for Europe)** had the aim of achieving coherence of the different telecommunication systems and services being developed in the Community.
- **EUREKA (European Research Co-ordinating Agency)** launched as a nonmilitary European response to the US's SDI to identify, support, and co-ordinate military industry protects to increase European competitiveness.

An attempt to integrate the different efforts to develop state-of-the-art technologies into a coherent framework is the concept of "European Technological Community," incorporated in the text of the Single European Act of 1985:

> The Community's aim shall be to strengthen the scientific base of European industry and to encourage it to become more competitive at the international level. (Article 130)

The broad objectives of a coherent policy for the Community in technology have been largely praised, but the results of specific programs have received mixed reviews. Still, in contrast to the cases of sectorial policies for coal, steel and agriculture, there is largely consensus that a unified effort to promote European technology interests is necessary and advisable, and preliminary results have been positive.

INDUSTRIAL AND TRADE POLICY

Earlier in this paper, reference was made to the interaction between industrial and trade policy. The Commission can not only formulate and implement sectorial policies, but also has responsibility for European trade policy. Among other duties it represents the EU in GATT negotiations, and has sought to enforce "reciprocity," which means access to specific foreign markets, similar to access the EU grants to actors from those markets. Japan has been targeted specifically as an unfair player.

The previous discussion has shown that the necessary mechanisms for the formulation and implementation of a "European Industrial Policy" have in fact existed at the level of the European Union since the founding of the EEC. Nevertheless, it is likely that EU officials would object to the suggestion that such a policy exists. However, there are clearly defined sectorial policies, of which some, as in the cases of coal, steel, and agriculture, can be traced back to the founding of the Community in 1957.

Before turning to the modifications introduced in the Maastricht Treaty it is useful to examine a further question: Does the European Union have sufficient ideological coherence to warrant a unified industrial policy?

EUROPEAN INDUSTRIAL POLICY: IDEOLOGICAL CONCERNS

It is evident that there is a continuum of ideological variants across the current twelve Community members. Nevertheless, it seems appropriate to consider all EU members as belonging to the tradition that Lodge has defined as "communitarianism." It is also possible to recognize the mechanisms of a welfare state in most, if not all instances. In practice, the interaction between government and business, and the role of government in the economy are very active, much more so than in the United States. At the very least, EU governments heavily regulate industries directly linked to the common good, such as health care. Essentially, there is universal health care across the EU, as well as educational opportunities for all citizens (including higher education), which are heavily subsidized by the state. Despite its evident political fragmentation, the EU offers a more ideologically appropriate ground for the implementation of an industrial policy than does the United States.

Although in most cases there is agreement in principle on fundamentals, such as the need for general welfare (a minimum standard of living for all citizens), universal health care, and education, there have been disputes regarding specifics. For example, the United Kingdom has heavily opposed Community-wide legislation that would have extended fringe benefits such as health care insurance to all part-time workers, or would have implemented a co-determination program (worker representation at the board of publicly owned companies) following the German model. These issues are part of the European "Social Charter" that has not yet gone far beyond agreement on principles.

THE MAASTRICHT TREATY

The Maastricht Treaty, signed February 7, 1992, represents a step forward in the process of European integration. There is a clear movement toward further unification of policies, such as community-wide research and development and the creation of an environment favorable to industrial development.

Article 130, a final compromise between a stronger French proposal and a weaker German one, provides a new legal framework to create an appropriate environment for European industrial development:

The Community and the Member States shall ensure that the conditions necessary for the competitiveness of the Community industry exist.

For that purpose, in accordance with a system of open and competitive markets, their action shall be aimed at:

- speeding up the adjustment of industry to structural changes;
- encouraging an environment favorable to initiative and the development of undertakings throughout the Community, particularly small and medium-size undertakings;
- encouraging an environment favorable to cooperation between undertakings; and
- fostering better exploitation of the industrial potential of policies of innovation, research, and technological development.

The Member States shall consult each other in liaison with the Commission and, where necessary, shall coordinate their action. The Commission may take any useful initiative to promote such coordination.

The Community shall contribute to the achievement of the objectives set out in paragraph 1 through the policies and activities it pursues under other provisions of this Treaty. The Council, acting unanimously on a proposal from the Commission, after consulting the European Parliament and the Economic and Social Committee, may decide on specific measures in support of action taken in the Member States to achieve the objectives set out in paragraph 1.

> This Title shall not provide a basis for the introduction by the Community of any measure
> which could lead to a distortion of competition.

Starbatty (1993) provides a critical analysis of recent developments toward the development of a European industrial policy by the Commission, under the framework provided by Article 130 of the Maastricht Treaty. He argues against the so-called "new" horizontal form of industrial policy proposed by Commissioner Bangemann, which integrates elements such as mutual recognition of technical standards and environmental policy. According to Bangemann, such "new" horizontal industrial policy is different from the "old" vertical form of industrial policy. It is comprehensive (horizontal) and not directed to the preservation on specific (vertical) industrial sectors, and does not affect free competition.

Starbatty, however, argues that the commonality between "old" and "new" industrial policy lies in the fact that in both cases the process of innovation is not ruled simply by market forces, but that policies play an active role. He is skeptical about the fundamental differences between both approaches, and how the new policy will be kept free from the negative consequences of the former.

THE WHITE PAPER OF 1993

The celebration of the "Completion of the Internal Market" by January 1, 1993, was subdued by the reality of a deep economic recession, which made the promises of the Cecchini report of 1985 seem like a distant dream. The Community now comprised a total of 17 million unemployed workers, 40% more than the 12 million of the late eighties. The crisis affected particularly the younger European workers. One out of five had to wait over two years for a job opportunity. The Commission was asked to develop a new set of policies to solve the critical situation.

The *White Paper on Growth, Employment and Competitiveness*, presented by the Commission and approved by the twelve member states of the Community in December 1993, is an ambitious agenda to restructure the European economic environment and create 15 million jobs by the end of the century. The Paper calls for a high level of concerted action throughout the Community, the type of actions referred to in the framework for cooperation and planning at the Community level as laid down in Article 130 of the Maastricht Treaty. The call for support of small- and medium-sized enterprises, investment in infrastructure, coordinated R&D efforts, and a coherent quality policy was built on previous efforts. But it reaches new levels of coordinated policy formulation and implementation, representing a clear example of the new, horizontal industrial policy Commissioner Bangemann had described.

A few examples of the analysis and policy recommendations included in the White Paper will illustrate the European agenda for the next decade:

1. The key handicap for Europe is the fragmentation of the different markets and the absence of inter-operable electronic communication networks. The solution will have to rely on significant public and private joint action.
2. The proposal does not call for remedial action as a consequence of a failure of the Europe 1992 program to achieve its objectives. The Europe 1992 program is seen as an objective building stone, an example of the degree of success that can be achieved by such concerted action. Some positive results of Europe 1992 are:

- 9 million jobs created between 1986 and 1990
- One-half extra percentage of annual growth
- 3% savings in transportation costs
- One-third more investments between 1985 and 1990
- 70 million fewer custom documents

Highlighting the success of the 1992 program is critical for the Commission, since Euro-skeptics are prone to oppose any further transfer of powers to Brussels.

3. The Paper integrates into a coherent framework different current models, such as sustainable development, that relate to the conditions necessary for industrial competitiveness and the creation of high value-added employment:

(a) A technological "standardized" information flow infrastructure is critical to future competitive success. An "information highway" is to be created and a 67 billion ecu investment for the period 1994–1999 is called for.

(b) Trans-European networks for transportation and energy need to be strengthened. Fast access to natural and technological resources has been a traditional source of advantage for Europeans. An investment of 20 billion ecu is planned for the period 1994–1999, out of which 5.3 billion will come directly from the Community budget.

(c) Stronger links must be achieved between basic research and commercial technological application. As well, a "quality policy" should be developed, building upon the significant steps already taken toward standardization (CEN, CENELEC) and mutual recognition of technical standards under the "new approach" directives.

(d) Small- and medium-size enterprises need to be supported through access to critical factors of competitiveness such as information and management expertise. These enterprises represent an important source of new employment opportunities for Europeans.

(e) The development of eco-industries is to be fostered. This will be a step further in the initial investment already committed to such purposes, the expertise developed by European organizations, and legislative action such as the regulation on voluntary eco-audits by companies.

The White Paper of 1993 provides a new framework for concerted action in Europe, which differs from traditional "vertical" industrial policy. However, the degree of guidance and intervention by the European supra-national organizations such as the Commission seems to indicate a new form of inter-governmental cooperation, which may be termed "horizontal industrial policy."

CONCLUSION

A strong argument can be made that a de facto industrial policy exists in the European Union. Two factors that demonstrate its presence are the different sectorial policies currently implemented and the framework for industrial competitiveness and economic growth developed in the White Paper of 1993.

The existence of such a policy does not presuppose that it may be economically efficient. On the contrary, some sectorial policies such as those for coal, steel and agriculture can be considered largely ineffectual and even detrimental when viewed from an aggregate economic perspective. The coordination of research and development efforts, however, looks more promising. The ambitious goal of sustainable industrial development laid down in the White Paper of 1993 cannot yet be evaluated, except for the relevance of its stated objectives.

The existence of concerted economic action in Europe must be explained from more than the solitary position of economic rationality. It also requires the analysis of several other causal variables, such as regional or national, economic and political interests, as well as the effect of the long welfare tradition of most EC members. In other words, the analysis of European history, ideology, and specific political interests is key to the understanding of sectorial policies and other forms of concerted economic action in the Community, or of a Community-wide industrial policy.

BIBLIOGRAPHY

Bangemann, Martin. "European Industrial Policy Is Neither a Copy of Japan's M.I.T.I. Nor a Market-Forces Free-For-All." Speech to the European Parliament. March 7, 1989.

Bizaguet, Armand. *Le Grand Marché Européen.* Presses Universitaires de France. Paris: 1993.

Burstein, Daniel. *Euroquake.* Touchstone. New York: 1991.

Cecchini, Paolo. *The European Challenge: 1992.* Wildwood House Ltd. Aldershot, Hants: 1988. United Kingdom.

Commission of the European Communities. *Croissance, Competivité, Emploi: Les Défis et lesPistes pour entrer dans le XXI Siècle - Livre Blanc.* Bulletin des Communautés européennes. Supplement 6/93.

The Economist. "A Survey of Agriculture." December 12–18, 1992.

The Economist. "The End of Europe's Iron Age." March 6–12, 1993, pp. 17–18.

The Economist. "Steering the EC's Industry." Editorial note, January 25, 1992.

The Economist. "A Survey of Europe's Internal Market." July 9, 1988; July 8, 1989.

The Economist. "A Survey on the European Community." July 7, 1990.

The Economist. "A Survey of Business in Europe." June 8, 1991.

Harvard Business School. "Background Note on the Common Agricultural Policy of the EEC." Note 9-580-058 Rev. 11/79.

Harvard Business School. "Technology Collaboration in Europe." Case 9-389-130, 1989.

Hufbauer, Gary Clyde, ed. *Europe 1992: An American Perspective.* The Brookings Institution. Washington, DC: 1990.

Finn, Jensen B., and Ingo Walter. *The Common Market: Economic Integration in Europe.* Lippincott Co. Philadelphia: 1965.

Kelly, Margaret, et al. *Issues and Developments in International Trade Policy.* Occasional Paper 63. International Monetary Fund. Washington, DC: 1988.

Lodge, George C. *Perestroika for America.* Harvard Business School Press. Boston, MA: 1990.

Ludlow, Peter. "The European Commission" in *The New European Community: Decision Making and Institutional Change.* Robert 0. Keohane and Stanley Hoffmann, eds. Westview Press. Boulder, CO: 1991.

Marchipont, Jean-Francois, et al. "Politique Industrielle: Interet Communautaire" in *L'Evenement Europeen* "Apres Maastricht." N. 17. 1992 Eds. Seuil. Paris, France.

Mayne, Richard. *The Community of Europe.* Norton. New York: 1963.

Owen, Richard, and Michael Dynes. *The Times Guide to 1992.* Times Books. London: 1989.

Pfeffer, Jeffrey, and G. Salanzick. *The External Control of Organizations.* Harper and Row. New York, NY: 1978.

Porter, Michael. *The Competitive Advantage of Nations.* The Free Press. New York, NY: 1990.

Rostow, W.W. *Stages of Economic Growth.* Cambridge University Press. Cambridge: 1960.

Starbatty, Joachim. "Europäische Industriepolitik und die Folgen - Zur Immanenz industriepolitischer Dynamik" in *Kartenhaus Europa?* Manfred Brunner, ed. Bonn Aktuell. München: 1994.

Sutherland, Peter. "European Unity and EEC Competition Law." Remarks to Meeting of the St. Louis
    Bar Association. May 10, 1985.

Thompson, James. *Organizations in Action.* McGraw-Hill. New York, N Y: 1967.

The Wall Street Journal. "The Hidden Dangers of Industrial Policy." March 1, 1993, p. 1.

Wistrich, Ernest. *After 1992: The United States of Europe.* Routledge. London: 1991.

READING 15

Marketing Issues and the European Common Market

KIP BECKER

CONCERNING THE DEVELOPMENT OF THE SINGLE EUROPEAN MARKET

What makes the European goal of a common market so unique for the business person? Perhaps it's because Europe has embraced a belief that the use of armed conquest to achieve greater wealth is no longer acceptable. Enthusiasm is centered around the hopes that peace, and wealth, can be achieved as a result of orderly win-win business interactions. To most non-Europeans, and particularly Americans, this may not seem overly significant. It is easy to forget that Europe is currently experiencing its longest peaceful era. In historical terms, the desire to maintain this condition through trading agreements and mutual respect is extraordinary! Neither Caesar, Napoleon, nor Hitler ever envisioned that European nations could be bound together by an appreciation that trading cooperation is paramount to success, the North must share with the South, and that individual cultures must be transcended for standardization. Inter-Europe trade helps to move toward these goals with an acceptance of a business infrastructure based on a single code.

Western Europe, one-third the size of Australia and one-quarter the size of the United States, is home to over 340 million consumers. Its viability as the largest unified buying power in the world rests on the ability to coordinate the massive rules and trading practices designed to protect national markets from outside disruptions. The EC market's potential for new internal and external businesses is staggering. Consider, in addition, to its huge consumer base that:

- The GNP is roughly $4.1 trillion
- 22% of world imports are to the EC
- 21 % of world exports come from the EC
- Employment is service oriented with 58% of the labor force in services, 34% in industry and only 8% in agriculture.
- EC-U.S. service sector trade is $38 billion a year

While 1992 was to be the "Year of Integration," it was only a year in which the European States truly began to establish principles designed to establish the economic and political infrastructure required for a unified market. One of the documents, the Maastricht Treaty, has seven titles and seventeen articles (with thirty-three declarations) devoted to establishing these principles. Title I describes the amendments to the EEC treaty necessary to establish the European Community and provides for the free movement of goods. Title II addresses the difficult question of agricultural trade . Title III speaks to the free movement of persons, services, and capital. Titles IV (transport) and V (common rules on competition, taxation, and approximation of law) establish the conditions under which business operations will be conducted.[a]

THE COMMON MARKET'S IMPACT ON NON-MEMBERS

One of the most important trade issues of this decade will be how the common market responds to non-members. "Fortress Europe, closed to outsider trade, is frequently forecast but highly unlikely. It would simply not be in the EC's best interest to build walls around their internal market."[1] As depicted in Figure 15-1 and Figure 15-2, the volume of inter-EC trade is important (58% of the total trade of member states) but these nations also conduct a significant volume (10%) of the world's non-EC trade (See Figure 15-3).

The EC's main export customers are the United States and their EFTA neighbors. Together these markets account for over 40% of external EC trade. It is doubtful that member nations would want to risk the consequences of damaged external relationships. The United States, for example, has made its position clear and is prepared to take steps that would make access to its market difficult for firms from countries that discriminated against U.S. imports (section 301 allows retaliation against unfair trade practices). Several test cases presented themselves during 1993/94. Each drew quick promises of retaliation from trade negotiators if the United States was restrained (tariff or non-tariff) from European markets. Fortunately, both sides recognized the importance of continued inter-continent trade and open dialogue for trade enhancement that resulted in cooperative repositioning. In addition to other OECD nations, EC trading with developing nations is increasing in importance (31% of exports). Table 15-1; and Figure 15-4 and Figure 15-5 provide information concerning the major European importers and exporters.

While there is currently not a unified EC trade policy for non-member nations, Article 115 of the original Treaty of Rome permits member states to shield themselves from economic difficulties that could be a result of non-member trade. Thus, for example, some EC members limit the number of Japanese cars imported through "Voluntary Restraint Agreements" and block any flow of these cars via other members into their national markets. Similarly, the United Kingdom uses controls to assure that cheap bananas do not arrive via some other EC nation since it has a special trading arrangement with its Caribbean ex-colonies to import more expensive bananas.[2]

---

[a]While current terminology favors the use of European Union (EU), the author has chosen to use European Community (EC) throughout to provide consistency since pre- and post-1995 data and issues are presented.

FIGURE 15-1

Intra-European Union Trade (Jan.–Sept. 1993)

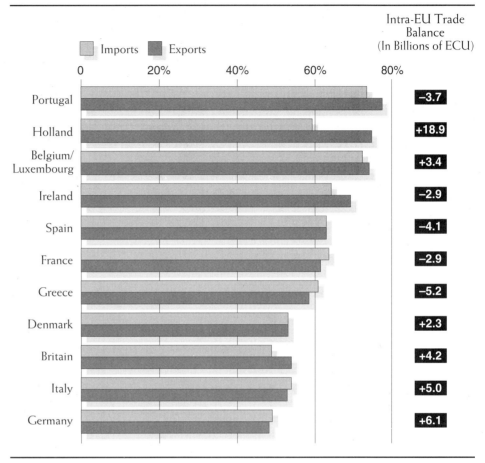

Source: *The Economist,* May 21, 1994, p. 69.

CONSEQUENCES FOR NON-MEMBER FIRMS

Of central interest to the Non-European community is the potential consequences for their *own* operations, not how European integration will help European firms. One concern is to eliminate protectionism. In the past, closed markets have been as much a part of European business as the three-hour lunch. Under Article 115 of the Treaty of Rome, members were granted the right to impose quantitative restrictions against each other as a result of third country (non-member) imports. In addition, they can inspect intra-Community trade to confirm the actual national origin of any questioned goods to prevent trade deflection (where external exporters can enter common markets through a permissive member nation).

Early indications from EC leaders were that "the new EC" would phase out Article 115 and new external trading relationships would be based on "reciprocity." That is to say "Trade unto others as they trade unto you." In 1988, the then Commissioner for External

FIGURE 15-2

Intra-European Union Trade, 1978, 1988, and 1992

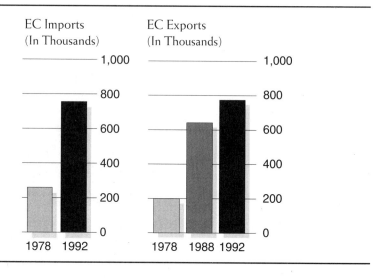

FIGURE 15-3

World Trade, 1990

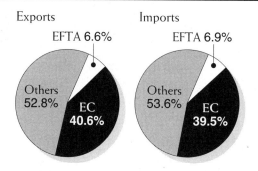

Relations, Willy de Clercq, stated that the internal benefits of trade liberalization should extend to non-member nations. "The Community is already the world's largest trading partner. Our exports of manufactured goods represent 26% of those of OECD countries, compared with 14% for the United States, and 17% for Japan. Our share of world exports of services is even greater. As a result, we have a vital interest in the maintenance of a worldwide liberal trading system."[3]

The following benefits of a single market are of significance to non-EC businesses:

1. **It Will Be Easier to Travel Within EC Internal Borders** External points of entry will most likely be strengthened, but once "inside" the EC, travel will be unrestricted.
2. **Business Access to 340 Million Consumers** EC firms will have open access to all EC consumers making the establishment of relationships with EC companies of considerable significance.

TABLE 15-1

Importing/Exporting Information for EC, EFTA and Selected Nations

	Total Import (in millions, 1992)	Total Export (in millions, 1992)	Import from EC	Export to EC	Import from EFTA	Export to EFTA	Import from Others	Export to Others
EC								
Belgium	$ 124,947	$ 123,286	$ 89,561	$ 90,223	$ 7,049	$ 6,643	$ 6,068	$ 7,413
Denmark	33,610	39,522	17,575	21,033	7,413	8,384	1,899	1,918
France	238,935	232,182	141,751	144,538	16,032	13,362	21,661	18,717
Germany	408,683	430,258	209,281	231,891	53,277	57,793	31,518	31,606
Greece	23,524	9,867	14,605	6,394	1,191	408	993	506
Ireland	7,517	8,786	4,878	6,434	232	147	1,181	851
Italy	183,000	170,000	102,000	96,000	15,000	13,000	10,000	14,000
Luxembourg	8,619	6,667	7,342	5,243	—	—	—	221
Netherlands	134,412	141,506	83,769	104,985	4,566	8,178	10,883	5,521
Portugal	29,991	18,171	21,972	13,316	1,756	1,583	1,077	774
Spain	94,475	60,799	55,667	42,924	3,575	1,433	7,525	3,360
United Kingdom	67,111	59,253	18,184	5,274	5,274	3,785	905	8,080
Total	$1,354,824	$1,300,297	$766,585	$768,255	$115,365	$114,716	$93,710	$92,967
EFTA								
Austria	$ 54,042	$ 44,364	$ 35,469	$ 28,718	$ 3,138	$ 3,289	$ 2,129	$ 1,170
Finland	21,194	23,987	9,251	11,629	4,009	4,345	1,293	1,421
Iceland	1,684	1,526	883	975	360	73	139	174
Norway	26,556	35,421	12,524	23,081	5,619	4,730	2,650	2,594
Sweden	49,815	56,015	24,541	30,207	8,122	9,614	4,356	5,252
Switzerland	67,398	62,373	46,900	36,177	4,625	1,539	4,944	4,944
Total	$220,689	$220,689	$129,568	$130,787	$25,873	$23,590	$15,511	$15,555
Others								
Canada	$122,309	$134,377	$ 11,379	$ 9,148	$ 2,885	$1,619	$ 79,764	$103,870
Israel	14,770	10,026	8,016	4,173	1,786	394	3,390	3,800
Turkey	22,872	14,715	1,098	1,084	100	33	379	126
United States	532,498	448,156	88,859	87,625	10,359	7,380	102,309	94,636
Total	$692,449	$607,274	$109,352	$102,030	$15,130	$9,426	$185,842	$202,432

FIGURE 15-4

Major European Exporters and Destination of Exports, 1989

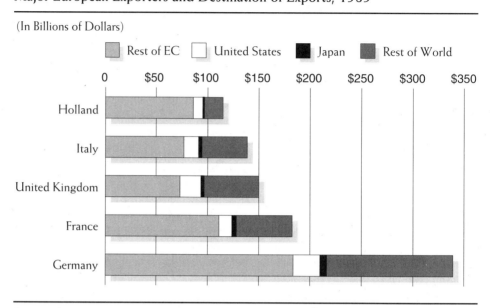

(In Billions of Dollars)

Source: Commission, Eurostats: *Basic Statistics of the EC*, 18th ed. (Luxembourg: OPOCE, 1991). From: Lynch, R. *European marketing*. Irwin: New York, 1993, p. 15.

FIGURE 15-5

Major European Importers and Destination of Exports, 1989

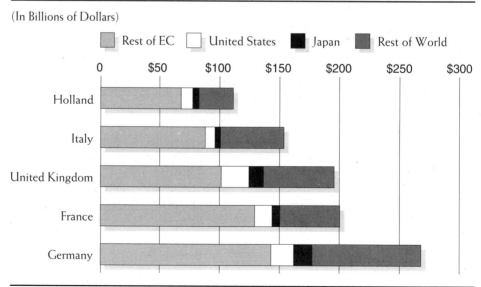

(In Billions of Dollars)

Source: European Commission, *Eurostats: Basic Statistics of the EC*, 28th ed. (Luxembourg: OPOCE, 1991). From: Lynch, R. *European Marketing*. Irwin: New York, 1993, p. 16.

3. **Lower Business Costs** It is expected that considerable savings will result from reducing border crossing delays (many heavy trucks wait over 8 hours at borders) and revisions in customs documents. Delays amount to an estimated annual cost of $25 billion, and changes in public contracts should save $90 billion yearly.

4. **Standardization** Attempts to design uniform standards to make life simpler within the EC are expected to benefit non-EC firms through consistent labeling, health, and safety standards. These previously acted as non-tariff barriers through unique national criteria designed to protect selected domestic industries. Standards will, additionally, simplify manufacturing as one specification will apply across member nations. Small differences such as different electrical plug fittings have created massive sales difficulties, higher costs and lost sales opportunities.

5. **Tax Rate Unification** Benefits to non-EC firms should result from attempts to standardize VAT tax rates. The Commission's proposal sets a standard rate between 14% and 20% and a reduced rate of 4–9% on basic goods and services. One difficulty facing EC nations is that free internal markets could result in heavy diversions of revenue unless indirect taxes are similar. More standardized rates should reduce the need for consumers to seek out low VAT nations for purchases, thus artificially building some markets and reducing others. Efficient business practices dictate that sales should occur in the country of residence, not the nation with preferential tax advantages. The shift of current duty-free sales in high-overhead locations will be diminished as these companies disappear due to a single tax structure.[b]

6. **Increased Competition** Three important Internal Market White Paper articles directly address the intent to increase competition within the EC. The importance of this to non-EC firms is two-fold. Article 92 clearly forbids members to "spend large amounts of public funds on state aid to uncompetitive industries and enterprises." Doing so, the article states, distorts competition and undermines efforts to increase European competitiveness. Non-EC companies will no longer face government subsidies solely designed to protect non-competitive industries, thus opening the door for improved, less expensive, and innovative products.

The intent of the EC union is to promote efficiency through consolidation across national boundaries, reducing duplicate or excess capacity and promoting economies of scale. Articles 85 and 86 are designed to insure that this does not cause a loss of competition due to mergers and abusive tactics due to dominate market positions. The Commission has overseen a decade of enforcement of the Articles that has strengthened the position that member nations cannot restrict competition solely to assure the survival of their outdated companies. The non-EC firm will gain when market conditions are free-trade oriented and may lose when intentions are to dominate market position in order to control price, distribution, or other non-competitive areas. In 1986, British ICI and Shell, for example, were restrained from a merger. However, in 1987 ICI was permitted to align with the Italian Enichem. Their joint venture, Vinyls, resulted in the closing of 300,000 tons of excess capacity.

---

[b]Sales will diminish, not disappear, as duty-free shops with their estimated $250 million in revenue will continue to operate in huge offshore superstores, possibly in roll-on-off converted ferries.

Unique Issues Face the Service Multinational

Service markets will also be dramatically altered by changes in EC regulations. According to Articles 59-66, members must remove quantitative restrictions that obstruct the free trade of services. Restrictions on capital movement have been lifted and television and broadcasting technical standards are to be synchronized so that the member nations cannot obstruct sales and communication through artificially contributed standards. The telecommunications market, with an estimated value of over $25 billion, was recently tied to new organizations such as CEN[c], CENELEC[d] and ETSI[e] after initial attempts to standardize telecommunications technology failed under the direction of CEPT. This was not surprising as CEPT was a federation of Europe's major governmental telecommunications agencies and each had vested interests.

The $100 billion construction sector (which is both service and product) has had two types of barriers to foreign entry. Technical specifications and certification have been considerable obstacles to trade. Firms often waited five years to receive certification. The Internal Market White Paper has set forth a uniform set of technical standards while the standards organization (CEN) has been drafting a European code that will ultimately define criteria of stability, safety, and health.

The second barrier, the lack of acceptance of professional credentials among EC members, has been fairly unique to Europe. Engineers, accountants, lawyers, and architects all were nationally licensed with a minimum of cross-boundary reciprocity.

Public sector spending is one area that has been especially resistant to a more open flow of goods and services. Governments have held strong convictions that buying domestic products and services is good for the national economy, regardless of price. This prized sector often exceeds the value of all commercial intra-community trade ($550 billion). While Articles 30-36 specifically prohibit discrimination against non-national (but EC) contractors or suppliers, actual resistance necessitated the implementation of two additional directives to curb violations to free trade.[f]

Services provided to businesses tend to be more standardized than those provided to the consumer. Of particular interest to non-EC companies is what was once applied only to the goods sector is now characteristic of many service markets. International mergers have become a natural way of life to service industries such as publishing, law, communications, and advertising. In addition franchises such as Dunkin Donuts and Kentucky Fried Chicken have obtained some of their highest returns from European operations.

Transferring services across international markets is a complex task. Services are very susceptible to marketing mistakes resulting from language, culture, and regulations. Even a service company as knowledgeable as Disney may fail to understand the European customer. When Euro Disney was built the company believed visitors wanted sit-down meals and souvenir sweatshirts with small logos of the famous mouse. It turned out that

---

[c]CEN (European Committee for Standardization).

[d]CENELEC (European Committee for Electrotechnical Standardization).

[e]ETSI (Telecommunications Standards Institute).

[f]In an attempt to enforce the free trade of public contracts above the legislation contained in Articles 30–36, the 1971 Directive on Public Works and the 1977 Directive on Public Supplies were enacted.

they wanted take-out food and huge, chest-size Mickey Mouse pictures. The Euro Disney Chairman stated, "Each time we tried to Europeanise the product we found it did not work. Europeans want American and they want Disney."

Euro Disney executives say they now have a clearer concept of what visitors want: branded souvenirs to general merchandise, cheaper meals, and a chance for children to shake a Disney character's hand. While American children seem to be heading toward computer animation and graphics, Europeans still favor the classic Disney characters such as Sleeping Beauty, Goofy, Minnie, and the timeless Mickey. Other changes were made to adapt to European styles. Americans, for example, prefer lunch at 11:30 to 3 PM. Europeans, however, want to eat between noon and 2 PM. Attempting to alter lunch hour habits, the park now has a parade that ends at 11:30 so visitors will "decide" to eat before going on to other park adventures.[4]

Service industry firms have found interesting ways to differentiate their products." When the last episode of TVs hottest American hit, *Twin Peaks*, was shown in Europe and in the United States at the same time, the producer altered the two endings so that the time difference between the two continents could not be used in the United States to give the ending away.[5]

When the film *Wayne's World* opened in Paris the soundtrack was dubbed in French by a pair of young Frenchmen calling themselves "Les Nuls," or "the nothings." The success of the film in America was based on the distinctive American slang. To overcome this problem film distributors invented their own French slang. Wayne's "Party On!" became *Megateuf "teuf"*—something like the reverse of *fete*, or party. Weird is *Zarb* and "A babe" is *Une Bombe*. The famous "Not" at the end of so many of Wayne's sentences was replaced by *Nul*, which lost something in the translation![6]

THERE REALLY IS NO "COMMON" MARKET!

It is important to realize what a common market is and what it is not. By definition a common market is a higher order form of economic integration with free movement of labor and capital. "Higher order" means higher than a free-trade area or customs union. It is not a market common, in the sense of consistency. One of the greatest mistakes a business could make is to embrace the idea of a single European market— meaning an undifferentiated one. In reality, it is quite the contrary. There are, in fact, reasonable arguments for considering each country as unique and separate with its own languages and customs. Lander, Terpstra, Yoshino and Sherbini,[7] and Keegan [8] have reported that to think of Europe as a single entity does not properly provide for significant differences. Geroski[9] stated in a 1992 article that the benefits of opening up the internal market would actually be the ability to "enhance the diversity that can be offered to customers." In addition, a 1989 survey that polled Europeans from various professions clearly demonstrated that there is no consensus even in the perspectives of the different EC nations about the importance of cooperation (Table 15-2).

Even companies within the EC have different viewpoints concerning the benefits of unification. Kellogg, Johnson & Johnson, and Mars all have adopted pan-European branding. Other companies have chosen to remain more locally oriented. When individuals from the member states were asked in 1992 if they felt that the internal market would provide benefits, there was significant national diversity and only slightly greater than 50% of the

TABLE 15-2

EC Members' Attitudes toward Cooperation

NATION	FUTURE LINKED TO EC	GREATER ECONOMIC INTEGRATION	GREATER FOREIGN POLICY COOPERATION	PROTECT AGAINST NON-EC NATIONS
Belgium	Yes	Yes	Yes	o
Denmark	o	No	No	o
France	Yes	Yes	Yes	Yes
Germany	Yes	Yes	Yes	No
Greece	o	o	No	o
Italy	Yes	Yes	Yes	Yes
Ireland	Yes	Yes	No	No
Luxembourg	Yes	Yes	Yes	No
Holland	Yes	Yes	Yes	No
Portugal	Yes	Yes	Yes	Yes
Spain	Yes	Yes	Yes	Yes
UK	o	No	Yes	Yes

o = Neutral opinion.

Source: Henley Centre, London, 1989.

EC were in agreement. It seems that in 1993 attitudes were mixed but slightly better for the general population (Figure 15-6).

Europe is more sociopolitically and culturally fragmented than the United States, with 50 states sharing a common language, constitution, and legal system or even the Japanese, with 47 perfectures but a highly organized social and political structure. Of particular concern to marketers are differences relating to both (1) cultural/geographic and (2) economic/demographic differences.

CULTURAL/DEMOGRAPHIC DIFFERENCES

Perhaps the most crucial step of any marketing research project is to obtain sufficient information about the EC consumer. With so many variables to consider, it is no surprise that most initial exporting is to markets with similar consumer profiles. In the case of the United States this usually means the United Kingdom. An accurate understanding of the actual market potential is essential and is affected by many factors. Simply estimating population is insufficient to comprehend nations with different cultures. In Saudi Arabia, where alcohol is forbidden for religious reasons, a beverage firm could be totally misled by population figures. There is no legal market for alcohol regardless of the number of citizens. Europe has its research traps as well. Switzerland, for example, with excellent public transportation and high-import tariffs on automobiles, has a smaller number of cars per capita than other Western nations. It is important to realize that even what may appear to be

FIGURE 15-6

Public Response to the Maastrict Treaty, Autumn, 1993

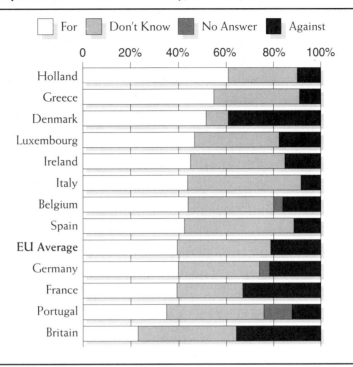

Source: Eurobarometer national polls.

similar may, in reality, be quite different. A Spanish Catholic is different from an Italian or French Catholic. Each shares cultural similarities but may not constitute similar consumers.

European business life is even more complex because some countries are bi- or even tri-cultural. Many have two official languages and several distinct segment groups (for example, Belgium). Other countries find that populations along borders often have more in common with the adjoining country than they do with their own. It is often advisable to draw an EC marketing map highlighting customer characteristics as well as national boundaries. Significant groupings can be drawn according to such factors as age, education level, family structure, area customs, religion, and ethnic backgrounds. Differences in languages alone provide for numerous possibilities of miscommunication, and differences in cultures enhance the possibility for error. It is interesting to note that the Economist Intelligence Unit determined in a survey of international managers that marketing skills were considered much less important than human relations skills.[10]

The implicit assumption is that differences between consumers of a particular nation are always less significant than differences between citizens of two different countries. Those who disagree would point out that in some cases greater similarities might exist between, for example, the residents of the major metropolitan areas of New York, London, Paris, and Milan than might exist between those consumers and their fellow citizens in the countryside. These critics would ask, "Who shares more similar customs? Citizens of Clarksville, Tennessee, and New York City or those of Boston and Paris?"

ECONOMIC/GEOGRAPHIC DIFFERENCES

One of the most important differences in the EC is between the affluent North and the less fortunate South (Ireland is often classified with Southern nations). The EC has gone to special lengths to avoid the Classic North-South nomenclature by incorporating such ter- minology into the 1992 policy as "cohesion" and "convergence." Whatever the terminology, the distinction remains that Britain, France, Germany, the Benelux nations and Denmark find themselves separated economically from a more agricultural Greece, Spain, Portugal, portions of Italy, and Ireland. The per capita difference in income between the richest and poorest EC nation in 1987 was 138%. An EC study that ranked EC nations and cities placed Hamburg, Germany, at a 182.6 (EC wealth index where EC 12 = 100) and Norte do Continent, Portugal, at 42.1. Major economic differences also exist within EC nations as the EC study placed Lombardy in northern Italy with a wealth index of 137.1 and Calabria, southern Italy ,with an index of 58.6.[11] Figure 15-7 presents GDP information for the twelve EC nations and Figure 15-8 presents data about each nation's population and size.

The research group, Mintel, has pointed out in the *Mintel Regional Lifestyles Report, 1988* that EC integration could easily act to widen the economic gap. The company points to such factors as the Channel Tunnel as possible factors that could divide individual countries strengthening a division between the richer southeastern United Kingdom and the north- ern areas. The use of technology will, undoubtedly, serve to widen gaps between the rich industrial centers of the north and the more agriculturally oriented south.

While there has been significant debate over the use of EC funds to assist the less- developed nations of the EC, the importance to businessmen and women pertains to trade more than to politics. In this, three significant areas stand out:

1. The European Social Fund has the objective of job creation and technology enhance- ment by providing funds to encourage job creation in areas of high unemployment.
2. Article 130c states that the European Regional Development fund is to address regional imbalances in the Community through development, structural adjustments, and con- version of declining industrial regions. Title V notes that the Community shall aim at reducing disparities between the "various regions and the backwardness of the least favored regions."
3. The grouping of Greece, Ireland, Portugal, as well as special regions of Spain and Italy, Corsica, and France into category 1 relationships. This makes them eligible for struc- tural funds designed to promote technology growth. Firms should consider that previ- ous stumbling blocks such as lack of infrastructure and poorer customer base could become business opportunities, due to grants and funds flowing to these areas.

As discussed, it is increasingly difficult to identify the Euro-customer as a single entity. Within this premise, EC methods of assuring free movement of communication, television, and movies will have a continued affect on the development of preferred brands and shared tastes. Vandermerewe and Huillier believe that instead of one homogeneous market, or even a collection of small specialized markets, segments of specific likes and dislikes will emerge,

FIGURE 15-7
GNPs of 12 EC Nations, EFTA, and Selected Other Nations

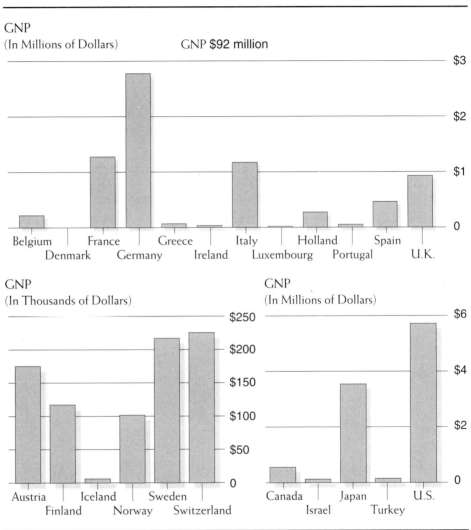

grouped not by country but by similar demographic and economic characteristics cutting across cultural and national boundaries.[12] It is important to note that EC 92 will likely turn into EC 97, EC 99 and maybe even EC 2000. Companies must appreciate that they are entering a changing environment that will have more than it's share of surprises. As such, companies will have to be flexible and design strategies and operations to meet shifting market needs.

In response to EC integration measures, foreign firms face either the lonely and difficult task of "going it alone" or of joining other experienced EC or even non-EC firms already in the marketplace.

FIGURE 15-8
Population and Size of 12 EC Nations and EFTA

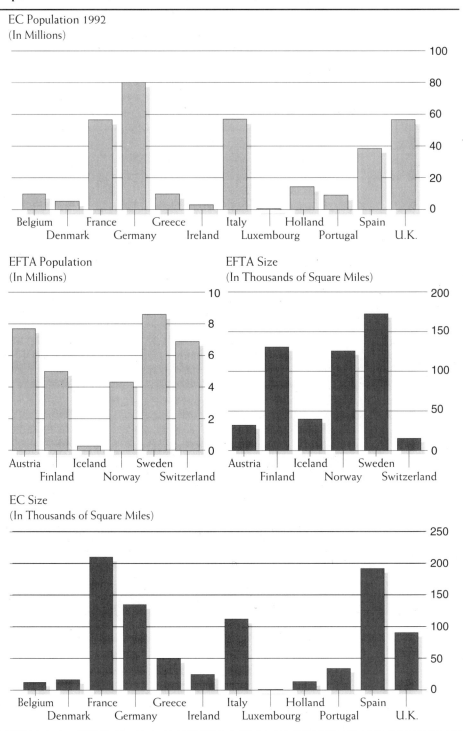

Those who choose to enter as a single company can adopt strategies of either selling in the general marketplace, going head-to-head against domestic competition, or seeking niche markets. Placing products or services in the general marketplace is a difficult task normally reserved for the more experienced company. These firms have either brand recognition or the resources necessary to: (1) improve current domestic products, (2) provide innovation to the marketplace, or (3) allocate sufficient marketing funds to "power their way" into an established market. The important question that must be answered is, "What would cause established EC customers to shift to a foreign-produced product?" The answer is: quality, price, or sales/after sales service.

For smaller firms and those unfamiliar with European sales, specialty markets can be carved from unserved markets or meeting specific consumer characteristics. Market research is essential to develop niche markets as well as to gain a thorough understanding of consumer needs and interests. The firm lacking confidence or resources for extensive research may wish to consider strategic alliances with companies currently in the marketplace with inferior goods or "holes" in product lines. Such alliances can provide an introduction to the EC market at a minimal risk (but, of course, at reduced profits). There are essentially four markets to consider: (1) local, (2) national, (3) regional/Europe, and (4) European. Each marketplace will have different consumer characteristics and competition.

The local market is comprised of small markets no larger, and usually smaller, than a city. Competition is domestic and tends to remain local as it is based on knowledge of limited consumer needs (for example, the corner restaurant). National markets tend to focus on broader consumer tastes (for example, pasta) that are, for the most part, confined within national borders. Competition tends to be with firms that have national reputations; often foreign companies find tariff and non-tariff barriers designed to protect domestic firms. Regional/European markets focus on similar buying characteristics within the EC as a whole. These may be ethnic or cultural in nature or may even be based on similar national tastes of people throughout Europe. Competition in this market tends to be from national firms that are exploiting their national reputations or European firms that have Euro-brand recognition. The European market is home to the MNC and the playing field is competitive, often price and marketshare sensitive and entry is difficult. As foreign firms seek a position within the EC they should know exactly which market they are in and be able to describe the strengths and weaknesses of their competitors. Regardless of the size of the firm, quality consumer research will be an essential element to any successful entry attempt.

THE GOAL OF EUROPEAN MARKET RESEARCH

The goal of a successful research program is to provide information that is current, useable, and reliable. It is quite difficult to obtain accurate information in unfamiliar markets, and differences in cultures increase the problems of assessment. This is particularly true for small- and medium-sized firms with limited marketing resources because most employees will never visit the country of their foreign customers (let alone meet them personally). For these firms the problem of attempting to understand consumer needs, distribution channels, and promotional activities may be the greatest difficulty facing small- and medium-sized businesses today. Private sector information is expensive and public information is often confusing and dispersed among many governmental agencies.

MARKETING RESEARCH AND THE EUROPEAN COMMUNITY

Gathering information about members of the European Community can be extremely expensive. As such, managers must determine at what point the cost of additional information surpasses the marginal benefit of reduced uncertainty. Research can be obtained from both private and government sources to assist in the development of marketing information systems. For a firm to determine the best market mix strategy for its products and services in the most appropriate European markets requires that a company-wide system be implemented. Information can be obtained from company internal records and external sources such as banks, government agencies, commercial research services, or private economic data collectors. Many new companies established during the past decade provide timely and orderly information at reasonable costs. Data Times, whose slogan is "a world of information," is just such a company. Users are able to automatically track information through fax or electronic mail services on industries, products, clients, competitors, or many other points of personal interest.

The value of international research is directly related to how well it reflects a factual representation of the foreign market conditions. The manner in which European research is collected and the quality of the research can be affected by numerous problems including the availability and quality of data, the ability to compare data across nations, and the costs of collection.

FOR ALL BUT THE LARGEST MNCs, IT IS IMPOSSIBLE TO ACCEPT THE RESEARCH CHALLENGE OF THE COMMON MARKET!

It is impossible, for any except the very largest of companies, to consider undertaking market research on every nation in the EC. Not only would the direct costs be prohibitive but also the firm would quickly be buried under too much information to interpret meaningfully. Two techniques seem most suitable to evaluate EC opportunities: (1) customer orientation and (2) market orientation.

Customer orientation. Firms with clear profiles of their customer base may select the customer orientation whereby the firms examine EC nations with large populations matching those profiles. This does not evaluate country differences, languages, customs, and so forth. Companies that lack either specific customer characteristics or are concerned about political, demographic, or cultural differences will find the market orientation more suited to their needs.

Marketing orientation. The market-oriented firm determines which markets are best suited for the firm. Some of the characteristics that may be considered important are similarity of language, customs, or distribution systems. It is the task of the marketing firm to determine how many characteristics of either the customer or market research should be included in a research study.

In any event, a company's research should not only provide information about customers and markets (domestic focus) but offer information concerning the following issues:

1. What is the importance of European expansion to the firm's future?
2. What is the cost of expanding? Not expanding?
3. How many markets (countries) can a company financially afford?
4. To what extent is the competition government supported/protected?

5. What are the alternatives to going it alone?
6. How will your market entry be received by domestic competitors?
7. How suitable is your product/service for unmodified distribution?
8. What will be the costs for any modifications (product, packaging, advertising)?
9. What are the licensing, testing and government fees?
10. Do you understand the distribution issues for your selected markets?
11. How will your cash flow be affected (delays in payment, shipping, and so on)?
12. Do you understand the potential costs of currency exchange changes?
13. Do you understand the use of foreign banking and payment protection?
14. What are the transportation alternatives and costs (FOB, FAS, CIF, and so on)?
15. How will tariffs and additional taxes affect your selling price?
16. How will geographic and business infrastructure affect business activities?

SOURCES OF INFORMATION

While Europe has only 6.2% of the world's population, its wealth makes it one of the most powerful purchasing centers in the world. This population is located primarily in urban areas with 60 cities, having a population of more than 500,000 and 157 cities with a population over 200,000. This concentrated buying power makes the European consumer fairly accessible.

Each EC country maintains a Center for European Business Information that provides data and information on EC legislation, product standardization requirements, EC industrial research, and training facilities. Additionally, the centers store all EC documents, and new businesses would find the *Official Journal of the European Community* to be a helpful guide for public sector contract information. European Banks, unlike in the United States, can be an interesting source of business information. When selecting a bank it is useful to consider one with branches in EC countries that are potential markets. Frequently, EC banks will point customers in the right direction —helping them locate research information, distribution networks, and legal/advertising offices.

Other low-cost sources of trade information come from individual trade associations related to the exporter's product line, Dun and Bradstreet directories of companies for specific EC nations, and the International Chamber of Commerce. The International Chamber of Commerce, through its national affiliates, can provide members with various publications and statistics concerning specific national markets. Many national Chambers operate offices in the countries of major trading partners and offer excellent information about the nation's markets and consumers. The complexity of EC trade has fostered several private information agencies. The Economist Intelligence Unit (with offices in the United States) and Croner's Europe (with U.S. offices in New York) are two of the better known.

The U.S. Department of Commerce and individual European nations all generate a considerable amount of general and specific market data that is available for private use. The following list provides examples of reports published by the U.S. Department of Commerce:

- *FOREIGN TRADE REPORT* provides information on U.S. exports and - commodities by country and provides a statistical record of more than 3,000 products that were shipped to over 150 foreign countries. All EC nations are included.
- *INTERNATIONAL ECONOMIC INDICATORS* offers basic economic data on the economy of the United States and seven other major countries to include gross national product industrial production, trade, prices, finance, and labor. The report highlights trends and changes in competitive indicators for eight nations.

- *MARKET SHARE REPORTS* show U.S. participation in foreign markets for manufactured goods during the last five years.
- *INTERNATIONAL MARKETING INFORMATION SERIES* assembles under a common format a diverse group of publications concerning European (and other foreign) market opportunities for U.S. suppliers. Some of the topics and titles of these reports are: *Global market surveys, country market sectoral surveys, Overseas Business Reports,* and *Business America.*
- *TRADE OPPORTUNITIES PROGRAM (TOP)* by which U.S. firms may communicate through American embassies and councils about products they wish to export.
- *COMMERCIAL INFORMATION MANAGEMENT SYSTEM (CIMS)* is a new computer system linking the Department of Commerce to worldwide resources. Through the use of CIMS databases companies interested in European trade can obtain timely data concerning these markets.[13]

The Difficulty of Interpreting Data in an Area as Diverse as the EC

Collecting consumer data is only half of the job. The real task is understanding what the data means to the company. It is often difficult to reconcile differences in contradictory or incomparable data. Often European data cannot be easily compared due to different reporting methods (kilos vs. pounds, liter vs. gallon) or coding differences due to language. An example of one source of linguistic confusion is that in one country a secretary might type, while in another a secretary would run a government agency. Educational levels, often a socioeconomic index, are difficult to aggregate since educational systems are diverse among EC nations. Some nations collect data on the number of school years, some on examinations passed and others on the number of annual graduates. Data may also be distorted. Items may be renamed in order to shift from a higher tariff classification to a lower one. Something as simple as marital status may not be easily comparable as not all countries recognize all possible marital status. The Irish Republic, for example, only publishes data under single, married, and widowed. How do you compare this with France who includes separated, cohabiting, and divorced?

Methods of data collection are as diverse as categories of data. In some nations, for example, income data is collected by government agencies and in others by private sources. In some European countries participation in data collection surveys is voluntary and this creates sample sizes that tend to be small and unreliable. The European Society for Opinion and Marketing Research (ESOMAR), located in Amsterdam, can assist the new exporter and is an excellent source of data. The Society publishes EC survey material and can provide guidelines for analyzing comparative data.

A firm should continually bear in mind, throughout any research effort, that the goal is to understand how many potential consumers with the means (income) and ability (distribution system) to purchase goods/services exist. The goal is not to own impressive, but unusable, lists of sociodemographic data.

References

[1]Heilbrunn, F. E.C. '92 Success to Depend on Marketing Strategies. *Marketing News,* Vol. 23, (14), (July 3, 1989), pp. 4, 22.

[2]Op Cit, pp. 12–13.

[3]de Clercq. Speech in London as quoted by Owen, Richard and Dynes, Michael (July 1989). The Times Guide to 1992, *Times Books,* London, p. 181.

[4]Skapinker, Michael, and Alice Rawsthorn. "An Older, Wiser Micky Mouse," *Financial Times*, April 10–11, 1993, p. 8.

[5]*Newsweek.* April 30, 1990.

[6]Jones, Terril, Paris. "Whoa, Excellent Dude! Parlez on Wayne!," *The Boston Globe*, October 25, 1992, p. B8.

[7]Lander, B., V. Terpstra, M.Y. Yoshino, and A. Sherbini. *Corporate Analysis for International Marketing.* Boston: Allyn & Bacon, 1967, pp. 67–90.

[8]Keegan, W. *Multinational Marketing Management.* Englewood Cliff, NJ: Prentice Hall, 1980.

[9]Geroski, P. "1992: Europe Becomes One," *Advertising Age*, 1989, p. 45.

[10]Wood, L. "Search for Wordly, Wise Company Executives," *Financial Times*, management supplement, April 9, 1991, p. 4.

[11]European Commission. *Eurostats: Basic Statistics of the EC*, 28th ed., Luxembourg: OPOCE, 1992, pp. 53–59. In Lynch, Richard. *European Marketing*, New York: Irwin, 1994.

[12]Vandermerwe, Sandra, and Marc-Andre L. Huillier. Euro-Consumers in 1992, *Business Horizons*, Jan./Feb. 1989, pp. 34–40.

[13]Cateora, Philip. *International Marketing*, 7th ed. Irwin: Homewood, IL, 1990, p. 377.

The Marketing Mix and the European Marketplace

KIP BECKER

PRODUCT ISSUES

Firms may produce several different products in a number of foreign markets or attempt to sell a single "global" product in many countries. Having the *right* product for the European market at the price is a key concern to both the multinational corporation and the small exporter. The game of Monopoly, for example, is manufactured in 23 languages and has enjoyed sales of 150 million sets in 80 countries, including all of the EC. While the rules remain the same, the places change. "Boardwalk," known to Americans becomes "Mayfair" in England, "Rue de la Paix" in France, and "Schlossalee" in Germany.

Most products, unfortunately, require significant modification for the European marketplace. Thus, specializing in niche products for specific markets can be the most favorable strategy for the smaller company. General Foods, for example, makes a chewing gum sold only in France and a pasta for the Italian market. Each product is successful in the national market, but has limited appeal for export to other EC nations.

CHOICE OF PRODUCTS FOR INTERNATIONAL MARKETS

Several studies have attempted to determine what factors influence a firm's choice of international products.[1] Two areas stand out with regard to a firm's ability to compete successfully in foreign markets. These areas include (1) the company's ability to meet efficiently the needs of the foreign marketplace and (2) the possession of competitive advantages. Table 16-1 shows management's responses when asked to assess possible changes in EC marketplace product policy.

PRODUCT TRANSFERABILITY

It is clear that firms must understand the needs of the local consumer and be able to relate those differences to product preferences and buying patterns. Non-European firms must be able to do this with a pricing or a quality advantage over available domestic products. An additional difficulty for non-European firms is a new European pride in buying EC goods resulting in domestic products having internal advantages over non-EC goods/services. Prior to the 1970s, products from different European nations, even those nations sharing

TABLE 16-1

Management's Assessment of Possible Changes in Products Issues

POSSIBLE CHANGES PRODUCT POLICY AND DEVELOPMENT	U.S. BASED	EC BASED	TOTAL
Standardized Euro-products will increase in importance	62%	60%	60%
Product line variation will be reduced (for a given supplier)	37%	33%	34%
On average, product variety available to customers will increase	63%	54%	55%
New products will increase (as % of sales)	50%	53%	52%
R&D spending will increase (as % of sales)	43%	34%	39%

Source: Quelch, John, Robert Buzzell, and E. Salama. *The Marketing Challenge of Europe 1992*, Addison-Wesley: New York, 1992, p. 411.

borders, were often viewed as "foreign competition." While the single market has not, and most likely will never, do away with an "us and them" perspective, it has certainly emphasized a "us first and then EC against non-EC competitive orientation." England may be the exception, finding itself in awkward situations pitted against its EC brothers over U.S. trading issues. The United Kingdom has traditionally had a Western orientation acting as a major source for both U.S. products and services. Language, customs, and heritage bond the United States and United Kingdom making it a primary funnel of U.S. goods to Europe and vice versa (Figure 16-1).

TRANSFERABILITY MAY NOT BE A SIMPLE TASK

The transferability of a product is dependent upon two basic factors: the degree of difference between the two environments, and the nature of the product itself. The degree of difference relates to cultural, economic, and political factors as well as differences in institutions such as the media, the law, and channels of distribution. Product issues relate to how the product is used, available substitutions, and the need that the product satisfies domestically. Firms selling to Europe find that while industrial goods (barring standard differences) may transfer fairly well, consumer products that rely on fashion, tastes, or preferences require adaptation. Failing to recognize this, American firms have attempted to sell items that were too large to fit in the smaller European ovens, pop tarts that burned in England's side-wired toasters, and condensed soups that seemed to be of poor value. Due to a lack of understanding about the concentrated product, Europeans heated the contents as they did with their regular canned soups (without adding water). This resulted in a strong taste and higher price when compared with the similar size can of English soup that already contained water.

An understanding of these marketing blunders helps a firm evaluate whether product adaptation is necessary and, if so, what type of adaptation is required. There are two types of product changes that may be needed. The first is an elementary adjustment and is limited to simple changes in the product. These may be a voltage change from

FIGURE 16-1

U.S. Goods to England Compared to Other EC Nations

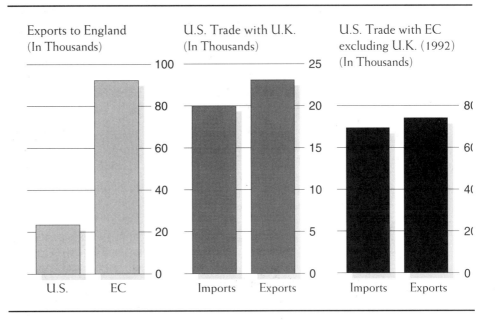

110 to 220, or a change in communication such as language translation. It is easy to assume, in some cases, that elementary adjustments may not be worth the cost or time, however, it is important that the firm not be complacent as even minor changes can have very important outcomes. Glass containers for products such as mayonnaise and mustard are important for Americans who want to see the product. Germans and Swiss, however, would not buy these products in bottles, as they prefer tubes. The elementary adjustment assumes that the basic home country product is, for the most part, adequate and transferable.

The second level of adaptation is more complex and requires a fundamental rethinking of a domestic product for the new market. Polaroid introduced the Model 20 Swinger Land camera in the United States and France at about the same time. The Swinger sold in the United States for $19.95 placing Polaroid in the mass market for inexpensive cameras (less than $50). This was an important market, accounting for over three-fourths of all still cameras purchased annually. Sales exceeded expectations and jumped nearly 15 percent in less than two years. The campaign capitalized on Polaroid's reputation emphasizing the camera's low price and "swinging" appeal.

The French market's price and theme were similar. Unlike the American, the French market was much smaller. In addition, it was heavily skewed at the bottom toward the lowest price range and at the top toward the older, wealthier segments of the population. To make matters worse a French adaptation of the American advertisement failed. This really should not have been surprising as marketing research had already shown that fewer than five percent of French consumers were aware of Polaroid's strong American image. A lack of understanding about the basic product and poor product information resulted in the mismatched product's failure.

COMPATIBILITY AND COMPLEXITY

Exporters find that the more compatible a product is with existing values and life styles, the more acceptable the product will be in markets. One might assume that the more complex a product is, the more difficult would be its introduction. That, however, is not necessarily the case as different cultures appear to value different levels of complexity. The Europeans appreciate products that provide user control. This often means that the item is rather complex. Americans, while priding themselves on their sophistication, normally do not like complex products when taking photos—most do not want to worry about light, film speed, or even focus. Europeans would find such "loss of control" unacceptable.

PRODUCT REGULATIONS

Regulations concerning adequate product standards, packaging and labeling can be confusing even for the experienced multinational corporation. The failure to properly identify the contents (and in some cases ingredients), to use the required languages or to meet size standards can all lead to problems. Coca-Cola found itself facing a significant loss of sales in the $120 million Italian market when an Italian judge in Genoa ordered the nationwide seizure of all bottled Coca-Cola on the ground that its ingredients were not properly labeled. The magistrate also banned any further distribution or production of bottled Coca-Cola, but allowed canned Coke, which listed the ingredients. The company claimed the bottled ingredients were listed on the cap but the judge stated that this did not meet Italy's label laws.[2]

Some countries with two official languages, such as Belgium, require that labeling be in both languages. Firms face severe penalties if labels do not adhere to language requirements. France has one of the most stringent language requirements. In France the law states, "in any offer, presentation, advertisement, written or spoken, instruction for use, specification or guarantee terms for goods or services, as well as for invoices and receipts, the use of the French language is compulsory."

Due to movements to standardize EC product, labeling, and packaging requirements, companies will begin to benefit as they no longer face separate standards designated by each EC nation. Article 30-36 prohibits members from establishing standards that act as an "arbitrary discrimination or disguised restriction on trade between member states." The purpose of this article has been upheld in subsequent court action. While the intent of the measure is to promote trade between EC members, non-member companies will find their EC access improved as the movement toward a standard set of rules develops. In the 1979 Cassis de Dijon ruling, the European Court of Justice decreed that Community law requires the mutual acceptance of goods from one member state to another. This ruling was based on the Internal Market White Paper statement "If a product is lawfully manufactured and marketed in one member state, there is no reason why it should not move freely throughout the Community." The court decision was a result of Rewe Zentral AG's desire to import Creme de Cassis into Germany. The Germans claimed that Creme de Cassis did not contain enough alcohol to be deemed a liqueur by their national standards, forcing the company to initiate legal proceedings. The European Court stated that Germany had no right to restrict the import of a drink sold in France except on grounds of health, fiscal supervision, fair trading, or consumer protection. A commission report, *The European Challenge 1992: The Benefits of a Single Market*, stated that European industry would save over $200 billion (5% of the GDP) by adopting unified standards. According to the report, which surveyed

11,000 business executives, technical standards were considered one of the most important obstacles to business in the EC. Standards required duplicated product development, lost economies of scale, and the inability to challenge domestic firms that were supported by contrived standards specifically designed to restrict competition.

The Single European Act states that, "The Council may decide that provisions in force in a member state must be recognized as being equivalent to those applied by another." Article 36 of the Treaty of Rome allowed countries the right to restrict imports because they did not conform to "essential requirements. "The new agreements on standardization of the *White Paper, Completing the Internal Market,* have brought Europe close to removing those standards that were designed to impede import trade.

Despite progress, technical standards remain a stumbling block as nations continue their interest in providing protection and preference to local firms. Three-pin electrical plugs will not, mutual recognition considered, fit into two-pin sockets! The type of cooperation necessary to achieve significant economies of scale by European-wide sales remains far in the future. The British Standards Institution (London) is an excellent source of information concerning EC standards. It can assist a company in understanding what standards a specific product must meet and what evidence would be required to demonstrate, satisfactorily, that the product has achieved the required levels.

PRICING ISSUES

Many firms believe that pricing is one of the most important elements of the international marketing mix. Europeans frequently comment that, generally, U.S. companies do not make the most of pricing in their overall business strategy, since most U.S. firms are used to a more normalized pricing environment. Prices are often established independently of the rest of the marketing mix. Pricing strategy frequently fails to consider the regional differences or global objectives of the company. United States and, often, European pricing tends to be cost oriented (cost plus some margin, or based on a target Return On Investment). This approach usually reflects a desire for regional profitability, as opposed to long-run global objectives. Figure 16-2 presents the location for the highest and lowest prices for 27 goods sold in all EC nations.

The basic subsidiary pricing strategy followed by Western European and North American MNCs places a major emphasis on achieving a satisfactory ROI. The second most common pricing strategy by a MNC for its subsidiaries is to maintain market share. The third is to meet a specific profit goal.[3] Some of the price differences experienced among national markets are a result of differential taxation. MNC pricing strategies that take into account domestic income levels, competition, attractiveness of the product, and company goals may also account for these differences. European Community rules stipulate that pre-tax price variation among members should not have a variance of more than 18%. A recent Brussels report, however, noted that new car prices in the EC varied as much as 70% and over 120% when taxes were taken into account. Table 16-2 provides an example of how new car prices compare across Europe.

Table 16-3 provides management's responses when asked to assess the prospective of possible changes in EC pricing issues.

Some areas of U.S. consumer pricing are becoming attractive to the European marketplace. One format, the warehouse club, is being tested in England and is expected to spread across the continent. This is in spite of the fact that the warehouse club culture is opposite

FIGURE 16-2

Highest and Lowest Prices (in ECU) of 27 EC Products

	LOWEST*		HIGHEST*		PRICE COEFFICIENT**
Bosch, 500-2 power drill	Brussels	70.94–56.75	Milan	99.34–83.48	1.47
Bosch 4542 washing machine	London	462.69–402.34	Milan	672.74–565.33	1.40
Braun Silencio hairdryer	London	18.44–16.03	Athens	50.60–43.62	2.72
Coca-Cola, 1.5l bottle	Amsterdam	.82–.69	Copenhagen	2.04–1.45	2.10
Colgate toothpaste, 100ml	Athens	1.33–1.15	Milan	1.88–1.72	1.50
EMI Compact disc: Tina Turner "Foreign Affair"	Athens	14.39–12.41	Madrid	21.72–19.39	1.36
EMI cassette of same	London	8.7–7.57	Copenhagen	21.84–17.9	2.36
Financial Times	London	.67–.67	Copenhagen	1.54–1.54	2.30
Gillette Contour razor blades, 5-pack	Athens	1.99–1.72	Copenhagen	3.53–2.76	1.60
Heinz ketchup, 570gm	London	.86–.86	Madrid	2.04–1.92	1.98
Hitachi 630 video recorder	London	452.17–393.19	Athens	749.64–551.21	1.40
Hoover 3726 vacuum cleaner	Luxembourg	118.31–105.63	Amsterdam	260.31–219.67	2.08
IBM 30-021 personal computer, 20MB, color display	Athens	1629.21–1404.49	Copenhagen	4065.75–3332.58	2.37
Kelloggs cornflakes, 375gm	Amsterdam	1.26–1.06	Cologne	1.95–1.82	1.72
Kodak 35mm Gold 100 film	Cologne	3.4–2.98	Copenhagen	5.98–4.90	1.64
Levi 501 jeans	London	50.01–43.49	Madrid	74.65–66.65	1.53
Mars Bar	London	.27–.27	Copenhagen	.67–.55	2.04
Nescafé, 200gm	Athens	3.67–3.16	Milan	7.78–7.14	2.26
Olivetti ET65 electronic typewriter	Brussels	331.37–278.46	Lisbon	638.37–545.62	1.96
Pampers, Midi 52, boy's	Dublin	10.47–8.51	Milan	11.70–10.73	1.26
Sony 2121 television	London	536.45–466.48	Copenhagen	1091.74–894.87	1.92
Timotel shampoo, 200ml	London	1.23–1.07	Amsterdam	2.09–1.76	1.64
Toblerone, 100gm	Amsterdam	.85–.72	Lisbon	1.49–1.38	1.92

*Prices in ECU, converted at rate of April 27, 1990. The first set of figures in each column is the retail price, the second the price before tax.

**Ratio of highest to lowest pre-tax prices.

Source: *Financial Times*, 1991. Data compiled by Runzheimer Mitchell Europe.

that of many U.K. retailers who have been attempting to increase operating margins. Costco, the third largest U.S. operator, as well as Price Club Canada and Nurdin & Peacock all began U.K. sales in 1993. The factory outlet, another U.S. idea, is being tested in the United Kingdom with expectations of wide acceptance. The U.K. Hornsea outlet mall was opened in the late 1980s with stores representing Aquascutum, Laura Ashley, and Wrangler. Prices are about 30% below street prices. The popularity of the concept is demonstrated by the 800,000 customers who visited the Hornsea Mall in 1993. While the

TABLE 16-2

Differing Auto Costs within the EC (1994)
Figures are tax free quotes with cheapest price = 100

COUNTRY	FIAT 900IE	FORD MONDEO	HONDA ACCORD	BMW 730i
Belgium	117.2	118.2	114.0	115.6
Britain	117.7	110.5	112.3	100.0
France	124.1	109.2	117.3	121.0
Germany	134.1	118.7	112.9	116.3
Holland	121.6	106.2	100.0	118.5
Spain	100.0	100.0	105.0	113.7

Source: European Commission/presented by *The Economist*, August 27, 1994, p. 43.

TABLE 16-3

Management's Assessment of Possible Changes in EC Pricing Issues

POSSIBLE CHANGES	U.S. BASED	EC BASED	TOTALS
Prices will tend to equalize among EC countries	57%	61%	60%
Average EC prices will decrease	40%	36%	37%
"Gray marketing" will increase	40%	21%	27%
Marketers will increase the use of deals as a means of varying prices	53%	69%	61%

Source: Quelch, John, Robert Buzzell, and E. Salama. *The Marketing Challenge of Europe 1992*, Addison-Wesley: New York, 1992, p. 411.

idea has enjoyed success, some remain skeptical—believing that the concept of buying out-of-season fashions from out-of-town malls is largely untested in Europe.[4]

ATTEMPTING TO SET A "EUROPEAN" PRICE

An important issue that still needs resolving is how to price products in a similar manner within European market regions. Different taxes and non-tariff barriers make uniform pricing difficult. Mars and Levi Strauss have begun to align their European prices with the goal of reducing the spread between EC countries to 10%. The motivation is to cut down on cross-border bargain hunting and the growth of parallel imports from low-cost countries to expensive ones. Many believe that deep-rooted economic and cultural differences within the European continent will ensure that price variations remain. It is clear that Europeans can "value shop" despite political attempts to standardize prices. It is extremely difficult to extract the same price, for example, from Greece and from Germany. A review of a particular EC nation's GDP and purchasing power parity is critical prior to establishing a pricing strategy. There are many different pricing issues that a North American firm could easily overlook. Consider, for example, that:

- Nescafé is expensive in Milan because as the Italian market for instant coffee is small.
- Coca-Cola's high price in Denmark is due to a requirement that drink containers be returnable.
- Recorded cassettes in Greece must be priced low to compete with "pirated" tapes.
- Levi Strauss' 501 jeans are expensive in Spain because they are considered "fashion" not clothes.

PRICING MUST REFLECT THE TOTAL COSTS

Advantages based on production location may be negated by the costs associated with exporting a product into foreign markets. At a minimum, these costs will include transportation, taxes, tariff, and additional channel members. Considering the possible substantial costs involved, it is no wonder that most international trade is conducted by rail and trucking with a nation's neighbors.

The cost of transportation will vary greatly as a function of the type of product sold. High-tech products and smaller costly items will not be as susceptible to transportation costs as commodities or large inexpensive items that require considerable shipping space in relation to their value.

CULTURAL DIFFERENCES

Due to the cultural diversity among EC countries, national preferences can also have significant effects on the actual price. Some cultures place higher value on specific products than others. The Shenandoah Valley Poultry Company, for example, ships their turkeys to the European market based on its preference for the moister dark meat of turkeys. Americans, who prefer white meat, would not be willing to pay the higher European price only to feed most of the dark meat to the family pet.[5]

THE ELEMENTS OF DELIVERED DUTY PAID PRICES

Having goods sold at the company's door (*Ex Works*) is always preferable to becoming involved in the problems, often extensive, of international sales. By having goods exchange hands domestically, there is no currency exchange risk and revenue from European sales can be compared directly to income from national or foreign sales. Establishing an accurate delivered duty paid price (DDP) is not an easy task as transportation, insurance, and duty must be calculated. Before EC unification it was very complicated to price goods that arrived in one nation's port and were transported over land through one or more nations to be sold in another. Unification measures have called for single tax structures, simplified paper work procedures, and clearance among EC nations once a good has been cleared by one member.

Companies should hope for the best and expect something less, for some time to come, as member nations sort out their economic and political differences. In spite of movement toward harmony it is not uncommon to find EC nations frequently pitted against other member countries relating to internal industry protection and tax revenues. Conflicts over Italian grapes entering France, British meat entering France, and Spanish products competing against those of Ireland and Italy have all resulted in internal tension and severely heated battles. There is little reason for North American firms to expect different treatment.

PROTECTING PAYMENTS

ESTABLISHING A EUROPEAN BANK ACCOUNT

Most firms, particularly smaller ones, find that having a bank account in Europe (preferably in the nations where trade is conducted) is essential. Both foreign currency accounts and ecu accounts can provide the inexperienced firm with several advantages. Among these are reduced currency conversion expenses within the nation for domestic advertising, traveling or legal expenses, ability to conduct ecu transactions as a hedge against currency depreciation, and ability to obtain local banking assistance. European banks, unlike American banks, can assist their clients with domestic market information, business referrals, and start-up assistance. Like U.S. banks, European banks can also be a source of loans (in the currency needed), provide letters of credit, and sell forwards and options.

INSURANCE AS A MEANS OF GETTING PAID

Goods and the payment for goods can be insured. Cargo insurance or marine insurance is available through the transportation company itself or the company's insurance agent. Payment insurance is often obtainable through private insurance companies or the U.S. export-import bank (EXIM). For firms operating out of the United Kingdom, the Export Credits Guarantee Department (ECGD) can provide this service. The ECGD insures about one-third of the U. K. exports to Europe and provides low-cost protection against foreign defaults. Private insurance companies have become increasingly important to European trade and usually can offer service advantages over government-run agencies. One important difference is that private insurance firms offer both domestic and export coverage under a single policy. A firm's insurance company should be able to give advice on types of coverage and costs of private insurances.[a]

The use of a letter of credit (LOC) is another alternative to assure payment through the use of a third party, normally a bank. North American firms should not be surprised if a European customer attempts to sidestep a requirement for a letter of credit. Such letters are cumbersome, add costs, may require capital to be tied up, and can be difficult to transact (particularly if a non-continental bank is involved). An account with a domestic bank can ease the pain of a LOC requirement but will not remove it. American firms, while knowing of the difficulties, are wise to rely on LOCs at least until relationships are well established and the firm becomes wise in the ways of European business! It is equally important to realize that banks will *not* release funds for letters of credit unless the documentation

---

[a]The largest private U.K. provider of export credit (located in London) is Trade Indemnity PLC (071-739 4311).

and other paperwork is *exactly* correct. This means that the foreign firm must thoroughly understand the materials and procedures needed for the transaction. The wise firm seeks bank assistance *to avoid* LOC problems.

The International Chamber of Commerce is an excellent resource for a company unfamiliar with international debt collection and problems. The Chamber offers arbitration experts to mediate disputes and has established guidelines for many international business transactions, such as the *Uniform Rules for Collection*. It is important to keep in mind that alternatives such as referring to the Chamber's guidelines or the use of arbitration are normally valid only when written in the contract.

FACTORING

Factoring provides a means whereby a firm can avoid many of the risks of non-payment. The company sells invoices, at a discounted rate, to a factor. In Europe they are normally sold at a 15% to 20% reduction. While the seller loses some of the revenue from the sale, he or she is protected from currency exchange loss, bad debt, and other inconveniences of attempting to collect payment. Many factors are connected to an international network that can pressure non-payers in their own language with court action in their own country. Even if they had the legal understanding to do it, this is something most companies could not afford to do. Most European banks either act as factors or can provide references. For those seeking English speaking factors the Association of British Factors maintains a membership list.[b] American factors are accessible through private companies and can be located in any large city's yellow pages. Companies can often find that factors offer interesting services that can result in justifying the factor's cost. Such services include pricing information, information concerning customers payment records, on-line computer demographic information, and assistance with documents.

THE EUROPEAN CURRENCY UNIT (ECU)

Non-EC companies should strongly consider the use of the ecu as a means to stabilize currency risk when payment in local currency is not possible. The usefulness of the ecu is that it is constructed of a basket of currencies representing all of the EC countries. The basket is weighted according to each nation's economic importance to the community. Importance is a function of the nation's GNP and extent of its intra-EC trade. The advantage of the ecu over a European currency is that its basket nature provides a greater measure of currency stability than a single national currency. ecu values can be applied to pricing and the invoicing of goods, as well as on loans. European businesses often have ecu accounts (with ecu check-writing ability) and those considering business within the European community are well advised to consider such an option. Unfortunately, not all member nations place the same value on the ecu, and a company must determine the financial importance of the ecu in the specific nation in which trade is being conducted. Italy, for example, places ecu value equal to any major trading currency (pounds, dollars, yen). Germany, on the other hand, is not as favorable in its treatment and has at times even prohibited citizens from holding ecu accounts. Firms (especially smaller ones unfamiliar with currency risks) conducting business within the European Community should consider the use of ecu for its ease of translation, stability, and EC status as a trading currency.

---

[b]Association of British Factors, 25-28 Bloomsbury Way, London, WC1A 2PCX (071-831 4268).

DISTRIBUTION/TRANSPORTATION ISSUES

The formation of a unified Europe has forced firms to reconsider new distribution system alternatives to better compete and reduce costs. Attention to distribution issues can have significant impacts. Rank Xerox, for example, estimated that it saved $200 million by reducing the number of carriers bringing components into its photocopier factory in Holland from 15 to 1. The reduction also resulted in improved control over suppliers and centralized deliveries of finished products. Many larger companies are requiring that the European distribution industry change its role from traditional transportation to become managers of a whole range of supply chain activities including forwarding, consolidation, warehouse management, picking and packing, transportation, and electronic data interchange. A trend is beginning for manufacturers and retailers to concentrate on their core business and contract out peripheral tasks. To respond to the increased pressures some logistical operations are seeking partnerships with other synergistic firms. European Transport Services, for example, has linked with the Mannheim-based German distributor Rhenania to form a new company, Trans-European Transport. Frans Maas, a Holland logistics firm, which Rank Xerox relies upon, states, "Our role is now to take care of the whole supply chain from manufacturer on to wholesaler or retailer. Transportation is only one item."

European distribution systems are becoming fairly complex and many believe that a maximum of ten companies will survive over the next ten years as a result of the need to develop pan-European infrastructures and multi-million dollar warehouse facilities.[6] The importance of distribution systems is illustrated by the responses of American companies doing business in Europe (Table 16-4). These firms rated the importance of different types of strategies to gain greater control and cooperation from distribution channel members.

Not all European distribution firms have found the changes during the first part of the 1990s to be in their best interests. Many had difficulties assimilating continental acquisitions into their systems, integrating computer systems, or maintaining profitability in an increasingly deregulated environment. It was believed that the rising fuel costs that followed the invasion of Kuwait (1990–1991) were solely responsible for the demise of hundreds of small European distribution companies.

DIRECT AND INDIRECT DISTRIBUTION CHANNELS

Companies can distribute in Europe through either direct or indirect channels. If the exporting firm deals directly with the foreign market, the relationship is considered direct. When companies utilize the services of foreign middlemen the relationship is considered indirect (Figure 16-3). The more important the foreign market is to the firm, normally, the greater the desire to gain control over the distribution process (making distribution direct). Direct distribution channels provide both influence over foreign markets and control over foreign pricing.

Indirect channels are comprised of the export merchant and the cooperative exporter. The export merchant buys directly from manufacturers and takes title to the goods. An important aspect of the export merchant is that he or she assumes the risk in his or her name and is paid by the markup obtained in the foreign market. Cooperative exporter relationships occur when firms agree to export their products into the other's markets. This is most common when both firms have similar but non-competing products. Colgate Palmolive Corporation, for example, distributes Wilkinson razor blades for the English firm. The distribution gives Colgate a highly competitive shaving razor compatible with the distribution system of their shaving cream.

TABLE 16-4 ———————————————————————

Manager's Assessment of Possible Changes in Distribution Policies

POSSIBLE CHANGES	U.S. BASED	EC BASED	TOTALS
Fewer distribution centers will be needed to service the EC	59%	73%	63%
Costs of transport and warehousing will be reduced	57%	73%	60%
Cross-border cooperative buying by dealers and distributors will increase	61%	73%	64%
Pan-European retailers and distributors will become more common	59%	73%	64%
Direct marketing will grow	50%	57%	56%

Source: Quelch, John, Robert Buzzell, and E. Salama. *The Marketing Challenge of Europe 1992*, Addison-Wesley: New York, 1992, p. 411.

FIGURE 16-3 ———————————————————————

Types of Distribution

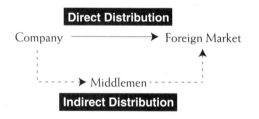

In any foreign environment the location of foreign channel members can be one of the most important exporting decisions a firm will make. EC businesses make use of both agents and distributors. An agent will work on a client's behalf by locating potential customers. Distributors develop more lengthy relationships and are independent companies authorized to sell a firm's products. Unlike agents, distributors actually take title of the products during the resale process. As title holders they become responsible for the condition, terms of sale, and bad debt. Lists of major agents and distributors are available from trade commissioners, local chambers of commerce, and a number of other sources. The U.S. Department of Commerce has an agent/distributor service that will assist in locating middlemen for companies. The U.S. Foreign Service post can also provide lists of domestic distributors for each nation a firm is considering. The U.S. Department of Commerce also maintains a master computer file, the *Foreign Traders Index*, which contains information on more than 100,000 foreign importing firms. The U.S. publications office offers *Overseas Business Reports* and other specialized information for specific countries a firm may be interested in. The U.K. Department of Trade and Industry (DTI) has an export representative service and also offers information concerning distribution agencies in specific EC nations. The International Chamber of Commerce publishes a guide dealing with differences in agency laws of EC nations; lists of lawyers specializing in common market agency legal issues can be obtained from the U.K. Law Society.[c]

A firm may also enlist the services of one of several types of indirect channel members. These are divided into export companies and trading companies.

EXPORT COMPANIES

Four major types of export companies offer services to businesses interested in obtaining assistance in the European Community.

1. *Export Management Company (EMC)* They operate under the client's own name and will even send letters on the client's stationery to handle the entire export function. They are up to date on issues relating to politics, customs, documentation, and shipping. There are thousands of EMCs worldwide with over 1,000 in North America alone.
2. *Manufacture Export Agent (MEA)* MEAs cover only limited markets and normally have shorter relationships with the exporting company. The MEA acts under their own name and could represent several manufacturers within the same industry.
3. *Foreign Freight Forwarder* The foreign freight forwarder handles overseas shipping arrangements between countries.
4. *Commission Agent* A Commission Agent represents foreign customers interested in purchasing a nation's domestic products. They attempt to locate goods throughout the world at the best price. They are paid by commissions received from the foreign client.

TRADING COMPANIES

Trading companies have assisted in the movement of European trade for centuries. They were especially useful during the colonial period of British and French expansion. The famous *Cie Francaise de L'Afrique Occidentale* was responsible for much of the raw materials trade between France and Africa. The famous Great Atlantic and Pacific Tea Company conducted trade between the American colonies and England. It is the function of the trading company to act as a source of market information, locate markets, sell goods, and perform the necessary transportation and documentation activities.

Channel members can certainly assist companies unfamiliar with the EC market, but increased costs for their services must be factored into pricing schemes. Campbell Soup Company, for example, found that their channel members repackaged their product according to the preference of European retailers who purchased soup in assorted soup cases as opposed to the single product-type case offered in America. Hand packing the assorted cases, however, increased distribution costs as much as 30%. Distribution systems can also affect inventory costs. Philips has found that it must maintain 23% of annual sales in Europe compared with 14% in the United States and Japan. Hopefully, advantages gained through integrated EC movement will work to reduce these high costs.[7]

---

[c]The Law Society, 113 Chancery Lane, London (071-242 1222).

TRANSPORTATION ISSUES

American firms who are used to fairly low transportation costs will find that the European Community has yet to unify transportation cost areas. This is partly due to the high level of government intervention in European transportation. EC governing bodies recognize that bringing a large EC market within reach of most European firms requires an affordable ratio between transport and product manufacturing costs.

Today, costs per ton/kilometer in the EC aviation industry are 50% higher than in the United States. Trucks carry approximately 80% of intra-EC trade by bulk and even more by value. Cross-border trips are frequently rationed by bilateral permits, valid for only one trip each way, and negotiated between nations. Border delays in the past have averaged 11.7 hours on a Belgium to Italy run and even the short trip from the Netherlands to Belgium requires 1.5 hours. The EC commission has estimated that 22% of the operating costs of a trip from England to Italy (18 hours) comes from delays. Under past EC constraints 35% of the trucks returned from their destinations empty and only some 16% of truck trips are allowed under EC-wide permits.[8] The Commission is attempting to provide for a rapid increase in EC-wide permits. Deregulation in the United States lowered interstate road transportation costs by 10%, and the Commission believes that EC prices will fall by about 5%. Due to the different costs involved firms need to explore a wide range of transportation alternatives to determine the most effective methods. Freight forwarders, listed in the yellow pages of most large cities, can provide valuable information concerning transportation-related costs.[d] Large freight forwarders normally have their own transportation systems and others rely on subcontracting. Fees for their services are typically paid by the transportation companies so shippers are assured that the methods used are in their best interest and not the freight forwarder's. Normally this is not a problem and freight forwarders can be a valuable source of free information concerning complicated transportation issues.

Several examples of transportation issues that most non-EC firms would have little experience with are the use of the England-France tunnel, the use of Ro-Ro ferries, and rail vs. air issues. The Euro-tunnel offers two significant advantages: speed and less handling. The English RD (road-rail-road) network and other European rail systems have formed a venture, Intercontainer, with the Euro-tunnel. Intercontainer can offer door-to-door service throughout Europe using special equipment designed for tunnel traffic and HERMES (the continental rail cargo tracking system).[e]

Ro-Ro ferries, located along the European coast, offer an effective and cost efficient method of transportation with roll-on roll-off convenience (hence, Ro-Ro). Most large ferry services offer door-to-door transportation services and customs clearing through networks of European companies.

Overland truck shipping, airfreight, and rail are excellent methods of inter-European transportation. Each method has advantages and disadvantages that need to be considered carefully. When reviewing airfreight, for example, it is advisable to recognize that most

---

[d]The Institute of Freight Forwarders (IFF) is a professional organization representing European agencies. A source of referrals, it is interested in standards of service and organizational improvement. The British International Freight Association located in Middlesex U.K. (081-844 2266) is the English association's contact.

[e]Information on Intercontainer services can be obtained from Intercontainer, Basle, Switzerland (010 41 61 452525).

European airlines belong to the International Air Transport Association (IATA), which, in theory, establishes freight rates. Companies, however, can often find "discounts" that are offered as a way to compete. Frequently the use of a freight forwarder, who can consolidate smaller shipments (called grouping), can also result in significant savings.

ADVERTISING AND PROMOTIONAL ACTIVITIES

PROMOTIONAL ACTIVITIES MUST BE PART OF THE OVERALL STRATEGY

Promotional policies must be part of the overall marketing strategy and relate directly to company goals. The promotional effort should assist marketing strategy by:

- Developing a portable communications program
- Developing product classes suitable for different cultures
- Positioning to be able to market in a number of countries

The objective of promotion should be to assist in the positioning of the product in each national environment. Knowledge of each market's unique features is essential for successful product positioning. For example, toothpaste in North America is believed to prevent tooth decay, so fluoride additives are necessary. In Great Britain, and the French areas of Canada, the purpose of toothpaste is to stop bad breath. In northern Europe consumers expect deodorants to reduce perspiration. In southern Europe where summers are humid and hot and this goal is essentially unobtainable, consumers look to deodorants to mask odors. Positioning and communicating the position may be the most important aspect of marketing. Figure 16-4 provides information concerning the allocation of funds to the three major promotional activities in the EC.

It is interesting to note that EC promotional activity spending has been the lowest per capita of the major nations. In 1989 the United States spent $317 ($79 billion) and the Japanese $222 (27 billion) while Europeans spent only $153 ($58 billion). It is highly likely that Europeans will increase their advertising budgets substantially with the increase of foreign and new EC business competition. Advertising in the EC is currently growing three times faster than U.S. spending and is expected to account for 30% of world advertising within five years.[9]

TO WHAT DEGREE IS A MESSAGE TRANSFERABLE?

As was noted in the preceding chapter, the common market contains vast differences among cultures, economies, and even the types of goods desired. Given the EC diversities, striving to achieve transportable advertising messages is an admirable goal but one that is difficult to achieve. Even Gillette, with years of advertising experience in Europe and around the world, has found that items as generic as razors encountered naming problems in the "common" European marketplace. "Trac II" was fine in countries such as Greece, but the razor had to be renamed for France, Spain, and other romance language nations since "trac" has a connotation of fragile in those languages. Gillette did not want its target group to think of the razor as anything other than strong and durable. The name was changed to "GII." Packaging designs were, however, kept the same so American tourists would recognize the product.

FIGURE 16-4
Allocation of Resources to Promotional Activities, 1991

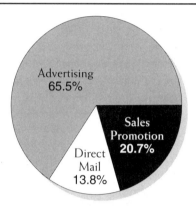

Source: European Commission, *Panorama of EC Industry* (Luxembourg: OPOCE, 1991). From Lynch, R., *European Marketing*. Irwin: New York, 1993, p. 223.

To what degree is a uniform advertising message and common image achievable? In a field study in Western Europe it was found that printed advertisements that were successful in the United States were surprisingly transferable to EC nations.[10] The American ads were strongly visual and promoted consumer products that varied little in positioning from country to country. While other research studies have been more cautious in their findings, the arguments for standardization are becoming more persuasive. Generally the advertising appeals of economy, comfort, advancement, and social approval are equally applicable throughout the EC. The widespread use of cable and satellite TV has promoted the use of standardized campaigns and created a desire for the products seen on popular American TV shows.

Gillette believes that they gained significant savings when one campaign was adopted for their Sensor razor. Contrary to the opinion of many who are less enthusiastic about global advertising and marketing, Gillette has come to believe that localization, while important, can be over done. Mr. Symons, who has had a hand in shaping Gillette's multinational expansion, is quick to point out that if Marlboro had conducted extensive national tests, their cowboy campaign would feature a matador in Spain, a boxer in Britain, and a sumo wrestler in Japan! Mr. Symons admits that, "There is no absolute right or wrong about global campaigns — their appropriateness varies from product to product." One of the features that enhances Sensor's more global approach is that men everywhere want pretty much the same thing from shaving: closeness, comfort, and convenience.[11]

DESPITE EC UNIFICATION, DIFFERING LEGAL ENVIRONMENTS REMAIN

Countries vary greatly as to their acceptance of promotional activities. With different laws and cultures there is almost no such thing as a simple adaptation. Kellogg's Cornflake breakfast cereal advertisement, for example, showed children eating the product, talked about vitamin enrichment, and used the slogan "The best to you each morning." In

Germany "The best to you" was considered a health claim and had to be removed. The segment praising the value of "extra vitamins" had to be deleted in Holland and the ad planned for France was cancelled because children could not endorse products. This difficulty was overcome in Austria by using midgets to play the part of children. While attempts to standardize promotions have met with some success, the regulations of individual nations will frequently interfere with the ability to transfer single advertisements worldwide.

Each EC nation has its own laws on advertising and the national differences can baffle even the most learned. Many EC nations ban ads on alcohol and tobacco. Some ban pharmaceuticals while others impose strict controls. France requires that advertisements be in French while the Netherlands has laws against sexism. National differences outweigh similarities and firms are cautioned to seek counsel prior to the implementation of any campaign.

The EC has instituted directives against misleading advertising and the European Commission has established guidelines for advertisements that enter the Community via satellite. An additional directive, the Cross-Frontier Broadcasting Directive, promotes freedom of transmissions across national boundaries, decreeing that control is the responsibility of the originating nation. The directive calls for a set of minimum rules including the amount of air time that can be devoted to commercials. It bans tobacco and prescription pharmaceutical air time and establishes guidelines for advertising to children.

WHAT TYPES OF CHANGES SHOULD BE CONSIDERED?

It is important to identify the target market that the company desires to capture. By now it should be clear that Europe is a combination of different tastes, incomes, languages, and customs and will remain so despite movements toward political unification. Once accepted, the issue becomes: What national markets within the EC are reasonable to address given customer needs, volume, and access? Once defined, the promotional issue becomes: What medium and what message is best to address that audience? Companies must thoroughly consider cultural, language, and educational differences in order to comfortably answer these questions. Many countries are bi- or even tri-lingual (Belgium, Netherlands), while some such as the United States continue to be mono-lingual (United Kingdom, Spain). Some nations have eclectic religious and cultural backgrounds while others maintain rather similar profiles. The issue for a company's promotional activities is that the degree of change will depend on the diversity of the consumer group addressed. Companies new to the European Community are well advised to specifically target their consumer market so as to minimize the amount of product or advertising change required. In an attempt to focus the advertising content, a company should understand the following:

1. **How the country will use the product** Tang was positioned in the United States as an energy drink for breakfast but positioned in France as a nutritious afternoon drink.
2. **How consumer needs differ among EC nations** London, for example, relies on in-house clothes dryers (much like the United States) while Naples, Italy, is famous for its outside clotheslines. In Munich, Germany, (which prides itself on miles of intercity bicycle paths) bicycles are commonly used for transportation to work. In Athens (which is noted for Europe's worst 24-hour traffic jams) few would risk their lives on a bike.
3. **How an advertisement's language can fall victim to translation errors** Consider "body by Fisher" as "Corpse by Fisher (Flemish), "Chrysler for Power" as "Chrysler is an

aphrodisiac" (Spanish), "Avoid embarrassment—use Parker Pens" as "Avoid pregnancy—use Parker Pens" (Spanish) or "Schweppes tonic water" as "Schweppes bathroom water" (Italian).[12] Language will often determine if the message is suitable across EC boundaries.

4. **How GDP differences determine if the product can be sold at similar prices** What may be a luxury good in one EC nation may be viewed as a necessity in another. Such perceptions will greatly affect the content of the advertising message. GDP can even impact the use of the product. Gillette found that in Northern Europe razor blades were used four or five times while in the poorer areas of Southern Europe the blades were made to last eight to ten times.

5. **How different country laws can significantly impact the method of promotion** In most EC nations, tobacco can not be advertised on TV. Laws can influence both the type of promotion (France prohibits the use of children in advertisements) and the message. The EC is currently considering legislation that would control the way women are portrayed, prohibiting auto advertisements that feature speed as a primary selling feature, and banning advertisements that undermine children's trust in parents or teachers.

The complexity of the European environment should not be underestimated nor be a perment barrier. The potentials of the largest single wealthy market in the world await those who are thorough in their research, targeted in their efforts, and focused in their promotions.

ADDITIONAL PROMOTIONAL STRATEGIES

INTERNATIONAL DIRECT MAIL AND TELEMARKETING

Selling directly to the international consumer by mail or telephone remains a practice dominated by the United States. Both direct mail and telemarketing have become increasingly successful in the European marketplace.

According to Services Postaux Europeans, the market for direct mail in France, Belgium, and France almost doubled during the 1980s and shows excellent potential through the 1990s. The European Direct Marketing Association is a good source of information concerning the advantages and disadvantages of Direct Marketing in Europe.[f] Names of EC brokers who can provide assistance are available from the British List Brokers Association.[g] In addition, the English Postal Service publishes a very interesting booklet, *International Mailing Lists: How to Use Them, Where to Find Them.*

The Pan American Experience   Direct mail campaigns must be undertaken with informed assistance in the country(ies) targeted. Direct mail has distribution, list arrangements, varying national fares, and language problems that can undermine effectiveness. When Pan American Airlines began its 1963 direct mail program in Europe the company experienced considerable difficulty. Among the problems: the letters were in English and sent to French

---

[f]The European Direct Marketing Association, 34 rue du gouvernement provisoire, B-1000 Brussels (010 32 2 2176309).
[g]British List Brokers Association, Springfield House, Princess Sreet, Bedminster, Bristol BS5 4EF (0272 666900).

speakers, foreign offices failed to report results to headquarters, and 25% of the letters were undeliverable as addressed. The company reorganized the campaign, rewrote the letters in several languages, improved the mailing lists and pretested copy and graphics.[13]

TRADE FAIRS

The international trade fair has become an extremely popular method of product introduction. This is particularly true for industrial type products. Over 2,000 trade fairs are held each year in Europe and exhibitors may book space years in advance. In Belgium alone there are about fifty trade fairs annually. The fair at Heysel to the north of Brussels, on the site of the 1958 World's Fair, has 50,000 square meters of exhibition space. Some companies will conduct up to 75% of their yearly business at one or two fairs.

It is important to recognize that, unlike the United States where customers come prepared to buy, Europeans tend to use fairs to browse, and exhibitors must exhibit patience and have a predesigned system to solicit names for follow-ups.

Small Business and Trade Fairs   Trade fairs are particularly useful to small businesses, which often lack the resources to hire salespeople or conduct market research. The trade fair can give a small company considerable exposure to potential distribution systems for their existing products. Attendance at the larger European fairs is fairly impressive and company participation is relatively inexpensive. Information concerning the most appropriate fairs can be obtained from state agencies. In many cases these agencies escort groups of exporting companies to fairs and supply translation, legal, and transportation assistance. State agencies and industrial trade organizations can also be a valuable source of information concerning which fairs are the most appropriate and draw the largest number of potential buyers.

REFERENCES

[1]Wortzel, Lawrence H. "Concepts and Sources for Teaching International Aspects of Product Policy," Proceedings American Marketing Association, Annual Educators Conference. Chicago: American Marketing Association, No. 44, pp. 178–182.

[2]*New York Times*, November 16, 1977, p. 5.

[3]Jenkins, Roger, and Sseed Samiee. "Pricing Objectives of Non-U.S. Manufacturing Firms in the U.S." Presented at Annual Conference of the Academy of International Business, June 1979.

[4]Buckley, Niel. "US Takes the Cut-Price Lead," *Financial Times*, June 15, 1993, p. 31.

[5]"World Report," *Wall Street Journal*, Jan. 20, 1977, p. 1; and Wells, Patricia. "Peddling Boursin to the French and Pizza to the Italians," *New York Times*, Sept. 16, 1979, p. 25.

[6]Terry, Michael. "Logistics Firms Don New Clothes," *Financial Times*, Nov. 6, 1990, p. 111.

[7]Tully, Shawn, Europe Gets Ready for 1992, *Fortune*, 1988, pp. 81–84.

[8]Pelkmans, Jacques, and Alan Winters. Europe's Domestic Market, *Royal Institute of International Affairs Chatham House Papers No. 43*, London: Routledge, 1988, p. 51; and Henley Center, *The United Markets of Europe:Transport*. London: Henley Center, 1988.

[9]Quelch, John, Robert Buzzell, and Eric Salama. *The Marketing Challenge of Europe 1992*, Reading, MA: Addison-Wesley, 1992, p. 81.

[10]Dunn, S. Watson. "Four Measures of Cross-Cultural Advertising Effectiveness." *Journal of Advertising Research*, Vol. 7, Dec. 1967, pp. 10–13.

[11]"On the Razor's Edge," *The Economist*, June 9, 1990.

[12]Ricks, D. *Big Buiness Blunders*, Irwin, Homewood: IL, 1983.

[13]Davidson, Robert. "Pan Am Soars into International Direct Mail." *The International Advertiser*, Vol. 11, No 1, 1970, pp. 19–22.

Researching European Issues: Guidelines for Students and Researchers

Kate Jones-Randall

When you begin a search for business information, you must have a purpose and a plan. The majority of business information is segmented into three areas: country, market, and company data. Once you have determined what type of information you require within these three areas, you can proceed with a research strategy that has a greater chance of success. Sometimes it is necessary to consult with an information professional to develop this strategy, and other times you need only to inquire where to start in a particular library or information center.

The most fortuitous beginnings take place in information-rich environments, such as libraries which hold government depository information on the European Community and trade information from the U.S. Department of Commerce in addition to basic reference sources for international business. Otherwise, you must consider purchasing the various publications which will be most useful, particularly those which are updated regularly. While this can be an expensive undertaking, it may be more cost-effective in the long run to have the materials available directly. Quite frequently, you may start your search with the telephone, connecting immediately with the right people or organizations. Never underestimate networks of people, especially international networks, where successful business is conducted once a personal connection is established.

International business information comes in a variety of formats, including print, microfiche or microfilm, CD-ROM, online electronic, telephone and fax. No single format is sufficient, although electronic information is clearly the most portable and, probably, desirable. In many cases, usefulness is determined more by the timeliness of a resource than by its format, and online electronic information is often updated daily or weekly rather than quarterly or annually, as are print formats. Timeliness is costly, of course, since online electronic access, with the exception of the Internet for students and faculty, is usually quite expensive. Also, one must factor in the time for the users and photoreproduction charges for non-electronic formats as well, as part of the total cost to the researcher. Theoretically, there will be a return on your investment of time and money. In this context, success is measured in your ability to do business abroad.

Two business bibliographies are essential in finding international business information. They may even substitute for a consultation with an information professional. Lorna Daniells' **Business Information Sources** and Ruth Pagell and Michael Halperin's **International Business Information: How to Find It, How to Use It.** While Daniell's book has been considered the "bible" of business information for some time, Pagell and Halperin's text makes a welcome addition to the "must have" list all business librarians maintain. In fact, the information which follows is only a sampling of the depth of information available in these two sources.

Country information, usually industrial and economic statistics, is often the first step to doing business internationally. Many print sources will be very useful in providing background information on the EC countries. The following sources are standard in most academic libraries, large public libraries or those with a business branch, and in special (corporate) libraries where the company is already involved in or wishes to become involved in doing business abroad.

- **Countries of the World**
- **CIA World Factbook**
- **Statesman's Year-book**
- **Europa World Year Book**
- **OECD Economic Surveys** (by country)

Always consult the information professional of a particular library to determine local resources.

The U.S. government is literally a gold mine of information with statistics and text available from the U.S. Dept. of Commerce on **CD-ROM**, in print, on the Internet, and by telephone. Since telephone numbers change nearly as often as Internet addresses, it is best to begin with the main Commerce telephone number, 202-482-2000, and proceed to contact directly the country desk officers and the industry desk officers for each country and line of business and to discover access to general import/export statistics. Commerce maintains an Office of European Community Affairs (202-482-5276 in Washington, D.C.) which offers direct access to EC information and guidance to businesses interested in the European Community.

The Dept. of Commerce has released recently some excellent CD-ROM resources. They include the **National Trade Data Bank (NTDB)** and the **Foreign Traders Index.** The first comprises two CD disks, with full text of publications such as the CIA World Factbook, trade agreements such as NAFTA, current country marketing reports, import/export statistics by country and by commodity using international harmonized codes. It contains many other useful documents geared towards doing business abroad, including current telephone numbers of country and industry desk officers and other points of contact. The second disk, the **Foreign Traders Index,** contains listings of individuals and organizations wishing to do business with the U.S., either as distributors, agents, partners, etc. Another recent **CD** is the **U.S. Dept. of Commerce Imports/Exports by Commodity,** which includes the following:

- recent month statistics by commodity/by country-port of entry
- year-to-date statistics also by commodity/by country-port of entry
- historical annual statistics back to 1989.

Many providers of information repackage some Commerce data, such as the **AT&T Export Hotline.** This is a free fax service which lists various sectors of country and industry marketing reports and offers customized industry analyses, trade information, Commerce trade opportunity leads, and an Export Hotline Directory listing 7500 different companies from over 80 countries. Dial 1-800-USA-XPORT to register.

Newspapers are a good source of current news, and are accessible both through print and **CD-ROM** indexes as well as online electronic databases. While full text is readily available online, most libraries maintain microfilmed back issues. Naturally, European publications such as **The Economist, The Financial Times,** and **The London Times** are most useful, since they regularly publish country analysis. U.S. publications such as **The Wall Street Journal** have a European edition as well. **The New York Times** offers international coverage and is usually held in most libraries. Newspapers can be helpful in pinpointing market and company information as well as country economic events and statistics.

While not always standard in most libraries, but extremely useful, the Economist Intelligence Unit produces **Country Reports, Country Profiles, European Trends, Global Forecasting Service, Global Outlook, World Outlook, World Commodity Outlook,** and **World Commodity Forecasts** in addition to numerous other industry-specific publications directed toward an international market.

Euromonitor is another major provider of European market information, noted for the print **Euromonitor European Marketing Data and Statistics** and **International Marketing Data and Statistics.** They also produce many industry-specific market publications. Other notable publishers of country and industry analysis include *Europe Magazine,* the International Monetary Fund, and the World Bank. The World Bank publishes statistics such as **World Debt Tables, World Development Indicators,** etc., on diskette, and the **International Monetary Fund** recently introduced a **CD-ROM** containing **International Financial Statistics** for over 100 countries with annual entries beginning in 1948. These new technological developments are relatively expensive and may not be found in all libraries. Print sources are still more widely available in most cases.

When it comes to providing market information, online electronic databases are essential. Most offer direct access to market research reports, either in full text or abstracts, and to market analyses through a variety of international publications. International news, company directory and industry information as well are available from the major online vendors such as **DIALOG, BRS, Data-Star, M.A.I.D., Dow Jones News Retrieval, Lexis/Nexis, Extel,** etc. Many bibliographies list the variety of databases which are included; refer again to **Business Information Sources** and **International Business Information: How to Find It, How to Use It.** These sources are not generally free to students or the general public unless subsidized by the library; fees for individual databases vary. Frequently libraries offer what is known as 'fee-based services' which allow researchers access to the databases hosted by these vendors for charges which include the direct access costs as well as the information professional's searching time.

Company information is also available through a variety of print and electronic resources. Most libraries own the following print items:

- **D&B Dun's Principal International Businesses**
- **Dun's Europa**
- **International Directory of Corporate Affiliations**
- **CIFAR Global Companies Handbook**
- **Directory of American Businesses Operating Abroad**
- **Directory of U.S. Importers/Directory of U.S. Exporters**

Many libraries offer access to the following **CD-ROM** resources, or may be able to get to their online equivalents:

- **Worldscope Profiles,** from Disclosure Inc.
- **D&B-Dun's European Market Identifiers**
- **One Source International Public Companies**
- **Moody's International Company Data**
- **KOMPASS Europe**

The Internet, a key component of the coming "information superhighway," is something which must be included in any discussion of access to information. Provided without extra charge to students and faculty in academic institutions, it is also accessible to users through commercial gateways such as CompuServe, Delphi, etc. So much has been written about the Internet that no more need be added here, but to remark that many guides for this service are available. Ask an information professional for recommendations.

There exist some specific Internet resources which deserve mention, however, as the Internet is not generally organized and indexed in the same manner (or at all) as the databases available through the major vendors. It has been primarily through the efforts of business librarians and other information professionals that such organization exists. The following is a selective list of pertinent international business information:

BSN—Business Sources on the Net: a guide to free sources of business information available through the Internet, organized by nine subject files based on Daniells' **Business Information Sources** (in print).

You can access BSN via anonymous FTP or gopher, which is housed at Kent State University; una.hh.lib.umich.edu. Most of the information is U.S.–related, but the most likely source is the BSN.STATISTI file, a "Guide to Foreign Statistics and Economic Trends and International Management." Types of sources included in BSN are discussion groups, bulletin boards, telnet files, gopher sites, FTP archives, electronic journals and newsletters, WAIS resources, World Wide Web, and freenets.

Also access the University of Missouri at St. Louis which has gopher sites to major files of business, economic and marketing data; umslvma.umsl.edu.

I am indebted to a recent article in *The Information Advisor* for its "Special Report: Business Information on the Net"; in actual fact, the entire issue is devoted to this subject. Equally essential was Mel Westerman's "BSN—Business Sources on the Net or Because It's So Needed" in the *Business and Finance Division [SLA] Bulletin*. I also found Jill Motton's "Top Ten List of Good Gophers" in *Library Management Quarterly* to be extremely helpful. I recommend all very highly, although, like any Internet gem, what is gold today may be gone tomorrow.

Increasingly, Internet tools have been developed which greatly aid information seekers. Most useful is the graphical universe of networked information, the World Wide Web, and the numerous "browsers" which have been created to search it. The web is explained in minute detail in the following article by Eric Lease Morgan ("The World-Wide Web and Mosaic: An Overview for Librarians." The Public-Access Computer Systems Review 5, no. 6 (1994):5–26. To retrieve this file, send the following e-mail message to listserv@uhupvm1.uh.edu: GET MORGAN PRV5N6 F=MAIL. Or, use the journals/ uhlibrary/pacsreview/v5/n6/morgan.5n6.)

Searchers with access to Netscape, Mosaic, Lynx, or other "browser" interfaces can make direct queries to multiple data collections about their specific areas of interest, retrieving ranked results which can usually be downloaded or pinted on a full-text format, often with accompanying graphics. In addition to these search "engines," lists or "guides" by subject area abound on WWW "Home Pages."

In general, the Internet will continue to improve, especially as information professionals add value to it, and as more information is added to the already vast stores of government data, economic statistics, and discussion groups or lists. You can learn of other Internet gems through discussion groups, such as BUSLIB–L: discussion group for business librarians. This alerts list members to sources such as **INETEL: Spanish electronic forum for librarians and other information professionals** or **Daily China Headline News** from AsiaInfo, to name only two which recently came across my screen.

Other discussion groups include Market–L for marketing and business research and country-specific groups such as E–EUROPE, the Eastern Europe Business Network for those interested in doing business in Eastern Europe.

Internet access also allows you to search the library catalogs of institutions such as the Library of Congress, major research universities such as the University of Massachusetts Amherst, Stanford, etc., and many other college libraries to determine the depth of their holdings in subject areas pertinent to the EC.

This section would not be complete without mention of information which comes direct from the European Community. The Commission of the European Communities has its central office in Brussels: Commission of the European Communities, Directorate-General X, Audiovisual, Information, Communication and Culture, Rue de la Loi 200, B1409 Brussels, Belgium. Other English-speaking offices exist in the U.K. and the U.S. as well as in other countries and in all member states in their native languages. The U.S. Information Services office is located at 2100 Street NW, Suite 707, Washington DC 20037 USA, tel 202-862-9500. You can either receive a general information package, or fax requests to 202-429-1766. Visitors are welcome, and telephone requests are graciously accepted as well.

UNIPUB is the U. S. distributor of EC publications and subscriptions. For catalogues, titles and price information, contact: UNIPUB, 4611-F Assembly Drive, Lanham, MD 20706-4391, tel (800) 274-4888.

Internet access is also possible to the EC. While there are many EC databases available through direct connection to the EC in languages other than English, the European Commission's host service, ECHO (European Commission Host Organisation), was created in 1980 to set up an information services market in the Community. It is part of the Community program, IMPACT: Information Market Policy Actions. Most of the databases are free of charge to users, and are available in English as well as the other EC languages. ECHO accesses the database categories listed below.

- **User Guidance**: inventories of databases, host organizations and information producers/products in Europe. These include CCL–TRAIN [Common Command Language Training], I'M GUIDE [database of all databases], NEWS ONLINE [current and archival from 1984], XIII MAGAZINE [describes Commission publications], DUNDIS [online Directory of United Nations Databases and Information Systems], and UNESBIB [UNESCO bibliographic references].
- **Research & Development**: R & D programs or projects, some of which are promoted by the EC. These include CORDIS: Community Research & Development Information Service (9 separate databases, currently free but to be converted to a feebased format after initial implementation), BIOREP [biotechnical projects], DOMIS [Directory of Materials Data Information Sources], EUREKA [Europe-wide, not just EC, research and development], and EURISTOTE [online directory of over 14,500 theses and studies].
- **Business & Economy**: economic and social aspects of the EC. These databases include TED [Tenders electronic Daily; 48 ecu per connect hour], JUSLETTER [European legislation and judicial events], MISEP [Mutual Information System on Employment Policies in Europe], and EMIRE [European Employment and Industrial Relations Glossaries].
- **Language Industry**: support users and further develop the language industry. These include EURODICAUTOM [online terminology databank] and THESAURI [analytical inventory of all current structured vocabularies].

One must register with ECHO to receive user documentation for each database and to receive a User Manual explaining the principles of the "CCL" (common command language). One may call (+352) 34 98 1200 or fax (+352) 34 98 1234 or write ECHO, Airport Center, 5, rue Hohenhof L–1736 Senningerberg, B.P. 2373, L–1203 Luxembourg, Belgium to register.

Sources of information on international topics are increasing rapidly, as U.S. interests expand and technological developments make digital access easier and more timely. In conclusion, there are clearly multiple, "free" sources of information, but most of them require some analysis to add value to the data gathered, or simply to access them at all. While students and some members of general public don't necessarily require "today's" data, to understand the availability and types of resources will give them an advantage in the marketplace or the academic community. For those researchers who need "yesterday's" information, information professionals are always available to assist in the sometimes labyrinthine process of acquiring it. Academic business librarians, information brokers or fee-for-service operations within college, university or public libraries, "cybrarians" who navigate the Internet, make up the networks of people who are as valuable, or perhaps even more valuable, than the data itself.

WORKS CITED

Daniells, Lorna. Business Information Sources. 3rd ed., Berkeley, University of California Press, 1993.

Motton, Jill. "Top Ten List of Good Gophers." *Library Management Quarterly*, vol. 17:2, Spring 1994, pp 13–15.

Pagell, Ruth and Michael Halperin. International Business: How to Find It, How to Use It. Phoenix, Arizona, the Oryx Press, 1994.

"Special Report: Business Information on the Net." *The Information Advisor*, vol. 6:6, June 1994, pp. 1–8.

Westerman, Mel. "BSN—Business Sources on the Net, or Because It's So Needed." *Business and Finance Division Bulletin*, no. 96, Spring 1994, pp. 7–10.

INDEX